Jack the Ripper **WITHDRAWN**
and Black Magic

D0874316

WITHDRAWN

# Jack the Ripper and Black Magic

*Victorian Conspiracy Theories, Secret Societies and the Supernatural Mystique of the Whitechapel Murders*

Spiro Dimolianis

*Foreword by* Stewart P. Evans

McFarland & Company, Inc., Publishers
*Jefferson, North Carolina, and London*

DEC 19 2011

PROPERTY OF
SENECA COLLEGE
LIBRARIES
@ YORK CAMPUS

LIBRARY OF CONGRESS CATALOGUING-IN-PUBLICATION DATA

Dimolianis, Spiro, 1957–
Jack the Ripper and black magic : Victorian conspiracy theories, secret
societies and the supernatural mystique of the Whitechapel murders /
Spiro Dimolianis ; foreword by Stewart P. Evans.
p.     cm.
Includes bibliographical references and index.

ISBN 978-0-7864-4547-9
softcover : 50# alkaline paper ∞

1. Jack, the Ripper.    2. Serial murders — England — London — History —
19th century.    3. Serial murderers — England — London — History —
19th century.    4. Whitechapel (London, England) — History —19th
century.    5. Conspiracies — England — London — History —19th century.
I. Title.
HV6535.G6L6354    2011        364.152'32092 — dc23        2011023794

BRITISH LIBRARY CATALOGUING DATA ARE AVAILABLE

© 2011 Spiro Dimolianis. All rights reserved

No part of this book may be reproduced or transmitted in any form
or by any means, electronic or mechanical, including photocopying
or recording, or by any information storage and retrieval system,
without permission in writing from the publisher.

Front cover: Claudia McKinney. *Jack's Treasure Hunt.*
Mixed media. 2010. *phatpuppyart.com*

Manufactured in the United States of America

*McFarland & Company, Inc., Publishers*
*Box 611, Jefferson, North Carolina 28640*
*www.mcfarlandpub.com*

# Table of Contents

# Acknowledgments

Many people supported me in the course of researching, writing and producing this book. I am particularly grateful for the assistance, contributions, informed opinion and good humor of the following individuals and organizations.

Richard Whittington-Egan, Stewart P. Evans and Paul Begg, leading authorities on the Whitechapel murders, for encouragement in the subject and their interest in this study. The staff of the National Archives, British Library, Bibliothèque Nationale de France, the New South Wales State Library and Sydney University Fisher Library, the Library of Congress, and UK Parliamentary Archives. Jonathan Evans and Kate Richardson, archivists of the Royal London Hospital Museum. Andrew P. Brown, historical archivist of the Metropolitan Police Service. Historians Dr. David Waldron, Professor Ronald Hutton and David Lewis. Dr. Donald J. West. Paul J. Gaunt, editor of *Psypioneer*. Dr. Lindsay Clutterbuck. Alan Murdie. Nicholas Connell. Keith Richmond of Weiser Antiquarian Books and Ben Fernee of Caduceus Books. Philip Hutchinson and the research archivist of the Ghost Club. Stephen P. Ryder and Chris Scott, editors of the *Casebook* website. Eduardo Zinna and the editorial team of *Ripperologist*. The Swanson family. Jack the Ripper researchers Chris Phillips, Roger J. Palmer, Graham Wilson, Joe Chetcuti, John Savage, Amanda Howard and David O'Flaherty. Phillip A. Garver. George Duguay and archivist Joan Sutcliffe of the Canadian Theosophical Association. Jennifer Hissey of the Campbell Theosophical Research Library. Melanie Aspey, director of the Rothschild Archive. Peter O'Donnell, author of *Modesty Blaise* and son of crime reporter Bernard O'Donnell. Kim Farnell. Laura James. Martha Sachs, curator of the Marshall Women's History Collection, Penn State Harrisburg Library. Claudia McKinney for designing original cover art.

# LONDON

I wander thro' each charter'd street
Near where the charter'd Thames does flow
And mark in every face I meet
Marks of weakness, marks of woe

In every cry of every Man
In every Infants cry of fear
In every voice, in every ban
The mind-forg'd manacles I hear

How the Chimney-sweepers cry
Every black'ning Church appalls
And the hapless Soldiers sigh
Runs in blood down Palace walls

But most thro' midnight streets I hear
How the youthful Harlot's curse
Blasts the new born Infants tear
And blights with plagues the Marriage hearse

William Blake (1757–1827)

# Foreword
## by Stewart P. Evans

Writing a book on the subject of Jack the Ripper and the Whitechapel murders of 1888 has been likened to entering a minefield. Any author with the temerity to embark upon this literary venture knows full well the meaning of these words. For not only is detailed research and reading on the subject required, a proper understanding of the subject matter, Victorian times, police, press, people and history is also needed. So it is with admiration that I have read this contribution to the genre by Australian author Spiro Dimolianis. Not only has he been brave enough to tackle this vexed subject; he has chosen to focus on one of the more controversial aspects of Ripperology — Jack the Ripper and black magic. He has done this with an understanding of the material that is to be applauded, and I thoroughly recommend this work to anyone with an interest in this subject. It provides a new and much needed insight on an area that attracts more than its fair share of madcap ideas and theories — and has thrown up one of the more colorful suspects for the identity of the unknown Victorian killer. Mr. Dimolianis has aptly subtitled it "Victorian Conspiracy Theories, Secret Societies and the Supernatural Mystique of the Whitechapel Murders."

He rapidly engages us in the proper historical context of the times. As anyone with more than a passing knowledge of the subject is aware it is bedeviled with myth and misinformation. Here fictions are identified and examined and source material is considered, very relevant these days when the searching of online digital archives seems to be totally replacing good old-fashioned and time-consuming scouring of dusty records, letters and manuscripts. The importance of the cultural conditions and context with regard to interpreting the meaning of the historical data is explained. This is very important when modern concepts such as criminal profiling and studies of modern serial killers are increasingly applied to this case. This is more than a mere study of the "black magic" aspect of the case; it is a study of the concept of "conspiracy theories" used as an explanation for the motive and the murders. The author has not restricted himself to searching the Internet for information — he has realized the importance of supplementing that with the old research methods. We find out whether the idea of a "secret society" explanation is credible, and what of the secretive Special Branch of Scotland Yard and its possible involvement as evidenced in the Littlechild Letter, written to journalist, author, playwright, poet and man of letters George R. Sims in 1913, in which the colorful Irish-American suspect "Dr." Francis Tumblety was revealed?

It will be helpful to the reader to be au fait with the basics of the case and the story of the murders, but if not, a copy of *The Jack the Ripper A–Z* or Sugden's *Complete History of Jack the Ripper* would be beneficial as a ready reference. The book takes you on an enjoyable journey of discovery through the back streets, alleys and courts of Ripperology and is very different from any other book published on this famous chapter of criminological history.

The reader will find all aspects of the occult case for the murders and will meet fortune-tellers, mediums, spiritualists and their ilk. The old favorite of occultists, "the Great Beast," Aleister Crowley is here in all his glory and his connection with the Ripper story is fully explained. Iconic areas of Ripper research such as the "Macnaghten Memoranda," the "Swanson marginalia" and Assistant Commissioner Robert Anderson's "Polish Jew theory" are analyzed. And the tyro need fear not — for he or she is in the safe hands of a reliable and objective guide through the labyrinthine twists and turns of this baffling and beguiling history. Anderson, an undoubtedly important player in the drama, is looked at in depth and the relevance of his theological writings considered. The status of Anderson's pronouncements is defined. Many connections are made for the first time here as we read of the mysteries of black magic and tangential personalities such as Arthur Diosy.

Perhaps one of the more important parts of the book is that which looks at Roslyn D'Onston Stephenson, regarded by many as the top candidate for a "Jack the Magician" suspect — but was he a black magician at all? The pioneering work of author Bernard O'Donnell, an early "champion" of D'Onston is looked at. D'Onston was a patient in the London Hospital, hard by the killing ground, and we find an answer to the puzzling question of whether he could get out of the confines of the hospital at night in order to commit the crimes. The book is a literary historian's delight as the author examines obscure references, sources and probable influences for later writers on the subject. So, to those who puzzle over D'Onston and his status as a suspect — puzzle no more. The whole black magic angle attributed to the Whitechapel murders is explored and explained. The mysterious character of Vittoria Cremers, to whom the main case against D'Onston is credited, is fleshed out and assessed. The equally mysterious "Cremers memoir" is explained, and we meet the Victorian Theosophists led by the influential but decidedly odd Helena Blavatsky. You will also find here the mysterious "Jesuit theory." The very popular idea of conspiracy theory in shaping the history of Jack the Ripper and the Whitechapel murders is properly looked at for the first time.

Among the other characters we meet are author William Le Queux, Rasputin, "Dr. Pedachenko," Betty May, the suspect Fogelma and many others. It is all rounded off with an examination of secret societies, Parnellism and crime, and the Victorian secret service and Special Branch police. Mention of Parnellism and crime immediately reminds me again of Sir Robert Anderson whose series of articles in *The Times* in mid–1887 resulted in the Parnell Commission of late 1888 and 1889, which inquired into libels against the Irish Party MP Charles Stewart Parnell and *The Times* publication of the infamous letters seeking to associate Parnell with the Irish terrorists and the infamous Phoenix Park murders. The letters were found to be forgeries written by the journalist Richard Pigott, who committed suicide in Madrid in 1889. It is in this connection that a good insight into the character of Robert Anderson may be found.

Anderson's famous words with regard to the identity of Jack the Ripper are to be found in his 1910 book of memoirs *The Lighter Side of My Official Life*. In this volume Anderson notably states of the Ripper, "In saying that he was a Polish Jew I am merely stating *a definitely ascertained fact.*" Many theorists regard this statement as the best indication that we shall ever have of the identity of the Ripper, bolstering it with the claim that Anderson would not have lied and that his statement carries much weight as he "was in the best position to know." However, in my copy of the second edition (1907) of Anderson's 1906 book *Sidelights on the Home Rule Movement*, there is a new preface in which Anderson comments upon the forged Parnell letter written by Pigott. Anderson states, "And as regards the Parnell 'facsimile letter' of May 15, 1882, I have received *definite confirmation* of my statement that it is in the handwriting of Arthur O'Keefe. I have obtained further proof, moreover, that at that period O'Keefe was employed by Mr. Parnell as an amanuensis." History shows us that Pigott and not O'Keefe was the writer. So, perhaps Anderson's "definitely ascertained fact" may not have been so definite as he claimed.

*Stewart P. Evans has researched, written and coauthored reference works on Jack the Ripper and the Whitechapel murders. He consults on books, documentaries and films on the subject and was employed as a historical advisor on the feature movie* From Hell. *He is a retired police officer with a distinguished service career.*

# Preface

Jack the Ripper was a leading and international conspiracy theory of the late Victorian and premodern period. The unsolved case continues to charm, acquiring its own mythology and fancied suspects. Fiction is transmuted into fact and history into firm beliefs. True crime events that produce tangled theories and attract modern forensic interest to a serial killer whose identity is still unknown. Any approach seems to mask rather than resolve the murders that happened in 1888 in Whitechapel, London's East End, the impoverished heart of Victorian London.

Though the overall case history of the Whitechapel murders has been examined and documented, less attention was brought to vague anomalies noted in official files, Home Office reports and in subsequent police press statements and memoirs. Stories of supernatural events and shady politics born of opaque senior police conclusions has further entrenched the mystery. Without the full details, conspiracies flourish and detract from the truth, however incredible. It is then useful to compare Jack the Ripper legends in their historic context with a fair variety of sources and established investigative reports to discern fact from fiction.

The Victorian era was also an age of the secret societies. A review of these period subcultures is important in considering the Whitechapel murders because of repeated police references. These clubs were political, mystical, economic, esoteric, fraternal, subversive, and friendly. Some were law enforcement agencies. If the Ripper was a local nobody as supposed, and Scotland Yard simply failed to capture the culprit, why make subsequent politicized statements in defense of evolving Victorian police methods? Why record responses to tabloid press theories well into the next century with official phantoms and cautionary high-level police fictions? Constantly, the known facts are overwhelmed and at odds with fantastic historical surmise.

Jack the Ripper lore has become linked with the study of Queen Victoria's British Empire. The subject is studied by those who are drawn to the era's cultural and social elements and hooked by the mystery of the Whitechapel murders. Release of the official police and government files on the case during the late 1970s brought further insights and scholarly attention. "Ripperologists" have made significant contributions to the subject much as amateur astronomers searching for supernovas in an endless sky have contributed to the efforts of NASA.

The advent of digital archives and search engines has added vast amounts of raw Victorian data to the mix. With ongoing online release of primary sources, such as the Old Bailey criminal trials and scanned newspaper collections, particularly of obscure American sources, new theories are born of curiosity. The ease of Internet searching has tended to dispense with the exacting research methods of past crime historians and created new approaches. However, research is thus narrowed to digitized sources and omits documents that have not yet been digitized from fragile archives.

The official case files transcribed and published at the turn of the millennium were helpful to Victorian scholars, criminologists, feminist academics, crime historians and in school curricula. The fascination with a serial killer of prostitutes and the death of female victims representative of poverty and social neglect in Victorian East End London has achieved mythical status but little historic closure. As mounting primary, secondary and unrelated sources are sifted and analyzed, more questions are generated than resolved. The mystery of conflicting Scotland Yard reports, medical autopsies and Victorian politics invites conspiracy theories that lead only to the next exciting discovery.

Obviously the real Jack the Ripper can now never be captured. This has encouraged application of modern forensics and criminal profiling to a cold case, a historic murder inquiry with no surviving material evidence. The responsibility to catch the elusive murderer was the ultimate job of the Home Office, but blame for the failure was laid at the door of the police, strongly vilified in parliament, local and international press. Press coverage of the Whitechapel murders created a false impression that Scotland Yard and the City of London Police were weak and incompetent bodies that failed to capture an ordinary serial killer. This is important because those contemporary press reports are now relied upon as primary sources.

This incorrect historic premise leads to attempts to identify Jack the Ripper through use of modern forensics and DNA testing of irrelevant, missing or contaminated evidence. Psychological, geographical and behavioral profiling of a long-dead serial killer derived from fragmentary investigative files is also ineffective. Rather than view Victorian police methods as archaic and dysfunctional, it is useful to regard the crimes as did the era's highly experienced detectives. The Victorian foundations of English law enforcement provided a system that in a sense "made up for" the absence of advanced forensic technology.

The mythical character of Jack the Ripper is known, for instance, only through period press portrayals or letters conjectured to be from the killer. The events of the Whitechapel murders are known as far as what happened, how and to whom in some detail. However, the subjective _why_ for an apparently motiveless series of murders and mutilations proves elusive yet crucial to its resolution. A comparison with modern serial killers is fraught with the pitfalls attending a Victorian cold case. Lines of period police inquiries and the nature of wounds on the Whitechapel victims are all that remains in determining a credible motive with some confidence.

This book traces relevant, obscure and discounted or unknown accounts to their official sources or compares them with surviving Scotland Yard and Home Office reports for clarity and leads. Where possible, rare internal official reports were consulted. Anomalies of the period expressed in official files legitimized wildly speculative ideas. Hence, this book is also intended as a definitive reference on alleged Whitechapel murder conspiracies and theories on ritual homicide, occult crime, political slayings and the supernatural mystique of Jack the Ripper.

For the Victorians, the Whitechapel murders were significant as indicators of imperial, legal, political and social change. These implications have become shrouded with time. Yet the thematic persistence of class and cultural Jack the Ripper legends that supported suspects detached from Scotland Yard inquiries embody social commentary. Consequently, the narrative journeys through a remote time, place and cultural perspective in search of some tangible ground. As we know through experience gained with modern police methods on cold murder cases, a reevaluation can only commence from reconsidering existing files and evidence collated by the original police investigation.

Victorian beliefs about Jack the Ripper embraced fortune-telling, gypsies, the demonic, political and occult secret societies, ritualized or religious murder and the supernatural. As these expressions are also found in official files on the Whitechapel murders, then it is probably a good idea to examine them as objectively as possible. This is rarely done effectively, even by those with a professed interest in the study of all aspects of the period. As the medical conflicts are pervasive in the unsolved Whitechapel murders, this is precisely the area most vulnerable to speculation and inviting of commentary shaded with dogmas. Historic mythologies that have grown with the identity of Jack the Ripper are also social and cultural expressions worthy of study because they can illuminate other unsolved serial murder cases and the critical beliefs that infuse them. When it is shown that beliefs held by senior police officials may influence serial murder investigations, the topic assumes some importance.

These cultural conditions are vital in reviewing Victorian documents where the crimes of an unknown serial killer are recorded and noted according to attitudes, beliefs and detection methods of the time. When they are further glossed with modern criminology and scientific methods, surviving primary sources on the Whitechapel murders are inclined to support views and case studies far removed from their social and historical contexts. It is fortunate that the subject of Jack the Ripper has attracted the attention of cultural historians Judith R. Walkowitz and Sir Christopher Frayling. Their piercing social commentary remains pertinent and crucial to exploration of the murders in the period. Though human nature may not change significantly over time, social perceptions and systems of criminal justice vary.

Walkowitz observed that the historical narratives, reactions and speculative theories recorded on Jack the Ripper tend to fall into two broad gendered categories; expressions of female political melodrama or male gothic fantasy. Material in this book likewise reflects on obscure accounts of mystical, occult and supernatural subcultures that in Victorian times were aligned with development of the early English socialist and feminist movements. The gothic literature of the period on Jack the Ripper was fused closely with the facts of the case. These theories were forms of Victorian social and utopian expressions on the nature of crime and evil. They intersected with the police investigation, government policies and reached the ear of Queen Victoria.

Sir Christopher Frayling regards Victorian perceptions as idealist melodrama steeped in literary traditions legitimized by press proprietors, Fleet Street editors, and West End clubs. He extended the observation to the police investigation on Jack the Ripper. According to Frayling, Melville Macnaghten's central police briefing document naming three likely suspects, known as the Macnaghten Memorandum, is more a cultural expression of the prevailing moods than the considered police conclusions of an extensive manhunt.

The Jack the Ripper murders occurred at a crucial and changing time for Queen Victoria's British Empire. Fascinating and informative as the Ripper stories are, they continue to mask historical events. Pre–modern politics of crime with their legal precedents in developing democratic systems of law enforcement and civil liberties were a fixture of the Whitechapel murders. The killer's identity was unknown, but he was regarded as a psychotic maniac or insane immigrant whose crimes deserved limited police resources. That is generally the official view. However, the East End was also a hotbed and asylum for revolutionaries. European anarchists, Irish Republicans, retired soldiers, passing sailors and a transient local population all came under strained police concern during the murder investigation.

The Littlechild Letter, the informed views of ex–Chief Inspector John George Littlechild, head of Metropolitan Police Special Branch from 1883 to 1893, was sent to crime journalist George Sims in 1913. It is probably the most decisive document on Jack the Ripper since discovery of the Macnaghten Memorandum, though it is not an official police report. Littlechild's suspect, Dr. Francis Tumblety, suggested Special Branch inquiries regarding the Whitechapel murders. Littlechild's suspicions supported traditional historic surmise of political intrigues for Jack the Ripper with release of Victorian secret service index ledgers in 2002 to academics confirming it.

James Monro, Metropolitan Police commissioner and successor to Sir Charles Warren from late 1888, was also privately reported in retirement as having special knowledge of Jack the Ripper. However, Robert Anderson, Assistant Metropolitan Police Commissioner and head of CID, took the limelight with widely publicized theories that were at odds with internal police reports on the Ripper case. The Jack the Ripper case had many shades not only within a social, cultural and press context, but also with senior police officials navigating the investigation.

This book grew from an observation that despite works published during more than a century on the Whitechapel murders that cite fantastic theories of occult agencies, covert conspiracies and psychic detections, the topic had not been approached definitively or in context. Suspects conjured without reference to primary sources and with little regard for historic traditions of non-mainstream subcultures and personalities were the norm. When these theories approach flagrant fabrication and hoax, they become untenable, and fragile mainstream and official theories are afforded tenuous support as the best or only solutions. Yet behind almost every political conspiracy or fantastic occult crime theory lies some element of truth. When reputable contemporary sources considered them, then we must address them with fairness and objectivity and view them in a Victorian social and cultural context. Sensitive political and historic events often generate conspiracy theories with a tendency to record partial views as facts. This trend of historical bias must be taken into account in reviewing the Whitechapel murders with their reliance on conflicted primary sources and official period assurances.

Research for this book involved sourcing obscure periodicals, press reports, and antiquated works and official records omitted or excluded by other authors because their subject matter was dated or had fallen out of mainstream political, social and religious history. In any era, subcultures that are orphic, secret, mystical and politically subversive are the least documented or accessible. When they are noted, advocates of conservative principles, popular political scapegoats or the detractors of heretics usually record them for curious future historians.

Jack the Ripper was considered a renegade of a Victorian London's subculture due to the macabre and extensive mutilations of the victims. In the Victorian period, this naturally led to suspicions of secret societies. Probably the most obscure official files on the Whitechapel murders are the police and government inquiries into political secret societies steeped in esoteric designs. Covert and subversive groups are more impenetrable to historic research than a study of Victorian Freemasonry, the occult or supernatural. They are underground streams that all had cause to blend with period Ripper legends and the investigations of Metropolitan Police Special Branch detectives.

I reasonably assume that readers will have some knowledge of the Whitechapel murders. For that reason, a list of recommended texts is included for reference and further reading. Otherwise, the narrative seeks to be as accessible as possible in examining Victorian ideals and motives found in official documents, press reports and unpublished sources as a stand-alone study of the Whitechapel murders. Though several suspects, including some who are unknown or obscure, are covered in this work, I emphasize crimes committed by and efforts of the police to apprehend the killer known as Jack the Ripper. Credible suspects who came to the attention of Scotland Yard are considered, though it is misleading to chase imaginary and romantic Victorian Jack the Ripper figures around an East End landscape. Only related personalities who form part of a lost Ripper apocryphal tradition have been examined in some further detail.

A search for the historic reality of Jack the Ripper cannot be a partial attempt to extract reprisal for Victorian class inequities, gender conflict or the religious struggle between good and evil. It is rather a sustained vindication of the adapting justice system and its appended law enforcement agencies. Nor can it absolve charges of official corruption, suppression and political mongering at the expense of the murdered citizens of East End London. Historic consideration of Victorian subcultures, which are known to have harbored accounts of suspects during the murders, discounts imaginative theories on firmer ground. Cultural sensitivity for conflicted and opposing social and political forces active in the Victorian period and influential to its modern estimation, affords the killer, victims and motives sharper relief.

In knowing the broad context of a historic event, whether social or criminal, it is vital that period worldviews and legitimate expression of subcultures are allowed without antiquated bias and with informed fairness. Similarly important is a sound grasp of past places, dates and events noted with actions, reports and beliefs of individuals during the Whitechapel murders of 1888. Historical sources, for these reasons, are as reliant on a balanced assessment in hindsight and, as projections of future conclusions on Jack the Ripper, as they are on their documentary survival and archival preservation.

# 1

# Ghosts of the Ripper Wake

On the night of Sunday, October 28, 1888, Sarah Tanner, a 53-year-old married woman of 49 Bowsell Street, Bow Common, was charged on a warrant for fortune-telling. On the following day, Detective Sergeant Breed of K Division stated before Thames Police Court magistrate Mr. Lushington that during the last fortnight he and a Sergeant Duck had kept surveillance on the prisoner's house. The police had diligently employed the services of Mrs. Sarah Ann Bromley and her daughter of Poplar as decoys in the operation.

The Bromleys proceeded to Tanner's house ostensibly for a "reading" and to obtain evidence after letters of complaint were sent to the commissioner of the Metropolitan Police, Sir Charles Warren. When Breed and Duck arrived to apprehend the prisoner they found in a desk in the front parlor two packs of playing cards, the popular Victorian book of divination *Napoleon's Book of Fate*,[1] and a number of pieces of paper on which were written dates. Tanner said they were dates for the people to watch out for. The papers were included with the exhibits presented to the court in the case against her.

Mr. George Hay Young in Tanner's defense before the magistrate argued that it was difficult to accept that people still believed in fortune-telling. Detective Inspector R. Wildey, prosecuting on behalf of the Criminal Investigation Department, gave evidence that the accused told Mrs. Bromley that her mother, who had lived for over ninety years, did nothing but fortune-telling for a living. Sarah Tanner charged a respectable 6d for her services and it seemed a modest source of income especially for women if undetected. Little more than half that sum would have bought a destitute prostitute in the East End a bed for the night in a Common Lodging House, so fortune-telling was hardly a significant part of the Victorian black market economy or means of survival.

Mr. Lushington, however, sentenced Sarah Tanner to the minimum one month's imprisonment with hard labor for acquiring money by telling people "utter nonsense."[2] She was lucky for now, but the court and police were still expected to uphold the law of the land despite the added burden of the Whitechapel murders investigation that was unfolding nearby.

Detective Inspector Frederick George Abberline, in charge of inquiries into the White-chapel murders from September 1888 to March 1889, was also investigating criminal breaches of fortune-telling. Abberline, along with Detective Sergeant Stephen White[3] and Constable Henry Payne, all of the Whitechapel H Division, arrested the serial fortune-teller James

Ball of 62 Ocean Street, Stepney, on June 6, 1884. They were armed with a warrant for "obtaining money from various persons under the pretence of telling their fortunes." Ball had also charged 6d for his services.

At the Thames Police Court on June 9, 1884, witness Constable Payne testified that James Ball had previous convictions for fortune-telling. He had received sentences of three months' imprisonment with hard labor in 1878, six months in 1879 and ten months in 1880. Magistrate Lushington remanded Ball to appear for trial at the Middlesex Sessions and stated the witness "would be bound over in the sum of £20 to give evidence," supplementing the constable's income in the days before secure and fair Metropolitan Police pensions were established. The following week the assistant judge sentenced Ball to twelve months' imprisonment with hard labor for the proven indictment of being an "incorrigible rogue and vagabond."[4]

Antonia Spea and Emily Rachel Howies of St. George's were arrested on a warrant for fortune-telling on February 1, 1886. Detective Sergeant White of H Division sent Ellen Moore, a cook, of 78 Leman Street, to gather evidence at their respective homes. Moore stated that she first went to see Spea who had told her in a reading that there would be a death in the family and after some difficulty she would receive money left to her. Inspector Abberline, who had watched the case on behalf of CID at the Thames Police Court, had arrested them in the company of White and other officers. They found her sitting at a table, cards and a book in front, opposite 18-year-old Alice Woods of St. George's who most anxiously explained that she was having her fortune told.

At Howies's house, White reported, the police entered her room and she tried to pass the cards over his shoulder. However, they fell into the hands of Inspector Abberline. For their trouble and 6d, magistrate Lushington sentenced Antonia Spea to three months' imprisonment with hard labor and Emily Howies to one month. In her defense Howies stated, "I did not extort money. I am reduced in circumstances. I acknowledge I have cut cards for ladies. The witness [Ellen Moore] importuned me to do the same for her."

Victorian trial transcripts on protecting the Queen's subjects from the curse of fortune-tellers and spiritualist mediums, quantified to an extent beliefs by all classes in the occult and supernatural. At a time when the Whitechapel murders were calling for the transfer of police manpower to the East End from other divisions, invisible Jack the Ripper was gathering a cloak woven of mystical threads from the exotic slums of East London and lavish parlors of the West End. Based on Victorian superstitions and alternate beliefs, these interpretations and theories on the Whitechapel crimes were brought to official notice, reported by the press and documented in the archives of their associations.

Mainstream religious and rational purists had frowned upon fortune-telling, genuine or not, and regarded it as satanic. Their reports on alleged fraudulent mediums relied upon statutory duties of the Metropolitan Police. Catching fortune-tellers diverted a portion of police attention and resources. The commingling of Jack the Ripper, supernatural beliefs, ghost sightings, and ritual murder made plain the burden on the police. Encouraged by rising press coverage of mutilations and the extraction of internal organs of victims, gothic folk traditions of a "Jack the Reaper," were assured to attract the attentions of Victorian London's true believers.

The belief that paranormal or psychic abilities could solve the mystery of the Whitechapel murders originated with Victorian London's spiritualist, occult, and artistic subcultures. It has formed a part of a prolific literary tradition and fabled morality play ever since.

The affair with alternate religious views of Jack the Ripper, as the diabolical antagonist in an afterlife where dwelt his murdered victims, produced medieval gothic horror stories. As the specter of the unknown murderer grew, the police investigating the crimes were inundated with "clues" from psychic mediums. Where scientific, medical and practical police work could not settle the mystery of an unseen Victorian serial killer, detection by supernatural means was worth a try.

Fraudulent fortune-tellers and psychic mediums for gain were convicted under sections 4 of the Vagrancy Act, 1824, and Witchcraft Act, 1735. They were eventually repealed and replaced by the more tolerant Fraudulent Mediums Act[5] on June 22, 1951. But as late as 1921 a judge on appeal had stated, "I cannot reverse the decision on the claim that the intention to deceive was not necessarily to be proved. The act of fortune-telling is an offence in itself."[6] Clearly all Victorian fortune-tellers and mediums were not dishonest hustlers. Some made a modest living from entertaining and reading for consenting participants. Indictment had recognized the claim for supernatural abilities as a legal basis for a case and in so doing, continued in the Victorian legacy of archaic English witchcraft trials, beliefs and religious hegemony.[7]

The police in the East End during the reign of Jack the Ripper were in significant contact with beliefs of all persuasions, including immigrant folk superstitions and ritual practices. Dealing with fortune-tellers was as much a part of the work of detectives as was dealing with political extremists and the Whitechapel murders. Masses of information on the psychic detection of the killer's identity or that of his victims had either to be regarded as impossible nonsense and thus eliminated or selectively considered as possible leads in an unsolved serial murder case. (This is still a problem for modern police forces.) The investigating officers of the murders had little experience in processing mass media reports and voluntary information on such a scale. Scotland Yard was overwhelmed with reports, tips, and other paperwork, and reliant upon the subjective positions, religious beliefs and experience of their police officers to interpret them. Victorian East End crime policing during the murders of Jack the Ripper was anything but dull within its multicultural ghettos and slum setting.

Robert Anderson, head of CID and Assistant Commissioner of the Metropolitan Police during the Ripper murders, wrote in an internal report for the Home Office dated October 23, 1888:

> That a crime of this kind should have been committed without any clue being supplied by the criminal, is unusual, but that five successive murders should have been committed without our having the slightest clue of any kind is extraordinary, if not unique, in the annuls [sic] of crime. The result has been to necessitate our giving attention to innumerable suggestions, such as would in any ordinary case be dismissed unnoticed, and no hint of any kind, which was not obviously absurd, has been neglected. Moreover, the activity of the Police has been to a considerable extent wasted through the exigencies of sensational journalism, and the action of unprincipled persons, who, from various motives, have endeavoured to mislead us.[8]

An index to files on the police investigation of the murders dated October 19, 1888, was included with Anderson's report to the Home Office prepared by Chief Inspector Donald Swanson of CID, who supervised the case. Though the files have not entirely survived, these index entries and Anderson's report give a reasonable impression of the police activity up to that time. Apart from the expected socialists, slaughtermen, Asiatics, opium dens, sailors and touring cowboys from Queen Victoria's 1887 Jubilee American exhibit of William

F. "Buffalo Bill" Cody's Wild West Show, Swanson noted inquiries on "Gipsies Greek." In a summary report for the Home Office also dated October 19, 1888, Swanson gave further details: "Inquiries have also been made as to the alleged presence in London of Greek Gipsies, but it was found that they had not been in London during the times of the previous murders."[9]

A clear reason for why gypsies, let alone any specific nationality as they were a wandering people, were suspected and eliminated for the Whitechapel murders is not available. Their presence in London as vagrants, fortune-tellers and convicted criminals was already established in the courts when the October 19, 1888, summary report was made.[10] Though Swanson's report does not specify inquiries on immigrant Jews, East Enders were distrusted by English-born police and the native population. Institutionalized xenophobia stemming from imperial issues and Victorian political policies was and still is a central theme in the attempt to locate Jack the Ripper in the context of his social landscape.

In a letter to the editor of the *Evening News*, October 9, 1888, an explanation for the inquiries and suspicion that fell upon the fortune-telling gypsies might be found. It was sent by a contributor identifying himself as "An Ex-Superintendent of Special Constables and a Volunteer Officer." Special Constables were employed at the Chartist workers' demonstrations earlier and at the 1887 Trafalgar Square socialist riots.

The contributor offered his services as a "special detective" and the benefit of his previous experience to Scotland Yard to help in the capture of Jack the Ripper. A system of plainclothes informers, such as employed by the Whitechapel Vigilance Committee, he suggested, should be "empowered with the same authority for the time being as a real detective." He elaborated, "My system, if practicable (as I venture to say it is), would also put a stop to a great deal of illegality which is carried on in several places

Donald Sutherland Swanson as a Metropolitan Police Inspector in November 1881. Advancing to the position of Chief Inspector, Scotland Yard CID, he held overall supervision of the Whitechapel murders case. He left an important note in retirement naming Kosminski as a suspect (courtesy the Swanson family).

openly, and winked at by the police because they wish to keep themselves in good favor with the neighbourhood."

The "ex–Superintendent of Special Constables" illustrated the effectiveness of his plan by citing a few anecdotes, one of which referred to gypsies. Regardless that the police had already covered the East End with plainclothes detectives, it is difficult to say whether or not this anonymous contributor brought the matter to the attention of the police investigating the Whitechapel murders. However, he managed to use twice the Victorian colloquial spelling "Gipsies,"[11] as Chief Inspector Swanson did in his police summary report and file index of October 19. He stated, "On another occasion, also on which a friend of mine (who is a J.P.) had occasion to complain at the same police station of the destruction of his hedges in a lane adjoining his premises by a horde of gipsies, who made it a regular halting place, a constable in full uniform was placed on special duty in the aforesaid lane with the result, of course, that the gipsies, being fully aware that the place was watched, did not come near it."[12]

The multicultural mix of East End London was the setting of the widely publicized Jack the Ripper murders. News reports of the murders included descriptions of the area's destitution and foreign ways. As the news spread far and wide the accounts of the police investigation merged with sensational suspicions, beliefs, and extremist political ideals. This is commonplace in societies where the "other" is demonized for any local controversy or crime, be he an actual killer or a prospering immigrant shopkeeper. The undetected criminal in this way becomes the scapegoat for unrelated and negative cultural beliefs.

Efforts by police and a concerned public in the East End to find suspects in a case with few clues were inevitably influenced by these cultural beliefs, and they continue to blur scarce facts. Jack the Ripper may have been a local Jew, a gypsy or a deranged fortune-teller determined to eviscerate those he considered expendable. He may have been psychotic. It did not matter that legal evidence was lacking to convict the culprit. Victorian beliefs and press sensation would connect the dots as surely as the Whitechapel murderer remained invisible.

The inquest into the murder of Elizabeth Stride, only sometimes regarded as a victim of Jack the Ripper due to her lack of mutilations (unlike other victims), showed the difficulties in official handling of cultural beliefs and psychic clues. Stride's identity was unconfirmed when Mrs. Mary Malcolm entered the scene with her declared premonition that the victim was her sister. It is not known when she had first reported the supernatural event she claimed to have experienced, either to police or at the inquest. Two days earlier, Malcolm had examined Stride's body at St. George's Mortuary but was not sure. When she changed her mind, her insistence proved obstructive to the identification of the victim.

Mary Malcolm had approached police claiming to be the victim's sister after reading of the murder in the newspapers on September 30, 1888. Her sister Elizabeth Watts did not visit as expected, and Malcolm gave inquest testimony that she had a premonition at 1:20 A.M. on Sunday, September 30, 1888, the night of Stride's murder. She stated that she had experienced a "pressure on my chest," heard and felt three kisses on her cheek and was convinced it was a visitation of her sister, the murdered woman. The mortuary photo of Elizabeth Stride, which still exists, is unmistakable in the outline of her features and her face not mutilated, as was the case with Catherine Eddowes and Mary Kelly. So how did Mary Malcolm not recognize the face of her own sister when she testified that she had last seen her on the previous Thursday night?

At the inquest on October 2, 1888, Malcolm confirmed, "I can now recognize her by the hair" with other distinguishing marks. She included personal details that matched closely the inquest statements of other witnesses who had known Stride. The coincidences were so conspicuous that they prompted coroner Wynne Baxter, who conducted the inquest, to remark, on the final day, October 23, 1888:

> The first difficulty which presented itself was the identification of the deceased. That was not an unimportant matter. Their trouble was principally occasioned by Mrs. Malcolm, who after some hesitation, and after having had two further opportunities of viewing again the body, positively swore that the deceased was her sister — Mrs. Elizabeth Watts, of Bath. It had since been clearly proved that she was mistaken, notwithstanding the visions which were simultaneously vouchsafed at the hour of the death to her and her husband. If her evidence was correct, there were points of resemblance between the deceased and Elizabeth Watts, which almost reminded one of the Comedy of Errors.

Mrs. Malcolm did not appear on that day.

Elizabeth Stride's identity was finally established, though her name was known before Mary Malcolm gave evidence at the inquest. On the first day of the inquest, October 1, 1888, coroner Baxter asked Detective Inspector Edmund Reid,[13] Local Inspector in charge of H Division CID throughout the time of the Whitechapel murders, if the body had been identified. Reid replied that it had not yet, but the foreman of the jury intervened. "I cannot understand that, as she is called Elizabeth Stride." The coroner responded, "That has not yet been sworn to, but something is known of her. It is known where she lived. You had better leave that point until tomorrow."

Mary Malcolm attended the inquest the following day and was closely examined by Baxter who enquired, "Did not you have some special presentiment that this was your sister?," admitting Malcolm's testimony on premonition. "The only reason why I allow this evidence," Baxter said, "is that the witness has been doubtful about her identification."[14] Was there any way to know if Malcolm's premonitions were genuine because the time of her alleged experience, 1:20 A.M., was within half an hour of the victim's time of death? Malcolm did read of the murder in newspapers and would have been questioned before the inquest to explain this anomaly. However, another witness who was tentatively considered a suspect for Stride's murder — her partner Michael Kidney[15] — was asked the question, "Do you know of any sister who gave money to the deceased?" He answered, "No. On Monday I saw Mrs. Malcolm, who said the deceased was her sister. She is very like the deceased."[16]

These coincidences merged with Mrs. Malcolm's claim of a premonition about the murder of Elizabeth Stride. Though the police and coroner eventually rejected her claims, the popular theory and belief that psychic phenomena graced the mystery of Jack the Ripper was born, legitimized and widely circulated. The press delighted in this angle in reporting to a Victorian readership with amply held beliefs in the supernatural and occult. A contemporary account read:

> Mr. Percy Greg, in a recent magazine article says: "One class of apparitions, the most common and the most easily authenticated, do give one piece of information: the ghost's appearance or its disappearance makes known the death. A majority of apparitions are coincident, or nearly so, with the moment of dissolution. A soldier killed in battle appears to his mistress with a wound in the breast or a bandaged head; a drowned son or brother passes dripping and shivering through hall or chamber, and leans over the fire. A friend or relative expresses with his last breath a passionate wish to see the object of his special affection, and within the same hour, his appearance in the cabin of a ship a thousand miles from land, at a bedside in the Antipodes, or in the midst of a quiet, domestic party, conveys, quicker than the telegraph itself, the tidings of his death. Series of such cases are on record,

in which neither coincidence, nor superstition, nor imposture, nor imagination, supplies a rational explanation. In most of these cases the living person sees a vision of the dead, but occasionally some other token or sign conveys the needed intelligence. The case of Elizabeth Watts's sister is now, however, a strong one, for the alleged pressure on the bed, and three kisses did not convey any vivid impression; it was only when the sister read the newspaper in the morning that the kisses were said to have led her to think that the victim was her sister.[17]

Immediately after the murder of Catherine Eddowes and Elizabeth Stride on the night of what has come to be known as the "double event," letters to the press and police suggesting the use of clairvoyants surged. Mary Malcolm's premonition story had caught the imagination of the public. Spiritualists and seers were urged to "help" the police. The Metropolitan and City Police received numerous letters about Jack the Ripper, the supernatural, and varied occult speculations. Though these Ripper letters documented a social history of alternate Victorian spiritual and religious beliefs, they were of little assistance. In fact, they were a hindrance to Scotland Yard in investigating the Whitechapel murders.[18]

Soon the *Daily Telegraph* was printing summaries of letters sent to the editor.

Mary Malcolm's suspicion "that the woman who had been murdered was her sister" because, when she was in bed, she fancied the poor creature came and kissed her three times, has evidently inspired many of our most recent correspondents with suggestions for calling in the aid of Spiritualism and other more or less occult agencies.

"A Clairvoyant" is of opinion that "if the Ripper's letters were submitted to an efficient medium, the writer might be discovered." "Spiritualist" writes "that there are both male and female practitioners who might be of great service. Of course it is the fashion to scoff at Spiritualistic revelations; but there are on record many authentic cases in which the acute and sensitive medium has been enabled to unravel mysterious occurrences as dark at the outset as is the black and awful mystery that surrounds these current London tragedies. "Inquirer" asks "the Spiritualists of London" to "investigate these murders in their own way, and see what they make of them. If they can, as they unblushingly affirm, call spirits from the vasty deep, why not at once communicate with the unhappy women who have been hurried all untimely to their last account?" "S." writes: "I have read at different times, and also have been told, that when under the influence of mesmerism the medium can describe what has taken place on any day and at any locality at the will of the mesmerist. If this is so, cannot mesmerism be applied in tracing the murderer?"[19]

A report ran in several newspapers that

an extraordinary statement bearing upon the Whitechapel tragedies was made to the Cardiff police yesterday by a respectable-looking elderly woman, who stated that she was a "Spiritualist," and in company with five other persons held a seance on Saturday night. They summoned the spirit of Elizabeth Stride, and after some delay it came, and, in answer to questions, stated that her murderer was a middle-aged man whose name she mentioned, and who resided at a given number in Commercial-road or street, Whitechapel, and who belonged to a gang of twelve.[20]

Another widely syndicated press story was titled "A Spiritualist's Clue."

At another spiritualistic séance held at Bolton yesterday a medium claims to have revealed the Whitechapel murderer. She describes him as having the appearance of a farmer, though dressed like a navvy, with a strap round his waist, and peculiar pockets. He wears a dark moustache and bears scars behind the ear and in other places. He will, says the medium, be caught in the act of committing another murder.[21]

*Pall Mall Gazette* editor, avowed nonconformist and spiritualist W.T. Stead asserted that

Suggestions from the public as to the Whitechapel murders, their perpetrator, and their prevention are becoming positively idiotic.... Several correspondents suggest that the spiritualists should be called in. Where are Messrs. Stuart Cumberland and Irving Bishop?[22]

Stuart Cumberland was an editor and journalist, among other occupations, whose real name was Charles Garner. Under his stage name, he had worked with the great showman W. Irving Bishop, "The World's Most Eminent Mind-Reader," and learned the art of "contact mind-reading." This is a technique that ostensibly allows the expert to find hidden objects and solve problems. He then developed one of Bishop's acts, which linked stage magic and crime into the famed "Murder Game" that was acted out in theaters and large private houses. In his absence, an imaginary murder would be staged, and on his return to the scene of the "crime," the blindfolded Bishop would find the victim, the killer, and the hidden murder weapon.

Cumberland had a professed interest in the supernormal detection of crime and found the Whitechapel murders particularly suited for his talents. Less than a week after the murder of Elizabeth Stride and Catherine Eddowes, he was giving interviews to the press. An early tabloid newspaper reported that "Mr. Stuart Cumberland, being asked whether 'thought reading' would be of any avail for the detection of the Whitechapel murderer, answers very naturally that a thought reader is not a clairvoyant, and must first have his suspected murderer to hand to operate upon. Thought reading then might be applied to advantage at a later stage — when the hare is caught."[23]

Stuart Cumberland later returned from a successful tour in Scotland to give an interview on November 10, 1888, a day after the murder of Mary Kelly. He spoke about "thought reading and the detection of crime," and gave his thoughts on the Whitechapel murders.

> A representative of the Evening News was dispatched to interview Mr. Cumberland as to the possibilities of thought reading being used for the detection of a real murderer, with special reference to the recent horrible crime in the East end.
>
> "Well," said Mr. Cumberland, "how can I help justice in the matter? There is, at present, positively nothing to go upon, and unless I had something to go upon I could not bring my powers — as you are pleased to term them — into play."
>
> "What do you mean by something to go upon?" asked the *Evening News* reporter.
>
> "Well, it is just this way," he replied. "Like the hare that is to be cooked in the various tempting ways described in the cookery books — you must first catch the murderer before I could read his thoughts," he added, "and I can no more read the future than I can see through a brick wall. All I do is to interpret the unconscious physical indications given by my subjects while under the influence of emotion or concentrated attention. More I cannot do. With respect to these horrible murders which have startled not only London, but the whole of the United Kingdom, the friend who has perpetrated them is evidently no ordinary murderer; and I really cannot say what I should be able to make of him were I brought in contact with him. Time enough to speak of that when he is caught, or they, as the case may be."
>
> "What, do you think there is more than one in it?"
>
> "I cannot say; but the spirit of emulation is strong in human nature, and there may possibly be found among the criminal classes who, struck with the fact that the previous horrible murders have remained undetected, may be inspired to do some Jack the Ripping on their own account. It is, however, just possible that all these horrors are the work of one hand. In such case you may depend upon it that the murderer has some grievance against the class of women among whom he selects his victims. You, as a man of the world, will understand the nature of that grievance. I can only tell you, in conclusion — and I must be off in a minute — that I should be pleased to help the police all I could if an opportunity offered. In fact, I am postponing my journey to Berlin for a week or so on the chance of services being of any use. Goodbye."[24]

Cumberland was becoming a celebrity, and it was reported briefly on September 12, 1889, that he had visited the Pinchin Street murder victim.[25] "Mr. Stuart Cumberland managed to gain an entrance to the mortuary and viewed the remains, but for what object is not known," *The Times* reported.[26] As he had friends in high places and enjoyed experiments, it is probable he had permission by the police to "examine" the body telepathically for clues. Assistant Chief Constable Magnaghten, who attended Cumberland's evenings of thought-reading demonstrations on the detection of crime, was known to be enthusiastic about new methods for Scotland Yard.

Cumberland was also approached to apply his skills to other crimes of the period, such as the famous but flawed trial of Florence Maybrick, in 1889, for the alleged arsenic murder of her husband James for which she was convicted. An article Cumberland wrote titled "Maybrickism" included a letter he was sent by a Mr. Miller from Liverpool. "You call yourself a thought-reader and claim to know all about that bloodthirsty scoundrel 'Jack the Ripper'; but up to the present I have seen no sign from you respecting the innocent woman who lies in agonised suspense in Walton gaol.... You can have visions about the Whitechapel murderer, but poor Mrs. Maybrick in your idea is apparently unworthy of a dream. It ought all to be clear to you but perhaps you don't want it to be so."[27]

An alleged three-volume Florence Maybrick diary, in which James Maybrick was named as Jack the Ripper, was brought to Cumberland's attention in September 1889 and, given his interest in the crimes of Jack the Ripper, added some interest to the shaky provenance of the modern "Maybrick Diary," published in 1993 as *The Diary of Jack the Ripper* (later proven to be a hoax). As the Whitechapel murders scare had not abated after the death of James Maybrick and the sentence of Florence, any period connection with the Ripper would at best be prophetic.

It is not a credible solution to the Whitechapel murders and Stuart Cumberland was apparently not convinced either. On the contrary, he went on to lay bets challenging spiritualists and Theosophists to prove ability to detect by any supernatural means the unknown Jack the Ripper. On September 25, 1891, the *Glasgow Herald* reprinted a *Chronicle* debate between Cumberland and Annie Besant, the new head of the Theosophical Society, titled "Occultism and Jack the Ripper."

> Mr. Stuart Cumberland writes in the *Chronicle* this morning—"While sincerely hoping that Mrs. Besant may provide a clue to the Whitechapel miscreant, I must ask to be permitted to explain the part I played in connection with unravelling the mystery. I had a dream of Jack the Ripper, with a portrait of the individual who appeared to me in my dreams. I stated as the result of that dream that the Ripper would commit a ninth murder, but would not a tenth without being captured. A fortnight before the ninth murder was committed I had another dream, in which it was presented that on such and such a day a murder would be perpetrated. The next evening, when supping with some friends, I made known what I had dreamt, and my statement was taken down in writing. I also communicated with Scotland Yard, but no notice was taken of my communication. By a curious coincidence the ninth Whitechapel murder was committed on the very day mentioned in my dream. And it will not be forgotten that I at the time called attention to the fact that, had the police acted upon the suggestion I had made, they could not have failed to have captured the murderer. The murderer, however, remained uncaught, and, what is really extraordinary, he has not since attempted to commit another murder.
>
> If therefore, "Jack the Ripper" is still alive, it may be presumed he is a fatalist, and is convinced that if he attempts another murder, no matter when, he will be captured. If I did not succeed in unravelling the Whitechapel mystery, I can in all fairness claim to have stayed his hand; and what is more, that he would not have escaped the last time had my communication been acted upon. I shall, of course, be asked if I believe in dreams. Well, not much. Sometimes a dream may come true, but in ninety-nine cases out of a hundred they end in nothing. But we are too apt to remember the one instance that is realized, and to entirely forget the 99 other dreams, which are not realized at all. With respect to my Jack the Ripper dream, I simply gave it for what it was worth. It by a curious coincidence turned out to be worth something, and if it has proved to have been the means of staying the Whitechapel murderer's hand, it will not have been dreamt in vain."

Mrs. Besant writes in the *Chronicle*—"As a matter of fact, no person known as a Theosophist, or a member of the Theosophical Society, has claimed the possession of any 'supernormal' powers, and Mr. Stuart Cumberland's bet was made with the knowledge that no one would take it up. He may make a similar bet with the Archbishop of Canterbury to-morrow, and declare that Christianity is destroyed if the Archbishop does not accept it, but no one will be any the worse for such vapourings, and Theosophists will not disbelieve in the Mahatmas, because they have something better to do than accept vulgar wagers. I believe there are some social circles in which your opinion is regarded as worthless if you do not "back" it, but these circles do not rank high in the intellectual world."[28]

Scotland Yard, in the meantime, still could not find a credible lead on Jack the Ripper despite their capable efforts during a time of considerable administrative and social change. The Whitechapel murders continued, and the deeper the mystery became, the more deter-mined were psychics to help the police solve it. The dramatic and arcane events in the East End engrossed the population. It would surely take a miracle by "seers of the unknown," it was supposed, to solve the mystery of Jack the Ripper, who had successfully eluded the combined detective forces of the Metropolitan and City Police with stealth and cunning.

Supernatural accounts of the Whitechapel murders became popular after the murders of Elizabeth Stride and Catherine Eddowes on September 30, 1888. This was the second wave of press sensation that began with anonymous letters sent to the Central News Agency with the signature "Jack the Ripper." The offer of rewards also prompted the public to pro-duce elaborate theories about the killer. During the first wave, after the murders of Martha Tabram (whose status as a Ripper victim is doubtful), Mary Ann Nichols and Annie Chap-man, reported beliefs of psychic intervention were scarce. There were stories of ghost sight-ings at crime scenes or of contacting the spirits of victims in séances.[29] Early on, Jack the Ripper was not invested with mystique. If the killer were simply a man, perhaps a local immigrant, he might be captured. But as more murders were committed — as well as other East End crimes attributed to the invisible killer — psychics were becoming a viable option for the terrified populace.

The October 10, 1888, edition of the *Evening News* carried the headline "Spiritualism as an Aid to Detectives" printed over this letter to the editor.

In connection with these crimes, I am positively to state that several members of the London Spiritu-alist Alliance, the Vice-President of which is the Hon. Percy Wyndham, late M.P. for Cumberland, have for several days past been investigating with several clairvoyants with a view to the discovery of the murderer, and that some startling information has been revealed to them. It must not be under-stood that they accept the statements made, but there is such an air of probability about the revela-tions [that] the "clues" are being followed up with the aid of the officials of Scotland-yard. Whatever may be said to the contrary, I am in the position to state that a mere intellectual or keener body of men cannot be found than the spiritualists, and the fact that in cases of extremity, recourses is had to the aid of the psychical people proves that there is a lurking belief in their pretensions. *The Tattler*.[30]

In 1892, the retiring Chief Superintendent of the City of London Police, Alfred Foster, gave a press interview on his official career and the detection of vice. He indicated that police co-operation with psychics was not unknown.

And crime?— With the exception of Jack the Ripper's Mitre-square tragedy, and the Cannon-street and Arthur-street murders, we have had nothing out of the ordinary in that way. But that Mitre-square murder fairly puzzled me. I have been interviewed by eminent spiritualists and others on the subject, and have had great hopes at different times of lighting upon some clue, but have completely failed. In fact that crime is as great a mystery to-day as ever it was.[31]

If miracles and oracles could not divine the nature of the Whitechapel murders because faith was lacking, perhaps a more systematic approach would be effective. Challenging the moral and practical use of the supernatural for finding Jack the Ripper became a trend among detractors of spiritualism. They had voiced concerns in the mainstream press and specialist periodicals while taking the opportunity to advance their own theories on the murders by extolling the virtues of a "scientific occultism."

F.J. Gould, at the forefront of an embryonic humanist movement in East London during the murders, lamented the loss of faith in intangible qualities. In his autobiography he quoted a pamphlet he had written in November 1888, titled *Religious Instruction in Board Schools* (signed "Mirabeau Brown").

> The decay of faith in miracles is proceeding with a significant speed. The breeze of scepticism is sweeping out of the avenues of modern thought these sere and yellow superstitions, leaving still green and bright the moral sentiments which are the glory of true religion.... If scepticism as to the miraculous elements of religion is thus widely extended in present-day society; if, with the decline of theology and dogma, a more sympathetic and intelligent interest is felt in the application of moral forces to the bettering of man's condition in body and mind, surely this tendancy ought to be reflected in the character of the religious teaching imparted in our popular schools.[32]

The *Pall Mall Gazette* captured the discordant mood on October 4, 1888, with another striking W.T. Stead editorial.

> There is some sense, though not much importance, in the suggestion that the Whitechapel murders afford the practitioners of occult science (or religion) an unexampled opportunity to prove and advertise the genuineness of their pretensions. If spiritualists, clairvoyants, and thought-readers all "lie low and say nuffin'," we may at least conclude that, whatever spirits may be present at their séances, public spirit is notably absent. Interviews with Carlyle and Shakespeare may be all very interesting, but a short conversation with one of the six spirits so recently sent to their long abode, "unhousel'd, disappointed, unanel'd," would for practical purposes be worth more than a volume of trans–Stygian Carlylese. Clairvoyants, even if the mere local influence be sufficient to unseal their spiritual eyes, might set to work upon "Jack the Ripper's" letter and determine whether it be genuine or a hoax. Why does the Society for Psychical Research stand ingloriously idle?

The Society for Psychical Research[33] sixty years later commissioned a study by forensic psychiatrist and criminologist Dr. Donald J. West to investigate published claims of Scotland Yard's psychic detection of Jack the Ripper. Reports widely circulated in the U.S. and UK from 1895, based on the legends of clairvoyant Robert James Lees,[34] were derived from accounts made during the Whitechapel murders. The press story was revived and elaborated upon, notably in the tabloid *Daily Express*, during the 1930s. It was reprinted in subsequent and obscure publications as a validation of the psychic detection of crime and authenticity of spiritualism. The Lees story, probably the most famous example of a psychic connection in the Whitechapel murders, was perhaps the origin of the late 1970s Royal Masonic conspiracy theory of author Stephen Knight.[35] In turn it produced high-profile fictions, a recent one being the 2002 movie *From Hell* starring Johnny Depp and Heather Graham.

West's report was published in an internal research periodical in 1949 as *The Identity of "Jack the Ripper": An Examination of an Alleged Psychic Solution*.[36] It would appear to be the earliest documented public inquiry to the Home Office and New Scotland Yard on the then-closed official files of the Whitechapel murders. West, due to his inquiries, received in reply two letters stating the official position at that time and before the public release of the files from the late 1970s.[37]

After Lees died in January 1931, his daughter Eva Lees was interviewed by a Mrs. Brackenbury, research officer for the Society for Psychical Research. In November 1948 Eva was interviewed by Donald West. She encouraged the belief that Robert Lees acted as Queen Victoria's royal medium (for which some evidence exists), and that he knew the identity of the Ripper. Victoria herself held supernatural beliefs and conducted séances after the death of her husband.[38] Cynthia Legh, a friend of the Lees family, expanded on the "Royal Ripper" tale and published in the spiritualist periodical *Light*[39] in 1970. This was just six weeks before[40] Dr. Thomas Stowell released his influential Royal Ripper conspiracy theory in *Criminologist*,[41] implicating Prince Albert Victor, the grandson of Queen Victoria. Syndicated news accounts had apparently prepared the ground for the theories early in 1935 with the death of Dr. Thomas Dutton, allegedly a friend of the prince and a source for maverick journalist and author Donald McCormick.[42]

Brackenbury reported for the Society for Psychical Research in May 1931, the results of her inquiries to New Scotland Yard officials. She also questioned ex–Chief Inspector Frederick Porter Wensley, a Metropolitan Police constable in Whitechapel during the murders in 1888. No one had ever heard of any involvement by Robert Lees or a psychic in detecting Jack the Ripper despite Lees himself confirming the claim before he died.[43] However, Wensley at the time was also advising Bernard O'Donnell, an Old Bailey crime reporter for the *Empire News*, on O'Donnell's unpublished work on occult Ripper suspect Dr. Roslyn D'Onston. Wensley considered the black magic theory as the most feasible to have emerged in the early 1930s.[44] Wensley,[45] along with another former detective turned author, Edwin T. Woodhall, were ostensibly basking in post-retirement Ripper media attention.

In the March 9 and 10, 1931, editions of the *Daily Express*, crime reporter Cyril Morton rehashed the early 1895 American press versions of the Lees story, claiming an exclusive for his British readers. E.T. Woodhall included Morton's version, somewhat differing in detail and expanded upon, in his 1935 book *Crime and the Supernatural*.[46] Woodhall wrote of the Lees story, "I have no actual proof of its truth, but during my years at the Yard it was more than once recounted to me as I have related it, and I have not the slightest doubt that it is true, and that psychic science, even 45 years ago, was enabled to step in where police work had lamentably failed." Woodhall's account also mentions a private file in the Home Office that is said to provide evidence of the truth of the Lees story. On written inquiry to the Home Office to test Woodhall's claims for the 1949 Society for Psychical Research report, the following reply was received:

Home Office
Whitehall
December 29th, 1948.

Sir,

I am directed by the Secretary of State to refer to your letter of the 30th November about the nineteenth Century murderer known as Jack the Ripper and to say that there is no reference in the records of the Department to the statement said to have been left by a medium named Lees and that no such file as you mention appears to exist.

I am, Sir,
Your obedient Servant
C. S. Brown.

The reply from New Scotland Yard in the following year was as dismissive of the reported use of a medium in tracking Jack the Ripper but added further detail. With reference to Donald West's request on the stories of Woodhall and the *Daily Express*, the letter denied any police knowledge of the killer, which Sir Robert Anderson was not prepared to do earlier in the century. Anderson claimed as fact that the Ripper was known, caged in an asylum, and was a "low-class" Polish Jew.

New Scotland Yard, S.W.I
17th March, 1949

Sir,

With reference to your letter (unsigned) of the 8th March, regarding the "Jack the Ripper" murders, I am directed by the Commissioner to inform you that, according to the records in this office, there is no foundation for the newspaper stories that the murderer was known to the Police, and traced through the aid of a medium.

I am to add that there is no record of the person named [Robert] James Lees to whom you refer in your letter.

I am, Sir,
Your obedient Servant
[Illegible]
Secretary.

In his 1949 Society for Psychical Research report, Donald West concluded,

At first sight it might not seem feasible that a famous murderer could be apprehended and shut away without any public announcement, but such informed opinion as we have been able to secure on this point is varied. If it were true that the identity of the Ripper was known to the police immediately after the commission of his last crime (9 November 1888), this would be difficult to reconcile with the fact that subsequent arrests were made of persons believed to be involved in the murders."

As the Whitechapel murders became muddled with the dichotomy of scientific rationalism and faith in supernatural events, press reporting gathered mystique. Even the conservative *Times* in 1888 did not refuse an advertisement for the popular *Zadkiel's Almanac* that purported to predict the murders: "Zadkiel's Almanac 1889 — Enormous circulation. Voice of the Stars, Weather Forecasts, Nativity of the Emperor of Germany, &c. Zadkiel foretold the rainy summer, the Whitechapel murders, &c. London, Cousins and Co., 6 helmet court, Strand. Price 6d."[47]

Victorian astrological almanacs were the weather forecasts of their day. Popular astrology forecasts had originated in late Victorian and Edwardian newspaper columns. Richard J. Morrison, founding editor of *Zadkiel's Almanac*, was also a president of the Astro-Meteorological Society and was influential in the study of astronomical events and weather patterning. Alfred James Pearce had published a weather almanac in the 1860s and wrote *The Weather Guide Book* (1864) as well as the *Textbook of Astrology* (1879). When Morrison died in 1874, Pearce became the editor of *Zadkiel's Almanac*. Pearce was also interested in meteorology, having joined the Astro-Meteorological Society in 1861. The almanac continued to predict the weather and events. It was Pearce who predicted the 1888 Whitechapel murders in the *Times* advertisement.

On December 2, 1888, journalist George R. Sims wrote of James Monro's appointment as Metropolitan Police Commissioner, "He succeeds to office at a time when the East-end Terror is in full swing and the West-end Terror is due according to the almanac."[48] The West End terror did not appear according to the forecast, but unfortunately for the predictions of *Zadkiel's Almanac*, in the East End — Whitechapel and Spitalfields — it did. The following day, *Pall Mall Gazette* editor W.T. Stead joined the celestial chorus. Defending his contributor Robert Donston Stephenson's occult theory against incursion by Mr. Arthur Diosy, Stead stated, "He also darkly hints that the dates of the crimes have some occult relation to magical astrology. It would be more to the point if Mr. Diosy would tell us when the next murder ought to occur according to the dates of magical astrology."[49]

*The Magic of the Horse-Shoe*, published in 1898 by Robert M. Lawrence, summarized the Victorian mood.

> In enlightened England there are still to be found many people who believe that the relative positions of the sun, moon, and planets are prime factors in determining the proper times and seasons for undertaking terrestrial enterprises. Zadkiel's Almanac for 1898 states that natural astrology is making good progress towards becoming once more a recognized science. [It was also observed during the reign of Queen Victoria] that practically no one among the "lower classes" did not possess an almanac, and most lived their lives by it, refusing to cut their grass if rain was predicted, declining to dose their cattle if the day was inauspicious.

Assistant Commissioner Dr. Robert Anderson, head of the CID during the Whitechapel murders, was also a keen astro-philosopher. He served for a time on the Royal Observatory of Edinburgh Commission in 1876 and later recalled, "In this connection I gained the friendship of the Royal Astronomer and Mrs. Piazzi Smyth. I should mention also the Chairman, Lord Lindsay (now Earl of Crawford),[50] and Professor Tait; and the acquaintance I then formed with Sir George Airy, the Astronomer-Royal, proved valuable to me afterwards in some of my literary work."[51]

Sir George Airy had coordinated Britain's involvement in the discovery of the planet Neptune in 1846. He later assisted Anderson in astronomical calculations on the biblical Book of Daniel referring to the coming of the antichrist. Anderson published in 1895 the results of his work under the title *The Coming Prince*.[52] It is highly reminiscent of the work of his friend Charles Piazzi Smyth, one-time Royal Astronomer and once a respected scientist and member of the Royal Society. In 1888, Piazzi Smyth became a pioneer of the geometric and proportional assessment of the heavens reflected in the study and measurement of ancient monuments. He was especially noted for his work on the Egyptian pyramids of Giza as prophetic biblical code.

Anderson was also a founding member of the Prophecy Investigation Society during his early tenure as Assistant Commissioner. Along with Dr. Alfred T. Schofield, Metropolitan Police surgeon and vice president of the society, Anderson "had readings of a slightly different character in his own house also with Anderson's family."[53] The society, which consisted of fifty members, some of them prominent churchmen, published a series of volumes on prophetic subjects, adding to the apocalyptic literature of the period.

Anderson wrote:

> In the lowest classes of the community sin is but another word for crime. At a higher level in the social scale it is regarded as equivalent to vice. And in a still higher sphere the element of impiety is taken into account. But all this is arbitrary and false. Crime and vice and impiety are unquestionably sinful; but yet the most upright and moral and religious of men may be the greatest sinner upon earth. Why state this hypothetically? It is a fact; witness the life and character of Saul of Tarsus.[54]

In this way he informed readers of his biblical commentary *Redemption Truths*, which discussed his views on the nature of morality, facts and crime. This passage is striking in comparison to his public statements on the "definitely ascertained fact" that Scotland Yard was in possession of historical evidence about Jack the Ripper. Sir Melville Macnaghten, attempting to allay the growing press speculations of the Whitechapel murderer, titled the relevant section of his memoir "Laying the Ghost of Jack the Ripper."[55] This only added to Anderson's mystique. The concept of "religious mania" as a motive for crime was not foreign to Victorian police officials, as Chief Inspector John George Littlechild is reported as saying:

I have always found the worst beasts to be those who have committed crime under the cloak of religion. They have been undoubtedly the meanest wretches I have had to deal with. Some of the blackguards recorded in this book of convictions before me have paid their subscriptions to churches, helped to raise steeples or build organs, and have lived upon canting religion; but they have been the blackest and meanest scoundrels that I have ever arrested, and until arrested actually lived lives, perhaps, of apparent respectability. My own record of arrests, and that of almost every officer, will prove it.[56]

Macnaghten, Dr. Thomas Bond and others were certain that Jack the Ripper was not possessed of a "religious mania." However, speculations driven by Victorian beliefs and comparisons with other cases of religious violence remained persistent. There is no hard evidence to indicate that Jack the Ripper was a religious fanatic or extremist bent on eliminating prostitutes. Nevertheless, the surety of some senior police officials that he was not entails perhaps some awareness of who the Whitechapel murderer was for the comparison, as Anderson took pains to suggest. Police statements to the press had helped more to legitimize conspiracy theories than to clarify the case for a global readership.

Detective Sergeant Stephen White's reported account of Jack the Ripper, published after his death on September 17, 1919, is a classic example of seeing more in an account than it warrants. White was involved with the Whitechapel murders investigation and it was said that he almost caught the murderer:

He was engaged on the whole of the Jack the Ripper crimes which caused such a grim sensation among East Enders. One night he was on what appeared to be a certain clue to the mysterious murderer of women in the Whitechapel region. He kept watch in an East End street, but the murderer's movements were not in accordance with anticipation. For about ten minutes only he left the street, and to his amazement he found on his return that a woman had been stabbed. He saw no man anywhere, and the mystery became even more baffling. As is well known, Jack the Ripper was never discovered.[57]

Another press report went further, claiming that it was written by an anonymous Scotland Yard officer. "'Steve' White as we knew our deceased colleague, Mr. Stephen White [is] believed to be the only man engaged in the hunt who met 'Jack the Ripper.'" Following are some pivotal extracts of the newspaper article.

One of White's reports on his nightly vigils contains the following passages: "For five nights we had been watching a certain alley just behind the Whitechapel Road. It could only be entered from where we had two men posted in hiding, and persons entering the alley were under observation by the two men. It was a bitter cold night when I arrived at the scene to take the report of the two men in hiding. I was turning away when I saw a man coming out of the alley. He was walking quickly but noiselessly, apparently wearing rubber shoes, which were rather rare in those days. I stood aside to let the man pass, and as he came under the wall lamp I got a good look at him.

The most striking thing about him, however, was the extraordinary brilliance of his eyes. They looked like two luminous glow worms coming through the darkness.

In the East End we are used to shocking sights, but the sight I saw made the blood in my veins turn to ice. At the end of the cul-de-sac, huddled against the wall, there was the body of a woman, and a pool of blood was streaming along the gutter from her body. It was clearly another of those terrible murders. I remembered the man I had seen, and I started after him as fast as I could run, but he was lost to sight in the dark labyrinth of East End mean streets."

The mystery, however, that baffled the police more than anything was how the murderer and the victim managed to get into the alley under the eyes of the watching police. It was clear that the couple had not been in any of the houses, and they were not known to any of the residents. Therefore they must have passed into the alley from the Whitechapel Road, and the two police officers were positive that in the four hours of their vigil not a soul had entered the alley.[58]

White's reported account appears to be derived from several conjectural sources and amalgamated over time. It is typical of the development of Ripper theories and press speculations supposedly based on police information. The claims found favor also with fans of the super-natural and macabre.

By 1928, an obscure newspaper in Ohio, USA, borrowed from White's apocryphal story on the Ripper's "glow worm" eyes with a report titled "Owl Eyed Children: Science's Most Baffling Enigma."

> Briefly, its symptoms are the inability to see in daylight, with a gradual "pick up" of the optic nerve as the sun goes down. In darkness sufferers from "owl eyes" can usually see with an amazing clarity. Their gaze, like that of the bird whose name the disease has taken in lay terminology, pierces the shades of night and discerns objects invisible to the normal eye. One of the most striking instances was that of the notorious "Jack the Ripper," the fiend whose inhuman butchery of women alarmed the London public during the last Century. Many optical and psychic investigators believe that this criminal suffered from "owl eyes"—and that this explained why his murders were invariable [sic] per-petrated at night.[59]

Perhaps the most curious theory based on White's story was developed to a remarkable degree by the British occultist Aleister Crowley. In conversations with Bernard O'Donnell, noted in his 1943 article on Jack the Ripper, Crowley had a theory that the Whitechapel murderer was engaged in sorcery and enchantments to such a degree that he was able to become invisible and thus escape the policemen's vigilance in the alley. The invisibility theory assuredly says more about Crowley than about the Ripper. But it shows the extent to which reported police accounts and vague official conclusions are taken to legitimize arcane theories on the Whitechapel murders.

By the time official case files were released during the late 1970s and early 1980s, the central document on credible police suspects, the Macnaghten Memorandum found in the late 1950s, had come to the forefront. Lacking further support or official documentation for its summary of the case, it was used with merged press reports to construct a patchwork of influential research precedents. The major published work on suspect Montague Druitt,[60] for example, accepted White's story and elements of Woodhall's account to conclude that Jack the Ripper was an "Apostle," a member of a clandestine Cambridge University mystical society. Crowley, no stranger to mystical societies, could not as a Cambridge student have passed up noting a Jack the Ripper theory of such esoteric magnitude if it were true. We can see, therefore, how Victorian beliefs in the occult and supernatural enhanced the morality play born of the East End events during the autumn of 1888. They are a part of social history as they were ingrained in the subcultures that held them. How and to what extent their period associations and secret societies involved themselves in suspicions, perceptions and theories on the Whitechapel murders, became lost in the politicized labyrinth of inter-vening years.

# 2

# Sacred Prostitution

The women who are believed to be victims of the Whitechapel murders[1] have a legacy of some historical importance. They met death at the hands of Jack the Ripper sooner than they likely would have, given their poor health and the squalid conditions they survived daily in Victorian East End London.

The victims' lives and deaths reflected the times but were imbued also with the symbols and hopes of Victorian London's early feminist, socialist, religious and political movements. Since then the stories of the Ripper's casualties have served as sources for popular histories, fictional treatments and academic feminist gender studies. Each group has projected its own agenda onto the victims.

Some have opined that the Ripper's motivating impulse to kill and mutilate numerous prostitutes in the space of a few months in 1888 was sexual. Influential criminal case studies are sources of abstract theories and speculation on the nature and inclinations of sexual serial killers.[2] As vendors of sex to any man with a few pence in dark spaces, they were available victims for Jack the Ripper.

Knife murder, shocking mutilations, extraction of internal organs including uteri — all would result in copious amounts of warm blood. It is plausible to theorize that the Whitechapel murderer had a deeply disordered sexuality who devoured the sensations of killing. Yet no evidence of sexual assault was noted in the inquests, autopsies, or police reports. Today the theory is just that. There is simply no hard evidence for that position, except perhaps for the notion that even Jack the Ripper was not devoid of sexuality, frustrated and deviant as it may have been, or that every serial mutilating murder case is sexual in nature. Though senior police openly concluded that Jack the Ripper was a sexual maniac, the internal investigation pursued other motives as credible that cannot be dismissed in considering the Whitechapel murders.

Because sexual serial killers, especially of prostitutes, are known to find pleasure in cruelty, the argument goes that the Whitechapel murderer must also have been of this type because of the victims he chose. It is not a new concept; the first to make the assertion were Scotland Yard police surgeon Dr. Thomas Bond and Melville Leslie Macnaghten. The publicized and idealized portrayal of the sexual killer of fallen women was thus born. The theory, however, was not confirmed by the identification of a suspect or supported by contemporary medical reports.

As the murderer's count is also a contentious issue with only three victims known for certain,[3] the interpretation of the Ripper's motives becomes even more problematic and less likely to indicate or confirm the identity of the killer. The cautious police conclusions on the number of Ripper victims were dependent on the opinions and experience of Victorian police surgeons. The wounds inflicted by the Whitechapel murderer were so savage and of such deliberately crude precision that they divided the doctors. They had no way of knowing the extent of medical or anatomical knowledge of the killer. Thus they could not deduce why the murders were committed. The bodies of the victims were literally the only substantial evidence of the crimes and therefore were of paramount importance to inquests, inquiries and verdicts.

It is with the subjective question of motive that conspiracy theories are born in unsolved murder inquiries and it was no different for the Whitechapel murders. The circumstantial or moral suspicions of a serial murderer may be sufficient to legally convict and execute a suspect or incarcerate him as insane, but it is the behavior of a killer that constitutes a crime against victims and society. Jack the Ripper was criminally responsible for what he did, not for what he thought, was inclined to believe, or led others to believe, surmise or report.

The sensational news articles and wild theories were in this way an attempt to rationalize highly abhorrent and shocking events for an outraged society.[4] The modern tendency, however, involves attempts to determine the type of serial killer Jack the Ripper was. It continues to unduly influence interpretation of surviving and inconclusive official sources. Although useful, a criminal profile of the killer cannot determine who Jack the Ripper was. Nor is it certain to fit with numerous suspects and theories at the time or since because there is a lack of forensic material to make that determination. For these reasons, credible suspects who were a part of the original investigation and who lacked an alibi cannot now be eliminated from the case.

Without sufficient clues, it was left to Scotland Yard police surgeon Dr. Thomas Bond, on the request of Assistant Metropolitan Police Commissioner Robert Anderson and later Sir Melville Macnaghten, to fix police opinion and press reporting. The murders of Mary Ann Nichols, Annie Chapman, Elizabeth Stride, Catherine Eddowes, and Mary Kelly, now dubbed the five "canonical" Jack the Ripper victims, had set the count during the investigation. These official positions, based on conflicting medical and autopsy reports, became the mainstay of diverse police opinions and theories on suspects. They are also the direct source of erroneous speculations and the growth of conspiracy theories.

As the panic of the Whitechapel murders spread, it threatened to inflame the region with rioting and violence and was a real concern to Metropolitan Police Commissioner Sir Charles Warren. The failure of Scotland Yard to catch Jack the Ripper added to the international press vilification of British imperial policies. Government police structures and questionable results encouraged political murder theories at the expense of the victims. The necessity of prostitution for poor East End women and their awful living conditions prompted an international public outcry. Queen Victoria's subjects dead at the hands of Jack the Ripper were immortalized as unfortunates, their unknown assassin destined to become the prototype of the modern sexual serial killer.

However, the continuing din of press and political criticism of Scotland Yard's failure to catch the culprit has unfairly instilled a stain on the abilities and experience of a diligent police force. These perceptions unfairly view early police methods as primitive, applying

*Opposite:* Homeless in the East End in 1888. A realistic portrayal of a police officer attending an unfortunate in the slums (courtesy Stewart P. Evans).

modern standards to the tools of over a century ago. Scotland Yard detectives and beat police officers did manage to contain the panicky public in 1888, but could not capture the murderer known as Jack the Ripper. The ambiguity of senior police conclusions on the Whitechapel murders is apparently then an outcome of Victorian class structure and the defense of Scotland Yard traditions by public officials with broader political concerns.

Casual prostitution,[5] a way for poor, alcoholic women to support themselves, was an attraction for Victorian slummers and explorers of the macabre as it was for religious philanthropists and the upholders of purity and temperance laws. That Jack the Ripper chose or found his victims from the most vulnerable of East London's streetwalkers shows that this serial killer was concerned with their movements to some degree. These considerations have led to derived press theories on marginal suspects from the Victorian upper classes as well as from the local charitable institutions and philanthropic West Enders competing for the souls of the fallen.

The lives of "unfortunates," as they were known, were also probed by the press, recorded in inquest transcripts and investigated by the police. That five impoverished prostitutes are now perhaps better known and studied than even some politicians of the period is, in effect, a form of deferred justice and tribute. Unmarried women were especially vulnerable in the poverty-stricken East End. Coverture, a concept introduced in William Blackstone's *Commentaries on the Laws of England* in the late 1700s, was part of the common laws of England and the United States through most of the 1800s. Coverture is the archaic principle that in marriage a woman's complete existence is integrated into that of her husband and that she has no existence outside of him. The wife had no individual rights, could not own property, vote, obtain an education, or enter into any contract. If a wife was permitted to work under the laws of coverture, she was also required to surrender her wages to her husband, effectively making her personal chattel under the law. In the event of divorce, the wife would lose any benefits she had worked for and the custody of children was denied her without mercy or consideration for the interests of the child.

With the writings of Henry Mayhew, Charles Booth and others, prostitution began to be viewed as a social problem. It also began to be seen as an early feminist issue in the work of such notable activists as Josephine Butler, who crusaded against ingrained double standards in sexual morality. Charles Dickens's novel *Oliver Twist* and Thomas Hood's poem "The Bridge of Sighs" presented sympathetic portraits of prostitutes as victims and survivors. Yet the continuing literary emphasis on the "purity" of women, found in works such as John Ruskin's *Sesame and Lilies*, led to the portrayal of prostitutes as corrupted creatures of the night to be cleansed. This has lead to a raft of unfounded theories regarding Jack the Ripper as a social or religious moralist. These Victorian views were usually expressed in letters to police in search of information, and press reports that became the primary sources for subsequent theories.

The first law that used the term "common prostitute" was the Vagrancy Act of 1824, which covered a multitude of crimes from loitering to fortune-telling. Subsection 3 of this act stated that "any common prostitute behaving in a riotous or indecent manner in a public place or thoroughfare" was liable to a fine or imprisonment. Incarceration usually included hard labor, and it was not unknown for convicted common prostitutes to be transported to populate, entertain convicts and labor in remote colonies of the British Empire.[6]

The next law of prostitution control was applicable to London's police districts; subsection 54 of the Metropolitan Police Act of 1839. This stated that "any common prostitute loitering or soliciting for the purposes of prostitution to the annoyance of inhabitants or passers-by" would be subject to arrest and, if convicted, to a fine which would increase upon further convictions. In 1847 the Towns Police Clauses Act was established for provincial England. Together, these "solicitation laws," as they came to be known, were used by police in England and Wales to control boisterous women in public places. The 1869 Contagious Diseases Act, intended to contain the spread of venereal disease among the military, was also used to control common prostitution. However, early feminists fought for its repeal either to maintain prostitution as illegal and therefore not government regulated or because it potentially forced degrading and invasive medical examinations upon any female generally.

In July of 1885, a year before the Contagious Diseases Act was repealed, William T. Stead, editor of the *Pall Mall Gazette*, published an early investigative report exposing an organized child prostitution ring in London and a white female slave trade from Europe. Titled *The Maiden Tribute of Modern Babylon*, it established Stead's reputation as a socialist crusader and advocate of government by the press. After Stead was convicted and imprisoned for procuring an underage child in an attempt to expose the ring, Parliament under intense public pressure passed the Criminal Law Amendment Act.

The new act raised the age of consent for sexual intercourse from 13 to 16 and created protective laws against "procurement and forcible detainment of women by third parties for the purposes of prostitution." Section 13 of the act, "Suppression of Brothels," stated that, "any person who kept, managed, or assisted in the management of premises used as a brothel, or was the tenant or landlord of such premises, was liable to a hefty fine or a maximum of three months' imprisonment." The meaning of the word "brothel" was not clarified until 1895[7] as "premises used by more than one woman for the purposes of prostitution." By 1888, the Criminal Law Amendment Act had contributed to available streetwalking victims of Jack the Ripper and attendant pressures on the H Division of Whitechapel police to regulate and enforce the law.

A Stepney brothel keeper had the dubious honor of having one of the Whitechapel victims killed on her property. The story of Bella Freeman was recorded in the memoirs of Irish rebel and confidence trickster May Churchill Sharpe, better known as Chicago May. In her 1929 book May wrote

> I went to a fence, Bella Freeman, in Whitechapel, and disposed of the stuff. She told me she had to be cautious of Yanks, because they were so sharp that they would sell her swag, and then steal it from her. She certainly was frank to me, thinking I was Irish. This gave me an idea, so I, when her back was turned, robbed her of a package of unset stones worth about two hundred and fifty pounds. This with what she paid me for the rings, etc., gave me a fair price for my work. When Bella died, she had diamonds worth a king's ransom. She left most of her estate to the Church, and spent a fortune trying to identify Jack the Ripper, who killed the unfortunate woman on her property.[8]

Though there is little to verify Chicago May's story, Charles Booth later recorded the information of Inspector James Flanagan of J Division. "Between Roseberg Place and Woodland St. is Mayfield Road. No 36 at the South end is a brothel kept by 'the notorious Bella Freeman.' This Mrs. Freeman said Flanagan used to keep brothels in Stepney and Leicester Square, she still has one in the city. From Stepney she was turned out by the efforts of "Charrington & Co."[9]

In a report to the Home Office dated October 25, 1888,[10] Sir Charles Warren wrote that Mr. Charrington had "been very active in evicting the holders of Brothels, and has cleared out 6 Ford St. Stepney & Lady Lake Green, the result however is not conducive to morality, the unfortunate women are driven to plying for hire among respectable people, or else exercise their calling in the streets." No victim of Jack the Ripper was known murdered at 6 Ford Street, Stepney. Though Bella Freeman was running East End brothels and may have taken an interest in the Ripper, Chicago May's embellished story is unfounded.

A notable suggestion for alternative employment options available to East End prostitutes was championed in a letter to *The Times* from a social activist and early feminist, Frances Cobbe. It brought a scathing *Illustrated Police News* editorial response:

> Female detectives! This is the latest idea. Sir Charles Warren has been urged to enrol women in his force, and the suggestion has the support of Miss Frances Power Cobbe. In a letter to the Times she says that a female detective would pass unsuspected where a man would be instantly noticed; she could extract gossip from other women much more freely; she could employ for whatever it might be worth that gift of intuitive quickness and mother wit with which her sex is commonly credited. We are bound to assume that Miss Cobbe wrote her letter in sober earnest and after mature consideration. But the communicated certainty reads more like a grim joke than anything else. It is the female employment question carried to a ludicrous extreme.[11]

Today, female detectives are a fact of life and of vast benefit to the efficiency of modern police forces, but in Victorian London the idea was considered absurd. Male detectives and journalists dressed up as women to hunt Jack the Ripper. Sir Arthur Conan Doyle, author of the Sherlock Holmes novels, advanced his own theory that the Ripper was a man dressed as a woman, and there was no shortage of theories that Jack was in fact "Jill the Ripper." It was conjectured that the killer was able to avoid detection in this way but there is little basis for this as the prostitute victims presumably took their killer to remote places for low paying sex.

Warren did not take the suggestion to employ female detectives. However, he introduced one of the first known uses of bloodhounds in police work. Nevertheless, women were known to be engaged as informers by Scotland Yard detectives. Catherine Eddowes, murdered at Mitre Square on the early morning of September 30, 1888, was thought to be acting as a police informer based on comments she allegedly made on seeking a reward for the capture of Jack the Ripper. Mary Kelly, an Irishwoman murdered in the early hours of November 9, was also reputed to have been an informer on supposed Fenian plots to murder the Whitechapel victims, but there appears to be no evidence to substantiate the theories. Landladies, though, were in a unique position to provide detectives with information about suspicious lodgers and were employed by Scotland Yard.[12]

It was reported that Detective Inspector Frederick Abberline, in charge of inquiries into the Whitechapel murders from September 1888 to March 1889, gave East End prostitutes his own money to keep them off the streets. He may have been handing out funds in return for information. These procedures were set out by Howard Vincent in his 1881 police manual: "Detectives must necessarily have informants, and be obliged to meet them when and where they can. But it is very desirable that the public house should be avoided as much as possible. Tap room information is rarely worth much. Occasionally, perhaps, refreshment must be given to an informant, but when possible it is best to give money."[13]

The word "harlot" occurs 122 times in the New King James Version of the Bible. This has led to speculations of a "Jack the Religious Ripper" attempting to rid Babylon of its "impure vermin." A recent conclusion reached is that a killer inspired by the Old Testament book of Ezekiel was Jack the Ripper. With Ezekiel's numerous references to whores and the wrath of the God of Israel as a motive for the Whitechapel murders,[14] the theory is certainly not new, nor is the suspect, Joseph Lis, credible. This examination of the case is a modern reflection of the influential comments of Sir Robert Anderson. He caused a storm with his "definitely ascertained fact" that the identity of Jack the Ripper was known to Scotland Yard and that he was most certainly "a low class Polish Jew."[15]

Though the police had considered a possible killer fueled by either Christian or Jewish zeal from one of the charitable East End institutions or synagogues, there does not appear to be any convincing historical evidence for it. Despite this, Jack the Ripper has attracted a raft of religious and anti–Semitic cant from minority interests to modern revisionists in search of archaic blood libels for use in propaganda wars. As the Whitechapel murders did occur in a confined multicultural space of slums and competing interests, inevitable press and official references to alien beliefs, immigrant superstitions and transplanted ways of life were not surprising. Though internal official statements were reserved, public comments by police and political officials were more overt in their partiality. However, without evidence in a criminal investigation, these Jack the Ripper theories remain rhetoric.

In June 1888, several months before Jack the Ripper's reign of terror and after the start of the police file on the Whitechapel murders with Emma Smith, Annie Besant, a social activist and feminist, wrote a scathing report titled *White Slavery in London*, on the conditions of women and girls employed at the Bryant & May match factory in Bow. Besant and her friend the nonconformist editor W.T. Stead mounted another press campaign similar in style to *The Maiden Tribute of Modern Babylon* of 1885, it eventually resulted in safe and equitable working conditions for legitimately employed East End females.

Prostitution was a constantly lurking proposition in East End London for destitute women and girls. The Matchgirls Strike of 1888 was pivotal, not only in setting labor union and working standards into the next century, but also in refining the liberal press campaigns that would mark the news reporting of the Whitechapel murders. In a

Annie Besant as portrayed in W.T. Stead's periodical *The Review of Reviews* in 1891.

*Pall Mall Gazette* editorial, Stead observed, "The story is full of hope for the future, illustrating as it does the immense power that lies in mere publicity. It was the publication of the simple story of the grievances of the match girls in an obscure little halfpenny weekly paper called The Link which did the work."[16]

Besant wrote of the match girls:

> Born in slums, driven to work while still children, undersized because under-fed, oppressed because helpless, flung aside as soon as worked out, who cares if they die or go on to the streets provided only that Bryant & May shareholders get their 23 per cent and Mr. Theodore Bryant can erect statutes and buy parks? Girls are used to carry boxes on their heads until the hair is rubbed off and the young heads are bald at fifteen years of age? Country clergymen with shares in Bryant & May's draw down on your knee your fifteen year old daughter; pass your hand tenderly over the silky clustering curls, rejoice in the dainty beauty of the thick, shiny tresses.[17]

Stead, who supported and introduced Besant to the Theosophical Society in May 1889, commissioned her for a *Pall Mall Gazette* review on the October 1888 release of Blavatsky's book *The Secret Doctrine*. Helena Petrovna Blavatsky, a founder in 1875 of the Theosophical Society in New York, herself was to open an East End refuge sponsored by the London Branch for poor and destitute girls before she died in 1891. She appointed Annie Besant as her Theosophical Society successor, who had since distanced herself from the shortcomings of socialism and political activism. These alignments of Victorian London's early feminist, socialist, mystical, religious, and liberal press associations are the fountainhead of many influential Jack the Ripper theories. The killer's seemingly ritual removal of internal organs had in effect sanctified the victims.

Casual prostitution in the East End during the "Autumn of Terror" of 1888 acquired for Victorian "new age" and religious subcultures a spiritualized Magdalene idealism. Press illustrations of the murdered victims alive were notably utopian. Press reports, combined with ideas on medieval sacred feminism, chivalry and socialist aims turned the Whitechapel murders into a cause. Conservative politics and values, press agencies and mainstream religious beliefs were devilish scapegoats.

The police investigation of the Whitechapel murders progressed through the latter half of 1888. Absence of credible evidence forced the police to rely heavily on the victims' wounds as clues. Witness statements conflicted with medical opinions on the time of death. From the onset of the crimes, Scotland Yard was at the mercy of opinions of divisional police surgeons and inquest testimonies. Police officials attempted to clarify the facts even as the press reported "medical murders" as an apparent attack on the establishment. The theories explaining the Ripper's extraction of internal organs that were aired at the inquest proceedings have formed the backbone of the legendary stories on the Whitechapel murders. Over time, these conjectures have become as pervasive as the few substantial facts on the case.

On October 25, 1888, Robert Anderson, on the authority of Sir Charles Warren, sent a request to a Scotland Yard Central Office police surgeon, Dr. Thomas Bond, to review the murders. Anderson stated, "In dealing with the Whitechapel murders the difficulties of conducting the inquiry are largely increased by reason of our having no reliable opinion for our guidance as to the amount of surgical skill and anatomical knowledge probably possessed by the murderer or murderers."[18] Bond's report was made on November 10, 1888, a day after he examined the Dorset Street crime scene and attended the autopsy of Mary Kelly. He also reviewed medical files on the previous victims.

Bond went on to say that in his opinion the murderer was "subject to periodical attacks of homicidal and erotic mania." The nature of the mutilations indicated a sexual perversion known as satyriasis, an abnormally intense sexual desire in men. He added the possibility that the Ripper's impulse to murder had "developed from a revengeful or brooding condition of the mind, or that religious mania may have been the original disease, but I do not think either hypothesis is likely."[19]

Bond's report is the first known criminal profile of an unknown serial killer. It was influential for senior police, government policy, modern criminal profilers and in legal and medical case studies. The report also shaped primary and pivotal police sources of Macnaghten and Anderson in forming their subsequent theories. However, the Whitechapel murders were also of interest as a case study for medical experts who recorded their impressions. These views indicate the level of proficiency in scientific criminal studies in the late Victorian period. They had likely informed both Bond and Macnaghten and, in turn, the official police reviews of medical evidence influenced further case studies.

A letter to the editor of *The British Medical Journal* summed up the state of medical research available to police surgeons examining the crimes of Jack the Ripper.

> An eminent surgeon writes to us: "The crimes which have lately been committed in Whitechapel have given rise to many theories and speculations, prompted rather by a desire to account for them — that is to say, to find some motive for them than by any knowledge of the subject. Most of those who have written to medical or daily papers have treated these occurrences, as though they were unprecedented in the annals of crime.
>
> Therefore, however revolting be the subject, it seems desirable to point out that such is by no means the case; but that a certain horrible perversion of the sexual instinct is the one motive and cause of such apparently aimless acts, and that the criminal is neither insane nor prompted by pseudo-religious rancour against an unfortunate class of women. The most exhaustive and judicial treatise on this subject [Psychopathia Sexualis, Von Krafft-Ebing, Stuttgart, 1886] divides this form of neurosis into three divisions: local, spinal, and cerebral; but the individual may be affected simultaneously by more than one of these forms. The cerebral neuroses fall naturally into four sub-classes: 1. Paradoxia, that is, untimely desire (in regard to sex). 2. Anaesthesia, absence. 3. Hyperaesthesia, excess. 4. Paraesthesia, perversion of desire; among these last are cruelty and murder. He says (omitting certain parts): "These cerebral anomalies lie in the province of psycho-pathology. They occur, as a rule, in persons mentally sound, in a variety of combinations, and in them originate many sexual misdemeanours. They are worthy of study by the medical jurist, because they so frequently produce perverse and even criminal acts." Krafft-Ebing then goes on to give, in sufficient detail, accounts of five trials with conviction for the murder of women (sometimes of children) and mutilation of their bodies, and he refers to three other such convictions, naming the authorities.
>
> Of these criminals, one, Verzenteli, condemned in January 1872, had murdered and mutilated three women, and had attacked five others with murderous intent. The escape of his last victim led to his detection. One of Lombroso's cases is a certain Grayo, who thus slew and mutilated five women, and was discovered on the murder of a sixth after ten years of immunity. Several of the condemned persons confessed the disgusting motive of the crime, and not one of them was found to be insane. These acts are not committed by women (save in one exceptional case), nor is it likely that any woman would have the nerve, bodily strength, and audacity to carry out two murders, at an interval of only a few minutes, as was done in October."[20]

William Alexander Hammond, a Civil War veteran, past surgeon general, and head of a sanatorium in 1888, published on theories of motive for the Whitechapel murders. This was part of the wide international interest of medical experts in the case. Hammond's opinions also reflect contemporary forensics and criminology and show how little the case has progressed with psychological profiling over time.

> A few months ago a murder of a peculiarly atrocious character was committed in the district known as Whitechapel, London. The victim was a woman of the lowest class of that particularly low section of the metropolis. Not content with simply killing the woman, the murderer had mutilated

the corpse and had inflicted wounds altogether unnecessary for the accomplishment of his object. Three or four months afterwards another woman of the same class was found dead with over thirty stab wounds in her body, and in quick succession other similar crimes were committed, until now the number amounts to nine.[21]

The efforts of the police to discover the perpetrator or perpetrators have up to this time been utterly fruitless, and every supposed clew that has been followed up has proved to be without foundation. All kinds of theories have been indulged in by the police, professional and amateur, and by legal and medical experts, who appear to have exhausted their ingenuity in devising the most strained hypotheses in their attempts to account for these murderous crimes. In the foregoing remarks relative to madness and murder I have brought forward examples in illustration of several forms of mental derangement, any one of which may have been the predominating motive which has been the starting point of the crimes in question.

Thus they may have been committed by a person who kills merely for the love of killing, and who has selected a particular class from which to choose his victims, for the reason that being of very little importance in the social world, they could be killed with a minimum amount of risk of detection. The fact that unnecessary wounds and mutilation were inflicted gives additional support to this theory. The more hacking and cutting the more delight would be experienced.

They may be the result of a morbid impulse which the perpetrator feels himself unable to resist, and which, after he had yielded to its power, is followed by the most acute anguish of the mind. It may be said against this view that if such were the fact the murderer would, in his moments of mental agony and repentance, surrender himself to the authorities; but in answer I think it may be properly alleged that fear for his own safety would prevent him doing an act which he might feel to be right, but which he would know would lead to his speedy execution. To test the correctness of this hypothesis it would be necessary to offer him free and unconditional pardon. If he is the subject of a morbid impulse which he cannot resist, he will give himself up if immunity be promised him.

The murders may have been committed by one who is acting under the principle of suggestion. He may have recently heard or read of similar crimes (for such murders have been committed before) and has been impelled thereby to go and do likewise, until after the first two or three murders he has acquired a love for the act of killing, and for the excitement attendant on the risk which he runs. This last incentive is a very powerful one, with certain morbidly constituted minds, and has apparently been the chief motive in some notable series of crimes.

Again, they may have been committed by several persons acting under the influence of the power of imitation. This force, owing to the extensive publication of reports of crimes through the newspapers, is much more influential at present than at any other period in the history of the world. The more ferocious the murder the more likelihood that it will be imitated. It is not at all unreasonable to suppose that there may have been as many murderers of these women as there are murders.

I am inclined, however, to think that the perpetrator is a reasoning maniac, one who has received or imagines he has received some injury from the class of women upon which his crimes are committed, or who has assumed the role of the reformer, and who thinks he can annihilate them one by one or strike such terror into those that remain that they will hasten to abandon their vicious mode of life. He is probably a person whose insanity is not suspected even by those who are in constant association with him. He may be a clergyman, a lawyer, a physician, or even a member of the titled aristocracy; a cashier in a bank, a shopkeeper, an officer of the army or navy. All apparently motiveless crimes are exceedingly difficult of detection. It is quite conceivable that this man may leave the dinner-table or the ball-room and pass a dozen policemen on his way towards the accomplishment of his purpose. The higher he appeared to be in the social scale the less he would be liable to suspicion.

If the perpetrator of the so-called Whitechapel murders were to cease now his career of crime, there is no reason to suppose that he would ever be discovered. But it is not at all likely that he will fail to go on in the course which has now become second nature to him. His love for murder has become overpowering, and immunity has rendered him bold. Little by little he will become less cautious, and eventually he will be caught.

There is but one way to deal with a person like this Whitechapel murderer, and that is, to hang him as soon as he is caught. He is an enemy of society and is entitled to no more consideration than a wild beast which follows his instinct to kill. Laws are not made for the purpose of enforcing the principles of abstract justice; they are enacted solely for the protection of society. Some fifteen years ago, in a little book entitled "Insanity in its Relations to Crime," I urged that certain of the insane are properly as much amenable to punishment as though in full possession of all their mental faculties unimpaired.[22]

An illustration of Mary Kelly and her killer from a contemporary source (courtesy Stewart P. Evans).

Statements of Chief Inspector Donald Swanson, Robert Anderson and Melville Mac-naghten,[23] the holy trinity of police opinion on the Whitechapel murders case, relied on psycho-medical thinking of the day. The motive was confirmed as *lustmord*, a pleasure of a depraved sexual nature experienced from killing and mutilation. This position finds resonance in modern psychological profiling of Jack the Ripper. However, the subjective motive has become ingrained as the only possible alternative to explain the crimes. Despite other motives considered, it determines the type of the Whitechapel murderer in comparison with today's serial killers.

These semi-official police comments also delineate prime suspects for the Whitechapel murders and have become the test of credibility for new suspects. The 1993 discovery of the 1913 Littlechild Letter, of ex–Special Branch Chief Inspector John Littlechild, revealed a further credible police suspect. It also supported the motive of *lustmord* for the Whitechapel murders yet challenged the official suspects and theories. The statements support a Scotland Yard position on the crimes of Jack the Ripper more than proof that the killer's identity was "a definitely ascertained fact," as Anderson suggested publicly after his retirement in 1901. Police did not appear to know with certainty the identity of the murderer then, as it is hard to know now without proof contingent on sparse Scotland Yard investigative reports.

Theories, conspiracies, speculations and hard conclusions on the motives of Jack the Ripper are based on these primary and official sources that are reliant on conflicted medical reports, but are they historically honest or sufficient? Though Jack the Ripper may simply be an ordinary and psychotic local East End resident or a visiting *lustmord* killer, the circumstances of the Whitechapel murders were anything but ordinary. These murders were set apart with unique signatures: deep throat cutting, extensive mutilations and the extraction of female and other internal organs. They were performed with speed, crude precision and in the dark on prostitutes in a confined slum section of the East End.

The official details of the police investigation were not widely known by Victorian society. They were not released, despite the emerging British "new journalism" pioneered by *Pall Mall Gazette* editor W.T. Stead. Yet ever since, a great deal of information has been obtained, and theories developed, based on press reporting and information from competing news agencies, though the known Scotland Yard and Home Office files on the case are now available.[24] However, ambiguity in combined police opinions on the Whitechapel murders is found emphasized with the perplexing sureties offered in later unofficial comments of Sir Robert Anderson. He referred to a tacit Scotland Yard investigation[25] of a serial murder case, whose motive was officially recognized and supported by medical reports as that of an insane "homicidal maniac" filled with *lustmord*.

An example found in the investigative files is a December 23, 1888, report from succeeding Metropolitan Police Commissioner James Monro to the Home Office on circumstances of the death of prostitute Rose Mylett in Poplar. Monro stated, "We are absolutely in the dark as to the circumstances of this murder, which at present appears to be devoid of motive, as were the outrages in Whitechapel. I need not say that the Assist. Comr. and officers of the Criminal Investigation Dept. are doing & will do, all they can to detect this mysterious crime."[26]

Macnaghten later wrote a police position statement on prime suspects for Chief Commissioner Sir Edward Bradford, should the Home Office require it for press stories of Jack the Ripper. The internal report, dated February 23, 1894, allowed for the fact that "no shadow of proof could be thrown on any one." Known as the Macnaghten Memorandum, this is the official Scotland Yard account. Senior police, historians, and criminal profilers have based theories about the Whitechapel murders on this report. A draft version emerged in 1959 when Macnaghten's daughter, Lady Christabel Aberconway, wrote a letter to the *New Statesman* saying she held her father's notes on Jack the Ripper. Macnaghten, she stated, "names three individuals against whom the police held very reasonable suspicion and states which of these three, in his judgement, was the actual killer." As the contents of the official version have been found to contain errors and are unverified by investigative reports, its tone is strongly regarded as a police policy statement for the Secretary of State, prepared in readiness for questions in the House of Commons. It came in response to serialized press reports in *The Sun* early in 1894 that claimed to have evidence on the identity of Jack the Ripper suspect Thomas Cutbush, and was filed when Macnaghten held the position of Scotland Yard's Chief Constable, CID.

The statements of Macnaghten[27] and Anderson have in common the view that the Ripper was insane and motivated by *lustmord*. Anderson's suspect replaced M.J. Druitt with the theory that Jack the Ripper was an East End Jew. Swanson's later notes supported Anderson's suspect. The theory of a poor local dweller, insane and thirsty for blood, found support in noted FBI criminal profiles developed over time that also took Dr. Bond's report into account. Sensational reports in *The Times* of alleged Jewish ritual practices,[28] supposedly part of the Ripper's murder rituals, merged with theories of Anderson, Macnaghten and Swanson in attempting to explain the horrendous nature of wounds found upon the victims.

Important statements made by senior police officers have been given excess historical weight simply because they appear the best primary sources on the Whitechapel murders: the Macnaghten Memorandum, an official policy document prepared by a Chief Constable without known support of investigative Metropolitan Police reports; the Swanson Marginalia, annotations written in the margins and back page of Anderson's memoirs after the events by a Chief Inspector in overall charge of the case for CID; and the press and published memoirs of Anderson which transmuted Scotland Yard theories into definitely ascertained facts on an immigrant Jewish Jack the Ripper caged in an asylum and untouchable to the English justice system. Unfortunately, they are not conclusive and have of necessity given rise to further conjecture and speculation.

As a result of Anderson's public comments during his retirement, when he stated as fact that the identity of Jack the Ripper was known to Scotland Yard, an exchange of letters was published that refuted the allegations and requested evidence for the assertions. Extracts presented in the *Jewish Chronicle* follow and set the mood of the times before World War I:

Sir Robert Anderson, the late head of the Criminal Investigation Department at Scotland Yard, has been contributing to Blackwood's a series of articles on Crime and Criminals. In the course of his last contribution, Sir Robert tells his readers that the fearful crimes committed in the East End some years ago, and known as "Jack the Ripper" crimes, were the work of a Jew. Of course, whoever was responsible for the series of foul murders was not mentally responsible, and this Sir Robert admits. But I fail to see — at least, from his article in Blackwood's — upon what evidence worthy of the name he ventures to cast the odium for this infamy upon one of our people. It will be recollected that the criminal, whoever he was, baffled the keenest search not alone on the part of the police, but on the part of an infuriated and panic-stricken populace. Notwithstanding the utmost vigilance, the man, repeating again and again his demoniacal work, again and again escaped. Scotland Yard was nonplussed, and then, according to Sir Robert Anderson, the police "formed a theory" — usually the first essential to some blundering injustice.

In this case, the police came to the conclusion that "Jack the Ripper" was a "low-class" Jew, and they so decided, Sir Robert says, because they believe "it is a remarkable fact that people of that class in the East End will not give up one of their number to Gentile justice." Was anything more nonsensical in the way of a theory ever conceived even in the brain of a policeman? Here was a whole neighbourhood, largely composed of Jews, in constant terror lest their womenfolk, whom Jewish men hold in particular regard — even "low-class" Jews do that — should be slain by some murderer who was stalking the district undiscovered. So terrified were many of the people — non–Jews as well as Jews — that they hastily moved away.

And yet Sir Robert would have us believe that there were Jews who knew the person who was committing the abominable crimes and yet carefully shielded him from the police. A more wicked assertion to put into print, without the shadow of evidence, I have seldom seen. The man whom Scotland Yard "suspected," subsequently, says Sir Robert, "was caged in an asylum." He was never brought to trial — nothing except his lunacy was proved against him. This lunatic presumably was a Jew, and because he was "suspected," as a result of the police "theory" I have mentioned, Sir Robert ventures to tell the story he does, as if he were stating facts, forgetting that such a case as that of Adolph Beck was ever heard of.

But now listen to the "proof" that Sir Robert Anderson gives of his theories. When the lunatic, who presumably was a Jew and who was suspected by Scotland Yard, was seen by a Jew — "the only person who ever had a good view of the murderer" — Sir Robert tells us he at once identified him, "but when he learned that the suspect was a fellow–Jew he declined to swear to him." This is Scotland Yard's idea of "proof" positive of their "theory"! What more natural than the man's hesitancy to identify another as Jack the Ripper so soon as he knew he was a Jew? What more natural than for that fact at once to cause doubts in his mind? The crimes identified with "Jack the Ripper" were of a nature that it would be difficult for any Jew — "low-class" or any class — to imagine the work of a Jew. Their callous brutality was foreign to Jewish nature, which, when it turns criminal, goes into quite a different channel.

I confess that however sure I might have been of the identity of a person, when I was told he had been committing "Jack the Ripper" crimes, and was a Jew, I should hesitate about the certainty of my identification, especially as anyone — outside Scotland Yard — knows how prone to mistake the cleverest-headed and most careful of people are when venturing to identify anyone else.

It is a matter of regret and surprise that so able a man as Sir Robert Anderson should, upon the wholly erroneous and ridiculous "theory" that Jews would shield a raving murderer because he was a Jew, rather than yield him up to "Gentile justice," build up the series of statements that he has. There is no real proof that the lunatic who was "caged" was a Jew — there is absolutely no proof that he was responsible for the "Jack the Ripper" crimes, and hence it appears to me wholly gratuitous on the part of Sir Robert to fasten the wretched creature — whoever he was — upon our people.

MENTOR[29]

## TO THE EDITOR OF THE JEWISH CHRONICLE

SIR, — With reference to "Mentor's" comments on my statements about the "Whitechapel murders" of 1888 in this month's Blackwood, will you allow me to express the severe distress I feel that my words should be construed as "an aspersion upon Jews." For much that I have written in my various books gives proof of my sympathy with, and interest in, "the people of the Covenant"; and I am happy in reckoning members of the Jewish community in London among my personal friends.

I recognize that in this matter I said either too much or too little. But the fact is that as my words were merely a repetition of what I published several years ago without exciting comment, they flowed from my pen without any consideration.

We have in London a stratum of the population uninfluenced by religious or even social restraints. And in this stratum Jews are to be found as well as Gentiles. And if I were to describe the condition of the maniac who committed these murders, and the course of loathsome immorality which reduced him to that condition, it would be manifest that in his case every question of nationality and creed is lost in a ghastly study of human nature sunk to the lowest depth of degradation.

Yours obediently,
ROBERT ANDERSON.[30]

I have read the interview with a representative of the Globe which Sir Robert Anderson accorded that paper in order to reply to my observations upon what he said in Blackwood's Magazine concerning the Jack the Ripper crimes. The editor of the Jewish Chronicle has also been so good as to send for my perusal Sir Robert Anderson's letter to him, which appears in these columns, on the same subject. With great deference to Sir Robert, it appears to me that he misses the whole point of my complaint against what he wrote. I did not so much object to his saying that Jack the Ripper was a Jew, though so particular a friend of our people would have been well-advised, knowing the peculiar condition in which we are situated, and the prejudice that is constantly simmering against us, had he kept the fact to himself. No good purpose was served by revealing it. It would have sufficed had he said that he was satisfied the murderer was discovered.

As I pointed out, the creature whom Sir Robert believes to have been the author of the heinous crimes was a lunatic — obviously his brain virulently diseased — so that if he was a Jew, however regrettable it may be that our people produced such an abnormality, in that there does not lie the aspersion. What I objected to — and pace Sir Robert Anderson's explanations still do — in his Blackwood article, is that Jews who knew that "Jack the Ripper" had done his foul deeds, shielded him from the police, and guarded

**Robert Anderson, Assistant Commissioner of the Metropolitan Police (courtesy Stewart P. Evans).**

him so that he could continue his horrible career, just because he was a Jew. This was the aspersion to which I referred and about which I notice Sir Robert says nothing. Of course, when Sir Robert says that the man he means was "proved" to be the murderer, and that upon that point he spoke facts, he also ignores the somewhat important matter that the man was never put upon his trial. Knowing what I do, I would hesitate to brand even such a creature as Sir Robert describes as the author of the Ripper crimes upon the very strongest evidence short of a conviction after due trial.

MENTOR

Jack the Ripper had attacked the poor and was progressively regarded as an economic by-product of the times and residue of Victorian parliamentary polices. Fantastic beliefs about ritual murders and Freemasonic plots emerged with the political tensions. The defensive Royal and Imperial positions on the growth of European anarchy and Irish nationalist terror strained English and U.S. immigrant and extradition policies. Tense conditions touched with class prejudice rendered several East End casual prostitutes both sacred and expendable.

The speculations of motive arising from wounds inflicted upon the victims of Jack the Ripper have varied over time from sexual homicide to satanic ritual sacrifice. Clearly the perpetrator of these crimes was deranged. His drive to complete abhorrent actions of cruelty created a widespread panic, aided by the press, in London and around the world. However, theories and inquiries did not end with Anderson's views in general interest publications that appeared to bring closure to free press conjectures. The mystery of these prostitutes was further imbued with significance and history.

The official ambiguity expressed by Scotland Yard, the Home Office and to some extent the Foreign Office on the Whitechapel murders, would be acceptable but for the open and incongruous statements of several senior police officials. Scotland Yard's failure to catch a serial killer could have been tolerable with a capable response that effectively contained the public panic. However, subsequent police theories and apparent high-level doublespeak had only fueled intrigue. But with the use of Scotland Yard officials and detectives during the Parnell Special Commission of 1888 and 1889 in the volatile East End, the undetected murders and identity of Jack the Ripper were considered also as acts of extreme political terrorism.

The Whitechapel murders occurred in a dangerous and sensitive social and political climate that urged official review of conflicting medical reports. Examination of the victims' remains became crucial to the police investigation. The shocking mutilations and continuing escape of Jack the Ripper made some suspect enemies of the Crown. The equivocal police theories did not quell allegations, conspiracies or press conjectures but rather encouraged them.

# 3

# Faith and Occult Crimes

The Whitechapel crimes of 1888 happened as strange new cultures were introduced to the British Empire. Immigration to the East End, the nature of wounds and the extraction of internal organs from victims fed into medieval presumptions and beliefs. Jack the Ripper's apparent post-mortem targeting of the victims' bodies caused suspicions of a ritualistic killer. Fantastic theories clashed with mainstream religious beliefs.

The series of murders were so unusual in the experience of the police that foreign and alien elements of the city came to be strongly suspected by conservative society. Scientific advances challenged theology and medieval superstitions while a series of messy, irrational prostitute murders in the East End signaled the end of days. English mainstream culture could not have nurtured a demonic monster such as the Whitechapel murderer, it was thought, so the killer had to be a product of an exotic subculture or of foreign origins. From a Victorian perspective, emerging psychological and "psychic" sciences saw Jack the Ripper as an excellent case study. Though advances in fingerprinting and blood analysis came too late to apply to the Whitechapel murders case, Scotland Yard was prepared to consider alternative hints and suggestions, as Robert Anderson had noted.

With Victorian beliefs on the nature of evil and crime in flux, Victorian London's "occult" subcultures, now largely consigned to obscurity in general historical studies of the period, took a marked interest in the murders of Jack the Ripper. As previously stated, the police investigation, combined with press allegations of ritual murder, ensured that the motive of the killer was as obscure as his identity.

The mystery of the Whitechapel murders was ripe for a Victorian society that valued discovery and explorations. As new archaeological finds were shipped to the British Museum and Library or housed in private collections from the far reaches of the Empire, discoveries that prompted the "Victorian Occult Revival" also influenced theories about Jack the Ripper. He was a scapegoat for the changing sentiments of critical and religious rationalism — a serial killer demonized for the social ills of the time by Christian and religious clerics and congregations.

Anderson, for instance, held to some moral views on the nature of crime and evil, which it could be said, influenced his role in the investigation. In his prolific religious writings, which he developed in his leisure time, he often taught in legalistic and criminal fables. In his *The Bible and Modern Criticism*, he had this to say:

A few years ago — I could give details of every part of my narrative — a certain London merchant killed an unfortunate wretch whom circumstances had placed in his power. He did not actually kill him with his own hands, but he had him brought to a secluded room which was deliberately prepared for the purpose, and there he stood by while his victim was strangled by a man whom he had hired to do the deed. I myself examined the place. I can testify, moreover, that all the facts were known, not only to the authorities, but to the Queen. And yet not only did the homicide go unpunished, but, with full knowledge of all I have narrated, Her Majesty singled him out for royal favor and conferred a title upon him.

What estimate will my readers form of such conduct on the part of one whom we have been taught to regard as a pattern and paragon of public and private virtue?

But before they pass judgement upon the facts they ought to know a few additional details. The victim of the tragedy I have described was a condemned murderer; the man who was paid to strangle him was the common hangman, the secluded room was in Newgate prison, and the merchant who received a knighthood was the Sheriff whose official duty it was to execute the criminal.

And now the meaning of the parable will begin to dawn upon the reader. Let these added details be suppressed, and a plain narrative which does not contain a syllable that is untrue or even exaggerated, may seem to endanger the reputation of Queen Victoria. And it is precisely by this sort of suppression that the Bible and the God of the Bible are misrepresented. Will any "person of culture" in our day dare to defend the extermination of the Canaanites? Will any one, I answer, dare to defend the strangling of a poor helpless wretch in a shut-in room?

It is not God's way to justify Himself at the bar of His creature's judgement. He acts and speaks autocratically. But in this matter He has deigned to explain His decrees. Men read the Bible story in the false light of the evolution craze. They picture to themselves a number of semi-civilised tribes on the upward path of progress, exterminated by an invading horde of religious fanatics. But the Christian knows that they were a degenerate and apostate race whose destruction was decreed by a God of infinite mercy, because they had given themselves up to unnatural and loathsome sin. Four centuries had passed since Sodom fell. And among the citizens of Sodom not even ten could be found who were clear of the evil. What then must have been the condition of the land when God at last called in the Israelites as His executioners?

Of the guilty nations there was one that seemed still to merit pity, and on account of that nation the judgement was delayed. If for four generations the favored people were left as strangers in a strange land, it was "because the iniquity of the Amorites was not yet full."

Anderson here adds a footnote:

This is not a subject for plain speaking. I will dismiss it with the strange confession that prior to knowledge acquired at Scotland Yard, these Divine judgements upon Canaan were a difficulty to my faith. There are some kinds of vice that seem to spread like leprosy, and to become hereditary.[1]

In 1987, *The Ripper Legacy: The Life and Death of Jack the Ripper*[2] presented a theory that suspect Montague John Druitt was a member of a Cambridge mystical secret society, the Apostles, who had conspired in the murders. Some of its members were also scholars of the 1881 Bible Revision team. This prompted the bulk of Anderson's religious writing in defense of the Authorized King James Version and on the "supernatural"[3] prophetic substance of the Old Testament as the basis for the New Testament. The Bible Revision team consisted of English and American scholars and clerics gathered to standardize the Bible in modern English. It was also part of the political dream of Lord Salisbury, British Prime Minister during the Whitechapel murders, in unifying English-speaking countries as a bloc.

Religious views on Jack the Ripper had a marked influence on interpretation of the case. Some of the most pervasive theories on the Whitechapel murders that have their origin in the period moral climate are the conjectures that the killer was possessed of a religious mania. Christian charities of every denomination were well established in the East End among the poor as Jack the Ripper was at work. The idea that he was clergy, part of a congregation, or otherwise religiously connected, took hold of the public emotion and was of some concern to Scotland Yard. Religious philanthropist Dr. Thomas Barnardo, for instance, whose charity work commenced in the slums of Whitechapel, has been accused of being the killer on the strength of a letter written to *The Times*[4] on meeting one of the supposed Ripper victims, Elizabeth Stride. These emotive responses to the panic had deeply affected the local population.

## SUICIDES IN WHITECHAPEL

Information was conveyed to the coroner for North-East Middlesex to-day that a weaver named Joseph Sodeaux, living in Hanbury Street, Spitalfields, had hanged himself. He had been very despondent since the suicide of his wife, who had hanged herself in the same way. The revolting murders and mutilations in the neighbourhood preyed on her mind, and she was afraid to go out, and when the woman Chapman was murdered a few doors away Mrs. Sodeaux took her own life.[5]

To the Victorian mind and religious worldview, the murders would come to mean something far more sinister and verging on the supernatural than a modern behavioral conception of crime and the nature of evil. They would signify acts of a living demon and monster of assassination.

## THE LONDON PARANOIAC

There is, of course, no question as regards the insanity of the Whitechapel murderer. In the time of the bitter vendettas of the Middle Ages, in savage border wars between the whites and Indians, and among the cannibalistic Polynesians, similar murders have been committed with equally cruel mutilation by men whose sanity could not be questioned.

But in this age and in the very center of modern civilization there could be no incentive to such horrible crimes in the breasts of sane men, however unruly their passions or revengeful their natures. In the series of murders committed by Maximilian in De Quincey's remarkable story of "The Avenger,"[6] the incentives to the deeds, terrible as were the wrongs to his family and race, were scarcely adequate to such wholesale butchery. The story is improbable, and were it true, its hero would necessarily be considered a lunatic.

The motives of homicidal maniacs are very diverse, and often difficult of analysis. Sometimes it is a melancholy mother who destroys her children under the delusion that she saves them from some threatening disaster, or because a voice commands her to sacrifice them. Sometimes it is some moral imbecile who delights in torturing innocent people to death. Often it is the victim of alcohol who "runs amuck," stabbing right and left through a crowded thoroughfare. Frenzied outbursts of violence in acute maniacs and general paretics are by no means infrequent.

But there is a class of lunatics, formerly known as mono maniacs, but to whom now the term paranoiac is applied, which constitutes the most dangerous of all the insane classes. The word monomania has been discarded because misleading from its derivation. Though the insane man may have but one dominating delusion, yet there are often minor delusions, defective reason and judgement centring about the so-called imperative conception, so that he can scarcely be said to be insane on one solitary subject, as the word monomania would imply. Paranoia is a form of insanity which develops in a person who from birth has a defective mental organization. In paranoia the intellect may be unimpaired; there may indeed be unusual intellectual capacity. John Brown, Benvenuto Cellini, Guiteau, King Ludwig of Bavaria, and many others, both notorious and famous, were undoubtedly paranoiacs. Society is full of them in every class, high and low, educated and ignorant, and they vary in their characters from the mildly eccentric individuals to the most troublesome "cranks," a person peculiar from birth in his speech and conduct. The great trouble is that most of them are so bright intellectually or so useful, and injure society in general so little by their presence that they cannot be incarcerated, Though they may be a life-long affliction to their immediate friends and companions. Happily their homicidal tendencies are upon the whole developed rarely.

The motives of homicidal paranoiacs are also various. For instance, Duborge, who, some years ago, stabbed a number of women in Fourteenth-street, had far other reasons for so doing than this Whitechapel murderer. The former had delusions of persecution and hallucinations of hearing. He fancied he heard people reviling him as he passed through the street. He heard them say, "There goes the wretch who is taking all the money out of the country."

The Whitechapel murderer is actuated by one of two motives. He kills to satisfy a religious fanaticism or because of a perverted sexual instinct, or there may be a combination of the two impulses. The fact that his victims have been selected from the lowest classes of immoral women in London certainly inclines one to the opinion that his desire is to immolate these creatures upon the alter of religion, his delusions being that they are the chief emissaries of the devil in the spread of evil. Under the fiendish penal code which he has established it seems necessary to kill and mutilate these poor creatures.

If this be really his sole imperative idea, however, it will be the only example of its kind in history. The religious paranoiac is not so apt to concentrate his reforms upon one vice alone. He usually makes war upon universal evil, but by insane methods; he harangues audiences, announces himself as a prophet perhaps, is constantly quoting the Bible to his associates, and often incites rebellion and riot. John Thom, who caused the bloody Canterbury riots in 1833, is an example in point of a religious paranoiac.

The fact that women of this class are selected should not be taken too seriously. That he selects women is a more important point. That they should be of a base type is quite as likely to be due to the necessities of the case. They are the only women he can induce to follow him into dark corners in the dead of night.

When, on the other hand, the motive is excited by perversion of the sexual instinct with cannibalistic or similar insane propensities, the crimes are limited to women and the lunatic is more secretive. Andreas Bichel murdered young girls, cut open their warm bodies, and ate their quivering flesh. The Westphalia murders, a few years ago, with most shocking mutilation of the bodies, of which more than twenty young women were the victims, are of similar origin. Only recently in Texas there was a series of butcheries of young women all perpetrated under circumstances so peculiar as to point to a homicidal lunatic as their author.

The remarkable cunning of the London paranoiac, his secretiveness, his ability to elude the vigilant officers of justice in one of the most crowded quarters of the globe, his careful selection of victims of one sex, the singular mutilation to which he subjects them, all indicate that he is actuated by motives partly religious perhaps, but more than likely for the devilish gratification of perverted sexual instincts, and at the same time demonstrate him to be one of the most daring and atrocious homicidal lunatics of which medical jurisprudence has any record.[7]

The Victorian tendency of blending religious themes with unsolved crimes of blood and the immolation, meaning sacrifice or ritual murder, of women is a hard cultural concept to define. Reports of ritual murder or religious mania were filtered through period understanding. Difficulties are introduced when one applies contemporary attitudes to Victorian primary sources. A historical case could be woven, for example, for the Bishop of Lincoln being Jack the Ripper within predominantly Protestant London.

The announcement to-day that the Archbishop of Canterbury has decided to cite the Bishop of Lincoln before him on a charge of ritualistic practices startles all ecclesiastical England. For the past two years a photograph of him, with a mitre, crozier, and elaborate vestments, surrounded by clergy in similarly Romish apparel, has been one of the familiar features in all the displays of portraits in the shop windows here.[8]

Public interest in "ritual prosecutions" has so greatly decreased of late years that people generally seem unaware that one of these, of a far more important character than one any which made famous the names of Bennett and Mackonochie, Purchas and Tooth,[9] is to be brought forward next month. For the first time for four hundred years, and therefore the first since the Reformation, a bishop is summoned to appear before the Primate of all England to answer charges which practically involve an accusation of heresy and false doctrine. It is at Lambeth Palace that the Bishop of Lincoln will have to stand before the Archbishop of Canterbury to reply to the charge of using illegal vestments; and the ceremony, which will take place on the day that the Convocation of Canterbury reopens at Westminster, will be surrounded with much that is picturesque, for the Primate will be clothed in his archiepiscopal robes and will wear his unaccustomed mitre, while his legal assessors also will be tricked out in official drapery.[10]

This referred to prosecutions under the Public Worship Regulation Act of 1874, which limited the growth of "ritualism" or introduction of Roman Catholic rituals and observances into the Church of England. Known as the Oxford Movement, this was a highly contentious issue and prompted debate for several decades that convicted clergy and generated conferences in the East End during the Whitechapel murders. Though prosecutions ended in 1906, the act remained in place until it was finally repealed on March 1, 1965, with the

Ecclesiastical Jurisdiction Measure of 1963. Lord Grimthorpe, who had opposed ritualism in the Church of England, had written incessantly to the press on the subject and was a part of the general anti–Catholic sentiment then current in England. Grimthorpe also received threatening letters from an insane Jack the Ripper suspect, Thomas Cutbush, whose exploits and stabbing of young women may have been triggered by such Victorian religious fanaticism and debate.

A religious theory also emerged during the first published hint of Melville Macnaghten's suspects, Kosminski, Druitt and Ostrog — albeit without names in Major Arthur Griffiths' 1898 *Mysteries of Police and Crime*. Griffiths was Inspector of Prisons between 1878 and 1896 and an authority on crime and offenders. He worked with and was a friend to Anderson and Macnaghten, and published several accounts on the Whitechapel murders during his retirement. Griffiths supported the idea that by that time, Scotland Yard did not know the identity of Jack the Ripper. In the vacuum of contrary police opinion on the murders (at odds with the claim of Anderson's "consensus" in Scotland Yard), theories were manufactured.[11]

## IDENTITY OF "JACK THE RIPPER" A SECRET OF THE CONFESSIONAL

To the long list of "solutions" of the great "Jack the Ripper" mystery there is now added another — possibly the final one; possibly not.

It comes from a clergyman of the Church of England, a north country vicar, who claims to know with certainty the identity of the most terrible figure in all the blood-stained annuls of crime — the perpetrator of that horrible series of East-end murders which ten years ago startled the whole civilised world.

The clergyman in question declines to divulge the name of the culprit, being unable to do so without violating the secrecy of the confessional. He states, however, that he obtained his information from a brother clergyman to whom the murderer made a full and complete confession.

The vicar writes: "I received information in professional confidence, with directions to publish the facts after ten years, and then with such alterations as might defeat identification.

The murderer was a man of good position and otherwise unblemished character, who suffered from epileptic mania, and is long deceased.

I must ask you to not give my name, as it might lead to identification."

The ten years were completed on November 9 last, the final murder of the "Ripper" series having taken place on November 9, 1888, in Miller's Court.

Actor Richard Mansfield in *The Strange Case of Dr. Jekyll and Mr. Hyde* whose performance at the Lyceum before the Jack the Ripper murders was so convincing it was believed he was capable of the Whitechapel crimes. On October 5, 1888, the City of London Police received a letter signed "M.P.," who, having seen the play, "felt at once that he was the man wanted."

The clergyman who now comes forward with the latest identification declares that the assassin died shortly after the last murder of the series.[12]

Victorians generally took their religion seriously, and instances of dogmatic views abound in press coverage of the Whitechapel murders. Mr. Spurgeon, for example, was a staunch disciple and preacher who was a close associate of Robert Anderson. He was also a friend of Anderson's British spy in America, Le Caron, who appeared before the Special Commission on alleged criminal associations of Irish members of Parliament during the period 1888-89. Anderson and Spurgeon were deeply immersed in defense of the King James Version from revisionist attacks of the Cambridge biblical review team from 1881.

London, Oct, 26.—Mr. Spurgeon has withdrawn from the Baptist Union. In announcing his decision to withdraw and replying to his critics, he says: "To pursue union at the expense of the truth is treason to Jesus. To tamper with His doctrines is to become traitors to Him. We have before us the wretched spectacle of professedly orthodox Christians publicly avowing union with those who deny the faith, call the fall of man a fable, and deny the personality of the Holy Ghost." Replying to the question why he does not start a new denomination, he says that it is a question for which he has no liking; that there are enough denominations already; and that if another were formed the thieves and robbers who have entered the other gardens walled around would enter it also, so nothing would be gained. Baptists generally regret Mr. Spurgeon's decision and are urging him to reconsider it.[13]

As the Whitechapel murders increased in tempo through the autumn months of 1888, so too did the press and moral rhetoric. It was led early by editor Stead of the *Pall Mall Gazette*, a nonconformist and pious spiritualist crusader. The unknown Jack the Ripper was clad in the rags of the poor and beliefs of the age.

## MURDER AS AN ADVERTISEMENT

There have been many theories about the Whitechapel murders, but so far no one has propounded as the most probable hypothesis the theory that they are the work of a Scientific Humanitarian. We may be in the presence of a Sociologist Pasteur, capable of taking a scientific survey of the condition of society, and absolutely indifferent to the sufferings of the individual so long as he benefited the community at large. We have yet to witness the evolution of the scientific Sociological Jesuit.[14] His advent, however, cannot be long delayed. We have been expecting him for some time. Who knows but he is already in our midst in Whitechapel?

Extravagant as this thesis may seem at first sight, let us consider for a moment the immensely strong case which such a Sociologist could make out for himself if once you can overcome the prejudice which men not quite emancipated from the theological stage have against taking life. Here in London lie certain foul slums, which The Times describes as "the kitchen middens of humanity," in which the human being putrefies, and where, as "S.G.O." tells us, "tens of thousands of our fellow creatures are begotten and reared in an atmosphere of godless brutality, a species of human sewage, the very drainage of the vilest productions of ordinary vice."

Philanthropists have repeatedly, and in vain, called attention to their existence. "The bitter cry of outcast London" has fallen upon heedless ears. Prayer, entreaty, and warning all were in vain. The condition of these horrible death traps, into which hordes of our fellow creatures are driven to be trampled out of all semblance of human existence, excited no interest. Day followed day, week passed after week, month after month, year after year, and still nothing was done. Last year those nearest to the grim Malebogic pool of the Metropolitan Inferno raised their voices in Trafalgar square and elsewhere, pleading plaintively for help. Sir Charles Warren amid the enthusiastic applause of the well to do, rode them down with his cavalry, smashed their heads with his bludgeons, and restored "order" in the Square. Parliament was deaf; the Press, with but few exception, was callous; the public conscience seemed hardened as a nether millstone.

If these cesspools of brutalized humanity were not to become a permanent source of poisoned miasma, it was necessary something should be done that would at once rouse public attention, create universal sensation, and compel even the most apathetic and self indulgent to admit the first postulate of the socialist's faith, that the luxury and the wealth of the West must be employed to mitigate the squalor and crime of the East. The only question was what this means should be.

The scientific Sociologist in answering this question would ask himself by what means a maximum effect could be produced with a minimum of expenditure in money and in life. If he were familiar with Bismarck's great art of creating the "psychological moment," in which alone the decisive stroke can be delivered, he would not hesitate. There must be blood. That was indispensable. The warning must be printed in letters of gore. But mere bloodshed would not suffice. There must be more than murder. The public cannot be impressed by a mere commonplace killing. There must be mutilation. That is where the sensation comes in.

We presuppose in our scientific Sociologist such a supreme devotion to the welfare of the community, that he cannot for a moment hesitate in sacrificing a few worthless lives in order to attain his end. Now, as in old time, he would argue, it is sometimes expedient that one should die for the sake of the multitude. Having arrived at this decision, he would naturally select as victims those whose lives were most worthless both to themselves and to the State, and whose habits in life afforded the most ghastly illustration of the vicious horrors of the criminals' lairs. This is exactly what he seems to have done.

The victims belong to the class which of all others suffers the most hideous and tragic fate in the human lot. None of them found life worth living. All were drunken, vicious, miserable wretches, whom it was almost a charity to relieve of the penalty of existence. He took them to the very center of the plague spots to the existence of which he was desirous of turning the public attention. There he seems to have killed them with the merciful painlessness of science, so that suffering was reduced to a minimum, and death came as a welcome release from the insupportable miseries of existence. After killing his victim he mutilated her, well knowing that a knife's slit in a corpse makes more impression on the vulgar mind than the greatest cruelties, moral or even physical, on the living. Then he seems to have waited to see if his action would have the desired effect. Finding his first essay unsuccessful in achieving his object, he repeated it, and again repeated it. Not, however, until his fourth experiment did he succeed.

The sluggish public is roused at last and The Times and The Morning Post vie with each other in writing articles of almost unmitigated socialism. "We cannot contemplate the life," says The Times, "which these unexampled horrors reveal without feeling a quickened sense of responsibility for such features of it as human effort rightly applied can either abate or remove. We have to consider how far our social organization is responsible for the preparation of the soil and atmosphere in which such crimes are produced." "S.G.O." cries "At last!" and the Rev. S.A. Barnett exclaims with a sigh "Whitechapel horrors will not be in vain if at last the public conscience awakes to consider the life which these horrors reveal."

What then is more reasonable than to suppose that these horrors may have been produced in this scientific sensational way to awake the public conscience? If this should after all turn out to be the case, the defense of the scientific Sociologist at the Old Bailey will be a curiosity in the history of criminal trials and may mark the beginning of the scientific era in social development.[15]

By the end of the year the religious rhetoric was converted to clues and leads. Scotland Yard, with the City of London Police, who had entered the case with the murder of Catherine Eddowes on their adjoining territory, were actively pursuing the evidence.

It is stated that the City police are making searching inquiries into what they regard as "the most important clue" yet obtained. The clergyman at the head of one of the metropolitan missions received a letter from a man who had attended the services conducted by him, but whom he had not seen for some time. The letter was in three different styles of writing, but it has been proved that it was penned by the same hand, and the interesting fact is that it most minutely tallies with the writings on the post-cards which were circulated by the police. The letter was first of all taken to the Scotland-yard authorities, and all the attendant circumstances explained, but, owing to the many false scents they are put upon, the matter was not taken up. The letter was then submitted to the detective department of the City police, and, after carefully considering the matter, Mr. McWilliams [sic], who has the case in hand, said, as mentioned in the opening, that it was the most important clue they had as yet received.[16]

Of the ritualistic theories on Jack the Ripper that had their roots in the Victorian period, a traditional aspersions were born of immigration and the suspicions of local Jews as possible perpetrators. The incrimination of Kosminski the Polish Jew, a derived theory that Sir Robert Anderson would give as a "definitely ascertained fact" held by Scotland Yard, had without proof reflected the social conditions of the times. Potential riots had also influenced Sir Charles Warren, Metropolitan Police Commissioner during the Ripper murders, who had erased a piece of wall writing in chalk found on the morning of September 30, 1888, in Goulston Street above the only piece of evidence left by the killer, a portion of bloodstained apron from the Mitre Square victim, Catherine Eddowes. The well-known writing on the wall has been reported in many versions and is the source for countless conjectures and conspiracy theories. A common rendering was "The Juwes are the men that will not be blamed for nothing."[17] Anderson would later in his memoirs decry Warren's decision, but in the local press and widely circulated stories the real danger was confirmed.

### A RIOT AGAINST THE JEWS

On Saturday in several quarters of East London the crowds who had assembled in the streets began to assume a very threatening attitude towards the Hebrew population of the district. It was repeatedly asserted that no Englishman could have perpetrated such a horrible crime as that of Hanbury-street, and that it must have been done by a Jew — and forthwith the crowds proceeded to threaten and abuse such of the unfortunate Hebrews as they found in the streets. Happily, the presence of the large number of police in the streets prevented a riot actually taking place. "If the panic-stricken people who cry 'Down with the Jews' because they imagine that a Jew has committed the horrible and revolting crimes which have made Whitechapel a place to be dreaded knew anything at all of the Jewish horror of blood itself," writes a correspondent, "they would pause before they invoked destruction on the head of a peaceful and law-abiding people. Since the return of the Jews to England in 1649, only two Jews have been hanged for murder, Marks and Lipski, and taking into consideration the origin of many of the poor wretches who fly to this country from foreign persecution, this is a very remarkable record. That the beast that has made East London a terror is not a Jew I feel assured. There is something too horrible, too unnatural, too un–Jewish, I would say, in the terrible series of murders for an Israelite to be the murderer. There never was a Jew yet who could have steeped himself in such loathsome horrors as those to which publicity has been given. His nature revolts at blood-guiltiness, and the whole theory and practical working of the Whitechapel butchery are opposed to Jewish character."[18]

That would have been the end of the matter but for the emergence of press speculations on historical anecdotes of Jewish ritual murder and blood libels. It all began with *The Times* correspondent in Vienna who sent through this report.

### VIENNA, OCT. 1

With reference to the recent atrocious murders in London, attention may be called to a crime of an exactly similar kind which preoccupied the public in this country for nearly three years. A Galician Jew named Ritter was accused in 1884 of having murdered and mutilated a Christian woman in a village near Cracow. The mutilation was like that perpetrated on the body of the woman Chapman, and at the trial numbers of witnesses deposed that among certain fanatical Jews there existed a superstition to the effect that if a Jew became intimate with a Christian woman he would atone for his offence by slaying and mutilating the object of his passion. Sundry passages of the Talmud were quoted which, according to the witnesses, expressly sanctioned this form of atonement. The trial caused an immense sensation, and Ritter, being found guilty, was sentenced to death.

The Judges of the Court of Appeal, however, feeling that the man was the victim of popular error and anti–Semitic prejudice, ordered a new trial upon some technicality. Again a jury pronounced against Ritter, and once more the Court of Appeal found a flaw in the proceedings. A third trial took place, and for the third time Ritter was condemned to be hanged, but upon this the Court of Appeal quashed the sentence altogether, and Ritter was released, after having been in prison 37 months. There is no doubt that the man was innocent, but the evidence touching the superstitions prevailing among some of the ignorant and degraded of his co-religionists remains on record and was never wholly disproved.[19]

The Jewish community responded promptly to allegations in the press and had the support of Sir Charles Warren.

The absorbing pre-occupation this week of our brethren in the East of London has been the ghastly mystery of the Whitechapel murders. It was reserved for the Vienna correspondent of the Times to give a still more sombre hue to their thoughts by a strangely imperfect reference to a Galician cause celebre. We reported on March 5th, 1886, the acquittal of Moses Ritter. He, his wife, and the Christian Pole, Stochlinski, were imprisoned for four years while the several trials were proceeding, and the unhappy Christian peasant who was accused of being the actual perpetrator of the crime, died during this long confinement. It was alleged that Ritter had outraged a Christian girl, and in order to destroy all evidence of the fact, had caused his victim to be murdered. The crime was thus of a very different nature both in its motive and circumstances from the six apparently purposeless and maniacal atrocities which have terrified London. But the correspondent speaks of it as "of an exactly similar kind," though in the recent atrocities there was no evidence of, and in the last crime no time for, the perpetration of any offence previous to murder. The correspondent goes on to commit still grosser errors. Evidence, he said, was given, and passages quoted from the Talmud to show, that a belief existed among ignorant Jews that an Israelite who had been intimate with a Christian woman might make atonement by slaying and mutilating her. The correspondent adds that there was no doubt Ritter was innocent, but that the evidence as to this superstition was never wholly disproved. How could it be disproved, one may ask, if the Jew was innocent as a fact. In that case any evidence as to what his motive might have been, assuming he had been guilty, would be immaterial. But Professor Delitzsch and Dr. Bloch did give evidence that no such superstition existed, though the correspondent fails to mention their testimony.

This telegram appears to us as dangerous a piece of composition as could be imagined. Of course it is not correct. The crime of which Ritter, his wife, and the unfortunate Polish Christian were accused, was quite different as we have pointed out from the series of murders in England. It is equally untrue that any such diabolical belief, as that imagined, exists among Jews. What witnesses can be found to swear to, and what falsifications they will make in Hebrew books to suit their purpose, appeared in the Tisza-Eslar charge which is known from subsequent events and confessions to have been an anti–Semitic plot from first to last. Dr. Herman Adler has written to the Times stating positively, as the fact is, that in no Jewish book is there any support for such a barbarity. Dr. Gaster has shown, in the same medium, that these calumnies were long since wickedly used by heathens against Christians, and were next employed by Catholics against Reformers. He might have added that such stories are still invented in Spain against Protestants, and in China against Europeans. The impropriety and injustice of the libel is only equalled by the danger involved in telegraphing it. Though it is a Jewish member of Parliament who offered the first reward for the discovery of the murderer, and Jews are active members of the Vigilance Committee, no one knows what an exited mob is capable of believing against any class which differs from the mob-majority by well-marked peculiarities. Many English and Irish workpeople at the East End are inflamed against the immigrant Jews by the competition for work and for houses, by the stories of the sweaters and the sweated. If these illogical and ignorant minds should come to believe in the report heedlessly spread by a writer who is obviously not quite just nor well-informed himself, the result might be terrible. Fortunately the press generally has treated the suggestion with the contempt which it deserves.[20]

Crime historian Robin Odell in 1965 presented the theory of Jewish ritual butchers, the Shochetim, suspected of the Whitechapel murders. Though Odell's theory was worth considering, it could not be verified with primary sources and earned mixed reviews.[21] However, Dr. Gordon Brown (his name variously spelt in press reports as Browne), the City of London Police divisional surgeon, had been called in to examine the ritual knives in use by Jewish Kosher butchers.

There are not wanting signs of a deliberate attempt to connect the Jews with the Whitechapel murders. A butcher writes to a periodical to suggest that the character of the incisions is such that they were made by a butcher, and thence he jumps to the conclusion that it was a Jewish butcher, a trade rival exclusively employed by Jews. Now we have made it our business to ascertain whether this could be. Dr. Gordon Browne, the City Divisional Surgeon, to whom the City detectives submitted the body and to whom the knives used by the Jewish slaughterers have also been shown, has authorized us to state that he is thoroughly satisfied that none of the knives have been used. We may add that the Jewish slaughterers are a very small, learned and respectable number of persons whom nobody acquainted with them would suspect. As a make weight the report has been thrown in that the murderer wrote on the wall in a neighbouring street "Shall the Jews be blamed for nothing?" But if this inscription ever existed, if it had reference to the murders, if it was the work of the murderer, it was written to throw the public off the scent, not to put them on. The peculiar horror entertained by Jews of any mutilation of the human body after death is either unknown to, or concealed by, the theorists. To us it seems wrong for respectable newspapers to lend their columns to such suggestions, which are the work of ignorance if not of malice. We observe with satisfaction that the more ably conducted journals refrain from reproducing them.

## THE CITY MURDER

We are authorized by Dr. Gordon Browne, the City Divisional Surgeon, to state, with reference to a suggestion that the City and Whitechapel murders were the work of a Jewish slaughterer, that he has examined the knives used by the Jewish slaughterers, all of which have been submitted to him by the City Detectives, and he is thoroughly satisfied that none of them could have been used.[22]

Though Brown, who had made the post-mortem examination on the body of Catherine Eddowes and testified at the inquest, dismissed the use of Jewish butchers' ritual knives in the Whitechapel murders, the legend continued and was to take an exotic twist.

## A NEW LIGHT ON THE CRIMES

The Vienna correspondent of the Standard states that Dr. Bloch, a member of the Austrian Reichsrath for the Galician constituency of Kokomea, has called his attention to certain facts which may throw a new light on the Whitechapel murders, and perhaps afford some assistance in tracing the murderer. In various German criminal codes of the seventeenth and eighteenth centuries, as also in statutes of a more recent date, punishments are prescribed for the mutilation of female corpses with the object of making from the uterus and other organs the so-called "diebalichter" or "schlafslichter," respectively "thieves' candles" or "soporific candles." According to an old superstition, still rife in various parts of Germany, the light from such candles will throw those upon whom it falls into the deepest slumbers, and they may, consequently, become a valuable instrument to those of the thieving profession. Hence arose their name. In regard to these "schlafslichter," quite a literature might be cited. They are referred to by Ave Lallement in his "Das Deutsche Gaunerthum" published in Leipzig in 1858; by Loffler, in "Die Mangelhafte Justiz" by Thiele, and numerous others. They also played an important part in the trials of robber bands at Odenwald and in Westphalia, in the years 1812 and 1841 respectively. The "schlafslichter" were heard of, too, at the trial of the notorious German robber, Theodor Unger, surnamed "the handsome Charley," who was executed at Magdeburg in 1810. It was on that occasion discovered that a regular manufactory had been established by gangs of thieves for the production of such candles. That this superstition has survived among German thieves to the present day was proved by a case tried at Biala, in Galicia, as recently as 1875. In this the body of a woman had been found mutilated in precisely the same way as were the victims of the Whitechapel murderer. At that trial, as at one which took place subsequently at Zeszow, which is also in Galicia, and in which the accused were a certain Ritter and his wife, the prevalence among thieves of superstition was alluded to by the Public Prosecutor. In the Ritter case, however, the Court preferred harping on another alleged superstition of a ritual character among the Jews of Galicia, which, however, was shown to be a pure invention of the Judenhettzer. Dr. Bloch, who for ten years was a rabbi in Galicia and has made the superstitions of that province his special study, affirms that the "thieves' candle" superstition still exists among robbers of every confession and, as he believes, also of every nationality. He considers, however, that it prevails most among German thieves. Among other German laws where the crime in question is dealt with, the "Code Theresiana," chap. xxii., clause 59, may be referred to.[23]

Eventually, *The Times* published a disclaimer that ended the affair but it was only the beginning of fresh theories and the investigation of ritual homicide as a motive for the Whitechapel murders.

On October 16 we published a summary of two letters on the Ritter trial, one from Dr. Josef S. Bloch, member of the Austrian Parliament, and the other, also from Vienna, from a "Lawyer of 20 Years Standing." Dr. Bloch denied, and our other correspondent affirmed the existence among the low-class Jews of Galicia of a superstition such as would account for the mutilation of the body of the woman for whose murder the Ritters were tried, and, it has been suggested, for the mutilations in the case of the Whitechapel murders. Dr. Adolf Stein, of Vienna, who acted as counsel for Ritter and his wife, now writes strongly corroborating Dr. Bloch's view of the case, and adding that, though the superstitions of thieves were mentioned at the trial, it was never asserted that the superstition was Jewish. Dr. Gotthelf Carl Mayor also writes from Vienna to the same effect, and states that the superstition in question was never proved at the trial as existing among the low-class Jews of Galicia, and that the Ritters were finally acquitted by the Supreme Tribunal on the merits of the case, and not because the only witness against them had died in prison. (We cannot allow this subject to be discussed any further in our columns.)[24]

Jewish immigration to the East End during the Whitechapel murders was mainly Russian, Polish, and of the Ashkenazi stream from central and eastern Europe. Yet, other minorities were also importing beliefs and superstitions that were strange to local inhabitants and which, to some extent, had an influence upon the mysterious perceptions of an invisible Jack the Ripper:

> Particularly strong among Roumanian Jews of the immigration was a belief that matched their Judaism with a brand of Shamanism. It would be too sweeping a term to explain this away as pure witchdoctory, but it appears that certain members, and in the main these were women, were practicing priest-doctors. When they practiced they offered a phrase in Hebrew or Yiddish, but the ritual performed had more in common with alchemaic ideas or ritual magic.[25]

However, it was with local and native superstitions that Jack the Ripper found root in mainstream occult theories, religious mania and ritual homicide.

## THE WHITECHAPEL MURDERS
## STARTLING THEORY OF THE CITY OF LONDON DETECTIVES.
## NOT ONE MAN'S WORK

Probably a Conspiracy to Murder Unfortunates Conceived by Religious Monomaniacs.

## SPECIAL CABLE TELEGRAPH TO THE TIMES

LONDON. December 2.—I have ascertained that the police have for some time past been working on a clue on which a more than plausible theory explanatory of the motive for the commission of the Whitechapel horrors has been built up. The city police are entitled to the credit of whatever results may eventuate from their discovery, but hitherto they have been exceedingly reticent as to the result of their investigations. To-day, however, I gathered the following details of the lines they are working on from a thoroughly reliable source.

The city detectives then early in the first week of October came to a definite conclusion, namely, that the two women [Stride and Eddowes] met their death at the hands of different men. It was but taking a single step further to conclude that these two men were acting in collusion. The long interval that had elapsed between this and the previous butchery, the fact that the women belonged to the same class and the coincidence that the killing was done within the same thirty-five minutes all pointed to the same conclusion—that the murders had been deliberately planned, probably to be consummated at the same moment, for if even a couple of hours had elapsed between the two crimes the neighborhood would on the discovery of the first, have become so "hot" that the perpetrator of the second outrage would have found the matter of his escape rendered doubly difficult.

The two brainy men who thus theorized, though they firmly believed they had at last opened the case, were still at a loss in what direction to look for the authors of the fearful crimes. With the utmost patience they sought out the degraded companions of the dead women, and bit by bit they learned all that probably ever will be known of their habits, tastes and mode of life.

After a week or more of this dreary work they struck a woman whose half drunken babbling seemed to suggest a possible clue to the unravelling of the secret they were so industriously working at. This woman had known Beddowes [*sic*] intimately, and only about a week before the day she met her death poor Catharine had in a fit of maudlin confidence told this companion that she meditated going into a reformatory. She had, she said, on the previous night got into conversation with a stranger, who had, as she put it, tried to convert her, and earnestly begged her to discontinue her mode of life. He had worked on the woman's feelings by drawing a fearful picture of the hereafter staring her in the face if she should be suddenly cut off in her life of sin and shame. On his leaving her she pleaded poverty as an excuse for her sinful mode of life, and he thereupon gave her five shillings, telling her to meet him again in a week's time, adding that if in the meantime she would give up her evil ways and decide to go into a home he would use his influence to get her into one. The woman could not fix the exact date on which Beddowes [sic] made this statement to her, but thought it was about a week before the woman was killed. At eleven o'clock on the night of Thursday, the day before the murder, she saw Catharine and took a drink with her. Beddowes [sic] was then much the worse for liquor. She left her shortly after that hour, saying she was going to meet a friend. She was never seen again alive, but less than two hours later her mutilated body was found lying in Mitre Square.

The detectives had no reason to doubt this story and every effort by advertisements and handbills was made to discover the man who had talked with Catharine Beddowes [sic] a week before the murder and given her five shillings. Up to the present the personality of this man remains shrouded in mystery. The detectives argued that if he was innocent in intent he would at once have come forward, most people will be inclined to agree with them.

Having got thus far, the detectives had a consultation with George Lewis, the great criminal lawyer, of Ely Place, Holborn. They went to him because it was well known that he had from the first held the theory that the murders were the work of a religious monomaniac, and the slender clue they had picked up seemed to point in that direction. No man has had so wide a criminal experience as George Lewis. He has been in every great murder case for the last twenty years and his father before him enjoyed the largest criminal practice in England. From a careful and exhaustive consideration of the facts laid before him by the city detectives, Mr. Lewis is understood to have deduced the following conclusions:

Positive — First. That the murders of Elizabeth Stride and Catharine Beddowes (sic) were not committed by one and the same person. Second. That the two or more murderers were acting in collusion and by pre-arrangement.

Probable — First. That the series of murder have been committed by two or more men whose motive is the checking of prostitution. The unprecedented barbarities practiced on the bodies are perpetrated with the view of terrifying the women of the district into abandoning their mode of life. Second. That the murderers are religious monomaniacs.

The city detectives have since been quietly working in this direction. For obvious reasons they decline to afford any information as to the result of their investigations. It is an open secret, however, that certain members of a quasi-religious organization whose eccentric methods have again and again encountered adverse criticism at the hands of the press and the public have been closely watched for some time past. As at present it is understood that not a tittle of direct evidence is forthcoming against these suspects no arrest have been made. The fact that so long a period elapsed between the murders of September 30 and the slaughtering of the latest victim on November 9 leads the detectives to believe that they are on the right track. The last murder, on November 9, came as a great surprise to them, but it was skillfully timed, as that being Lord Mayor's Day, on which the city is thronged with sight-seers, every available detective and policeman was on street duty.[26]

It is not known or discernable which particular "quasi-religious organization" the press report refers to. The report exemplifies numerous accounts that pointed the finger at subcultures of Victorian London that had come to the attention of the police. These reports were often merged with legitimate Scotland Yard inquiries on the murders. A private quasi-detective and rogue, Charles Le Grand, employed by the Whitechapel Vigilance Committee to investigate the Stride murder, had also approached the solicitor George Lewis to be employed on the Parnell Special Commission in early 1889. The details emerged under cross-examination at the 1889 extortion trial of Le Grand, who was later in 1891 rumored to be yet another suspect for Jack the Ripper.

The following report combines several elements of the occult, herbal homeopathy and an American Ripper suspect that may have been the quack doctor Francis Tumblety. The early mention of Jack the Ripper and the "elixir of life" may also have inspired the theory of Sir Arthur Diosy, noted as having approached Scotland Yard on October 14, 1888.

THE WHITECHAPEL HORRORS
Public Excitement Not Abating and the
Police Still Without a Clew.

SPECIAL CABLE DISPATCH TO THE TRIBUNE
[Copyright, 1888, by the Press Pub. Co., N. Y. World.]

LONDON, Oct. 6.— An American who used to live in New York keeps a herb shop now in the
Whitechapel district. A detective called at his place this week and asked him if he had sold any
unusual compound of herbs to a customer since August. Similar inquiries were made at other shops
in the neighbourhood. The basis of this investigation has a startling Shakespearean flavor. An eminent
engineer in London suggested to the police the theory that the murderer was a medical maniac trying
to find the elixir of life and was looking for the essential ingredient in the parts taken from the murdered bodies; that, like the witches in "Macbeth," he spent the time over a bubbling caldron of the
hellbroth made from the gory ingredients looking for the charm. The fact that the police are spending
time looking up wild theories like this only shows the utter absence of anything like a clew.[27]

Theories that try to explain unsolved murder cases with motives and signatures of the
occult, satanic or religious mania are usually concerned with suspects considered eccentric
or abnormal compared to mainstream society. Criminologists and the police[28] are familiar
with examples of ritual killing, but these types of homicide are rare and difficult to detect
because of the subjective nature of few and conflicting facts. Ritual homicide can be performed by those of any religious denomination or occult tradition but is generally committed
by a disturbed individual. Its investigation is a subjective evaluation of "signature" crime
scene evidence and profiling personality traits of an unknown killer. Unless obvious signs
of a religious or pseudo-religious nature are found connected to a victim's death, there is
no way to determine whether extreme mutilations or missing organs are in fact a serial
killer's intended metaphors. The mutilations found on the deceased bodies of the Whitechapel victims — the facial lacerations of Catherine Eddowes, the apparent arrangement of
viscera around Eddowes and Annie Chapman, and the missing heart of Mary Kelly — were
not so definite in their design.

When symbolic markings or materials are found at a murder, they can at best lead to
the killer's capture and conviction. In that regard, forensic specialists in ritual murder can
assist police investigations but not determine the identity of the suspect. Unless a certain
signature is associated with a particular "quasi-religious organization," obsession, or belief,
it is impossible to locate the killer with the signature alone. Ritual murder is more an obsessive personality disorder than a motive prompted by belief.

Satanism or black magic is often linked to murder rites but public display of victims
does not guarantee it. Organized crime and terrorists generally commit public displays of
ritualized murder as an example. In the case of the Whitechapel murders, there does not
appear to be any evidence for the conjecture, though persistent theories and inquiries of
the police were documented. A firmer theoretical case perhaps can be made for a Jack the
Ripper with religious mania or extremism because the East End had religious missions
devoted to rescuing sinners from prostitution and other crime, and alcohol. The Victorian
interest in occultism may be of historic interest but is not evidence of ritual murder. Yet
theories of a Ripper engaged in black magic became firmly entrenched during the period
and entwined with the emerging criminology.

Sir Walter Scott, in *Letters on Demonology and Witchcraft*, one of the last works he
penned before he died in 1832, stated,

Among much reading of my earlier days, it is no doubt true that I traveled a good deal in the twilight regions of superstitious disquisitions. Many hours have I lost — "I would their debt were less!" — in examining, old as well as more recent narratives of this character, and even in looking into some of the criminal trials so frequent in early days, upon a subject which our fathers considered as a matter of the last importance. And, of late years, the very curious extracts published by Mr. Pitcairn, from the Criminal Records of Scotland, are, besides their historical value, of a nature so much calculated to illustrate the credulity of our ancestors on such subjects, that, by perusing them, I have been induced to recall what I had read and thought upon the subject at a former period.[29]

That continued to be the case during the 1888 crimes of Jack the Ripper with the Victorian perceptions on murder with mutilations, the occult and criminal justice buried deeply in the United Kingdom's social, religious and cultural psyche. Supernatural theories said more about religious reform, immigration and the Empire during the late Victorian period than about a serial murder inquiry. What, then, was the Victorian progressive religious worldview and how did it become entangled with the Jack the Ripper legend and police investigation?[30]

The term "occult" in Victorian times included spiritualism, magic, animal magnetism, mesmerism, séances, early biblical research, hypnosis, ghosts, Satan, God, Celtic nature spirits and wicker men. The Victorian Occult Revival fused Christian, Gnostic, Eastern, Demonic, and Hermetic traditions with current and medieval scientific thought. In Elizabethan England, the resurgence and royal sanction of the occult as an alternative belief gave rise to the word "magick," derived from the Persian "magi." Though the movement was forced to go underground with the ascension of James I, the use of the term survived with the British occultist Aleister Crowley as a tribute to the Elizabethan magician, alchemist, court astrologer and statesman Dr. John Dee. Crowley also developed a Jack the Ripper theory of his own during the 20th century.

As studies and devotional practices of medieval alchemy were the younger sisters of chemistry, so were the occult and symbolic sciences of the 19th century a herald of emerging psychological clinical studies and criminology. A "scientific philosophy" had developed to explain religious experience, the nature of evil, biblical origins and divine creation based on ancient sources rediscovered by British explorers and missionaries.

Medical historian Rhodri Hayward stated that "the idea of a conflict between demonology and psychiatry has been a foundational myth in the history of medicine. Nineteenth-Century alienists [medical specialists in the insane] such as J. M. Charcot and Henry Maudsley developed critiques of supernatural phenomena in an attempt to pathologize religious experience.[31]

It was with changing religious worldviews that Jack the Ripper assumed a legendary persona woven of mystery and mesmerizing fibers in stories that cast the unknown serial killer as evil and demonic. The theories of an exotic occultist turned black magician and murderer, contrary to evidence, fed the fires of Victorian supernatural and alien allure. Tales of tribal ritual practices imported from Britain's colonies satiated the primal curiosities of ladies, lords and gentry. The substance of Jack the Ripper ritualistic conjecture was then readily available in curiosities nurtured with the disaffections of traditional religious mores and beliefs in the wake of Darwinist evolutionary science.

The London of Jack the Ripper was also inhabited by an assortment of occult groups, each claiming distinction and ancient lineage from either European or native roots. Christian and Hermetic influences were a major part of the Victorian Occult Revival, with a fascination for Eastern philosophies being fashionable though viewed as radical. To disentangle this sprawling web of occult threads and traditions, it is important first to consider four broad and sometimes overlapping traditions that coexisted in London during the late 1800s. They came to influence interpretations of the Ripper crimes and to supply theories and suspects.

First, there was regular Freemasonry, established in London in 1813 as the United Grand Lodge of England (UGLE). It joined the lodges of the British Isles into a cohesive association and emphasised traditional masonic values. Sir Charles Warren was a high-ranking regular Freemason and founding member of a research lodge called Ars Quatuor Coronatorum Lodge No. 2076. (The name translates as "the four craftsmen.") Warren supported the ideals of the association but rarely attended its meetings. His only submission to the research lodge was a paper presented at the meeting of March 1887, titled "On the Orientation of Temples" and based on his work for the Palestine Exploration Fund. He stepped down as master of the lodge in September of that year. There were also independent masonic study groups where members could explore other aspects of occult lore and hermetic subjects. Freemasonry, strictly speaking, has little concern with the occult and serves a symbolic and allegorical spiritual function with moral codes for its members. One of these study groups open to regular freemasons was the Rosicrucian Society, formed in 1865, which eventually contributed to the forming of the Hermetic Order of the Golden Dawn in 1888. Sir William Gull and Sir Robert Anderson were not Freemasons as conjectured in the 1970s with the Royal Masonic conspiracy theory.

Pope Leo XIII held the papacy during the Whitechapel murders and troubled Anglo-Irish relations of the period. In 1884 he issued the *Humanum Genus*, which banned all secret societies for Catholics. Driving them further underground promoted speculation that Jack the Ripper was a protected member of such a society (courtesy the Vatican Archives).

Secondly, there was what was known as irregular or fringe Freemasonry, which had developed in Europe and was gaining adherents in Victorian England. These bodies were pseudo-masonic and not officially recognized by UGLE, hence irregular. "Co-Masonry" was a term used to denote lodges that included women, which were not recognized but tolerated by UGLE. Under this heading was the French Occult Revival, led by the irregular Grand Orient of France, established upon medieval and hermetic manuscripts amassed during Napoleon's campaigns and the looting of the Vatican Library. Eliphas Levi (1810–1875) was the main author and protagonist of the French Occult Revival. It took root in 19th-century London, and Levi is known to have met author Edward Bulwer-Lytton on a visit to London in 1854. In 1876, the Grand Orient of France was disowned by UGLE after it banished the *Volume of the Sacred Law* from its lodges and deleted all references to the Great Architect of the Universe from its ceremonies. Freemasonry in a regular form was therefore unknown in France from 1877 until the National Grand Lodge of France was founded in 1913. On March 20, 1884, the Vatican issued a Papal Bull, *Humanum Genus*, banning all Freemasonry and secret societies. It was largely a response to the anti-papal French Jacobites of the Grand Orient, the irregular English lodges, and the growth of Irish Fenian secular and republican orders. Theories of anti-masonic conspiracies on the Whitechapel murders, popularized with the 1976 *Jack the Ripper: The Final Solution* by Stephen Knight and movies based on the book, are drawn from the spurious claims and "exposures" of these irregular and occasionally subversive lodges presented as regular English lodges and Freemasons. This fundamental and historical confusion of Royal Masonic Jack the Ripper conspiracy theory shows more an anti-establishment bias than an objective appraisal of the murder case.

Thirdly, paranormal investigative and Eastern esoteric associations were flourishing with Jack the Ripper theories of their own. Helena Blavatsky formed the Theosophical Society in 1875 in New York, and in 1884 established its English branch, the London Lodge, which became its European center in 1887. It was based on a ragbag of Eastern, occult, and anti–Christian ideas. It established an "Esoteric Section" in October 1888, of which Mabel Collins and Vittoria Cremers, who had developed a Ripper theory, were for a time members before they were expelled. When Edmund Gurney of the Society for Psychical Research died, the verdict suicide, it was in the wake of a damning report on the Theosophical Society. Allegations of Blavatsky being a fraud have since been withdrawn due to considerations of Victorian investigative procedures. The Theosophical Society's Aryan, Oriental and Russian early history clashed with Britain's interests in India. It had also audaciously named its internal journal *Lucifer*, issued in largely Protestant London from 1887. It drew sparingly from the writings of Bulwer-Lytton and Eliphas Levi, who were associated with Ripper suspect Roslyn D'Onston, but largely from rediscovered ancient Buddhist and Hindu sacred texts.

Lastly, there were the movements concerned with mesmerism, spiritualism, Christian mysticism and biblical research. Psychic sensitives, mediums, clairvoyants and spiritualists seeking guides and communication with the deceased populated West End parlors. Robert Lees, who is noted as having visions of Jack the Ripper, was very active within these circles, as was W.T. Stead, the editor of the *Pall Mall Gazette*, who predicted his own death on the *Titanic* in 1912. Séances were conducted in an attempt to contact the Whitechapel victims for clues to the identity of the killer and information offered to the police. D'Onston was also in contact with the Anglican bishop B. F. Westcott while researching his 1904 *Patristic Gospels*. Westcott and his colleagues of the Society for Psychical Research and its predecessor, the Cambridge Ghost Society, formed a biblical commission that issued the Revised Version of 1881. Sir Robert Anderson would refute the work of the commission in defense of the Authorized King James Version in the bulk of his religious writings.

It is useful to note that occult interests were also present with the Victorian media establishments and its representatives. Apart from Stead's enthusiastic concern for all things paranormal, Sir Edwin Arnold, a member of the Theosophical Society and author of *The Light of Asia*, founded the *Daily Telegraph*.

Theodor Reuss, a German irregular Mason, Socialist League activist and founding member of the Thule/Illuminati Lodges and O.T.O (Ordo Templi Orientis) early in the 20th century, worked as a journalist for the Central News Agency, which had received the "Dear Boss" Jack the Ripper letter. In early 1888, William Morris of the Socialist League printed an extensive list of alleged Prussian police spies in *The Commonweal*. He described Reuss as "Bismarck's political agent on the Central News of London; contributor to the *Suddeutsche Presse* at Munich and the *Berliner Zeitung* at Berlin."[32] The German Thule/Illuminati Lodges drew heavily from the works of Bulwer-Lytton and became a conduit for anti–Semitic and pre–Nazi ideals with later borrowings of the Jack the Ripper legend.

The Central News Agency, formed in 1871, was not the only supplier of newsworthy items to the mainstream press of 1888. It was in competition with the well-established Reuters News Agency (formed in 1851) and the rival Press Association, formed in 1868 on the invention of the telegraph. Senior police officials Melville Macnaghten, Robert Anderson and head of Special Branch John George Littlechild held suspicions about the involvement of a journalist in the production of bogus Jack the Ripper letters. This indicates that Scotland Yard conducted inquiries in media houses regarding the Whitechapel murders and formed contacts with media representatives.

During the "Autumn of Terror" of 1888, detectives investigated many theories advanced to them by the public, discarding the more fanciful assumptions. One line of inquiry was the possibility that Jack the Ripper was a black magician performing satanic murder rites.[33] The necromantic ritual practice of evisceration or disembowelment was widely known to senior members of the police force from their travels and campaigns around the world. The investigation into the murder weapon and extent of the mutilations considered acutely the travels of the Thames dockworkers. The alien customs of the local immigrant population were also regarded with suspicion. While Stuart Cumberland and other "psychics" were divining the Whitechapel murders for clues, in Victorian London's mystical and occult societies Jack the Ripper was donning the cloak of a black magic vampire thirsting for blood and transcendental potency.

The shadowy nature of the crimes had inspired horror fictions and macabre works of art with precedent in English, American, Continental and French literary and artistic movements during the 1800s. Much of it was derived from rediscovered manuscripts and revived studies on medieval occultism. In the late Victorian period science, religious beliefs and criminology were constantly interacting and merging. With the first 1886 edition in German of an early study on perverse human behaviors, *Psychopathia Sexualis*, and in a later English edition, the work inserted the crimes, albeit with discernable errors, as *Case 17. Jack the Ripper*, which established the killer as an erotic maniac.

Whitechapel murder stories of those disaffected and marginalized from mainstream religious beliefs had infused part of the Victorian Occult Revival. The mysterious deeds of Jack the Ripper suggested to Victorian occultists and, in time, to press and horror novel readers, that the murderer was enacting ritualistic kills. The motive for these ritualistic mutilations was thought to be his perverse supernatural needs and thirst for power. Victorian occultists were drawn from various professions and the clergy and attracted the attention of socialists and women of the early feminist movements. They included authors, painters, journalists, and performing artists; and, like most Londoners, were intrigued by Jack the Ripper and the Whitechapel murders. All concocted theories to solve the crimes. The development of popular modern treatments and a multiplicity of conjectures on a black-magic Ripper were derived from these period sources. But how extensive was the theory for the Victorians, and was it considered a credible motive by Scotland Yard?

Bram Stoker, the author of *Dracula*, wrote in a preface dated August 1898 and included in a 1901 Icelandic edition that states, "a series of crimes which appear to have originated from the same source ... created as much repugnance in people everywhere as the notorious murders of Jack the Ripper." Dracula himself utters, "I long to go through the crowded streets of your mighty London, to be in the midst of the whirl and the rush of humanity, to share its life, its change, its death." The preface also declares, "I am quite convinced that there is no doubt whatever that the events here described really took place, however unbelievable and incomprehensible they might appear at first sight. And I am further convinced that they must always remain to some extent incomprehensible, although continuing research in psychology and natural sciences may, in years to come, give logical explanations of such strange happenings which, at present, neither scientists nor the secret police can understand."

Stoker's notes for the novel have an entry headed "Gladstone/immortality." Though it is thought to refer to the famous black Gladstone bag of Jack the Ripper, it may refer to William Gladstone, the British prime minister who introduced Irish Home Rule. *Dracula* is partially set in Victorian London, Stoker may have created an allegory of blood and English imperial rule that feared Jack the Ripper as a foreign killer. Part of Stoker's narrative appears in the form of excerpts from the liberal *Westminster Gazette*, indicating the popular press's contribution to the allure of macabre murders and blood-sucking beasts.[34]

## A THIRST FOR BLOOD

The two fresh murders which have been committed in Whitechapel have aroused the indignation and excited the imagination of London to a degree without parallel. Men feel that they are face to face with some awful and extraordinary freak of nature. So inexplicable and ghastly are the circumstances surrounding the crimes that people are affected by them in the same way as children are by the recital of a weird and terrible story of the supernatural. It is so impossible to account, on any ordinary hypothesis, for these revolting acts of blood that the mind turns as it were instinctively to some theory of occult force, and the myths of the Dark Ages rise before the imagination. Ghouls, vampires, bloodsuckers, and all the ghastly array of fables which have been accumulated throughout the course of centuries take form, and seize hold of the excited fancy. Yet the most morbid imagination can conceive nothing worse than this terrible reality; for what can be more appalling than the thought that there is a being in human shape stealthily moving about a great city, burning with the thirst for human blood, and endowed with such diabolical astuteness, as to enable him to gratify his fiendish lust with absolute impunity?[35]

The first conjectured instance of ritualistic practices as a motive for the Whitechapel murders occurred with the brutal stabbings of Martha Tabram in George Yard Buildings, 7 August 1888.[36] Police surgeon Dr. Timothy Robert Killeen examined her mutilated body and found 39 puncture wounds. A larger blade such as a bayonet or dagger had also made a single wound to the heart. The press developed the theory that a bayonet had been used, as Tabram was last seen with soldiers. The dagger, however, was suggestive of arcane rituals of blood sacrifice to a superstitious public, Victorian occultists and later theorists. The 39 wounds of Tabram have also added to the numerology myths about Jack the Ripper. Even if these indications were true, and there is no clear evidence that Tabram's wounds were anything but frenzy, they still could not confirm the identity of the killer or that it was a Ripper murder. It is generally discounted as such.

In a *Times* editorial of September 27, 1888, about the inquest of Annie Chapman, murdered on September 8, 1888, it was reported:

> The lucid statement by the Coroner, which yesterday preceded the verdict of the jury in the inquest held upon the death of the woman Chapman, throws an altogether different light upon the recent murders in Whitechapel, and attributes an appalling motive to what must be in any event a terrible crime. If the Coroner is right,—and his opinion is formed upon no fanciful conjecture,—we must reject all the theories which have been ventured by society in its gropings for an adequate motive. We have been schooled to believe that a maniac was indulging a craze for human blood, or that the criminal was a creature whom constant practice at the shambles had hardened to habits of slaughter, or that the crimes were perpetuated by some jealous woman, the companion in vice of the victims, and the police were even advised to search for some heathen sect which practiced barbarous rites.[37]

*The Times* editorial went on to outline the motive advanced by the coroner, Wynne Baxter, based on the evidence of divisional police surgeon Dr. George Bagster Phillips. It was said that an American doctor and pathologist had ventured to extract the internal organs of victims — particularly the uterus — for medical research, as the killer appeared to have surgical skill. Baxter's obituary in the *Evening News* on October 1, 1920, noted he had also considered Fenian secret society involvement in the crimes, perhaps due to the use of surgical knives in the 1882 Phoenix Park murders. According to the 1920 report, "Dr. Baxter advanced his theory to the Home Office, who told him he was not alone in his opinion." *The Times*, however, gave its support to the coroner's call for police to investigate. In time it proved to be a false lead.[38] It is not known which "heathen sect" was suggested to Scotland Yard or if any inquiry resulted, but Baxter's widely circulated theory inspired more occult conjecture.

With the savage murder and mutilation of Catherine Eddowes in Mitre Square, in the City of London Police district west of Whitechapel, in the early hours of September 30, 1888, the time was ripe for supernatural and occult theories. A horror fiction pamphlet, *The Curse Upon Mitre Square: A.D. 1530–1888*, by John Francis Brewer,[39] was published in 1889. The press widely promoted the short work, which was reissued in New York the following year. It is possible that Bram Stoker was inspired by the ready readership for tales of supernatural and ghostly murders. Brewer's influential occult work was drawn on the landscape of ancient London during the October hiatus of Jack the Ripper. That is, until the horrific murder of Mary Kelly on November 9, 1888, changed everything.

> A blood red splash at the head of a long, narrow poster is at this moment attracting some attention in town. It is the sensational advertisement of a sensational shilling brochure, called "The Curse upon Mitre square." I have glanced over it in the interests of my readers, and may say that it is a far fetched story by Mr. J.F. Brewer. The pith of it is that the mysterious murder of Kate Eddowes in Mitre square was the outcome of the Curse called down on that spot by a monk's assassination of a woman on the altar steps of Holy Trinity Church (which stood on the same site) three centuries ago, in the reign of King Henry VIII.[40]
>
> Mr. John Francis Brewer, the author of the new "shilling shocker," "The Curse upon Mitre Square, A.D. 1530–1888," which is creating interest at present, is a grandson of the late Professor Brewer, the celebrated historian, and editor of the "State Papers," &c., whom Mr. Gladstone quotes in his interesting article on "Queen Elizabeth and the Church."[41]

Widespread, graphic press reports of the Whitechapel murders produced imitative "copycat" violence. However, the same effect applied to the production of Ripper theories. In a study of the influence of media representations of social violence, *The Copycat Effect*, Brewster's *The Curse of Mitre Square* is briefly discussed. It is described as giving a "vivid" account of the Whitechapel murders. Author Loren Coleman notes that "the telegraph-hastened, press-driven coverage of the Jack the Ripper story created its own mythos.... Researcher Jean-Gabriel de Tarde, soon after the Jack the Ripper murders, wrote that a "suggestion effect" had taken place.[42]

Behind the scenes in occult and mystical subcultures, beliefs about the Whitechapel murders were published in obscure journals. Helena Blavatsky and her Theosophical Society produced many influential theories and commentaries on the murders. In the December 1888 issue of the Theosophical periodical *Lucifer*, an article about the influences of the Jack the Ripper crimes upon children appeared. It was attributed to "Ariadna" in the journal and to the editor Helena Blavatsky in published lists of the journal.

It is not known who Ariadna was, if not Blavatsky, but "she" may have been either Mabel Collins, co-editor of *Lucifer*, or Vittoria Cremers, noted as a member of the newly formed "Esoteric Section" at the date of the article. Cremers was to convey a Jack the Ripper theory about Roslyn D'Onston to crime reporter Bernard O'Donnell in 1930. She was also noted as having read, with other members of the Theosophical Society, a December 1, 1888, *Pall Mall Gazette* article by D'Onston about a black magic Ripper theory. The following article mentions a "large seaside resort," perhaps Southsea or Brighton, where D'Onston, Collins and Cremers are said to have converged later in 1889.

## CHILDREN ALLOWED TO TRAIN THEMSELVES FOR MURDER

"ARIADNA" writes:— English folk are fond of maintaining the superiority of their national morals as contrasted with those of our Continental neighbours across the seas. Yet had one of the latter been strolling down a thoroughfare of one of our large seaside resorts but a few days ago he might have been inclined to doubt it. In a large shop an alluring tray of boys' knives was exhibited, ticketed "Jack Ripper's knives"! In an adjacent street, a merry gang of children, aged respectively from six to eleven years, were playing at "Ripper," jumping one over the other and knocking them down — a true rehearsal of the felonious act.

Of course the natural question would be, "Why did not their parents stop them and prohibit the ghastly play?"....

But they did not, it is evident; and the fond parents, children themselves of the present age, must have merrily laughed and felt amused at the "original idea." Good Christian people! They do not even think of uprooting the evil by lodging a complaint against the infamous speculators who are permitted to bring out such a toy! The translators and publishers of Zola's outlandish "immorality," which shows vice in all its hideous nakedness and ugliness, are condemned to heavy fines. "Jack Ripper's" knives are permitted to be freely sold to children: for what can be more innocent than a card-board or a wooden knife, gaudily painted, for boys and girls to play with, on its very face! Has any of the lookers-on while witnessing those children, bright things "fresh from the hand of God," the merry, playing babes, put himself the question:

"What wilt thou be hereafter?"

Yet, how many of these little boys and girls now openly sporting with knives and playing at "Jack Ripper" shall, directly in consequence of such "play" become candidates for gallows and swing in that "hereafter." Yea, LAW in all her majesty may claim, through her righteous judges, ten or twenty years hence, any of these light-hearted "little ones" as her lawful prey. "May God have mercy on your soul" will be the pompous but awful verdict of a black-capped Judge as the logical result of such play for one of those now innocent, then guilty, "Jack Rippers." Will any of the future judges or jurymen, we wonder, remember during such a possible trial that, when himself a boy, he may have longed to take the part, nay, perhaps actually has had a hand in the fun during a vacation in one of those fashionable seaside resorts?

The child is father to the man. It is the first impressions, visual or mental, which the young senses take in the quickest, to store them indelibly in the virgin memory. It is the imagery and scenes which happen to us during our childhood, and the spirit in which they are viewed by our elders and received by us, that determine the manner in which we accept such like scenes or look upon good or evil in later years. For, it is most of that early intellectual capital so accumulated day by day during our boyhood and girlhood that we trade with and speculate upon throughout later life.

The capacity of children for the storing away of early impressions is great indeed. And, if an innocent child playing at "Jack Ripper," remarks that his sport produces merriment and amusement instead of horror in the lookers-on, why should a child be expected to connect the same act with sin and crime later on? It is by riding wooden horses in childhood that a boy loses all fear of a living horse in later years. Hence, the urchin who now pretends to murder will look on murder and kill de facto, with as much unconcern when he becomes a man as he does now. There is much sophistry in Mrs. Stowe's remark that "children will grow up substantially what they are by nature," for this can only apply to those exceptional children who are left to take care of themselves; and these do not buy toys at fashionable shops. A child brought up by parents, and having a home instead of a gutter to live and sleep in, if left to self-education will draw from his own observations and conclusions for evil as for good, and these conclusions are sure to color all his after life. Playing at "Jack Ripper," he will think unconsciously of Jack Ripper, and what he may have heard of that now fashionable Mr. Hyde of Whitechapel. And — "...he who but conceives a crime in thought Contracts the danger of an actual fault."[43]

## DIAGNOSES AND PALLIATIVES

Zola's works are finally exiled in their English translations; and though we have not much to say against the ostracism to which his Nana and La Terre have been subjected, his last — La Bête Humaine — might have been read in English with some profit. With "Jack the Ripper" in the near past, and the hypnotic rage in the present, this fine psychological study of the modern male neurotic and "hysteric," might have done good work by way of suggestion. It appears, however, that prudish England is determined to ignore the truth and will never allow a diagnosis of the true state of its diseased morals to be made — not by a foreign writer at all events.[44]

The sobriquet Jack the Ripper, as a designation for a serial killer or personage of ill repute, is still in use today. It entered mainstream Victorian society as a title with publication of the "Dear Boss" letter dated September 25, 1888. The nickname was also becoming an East End rubric for vice and the primal human instincts among spiritualist groups and in journals of occult subcultures. The Theosophical Society was particularly observant from December 1888, as the following excerpts illustrate.

Both the suicide and the man dead of other violence are subject to astral liaisons with the living — the tendency to become connected with loosely organized human beings of the type called "mediums." Entering into such connections, they enjoy vicarious gratification from such passions as the medium may indulge in, and greatly stimulate those passions, so that in time the medium may become a monster. Few among such mediums are ever recognized as mediums, or realize it themselves. They appear as "Jack the Ripper" and the committers of other unspeakable horrors usually dealt with in legal and medical books of limited circulation.[45]

## THOUGHTS ON KARMA AND REINCARNATION

Our disbelief credits the Unseen Power instead of equity with fiendish cruelty. It makes of it a kind of a sidereal Jack the Ripper or Nero doubled with a human monster. If a heathen doctrine honors the Deity and a Christian dishonors it, which should be accepted? And why should one who prefers the former be held as — an infidel?[46]

## PSYCHIC AND NOETIC ACTION

This means that he would have to admit a lower (animal), and a higher (or divine) mind in man, or what is known in Occultism as the "personal" and the "impersonal" Egos. For, between the psychic and the noëtic, between the Personality and the Individuality, there exists the same abyss as between a "Jack the Ripper," and a holy Buddha. Unless the physiologist accepts all this, we say, he will ever be led into a quagmire.[47]

On June 7, 1895, at a meeting of the "Ghost Club" presided over by Thomas B. Har-bottle, "The President alluded to the Tooley St. ground, an account of which he had pre-viously communicated to the Club, as being the supposed seat of black magic in connection with the "Jack the Ripper" murders. This introduced remarks from various members on the subject of black magic and the composition of the Elixir of Life."[48]

The curious mention above of a black magic theory of the Whitechapel murders is notable for the president of the Ghost Club, who was a past functionary member of the Theosophical Society. Tooley Street is the site where the London Dungeon with an exhibition on Jack the Ripper now stands. Harbottle, with his "account ... previously communicated to the club," had resigned from Blavatsky's "Esoteric Section" in 1891 with Irish author William Butler Yeats. This was the same association, established in October 1888, that had included Mabel Collins and Vittoria Cremers, who were both expelled in early 1889.[49] Though this entry in the Ghost Club 1895 minutes forms a bridge in the development of the black magic Ripper theories of the Theosophical Society and Vittoria Cremers, the introduction of "black magic and the composition of the elixir of life" is an extraneous addi-tion to the legend. It was an element found in the occult Jack the Ripper theory of Sir Arthur Diosy, who is reported as bringing it to the attention of Scotland Yard during the Whitechapel murders.[50] The editor of the *Pall Mall Gazette*, W. T. Stead on 3 December 1888 had reported that

> Mr. Arthur Diosy is aggrieved. The ingenious contributor who discovered the nationality of the Whitechapel murderer said that no one had hit upon the suggested necromantic motive. Mr. Diosy says he told the police all about it on October 14, which of course is news to everybody else. He also darkly hints that the dates of the crimes have some occult relation to magical astrology. It would be more to the point if Mr. Diosy would tell us when the next murder ought to occur according to the dates of magical astrology.
>
> "One who Thinks he Knows"— the contributor in question — is an occultist of some experience. When he was a lad of eighteen he studied necromancy under the late Lord Lytton at Alexandria. It would be odd if the mystical lore of the author of "Zanoni" were to help to unearth Jack the Ripper.[51]

As far as is known, notwithstanding *The Times* report of September 27, 1888, advising police to "search for some heathen sect which practiced barbarous rites," Sir Arthur Diosy (1856–1923) first advanced the theory to Scotland Yard on October 14, 1888. The source for Stead's information on Arthur Diosy's theory is unknown, as it does not appear in pre-vious press reports or the official police files, but Diosy did confirm the claim that he had approached Scotland Yard with his black magic Ripper theory at a later date. It was followed by Stead's contributor dubbed "One who Thinks he Knows," Roslyn D'Onston, in his letter to the City Police on October 16 suggesting a necromantic motive for the Whitechapel mur-ders.

Sir Arthur's father was Martin Diosy, a Hungarian Jewish patriot who came to England in the early 1800s and was employed as an immigration official for east European refugees arriving through the port of Hull, the home of Robert Donston Stephenson. From the 1890s, Sir Arthur was a member of the Crimes Club, an association of police officials, jour-nalists, crime authors and coroners interested in the study and discussion of various aspects of crime.

Arthur Diosy was an eccentric and flamboyant man. His accounts of black magic sus-picions for the Whitechapel murders were also noticeable because of his status and could influence his reputation as the Queen's emissary on Japanese diplomacy. Diosy had founded the Japan Society, which grew from a meeting of the International Congress of Orientalists held in London on September 9, 1891. Among his prolific Eastern writings, he also wrote a book on the Japanese Shinto religion titled *Yamato Damashi*. A letter from Diosy to Mrs. George Cornwall West (Lady Randolph Churchill) dated July 5, 1903, thanks her for a copy of her article on a journey to Japan published in the *Pall Mall Gazette*. He wrote that he would have liked to have assisted her in correcting some Japanese words, and remarks about the truth of his predictions on the rise of Japan.[52]

Diosy was also a member of the English branch of the chivalric Order of Christ, the sole descendant of the Order of Templars in Portugal, and was instrumental in its English establishment during 1894. The explorers Christopher Columbus and Vasco da Gama displayed the banner of the Order of Christ on the sails of their ships. He was a close associate of fellow orientalist Lafcadio Hearn, who had written a commentary on the Theosophical Society and its establishment in France and England.[53] Diosy was fascinated by the occult, and he developed a theory for the Whitechapel murders. In a recently discovered 1903 letter from Hearn, he expressed that his friend Arthur Diosy was "on the side of Light, not Darkness"[54] and discussed the difficulties with the English establishment in forging closer cultural ties with oriental societies.

According to his reported statements, Diosy claimed that Jack the Ripper had left clear evidence indicating ritual murder as the motive. He listed the arrangement of certain articles and other occult features of the Whitechapel atrocities, suggesting he had a first-hand account of the crime scenes. It was also noted that Diosy was apparently commissioned to report for the *Star* newspaper, established in January 1888.[55] In some versions, he describes details that are blatantly inaccurate; such as the enacting of rites the killer would simply not have had time for and which would have entailed further risk. It was further claimed that his visit to Scotland Yard on October 14, 1888, resulted in the investigation of a London bookshop that specialized in the sale and procurement of books on black magic.

According to crime novelist and Crimes Club member Sir Max Pemberton:

One night Arthur Diosy walked into Scotland Yard, and being asked his business, declared that he had a theory about the Ripper murders which somebody in authority might like to hear. An inspector received him with great courtesy, as Scotland Yard always does, and told him that he was the two thousandth or so who had come with such an idea.

"Very well," said Diosy, "I will write down two words on a piece of paper, and if you find them interesting you shall hear the rest." The inspector agreed and the words were written. Five minutes afterwards Diosy was telling his story to one of the C.I.D. men engaged upon the case. In effect his theory as I had it from him was this.

He believed the person who committed the Ripper crimes, the maniac who cut so many wretched women to pieces, was the victim of black magic. He declared that the concomitants of the crime proved this beyond a peradventure. In every case, he declared, even when one of the murders was committed in the open street under the very nose of a policeman, there had been a pentagon of lights. In the street case, this pentagon had been formed of the stumps of five matches; in the houses themselves candles had been used. These lights were supposed to bestow invisibility upon the particular person favored of the devil, and so one murder was committed while a policeman stood but a few yards away. Goats' hair was found, I believe, in almost every instance, and all students of black magic will understand the significance of that. There were various other clues, but they are too intricate to be enumerated by the uninstructed; yet they seemed to have convinced the police that there was a great deal in what Diosy said and I am told that they began to make inquiries among those who vended books on black magic and among those who were their customers. In the end, Diosy averred that the names of five men were marked down and that one of them certainly was Jack-the-Ripper. Unfortunately, the matter ended there and "the One" was never taken.[56]

The London antiquarian book-dealer Bernard Quaritch, supplier and publisher of numerous occult books, medieval grimoires and ancient manuscripts, owned such an establishment. He was well known and respected as a major compiler in the Victorian occult community and was active on the boards of the British Library and Museum. Quaritch was also the initial publisher of Helena Blavatsky's miscellanea *Isis Unveiled* and the London agent for *The Theosophist*. He was Victorian London's major contact for ancient and medieval magical treatises and rare manuals of black magic throughout Europe and America.

Quaritch founded the London literary society "Sette of Odd Volumes,"[57] which numbered among its members luminaries of British arts, letters, and diplomacy. George Charles Williamson's papers on the business of the Sette of Odd Volumes are held in the Manuscripts Department of the Lilly Library of Indiana University. Williamson's correspondents included Arthur Diosy, Sir Max Pemberton, occultist John William Brodie-Innes, and Sir Edward Sullivan of Gilbert and Sullivan musicals fame, a Freemason and organist of the United Grand Lodge of England. Quaritch is also mentioned in an obscure booksellers' list of antiquarian manuscripts and rare books as "Librarian of the Sette of Odd Volumes." Diosy held a term as president of Sette of Odd Volumes from 1903 to 1904, shortly before he joined the Crimes Club, otherwise known as "Our Society."

Diosy was also mentioned in an article on the reminiscences of Arthur Lambton, a cofounder of Our Society, in describing its formation. Lambton was an author and amateur criminologist who wrote in 1923:

In Naples I met Mr. S. Ingleby Oddie, now Coroner for Westminster, who has always been an ardent student of criminology. When we renewed our acquaintance in England, he told me that he should much like me to meet a friend of his who lived in Norfolk, Dr. Herbert Crosse, and I responded by saying that he must meet H.B. Irving, the actor-manager son of Sir Henry, who was himself a respected crime historian. The result was that on Tuesday, 1 December 1903, I gave a lunch at the Carlton Hotel, to which Mr. Oddie brought Dr. Crosse, and the rest of the party consisted of Mr. Irving, Lord Albert Godolphin Osborne, Mr. H. Tunstill and Mr. Robert Lang — and I shall always say that that lunch was the kernel of Our Society.

On the following Friday, Mr. Tunstill asked me to supper with Mr. Irving. On that night, for the first time, I met James Beresford Atlay, son of the late Bishop of Hereford, who wrote the only account [to that date] of the Tichborne trial. He was a man with a very pretty wit. Here is an example. In the early days of Our Society, a certain man was very desirous of obtaining admission, and offered to read to us a paper on the Whitechapel Murders. We knew a great deal about — and against — this man, and did not want him, and the question was, how to stave him off. So Mr. Atlay undertook to draft a letter for me to send. This was the draft:

"Dear..., I am desired by the Committee to thank you very much indeed for your kind offer to read us a paper on the Whitechapel Murders, but you will appreciate the reason why we cannot accept it when I tell you that the Whitechapel Murderer happens to be a very near and dear relative of one of our most popular members."[58]

On the night following Mr. Tunstill's supper — Saturday, 5 December 1903 — Mr. Irving gave a dinner at his house, 1 Upper Woburn Place. We sat down six: Professor John Churton Collins, Mr. Atlay, Mr. Ingleby Oddie, Dr. Crosse, the host and myself. We were the original members of Our Society.

Churton Collins's memory was extraordinary, prose and poetry like, and he could give every date and every detail of any murder case without any mental effort. The dear old professor's enthusiasm for criminology was so intense that occasionally he ran past himself. For instance, he once suggested that we should invite the Public Executioner to be the guest of the Society. I gently pointed out to him that if the invitation was extended and accepted, I feared that that particular dinner would be of the tete-a-tete description.

After a short interval, the Society doubled its numbers, and, therefore, by simple arithmetic, we became twelve, the neophytes consisting of Sir Arthur Conan Doyle, Sir Max Pemberton, Mr. Fletcher Robinson, Sir Willoughby Maycock, Mr. Arthur Diosy, and Mr. F.W. Rose.[59]

The Crimes Club then extended its membership to forty, with such distinguished persons as Major Arthur Griffiths, the publisher Eveleigh Nash, George R. Sims and Sir Melville Macnaghten taking an interest. Eventually, membership reached 100 and included Ripper researchers and true crime authors Richard Whittington-Egan, Jonathan Goodman, Robin Odell and Donald Rumbelow. Until he died in 1935, Arthur Lambton was honorary secretary of the club for the first thirty-two years and was to miss only four dinners. But it was Sir Arthur Diosy's impromptu talk, "My 'Black Magic' Theory of the Whitechapel Murders, as submitted to Scotland Yard" given to the Crimes Club on November 8, 1914, which caused a stir.

Diosy's theory was also outlined in a book by the former coroner of Central London, S. Ingleby Oddie. Oddie, a friend of Dr. Gordon Brown, who had examined the body of Catherine Eddowes, had conclusions of his own about the Whitechapel murders. In *Inquest*[60] (1941), Oddie wrote "The most reasonable theory to my mind is that the man was a homicidal lunatic with some anatomical knowledge, acquired either as a butcher or a medical student, who obtained physical gratification from murdering women and slashing their bodies about with a knife." As the killer's mental condition worsened, conjectured Oddie, "he became suicidal and probably jumped into the Thames, just an unknown man."

Ingleby Oddie's book has a chapter on "The 'Ripper' and Other Murders" which includes the outline of Arthur Diosy's theory:

> Among the theories put forward was one by Arthur Diosy, a member of "Our Society." He thought the murders were the work of some practitioner of "black magic." According to him, among the quests of these people in the East is the "*elixir vitae*," one of the ingredients of which must come from a recently killed woman. Diosy got quite excited when he heard of the bright farthings and burnt matches which he said might have formed the "flaming points" of a magical figure called a "pentacle" at each angle of which such points were found, and according to ritual certain "flaming" articles had to be thus disposed. Diosy said later he had paid a visit to Scotland Yard to place his theories before the authorities, but had been received without enthusiasm, as one can well understand.
>
> There seems little doubt that the real explanation lies, as I have said, in some insane medical man, possibly a Russian Jew living in the East End, who was a lust murderer, a Sadist, whose insanity increased until it culminated in the wild orgy of Dorset Street and was followed by his own suicide in the Thames.

Oddie blends several theories of the time based on the writings of Macnaghten, Anderson and Le Queux[61] into a symbiotic synthesis. Diosy had alternatively combined the Victorian occult traditions of East and West to arrive at his. Diosy's highly original theory on Jack the Ripper, based on a wide reading of the available literature, does not match the facts of the police investigation and the known crime scene evidence. Is it any more extraordinary than the theory adhered to by Macnaghten, of a suicide found in the Thames, or that of Anderson, on the insane Polish Jew suspect? Or of the subjective psychological criminal profiling of today?

In a letter written by Lord Lindsay, the 26th Earl of Crawford and Balcarres, to Robert Anderson,[62] an unnamed lady was introduced who had approached him with a claim to have vital information on the author of the Whitechapel murders. Crawford implored Anderson to hear her account and implied discretion in any association on his part with her fears of a connection to the alleged suspect. Though the letter is undated, it seems to have been written sometime in 1889. The lady remains unidentified, and the only other fact known is the writer of the letter.

The "Crawford letter" alone proves nothing, but does exemplify Victorian interest in alternate beliefs and theories.

2 CAVENDISH SQUARE. W

My dear Anderson,

I send you this line to ask you to see & hear the bearer, whose name is unknown to me. She has or thinks she has a knowledge of the author of the Whitechapel murders. The author is supposed to be nearly related to her, & she is in great fear lest any suspicions should attach to her & place her & her family in peril.

I have advised her to place the whole story before you, without giving you any names, so that you may form an opinion as to its being worth while to investigate.

Very sincerely yours,

Crawford

In Crawford's silence in noting details traceable to crime historians and in view of his Victorian esoteric contacts, is it not possible that the lady in question was fearful not of someone "nearly related" but of guilt by association? Perhaps a fellowship of secret oaths, subculture requirements of loyalty and lack of publicity could explain her approach to him rather than directly to the police. As no evidence existed to convict any suspect or to connect the letter with the Druitt or Kosminski families, the possibility appears substantial.

In view of Crawford's standing in the occult community of Victorian London, he would be the obvious choice for discretion and official police contacts in such matters. Very few people knew of his friendship with Anderson, established while on the Royal Observatory of Edinburgh Commission. As the only known fact about this letter is the writer of it, a logical but tentative step would be to examine, without historical bias or prejudice, Crawford's associations for any Ripper anecdotes or suspicions that may have come to the attention of Scotland Yard.

Though Anderson and Crawford were the closest of friends, they were diametrically opposed in their views on spiritual matters. Anderson was a conservative and highly suspicious author of the "critical approach" to biblical research, and Crawford was a champion of liberal explorations of the maps of Theosophical alchemy and the occult. The Earl of Crawford also amassed a huge personal library and collections of archaic and medieval manuscripts. He was chairman of the Royal Observatory of Edinburgh Commission in 1876 and an ancestor of the royal house of Stuart. Restored to the peerage in 1880 by an act of Parliament as Earl of Crawford and Balcarres, he donated a large segment of his astronomical books and instruments to the commission from his library, the Bibliotheca Lindesiana, at that time the largest in the British Empire. Bernard Quaritch assisted him in the procurement of rare books and manuscripts and was a close friend of the family.

In her account of a meeting in December 1888 noted by crime journalist Bernard O'Donnell in the 1930s, Vittoria Cremers claimed that Crawford was discussed in a conversation with Helena Blavatsky and other members of the Theosophical Society. He was described as a "black magician" and the author of an article published in the *Pall Mall Gazette* on December 1, 1888, proposing an occult motive for the Whitechapel murders. It appears that Robert Donston Stephenson penned the article, though newspaper reports of the time also rumored the Earl's authorship. The confusion was disclosed in an article reprinted from the *New York Times* in the May 1889 issue of the American periodical *The Theosophist* titled "Dr. Keightley Speaks." Archibald Keightley was general secretary of the English Theosophical Society from 1888 and an acquaintance of Blavatsky, Mabel Collins, and Cremers. He aligned with the American branch in the split of the society after the death of Blavatsky in 1891.

Keightley remarked that those who would visit Blavatsky included "Mr. W.T. Stead, editor of the *Pall Mall Gazette*, who is a great admirer of the 'Secret Doctrine,' finds much in it that seems to invite further elucidation; Lord Crawford, Earl of Crawford and Balcarres, another F.R.S. — who is deeply interested in occultism and cosmogony, and who was a pupil of Lord Lytton and studied with him in Egypt — comes to talk of his special topics of concern; Mrs. Besant, whose association with the National Reform Society has made her famous, drops in to express her interest in theosophy as a power affecting the social life of humanity..." One of the indicators that D'Onston wrote the anonymous December 1, 1888, article was Stead's claim that he was a pupil of Lord Lytton, which was repeated in an 1896 issue of his *Borderland*. However, the suggestion that the Earl of Crawford was involved in satanic practices has drawn little consideration. His writing a letter to Robert Anderson with information on the murders at about the same time that Keightley was writing to the *New York Times* verges beyond a coincidence. It is a source for Cremers's December 1888 story about Crawford's connections with the Theosophical Society, Jack the Ripper, Stead and Roslyn D'Onston.

Crawford was also brought to the attention of the Society for Psychical Research when his name appeared on the allegedly hoaxed "Mahatma Letters" of the Indian branch of the Theosophical Society. Though the results of the inquiry, known as the Hodgson Report of 1885, do not mention him by name, he is listed as a functionary member of the early London Lodge of the Theosophical Society in memoranda and correspondence with its early British head, Charles Massey. Massey was to resign his tenure under the weight of his own misgivings on evidence submitted to the Society for Psychical Research.

One of the Mahatma letters stated:

This applies equally to the case of the Lord Crawford and Balcarres, an excellent gentleman — imprisoned by the world. His is a sincere and noble, though may be a little too repressed nature. He asks what hope he may have? I say — every hope. For he has that within himself that so very few possess: an exhaustless source of magnetic fluid which, if he only had the time, he could call out in torrents and need no other master than himself. His own powers would do the work and his own great experience be a sure guide for him. But, he would have to guard against, and avoid every foreign influence — especially those antagonistic to the nobler study of MAN as an integral Brahm, the microcosm free and entirely independent of either the help or control of the invisible agencies the "new dispensation" (bombastic word!) calls "Spirits." His Lordship will understand my meaning without any further explanation: he is welcome to read this if he chooses, if the opinions of an obscure Hindu interest him. Were he a poor man, he might have become an English Dupotet, with the addition of great scientific attainments in exact science. But alas —! what the peerage has gained psychology has lost.... And yet it is not too late. But see, even after mastering magnetic science and giving his powerful mind to the study of the noblest branches of exact science, how even he has failed to lift more than a small corner of the veil of mystery.... His Lordship's letter to you exhales an influence of sincerity tinged with regret. This is a good man at heart with latent capacity for being a far better and a happier one. Had his lot not been cast as it has, and had his intellectual power all been turned upon Soul-culture, he would have achieved much more than he ever dreamt. Out of such material were adepts made in the days of Aryan glory. But I must dwell no longer upon this case; and I crave his Lordship's pardon if, in the bitterness of my regret I over-stepped in any way the bounds of propriety, in this too free "psychometrical delineation of character" as the American mediums would express it...

P.S. — The "friend" of whom the Lord Lindsay speaks in his letter to you, is, I am sorry to say, a true skunk mephitis, who managed to perfume himself with ess-bouquet in his presence during their palmy days of friendship, and so avoided being recognized by his natural stench. It is Home[63] — the medium, a convert to Roman Catholicism, then to Protestantism, and finally to the Greek Church. He is the bitterest and most cruel enemy O. [Olcott] and [Madame] B. [Blavatsky] have, though he has never met either of them. For a certain time he succeeded in poisoning the Lord's mind, and

prejudiced him against them. I do not like saying anything behind a man's back, for it looks like back-biting. Yet in view of some future events I feel it my duty to warn you, for this one is an exceptionally bad man — hated by the Spiritualists and mediums as much as he is despised by those — who have learned to know him. Yours is a work which clashes directly with his. Though a poor sickly cripple, a paralysed wretch, his mental faculties are as fresh and as alive as ever to mischief. He is no man to stop before a slanderous accusation — however vile and lying. So — beware.
K. H.[64]

In a private letter to her friend A.P. Sinnett, organizer of the original London Lodge of the Theosophical Society,[65] Helena Blavatsky expressed feelings on her treatment by mainstream society. She was incensed by the acrimonious investigation and allegations of hoaxed letters from India as widely publicized:

And please remember, my dear Mr. Sinnett, that if those psychic asses offer after your letter in "Light" to show me any "letters" or to give me a chance of rising and explaining — I refuse to do so beforehand. I would have nothing to do with them, if it even lead to an entire vindication. I have enough of them, of their ungentlemanly, disgusting, Scotland yard secret proceedings, and do not wish to be any more troubled by anything coming from Cambridge, which be — condemned. The "Arundale group" is not altogether composed of geniuses as you know.[66]

Aleister Crowley was a lad of 13 during the Whitechapel murders but is sometimes regarded as a suspect. He wrote on Jack the Ripper in his adult life (courtesy the O.T.O.).

Blavatsky was herself regarded as a Jack the Ripper suspect, though this is a modern theory derived from a comment found in a 1943 article of the British occultist Aleister Crowley titled "Jack the Ripper." Crowley has also been suggested as a suspect, but as he was a mere lad living in London during the Whitechapel murders, and is known to have written fairly extensively on the black magic theory later, he was not brought to the attention of Scotland Yard. However, Blavatsky had confirmed Crawford's occult interests and contacts with her Theosophical Society, as Cremers noted to O'Donnell in 1930, discussing Ripper suspect Roslyn D'Onston.[67]

## MADAME BLAVATSKY AND HER OPINIONS

The ignorant may perhaps ascribe to Mme. Blavatsky "the power of working miracles"; but "miracles" we, Theosophists, leave to fools and believers in a personal god. We reject with the contempt of admirers of science everything "supernatural." It is also to be regretted that the Right Honorable Lord Lindsay, F.R.S., and President of the Royal Astronomical Society of London, who has had the great misfortune to fall under the ban of the influential and world-famed

Ceylon Observer, should thus have had all his prospects in life blighted, and his "once honored name" pronounced with prudent compassion by the pious Colombo Editor for having joined the Theosophical Society. But the fact of His Lordship's being in the good company of a number of English and other European aristocrats and men of science and high Indian officials — Generals, Colonels, Deputy Collectors, Magistrates, English Editors (many of them with their wives), who have also joined our Society, may afford some little consolation to the unhappy nobleman.

The "Occult Sciences" based on a knowledge of the natural forces in the universe may be "of the devil" only in the opinion of the Ceylon Observer, and a few well-meaning but ignorant padris [sic]; and if "the devil is not an idiot" we may perhaps account for the fact, by inferring that this much maligned, mysterious gentleman in black has generously ceded his full share of idiocy to some Editors, who despite the conclusions of the 19th Century still believe in this interesting though grim Christian myth.

H. P. BLAVATSKY,
Corresponding Secretary, Theosophical Society.
PANADURE,
May 29th, 1880.[68]

An editorial followed in the internal periodical *The Theosophist*: "Among the stupid falsehoods set afloat by our enemies, was one that the Right Honorable Lord Lindsay, M.P., F.R.S., one of the Councillors of the Theosophical Society, had repudiated his connection with us; the fact being that that eminent savant and nobleman, in a letter of May 20, accepts the position in question with 'cordial thanks' for what he kindly designates as the honor done him."[69]

So what lay behind Madam Blavatsky's written outburst to A.P. Sinnett about the "Scotland yard secret proceedings" of the Theosophical Society? Blavatsky herself gave the reasons in further correspondence as these excerpt show:

## LETTER NO. CVIII

Wednesday.

My Dear Mr. Sinnett,

There seems to be a fatality attached to all you do in the best and most friendly intentions — for me. And I knew it from the first. There's fruits No. I of the "Incidents!" Yesterday I received from my sister three columns cut out of the Novoye Vremya about those accursed Memoirs, a review of your book by Moltchenoff, the London Correspondent of that paper. Prominent among other chaff is the sentence in my letter you framed yourself (for the Times that would not have it) and published in the pamphlet, that "bad as the Anglo-Indian Govt. was the Russian would be a 1000 times worse."
Against its appearance in the pamphlet, I did not protest. No one read it except Theosophists; but its publication in the "Incidents" is a public slap on the face of Russia, of all Russian patriots — of which my sister and nieces are foremost. She is indignant and ready to repudiate me. She says she read the proofs and never saw that — I suppose not since you added it later on!

Well any how, it is my fault, the fault of my cowardice before the cowardly art of Hodgson & Co. [Society for Psychical Research] and of his accusation. If I have left or made to leave his attack on the phenomena unnoticed I ought to have left this beastly, vile lie and calumny untouched. Had I been hung by your Govt. in India on false suspicions I would have left at least good feeling for my memory in Russia; as it is now, I stand a spy, a beast in the eyes of England and a heartless, unpatriotic wretch in those of every Russian I honor and love, including my own sister — and Gaboriau including the translation of that same letter in his French Occult World! Now every Russian will read it. And it is a LIE; a horrid, disgusting cowardly lie of mine for which I will blush to the end of my days....

Your ever the same,
H. P. B.

## LETTER NO. CV I

[First part missing] ... her departed Jesus. Unless you ferret out for your own private amusement a new Leonard, or Crookes runs away with Mrs. Golindo and her wig, I do not smell any new rat in the shape of scandal ahead. Quite the contrary. For, above the black stormy clouds of your dirty

English political life — the great red harlot and Beast, with the Pope and Bismarck dancing the lanciers and Salisbury making his grand rond around them, I perceive a bright blue opening, a canopy of light over your own Theosophical head. This is no inspiration, but written in the Book of Destiny now open before me, and in which, notwithstanding young Fawcett upsetting books and furniture behind me, I see quite clear. Do not take this as a joke, for it is serious, I have just finished reading your "Blue Book" in the Pall Mall Gazette and I am full of it — fuller than I would be had I eaten at my dinner three pounds of lobster and green venomous mushrooms. But you — I can't help loving you. Only — what, in the name of mischief, have you been writing to Coues. Some great mischief from that letter in the U.S.A. Oh Lord, Lord — I wish my enemies would each write a book! which, according to Job, who for all he forgot to be born in your "superior" race and was but a dirty unwashed Arab spoke wisdom nevertheless — would be my best revenge. Now what have you been writing to Coues?...[70]

Meanwhile and notwithstanding I am,
Yours ever truly,
H. P. B.[71]

Following is an extract from the circular included with the letter above:

Private and Confidential

It would be well perhaps, if the Jesuits contented themselves with making dupes of Freemasons and opposing the Theosophists and Occultists using for it the Protestant clergy as "cat's paw." But their plottings have a much wider scope, and embrace a minuteness of detail and care of which the world in general has no idea. Everything is done by them to bring the mass of mankind again to the state of passive ignorance which they well know is the only one which can help them to the consummation of their purpose of Universal Despotism. An old page refused for insertion in the History of England in the XIXth Century, because of the blindness of its statesmen, will be added to it — when too late — in the XXth Century.[72]

The preceding extracts help to explain a Jack the Ripper theory involving Jesuits in London. It was formulated by W.T. Stead and noted in a 1907 letter to crime journalist George R. Sims. The Executive Superintendent of Scotland Yard, Charles Henry Cutbush, would likewise become obsessed with a perceived Catholic conspiracy before committing suicide due to chronic depression. There is no direct evidence of a Catholic plot in London as described, apart from the political and historic English machinations between the Vatican and the Tory government on the vexed issue of Home Rule for Ireland.

However, it does further illustrate the strained atmosphere that was a way of life for Victorians as Jack the Ripper was prowling the East End. The extent to which republican, separatist and socialist idealists were active, intermingling with occult subcultures and under investigation by Scotland Yard, are now largely consigned to obscurity. Alignment of some factions of the Theosophical Society with socialism, early feminism, Indian independence and the Great Game with Russia was of some concern to British authorities, who responded with vigilant surveillance of secret societies.[73] There is little evidence to suggest that Helena Petrovna Blavatsky was a Russian spy, as she said. Rather, she founded her society based on the principles of Eastern mysticism and humanism. Victorian Londoners had legitimate suspicions that the killer was housed within such associations when Crawford wrote to Anderson.

Allan O. Hume of the colonial secret service had infiltrated the Indian branch of the Theosophical Society. In a memorandum he referred to the "legions of secret quasi-religious orders, with literally, their millions of members, which form so important a factor in the Indian problem."[74] Back at home in 1887, the Maharajah Duleep Singh[75] was resisting advances from the Empress of India, Queen Victoria, and threatening to align with Irish republicans. Arthur Diosy's approach to Scotland Yard about a Jack the Ripper using "Eastern" customs of disembowelment and black magic rites using the bodily portions of British citizens was indeed not well received.

Of some further interest is the establishment of the early Theosophical Society on the Indian continent during a time when James Monro and Melville Macnaghten held official Indian positions. Monro was also consulted on the early formation of the Home Office secret service based on his police experience in India. They were later to join the Metropolitan Police as senior officials and would have noticed the society's growth in London during the Whitechapel murders. Robert Anderson would likewise have been aware of the Earl of Crawford's Theosophical Society membership when receiving an enigmatic letter from him about an unnamed lady with a Jack the Ripper story to tell.

"What should by now be quite clear," wrote author Colin Wilson in 1971, "is that the spirit of magic underwent a complete transformation in the nineteenth century. With Paracelsus it had been a science. With Cagliostro it became the instrument of his religion of the regeneration of mankind. But with

Helena P. Blavatsky in 1887 sitting in the home of Mabel Collins, "Maycot," at 77 Elgin Cresent, Crownhill, Upper Norwood, London. Vittoria Cremers likely stayed there the following year (courtesy the Theosophical Society).

Levi and Lytton it became a romantic literary property, surrounded by dense clouds of incense."[76] (Wilson later developed material on Jack the Ripper.)

It is the dearth of historic sources and obscurity of secret societies that makes commentators on the Whitechapel murders discount the value, quality or relevance of the period's subcultures. When a Jack the Ripper reference is permeated with occultism[77] or suspicion of religious mania, it is presumed apocryphal. As the suspicions intersected with Scotland Yard inquiries, the historical sources cannot be dismissed so lightly. The rational bias of modern thought may blind us to the Victorian worldview that Jack the Ripper was an enigma of supernatural proportions.

# 4

# Suspect
# Dr. Roslyn D'Onston

Dr. Roslyn D'Onston, alias of Robert Donston Stephenson,[1] was first brought to the attention of Scotland Yard as a suspect for the Whitechapel murders by George Marsh, an unemployed East End ironmongery salesman. In his statement to police on December 24, 1888, Marsh concluded, "From his manner I am of opinion he is the murderer in the first six cases, if not the last one." The questioning officer, Inspector Thomas Roots,[2] an experienced detective with the Criminal Investigation Department (CID), did not share Marsh's suspicions. Roots noted in his summary report of December 26, 1888, to the supervisor of the case, Chief Inspector Donald Swanson, that as D'Onston had voluntarily approached Scotland Yard, "I was under impression that Stephenson was a man I had known 20 years I now find that impression was correct."

Upon release of the official files in the late 1970s, crime historians decided that D'Onston's involvement, enough to generate a police file, deserved further attention. If he was not Jack the Ripper, what, then, was the nature of his interest in the murders? Why did he suggest his own tenuous suspect, Dr. Morgan Davies, in his police statement of December 26, 1888? The rediscovery of D'Onston in the Scotland Yard files (now lost) encouraged further speculation. However, neither his alibi as a patient of the London Hospital nor his plausibility as Jack the Ripper have been established. Compared to Roslyn D'Onston, wishful suspects such as James Maybrick, Walter Sickert and Lewis Carroll are rather symptomatic of novel and literary speculative treatments.

A suspect who presents himself cannot be discounted in an unsolved serial murder case. A confirmed police suspect may later be eliminated, however, the details add to knowledge of the historic police investigation. D'Onston since 1987 has been placed on an equal historical footing with the "Macnaghten three," Kosminski, Montague Druitt and Michael Ostrog.[3] Among other nominal police suspects such as Thomas Cutbush and George Hutchinson, Roslyn D'Onston has assured himself of a claim to infamy as a Jack the Ripper suspect.

As D'Onston can be firmly placed in the East End during the murders, he remains a credible but minor suspect without further corroboration. Until the rediscovery of Chief Inspector John Littlechild's American suspect Francis Tumblety in 1993, D'Onston remained a viable contender, despite being discounted on the tenuous grounds of his published claims and occult leanings. If one compares primary sources on D'Onston with substantial but flawed secondary suspicions noted during the 20th century, his suspect status degrades. Yet he resided as an inpatient at the London Hospital, Whitechapel — a location in close proximity to the first generally regarded Ripper murder of Mary Ann Nichols on August 31, 1888.

His association with W.T. Stead, for instance, as a long-time contributor and friend, is another important detail. D'Onston as a murder suspect, however, is generally not considered to have been Jack the Ripper. The question then arises; why did he put himself into the case? Did he acquire, with Stead, information about the investigation of the murders, if not the identity of the killer, or was he seeking official details for newspaper copy?

D'Onston also wrote a letter to the City Police dated October 16, 1888, after the murder of Catherine Eddowes suggesting that the motive for the murders was derived "from a French book, a use made of the organ in question — 'd'une femme prostituee.'" This referred

Roslyn D'Onston, alias of Robert Donston Stephenson. The portrait was published in *Borderland* in 1896 (courtesy Stewart P. Evans).

to the removal of Catherine Eddowes's uterus (and of Annie Chapman's on September 8, 1888) for supposed use in black magic. In the letter, he advanced a theory on the meaning of the Goulston Street wall writing, found on the morning of September 30, 1888, above a portion of Eddowes's apron. This further suggested, he claimed, a French connection to the crimes associated with anti–Semitic beliefs.

Today D'Onston is regarded as a potential suspect, though the possibility was seemingly dismissed at the time of the murders. Modern interest in D'Onston has been active since at least 1958, with the discovery of an unpublished manuscript by crime reporter Bernard O'Donnell.

Apart from theories based on secondary and press sources that were advanced and later developed by W.T. Stead and Vittoria Cremers particularly, D'Onston's likelihood of being a suspect rests on items from the official files. Though D'Onston's letter to the City Police on October 16, 1888, has a file reference at the London Record Office, his Metropolitan Police documents are now missing. However, they were copied and noted during the 1970s as "Under MEPO 3/141, ff. 32–135" and lost before the files were deposited at the Public Record Office in the late 1980s.[4]

*October 16, 1888:* D'Onston writes a letter to the City of London Police investigating the murder of Catherine Eddowes from his London Hospital bed introducing his theory that the Goulston Street wall writing on "Juwes" was made by a Frenchman. He cites as his source a circular issued in the press the previous day by Metropolitan Police Commissioner Sir Charles Warren. On October 5, 1888, the *Police Gazette* had issued a notice from the Commissioner of the City of London Police of a reward of £500 for information leading to the discovery and conviction of Eddowes's killer. This may have prompted D'Onston to write the letter as the question of rewards emerged in his further statements to Scotland Yard. He signed the letter "Roslyn D'O. Stephenson" and included a return address, "Major Stephenson 50, Currie Wards, The London Hospital E." As a postscript he adds, "P.S. I can tell you, from a French book, a use made of the organ in question — d'une femme prostituee, which has not yet been suggested, if you think it worth while." The entire letter outlined a theory he later developed for a newspaper article that was published on December 1, 1888. Arthur Diosy was reported to have approached Scotland Yard two days before the date of D'Onston's letter with a similar theory on removal and use of the uterus. There is a marginal note added at the top of the original letter that a reply was sent on October 17, 1888.[5]

*December 24, 1888:* George Marsh, an unemployed ironmongery salesman, makes a statement to Scotland Yard taken by Inspector Thomas Roots on suspicions that D'Onston was Jack the Ripper. Marsh based his accusations on several conversations with D'Onston at the Prince Albert Public House since D'Onston's voluntary discharge from the London Hospital on December 7, 1888. Marsh was directed to approach the police with D'Onston's information, perhaps in hopes of a reward, on suspicion that a Dr. Morgan Davies was the Ripper. Marsh, who described himself as an "amateur detective," had secured a sample of D'Onston's handwriting presumably to compare with the Ripper letters which the press believed were written by the killer. He adds that D'Onston had gone to see Dr. Davies and Mr. Stead with an article for which he expected £2. Marsh confirms that D'Onston told him of his authorship of the December 1, 1888, article signed "One who Thinks he Knows" for which D'Onston received £4. He also claimed he had seen letters from Stead concerning it. Marsh further noted seeing a letter from Stead refusing to allow D'Onston money to find the Whitechapel murderer and a discharge sheet from the London Hospital where the name of Stephenson was struck out and replaced with "Dr. Davies" written in red ink.

*December 26, 1888:* D'Onston voluntarily makes a statement to Scotland Yard that, like Marsh's, was taken by Inspector Roots. He draws attention to Dr. Morgan Davies who, D'Onston states, "was for sometime a House Physician at the London Hospital, White-chapel,"[6] and indicates that his accusations attach mainly to the murder of Mary Kelly on November 9, 1888. D'Onston was in a ward overseen by Dr. Davies.[7] He claimed Davies would visit and act out the murders to cause suspicion that he was Jack the Ripper. Finally, D'Onston offers as proof that Stead informed him that the victim was sodomized — gesture that Dr. Davies simulated during his hospital visits. D'Onston urged the police to see Davies before he left for Australia and said that he was a resident of the East End at Castle Street, Houndsditch. He adds as a postscript that he had mentioned the details to George Marsh, described as a "pseudo-detective," and that an agreement was made but signed only by D'Onston. It was attached to the statement, dated December 24, 1888, and read, "I hereby agree to pay to Dr. R. D'O. Stephenson (also known as 'Sudden Death') one half of any or all monies received by me on a/c [account] of the conviction of Dr. Davies for wilful murder." D'Onston informs Scotland Yard that he may be contacted via a Mr. Iles of the

Prince Albert Public House, St. Martin's Lane, but was reluctant to leave an address, which he indicated was near the public house.[8]

*December 26, 1888:* Inspector Roots writes his summary report and notes that the statements of D'Onston and Marsh were forwarded to Chief Inspector Donald Swanson of the CID. Though documentation of the outcome of the police interview or of Swanson's conclusions is not available, Inspector Roots's previous knowledge of him appears to discount D'Onston as Jack the Ripper. Roots also noted important background details on D'Onston, which in the main have proved historically reliable, as shown by the following extract:

> When Marsh came here on 24th, I was under the impression that Stephenson was a man I had known 20 years. I now find that impression was correct. He is a traveled man of education and ability, a doctor of medicine upon diplomas of Paris & New York: a major from the Italian Army — he fought under Garibaldi: and a newspaper writer. He says that he wrote the article about Jews in the *Pall Mall Gazette*, that he occasionally writes for that paper, and that he offered his services to Mr. Stead to track the murderer. He showed me a letter from Mr. Stead, dated Nov. 30 1888, about this and said that the result was the proprietor declined to engage upon it.[9] He has lead [*sic*] a bohemian life, drinks very heavily, and always carries drugs to sober him and stave off delirium tremens. He was an applicant for the [Metropolitan and City Police] Orphanage Secretaryship[10] at the last election. The statements were forwarded to Chief Inspector Swanson.

On September 24, 1888, the *Pall Mall Gazette* became one of the first London daily newspapers to report on the Gateshead murder. Soon to be widely publicized, the case had alerted D'Onston to Roots's investigation. The *Pall Mall Gazette* presented the story as the inquest into the murder of Ripper victim Mary Ann Nichols on August 31 was concluding. The inquest on the murder of Annie Chapman concluded two days later on 26 September 1888.

## THE POLITICAL MORAL OF THE MURDERS

The murder and mutilation of a woman near Gateshead yesterday morning will revive, in the provinces, the horror which was beginning to die out in London. The coroner in summing up the evidence in the case of the woman Nichols went through once more the points of suspicious similarity in the four Whitechapel murders. In some respects the Gateshead murder is said to closely resemble them; and already the people in the neighbourhood have begun, it seems, to be haunted with the idea that the murderous maniac of Whitechapel may have made his way to the North of England. The idea is natural, but improbable. What is far more likely is that the Birtley murder is not a repetition, but a reflex, of the Whitechapel ones. It is one of the inevitable results of publicity to spread an epidemic. Just as the news of one suicide often leads to another, so the publication of the details of one murder often leads to their repetition in another murder. Reading of means to do ill deeds makes ill deeds done. This, we suppose, was one of the motives which led to the Whitechapel doctor to suppress so long as he could the results of his post-mortem. The coroner ultimately insisted on the full facts being stated, and, in view of the many countervailing advantages which result from publicity, it is impossible to blame either the coroner for eliciting or the press for printing the particulars of the Whitechapel horrors. But news is one thing; literature is another. And if there is going to be either an epidemic, or a panic, of murder in the North of England, it will be strange if some of the public indignation is not visited upon the newspapers which set their readers to sup upon "Newgate Calendars"[11] and tales of crime.

Meanwhile, is there any reason to suppose that the lesson of the Whitechapel murders has been fully learned in London? Taking as the most faithful hypothesis that they were the work of a scientific and philanthropic sociologist,[12] can we say that he has reason as yet to stay his hand? The police, we know from the proceedings at the inquest, are at their wits' end; do not expect fresh evidence; and are frankly waiting for a fifth murder to give them a clue to the preceding four. But is this attitude of grim expectancy to be adopted also by the social reformer? The answer depends on the degree in which the morals of the murder are taken to heart during the next few weeks or months.[13]

Dr. George Bagster Phillips, a Whitechapel police surgeon, had at that stage conducted the autopsy and reported to the inquest proceedings on Annie Chapman, murdered on the morning of September 8, 1888. The similarity between Nichols's and Chapman's neck wounds and mutilations, tied to earlier Whitechapel murders by press and the police, combined to form the theory that a serial killer was at work in the East End. With the Gateshead murder of 27-year-old Jane Beadmore occurring north of London in Birtley, a mining town in County Durham, Dr. Phillips and Inspector Roots were sent by Scotland Yard to assist the Durham police. They reported on the neck and abdominal mutilations that were conjectured to be similar to those of the Whitechapel murders.[14] The press reported:

> The action of the London authorities in sending Dr. Phillips and Inspector Roots down to investigate the circumstances of the murder has unquestionably intensified the feeling among the public.[15] The London police appear to think that there may be some connexion between this and the recent outrages in Whitechapel, and Inspector Roots, of Scotland-yard, with Dr. Phillips, who conducted the post-mortem examination on the body of Annie Chapman, yesterday, in company with Colonel White, Chief Constable of the county, drove from Durham to the scene of the tragedy. Dr. Phillips saw the body, but the result of his investigation is not known. It is believed, however, that the examination must have failed to disclose any direct resemblance to the Whitechapel murders, for, though the wounds in each case were somewhat similar, those upon the body of Jane Beetmoor [sic] had been inflicted by brute force, and did not show any appearance of anatomical skill.[16] [...] Inspector Roots, of Scotland-yard, has also expressed the view that the Birtley affair is nothing more than a clumsy imitation of the mutilations that took place in the metropolis.[17]

The lengthy inquest on Annie Chapman conducted at the discretion of coroner Wynne E. Baxter commenced on September 10 and ended on September 26, 1888. The body of Jane Beadmore was found the morning of September 23, 1888. Baxter's inquest launched theories of a killer with knowledge of human anatomy. The medical evidence was reviewed when Robert Anderson commissioned a report from CID police surgeon Dr. Thomas Bond after the murder of Mary Kelly on November 9, 1888. Baxter's belief that an American doctor was in search of uteri and other anatomical specimens linked the extraction of the victims' internal organs to his inquiries at London hospitals.[18] Moreover, this appeared to exceed the main purpose of the inquest — to determine cause of death.

## TO THE EDITOR OF THE TIMES

Sir, — Is it not time that the inquest on Annie Chapman should close, and a verdict of "Wilful Murder against some person or persons unknown" be given? The question which the jury are soon to determine — viz., how, when, and where the deceased met with her death, and who she was — is virtually solved. The discovery of the murderer or murderers is the duty of the police, and if it is to be accomplished it is not desirable that the information they obtain should be announced publicly in the newspapers day by day through the medium of the coroner's inquiry. J. P.[19]

Because D'Onston, a newspaper contributor, is known to have closely followed press coverage on the Whitechapel murders, he would likely have read reports on the Gateshead murder and of his old acquaintance Inspector Roots. The reports on the murder of Jane Beadmore and D'Onston's police file tie Inspector Roots to the Ripper investigation. The Gateshead murder reports also included mention of the police surgeon Dr. Phillips, who testified at the inquest about the mutilations and removal of Annie Chapman's uterus. It was with Phillips's testimony and Eddowes's murder that D'Onston would develop his uterus theory. He had therefore directed George Marsh to seek out Inspector Roots as his Scotland Yard contact on the matter of rewards concerning Dr. Morgan Davies, though Marsh had instead developed his own suspicions.

As the Whitechapel murders inspired copycat killings, they also made original news copy. Items were elaborated and syndicated to local and international press agencies. The

*Pall Mall Gazette* coverage, however, encouraged a smear campaign on the police and government in advocating social, religious and moral reform. This resulted in financial difficulties for the newspaper going into 1889.[20] More importantly, reporting on the sensational aspects of the murders, the mutilations and the apparently skillful removal of internal organs had sprouted further mystery. Confusion at Scotland Yard had moved D'Onston to introduce his black magic hypothesis, for which there was no evidence.

The London Hospital was associated with the police investigation. The whereabouts of three medical students were looked into after suspicious details emerged during Annie Chapman's inquest. It was also reported that, "inquiries at the London Hospital, the nearest medical institution to the scene of the murder, have elicited the fact that no applications of the kind referred to by the coroner [Baxter] have recently been made to the warden or curator of the pathological museum attached to it."[21] Half a kidney was sent with the well-known "From Hell" letter[22] to George Lusk, the chairman of the Whitechapel Vigilance Committee, who is said to have worked at the hospital. Dr. Openshaw, "pathological curator" of the London Hospital Museum, examined the kidney portion, which the police eventually regarded as a prank. He, too, received a letter signed by "Jack the Ripper." The London Hospital registers, now kept at the Royal London Hospital Archives and Museum, preserve D'Onston's crucial alibi and medical details. But was he able to leave the hospital grounds at night, commit the murders and return undetected on at least three occasions?

On the day that D'Onston sent a letter to the City Police from the London Hospital, the *Daily Chronicle* printed a Jack the Ripper story on "Hypnotism and Crime." The theory, which was a subject of interest to D'Onston, drew responses, one of which came from a member of a London Hospital Medical College club, the Athenaeum:

> Sir — In yesterday's issue of the Daily Chronicle a correspondent suggests that the Whitechapel murderer may have been a hypnotised subject, and in so doing is apt to give a wrong impression as to the possibility of using hypnotism for criminal purposes. It is true that a hypnotist may command his subject to perform a given act at a given time, and that the subject will obey, even though the action is in itself opposed to the inclination of the hypnotised person; but hypnotism is of doubtful advantage to the criminal, since no steps that he can take can make detection impossible.
>
> It is also true that the hypnotised criminal, if commanded so to do, will deny that he was influenced; but under no circumstances is a criminal's word accepted in the face of evidence; and in the hands of an expert hypnotist a criminal who had acted under the impulse of suggestion, could be made to reveal and to trace the instigator. It would also be possible, according to the opinion of many hypnotists — and in this I myself agree — to hypnotise a very susceptible subject at the scene of any crime immediately it had been discovered, and if possible before the surroundings had been altered, and articles removed by the police or others, and by a remarkable phase of the hypnotic condition learn from the subject whether the sleep had been used in committing the crime, and in some cases by this means trace the offender.
>
> In a word, hypnotism, like most scientific discoveries, will be an advantage to society and humanity, not a terror and a danger, as is sometimes supposed. Apologising for trespassing upon your space.
>
> I am, yours faithfully, CHARLES REINHARDT.
> London Hospital Athenaeum, London, E., October 17.[23]

Five days after D'Onston walked out of Scotland Yard on December 26, 1888, the *Pall Mall Gazette* reprinted a report that may have referred to D'Onston's movements during this time.

> According to the Sunday Times, a gentleman who has for some time been engaged in philanthropic work in the East-end recently received a letter, the handwriting of which had previously attracted the attention of the Post-office authorities on account of its similarity to that of the writer of the letters signed "Jack the Ripper." The police made inquiries, and ascertained that the writer was known to

his correspondent as a person intimately acquainted with East-end life, and that he was then a patient in a metropolitan hospital. It is stated that on an inquiry at the hospital it was discovered that the person sought had left without the consent or knowledge of the hospital authorities, but that he has been latterly seen, and is now under observation. The police are of opinion that the last five murders were a series, and that the first two were independently perpetrated.[24]

Though D'Onston's letter of October 16, 1888, to the City Police gives his return address as "Currie Wards," the surviving hospital register and his statement to Inspector Roots both place him in the Davis ward. It seems therefore that he was transferred from Currie to the Davis ward sometime after the October 16 letter because his hospital patient register has "Currie" struck out and "Davis ward" inserted. The case notes on D'Onston have not survived, which is unfortunate as they could have provided further details. However, Inspector Roots' December 26 report documented an observation of D'Onston's illness and medication several weeks after his discharge as "Relieved" from London Hospital on December 7, 1888. The London Hospital inpatient registers transcribed for the 1888–89 admissions of D'Onston are as follows.[25]

London Hospital register of inpatients, 1888.[26]
Page heading: Physicians male patients
Date of admission: 26th July 1888
General number: 1146
Without ticket number: 735[27]
Name: Roslyn Stephenson
Residence: Cricketers Inn, Black Lion Street, Brighton
Age: 47
Civil state: U [unmarried][28]
Occupation: Journalist
Ward: Currie [struck out], Davis [substituted][29]
Case: Neurosthenia[30]
Physician: Sutton[31]
Date of discharge: 7th December 1888
Condition on discharge: Relieved[32]
Number of days in hospital: 134

London Hospital register of inpatients, 1889.[33]
Page heading: Physicians male patients
Date of admission 13th May 1889
General number: 713
Without ticket number: 472
Name: Roslyn D'Onston
Residence: Burdett Cottage, Burdett Road, Mile End
Age: 50
Civil state: S [single]
Occupation: Author[34]
Ward: Davis
Case: Chloralism[35]
Physician: Sutton
Date of discharge: 25th July 1889
Condition on discharge: Cured
Number of days in hospital: 73

The most obvious detail that can be gleaned from D'Onston's hospital record is that in a few instances the recorder was reliant on the information provided by the patient. This means there are some yearly differences in the name given, marital status, and occupation. Why D'Onston would change these identifying details is not certain, but it does support a known tendency to alter his personal information as time progressed. Though his statements to police on personal details are more accurate and precise, he also gave conflicting information on census returns that cannot be explained by a recorder's error and must be allowed for in reviewing his movements. He also complicated the historical record by using several pseudonyms.

D'Onston's inclination to fabricate details has been taken as circumstantial support of his guilt in the murders. It could as likely be for misdirection on his part in an attempt to stymie the recording of his movements and assets. His change of occupation from journalist to author in the hospital register does reflect his progress as a serious writer attempting to establish himself in the always competitive publishing climate. He also recorded personal details that contradict other documents. Some contend that this shows he was lying or covering up guilt for the Whitechapel murders and might be expected from a killer who had approached police about the case to avert suspicion. A comparable suspect was the alleged witness to the flamboyantly described killer of Mary Kelly, George Hutchinson, who had also involved himself in the police investigation.

D'Onston stayed at the London Hospital from July 26, 1888, in Currie Wards until he was transferred to Davis ward sometime after October 16, and before his discharge on December 7, 1888. That, of course, means that this alleged suspect is known to have resided in the area at the time of the crimes, unlike other, more fanciful suspects. The East End was densely populated so this alone does not make him Jack the Ripper. Still, because Chief Inspector Swanson drew no known conclusion, the possibility warrants attention. Perhaps Swanson accepted Inspector Roots's conclusion and let the matter rest. The Whitechapel murders investigation continued after D'Onston's December 26 Scotland Yard visit. Therefore, D'Onston's alibi becomes a contributing and crucial factor, if not the central issue, in any theory based on his police file and of his status as a credible Jack the Ripper suspect. Surprisingly, his residence at the London Hospital is the one point, lost in the raft of black magic theories, which has been most neglected.

The wards at the London Hospital during the Whitechapel murders usually had 28 beds, 14 down each side of a long narrow room. This would have been the case in the Currie Wards section that D'Onston initially occupied. "50, Currie Wards," the return address given by D'Onston in his October 16 letter to the City Police, was situated on the second floor of the Grocer's Company Wing.[36] Grocers Wing, the hospital's newest block, was built due to overcrowding. The London Hospital was a Whitechapel institution, the largest in the UK at the time, serving the East End poor. It is not known with certainty what the number "50" in the address refers to, but it could indicate a postal address for patients of that hospital section, or it could reference a name recorded in an inpatient register.

The red-pen alteration of D'Onston's ward placement from Currie to Davis was typical Victorian practice for rotating the transfer of patients from general to recuperative or other wards. This is consistent with D'Onston's noted diagnosis requiring privacy and rest in a smaller ward arrangement, which the London Hospital provided on his second admission in 1889, when he was sent directly to Davis ward. D'Onston was discharged on December 7, 1888, as "Relieved." This indicated he was not cured of the diagnosed condition but probably released because it was at the peak winter overcrowding of the hospital and he had occupied a bed for 134 days.

Though the Currie Wards were not numbered, the London Hospital during Victorian times was made up of wings consisting of several separate wards. It is made complex in the naming of sections and wards with similar titles. D'Onston's placements were in Currie ward within the Currie Wards section, which differ in the return address of his October 16 letter and his 1888 inpatient ward register entry. He was later transferred to Davis ward, in the Davis Wards section of the hospital. The 1889 annual report of the hospital[37] states that Davis Wards, named in 1870, were on the second floor and likely in the East Wing. The main care wards for children and surgical cases were on the West Wing. Davis Wards, where D'Onston resided after October 16, 1888, and during his 1889 admission, comprised four small wards for men and two small wards for women, with each ward known by a number.

In 1890, a House of Lords Select Committee[38] was appointed to investigate all hospitals, dispensaries and charitable institutions in the metropolis dealing with the "sick poor" and which had investments in property. They were to further enquire into their overall management. Though the committee did not conclude their work until a later session, its report preserved testimony of London Hospital staff and officials during the Whitechapel murders. Twenty-two sittings were held between May 5 and July 31, 1890. Fifty-four witnesses were asked 9,758 questions relating to charitable hospitals, management, staffing, records, funding and expenditure, accommodation and overcrowding, treatment, complaint charges, security and sanitary conditions. The Select Committee also heard testimony on the accreditation of and conditions for nurses. Improvements were realized with the efforts of Florence Nightingale, dubbed "Lady with the Lamp" on nurses' nightly rounds, and those of her close friend Miss Eva Luckes, matron of the London Hospital from 1880 to 1919.

The London Hospital where D'Onston stayed was subject to the London Hospital Act of 1884 and was governed under a royal charter granted by George II in 1758. The charter appointed a house committee to determine "by-laws, rules, orders and ordinances" regulating every aspect of the hospital's practical management. It relied on donations and was not a part of the National Health Service until 1948. In 1888 it had a capacity of some 800 beds but averaged about 650 patients. The night shift during the period of the murders consisted of about 50 nurses which included two supervising sisters, as well as ward sisters, staff nurses and probationers. Medical staff determined the nature or urgency of a patient's condition from the receiving rooms and outpatients department. The hospital was constantly under pressure but was reasonably efficient in admitting the poor for medical relief. According to the testimony of House Governor William John Nixon, the London Hospital was ever mindful of available beds in the event of major accidents occurring particularly in the East End.

Mr. G.Q. Roberts, who described himself as the secretary of the London Hospital since 1888, was sworn and examined by the Select Committee on July 3, 1890. He outlined the "Sisters and Night Nurses Standing Orders" with the following relevant extracts. Section 3, on supervising sisters, stated: "They shall comply with the instructions of the matron and other officers; they shall daily report to the matron as to the condition of their several wards, noting particularly any irregularities which may have occurred, or other matters to which her attention should be directed." Section 12 required of night sisters: "They shall keep in good order and fill up with care, regularity, and dispatch, as required, all papers, orders, and other forms placed in their charge, and shall see that their daily returns and diet books are delivered at the steward's office not later than 9 A.M. and 2 A.M. respectively." Section 19 included, "The night sisters shall superintend the night nurses in the various

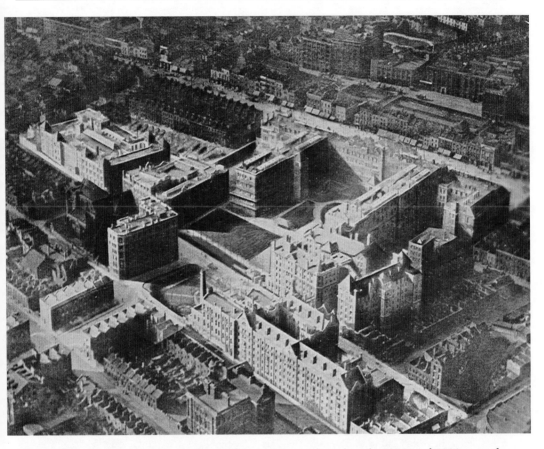

**The London Hospital, where Roslyn D'Onston was an inpatient in 1888 and 1889, was the major medical poor relief institution in East End London. The large complex fronted White-chapel Road near the murder site of Mary Ann Nichols, top right. D'Onston stayed on the East Wing, center right. (courtesy Stewart P. Evans).**

wards of the hospital, in such order of visitation as the matron may from time to time direct, or as circumstances may nightly require." Section 21 stated, "Night sisters shall make a daily report to the matron at 9.15 A.M., giving full information of such incidents as may have occurred, and duly calling attention to any irregularities which have come to their notice."

Victorian nurses were employed under similar disciplinary terms as police officers and probationary constables though the duties were different. They were required to pass a medical examination before appointment to the nursing staff of the London Hospital and were subject to dismissal for misconduct or negligence of duty. Mr. Roberts quoted a house visitor's [Inspector of the House Committee] report dated September 6, 1888, during D'Onston's stay, on conditions at the hospital: "During the last fortnight I have been all over the hospital, but not to the nursing home. The patients I spoke to said the doctors were attentive, the nurses kind, and the food good." A letter was also read to the Select Committee on the charges of negligence of the matron, Eva Luckes. "Dear Matron,—We all unite in condemning the conduct of those nurses who so unjustly attacked the hospital arrangements on Monday, 30th June [1890], and express our warmest sympathy for you in the charges against the hospital. Our deepest thanks are due to you for all you have done for the nursing staff since you have been here." Most of the sisters, nurses and probationers of the London Hospital signed it.

Nurses at the London Hospital in 1888 worked either day or night shifts of 14 hours duration. They had one day off a month and one week's holiday every six months. Night nurses who had their meals on the wards were also required, apart from nursing duties, to do domestic tasks, which included cleaning lamps, inkstands, taps, and lavatories, sweeping, and dusting, which were usually done around 3 A.M., the slackest time. Nurses and probationers of the hospital were also required to reside on the grounds, as was the case with lodgings for the head matron, Miss Eva Luckes.

The Select Committee report also yields testimony relevant to D'Onston's stay at the hospital and the night routine which determined his ability or otherwise to leave the institution and commit the murders.

Miss Ellen Mary Yatman was a probationer nurse at the London Hospital from April 1888 to October 1889. She left the position because of illness due to blood poisoning from suspected defective sewerage drains, and was later sworn and examined by the Select Committee. From her evidence, it was apparent that Yatman had worked the Davis Wards during D'Onston's 1889 admission and knew the routine of the ward that he was in during the murder of Mary Kelly.

On 10 July 1890, Matron Eva Luckes, who was known to conduct night shift surprise inspections, was cross-examined on Yatman's testimony on the use of night nurses' time for the early bathing of patients:

> Now, upon another matter: in Miss Yatman's evidence, which begins at 4876 and 4877, without going through all the questions and answers, you will see that she says this: "In many cases I have known the adult helpless patients begun to be washed about four in the morning; the children begun even earlier;" and then, further on, she says in answer to 4882, " the babies required to be fed in the middle of the night, and so they were washed then to economise time; and the other children were woke about 4 o'clock; they had their breakfast given them, and then were washed; the children did not mind it so much as the adult patients, but the adult patients often complained very much of being woke so early." Can you tell us what the practice in the hospital is, and whether Miss Yatman has correctly described it?—[Matron Luckes:]—I carefully asked various night sisters, and those who had taken night duty, and they say that it is not the case. I found that there was a case of a patient, who complained that she was disturbed at five o'clock; the doctor reported it to me, and asked if I supposed that it was justifiable; I made an inquiry, and found that they were getting lax on the subject. The rule in the hospital, not my rule, not the nurses' rule, but the rule in the hospital is, that all patients should breakfast at 6 o'clock. I then called the night sister's attention to the point, and asked how it had happened, because, having been night sister in the hospital myself, I knew perfectly well that it was not the regulation of the hospital that patients should be disturbed before that time. But the patients themselves asked me, before this went on, if, when the men woke up early, they might not get up and go to the lavatory where their washing arrangements are, and wash themselves before breakfast; I said that if they woke they might certainly do so, but that the gas was never to be turned on till 6 A.M., when the breakfast was quite ready: after that, the water would be handed round to the patients who were in bed.

With the close time frame of the discovery of the body of Annie Chapman, noted in witness and medical inquest testimony for her murder on 8 September 1888 around daybreak, it would have been impossible for D'Onston to comply with this London Hospital rule for breakfast at 6 A.M. without alerting staff if he was the killer. As the murder and mutilation of Chapman is a confirmed Jack the Ripper crime, this fact alone discounts and eliminates D'Onston of suspicion for the Whitechapel murders.

Miss Marion Barry Mackey, one of the two supervising night sisters covering the Eastern,

Western and Grocers wings of the London Hospital at this time, was sworn and examined by the Select Committee on July 21, 1890. Bradley described herself: "I was night sister at the London from the 30th of April 1887 till I left to take my present post; I was recommended for it by the matron of the London Hospital." The post she had taken up was matron of the Throat and Ear Hospital, Golden-square, "since November 1888." *The London Hospital Register of Sisters and Nurses, 1880–1902,*[39] confirms that Mackey was appointed as a night sister on April 30, 1887, and is noted as having left for her new post on October 27, 1888. She began her training in 1872 at Bradford Infirmary in Yorkshire and perhaps shared stories with D'Onston who was from nearby Hull. Though Mackey testified that she was recommended by Matron Luckes for her new post, the register also notes the matron's comments on Mackey: "a violent temper, a great want of self control, an injudicious way of making favorites and that of most undesirable persons but thought her capable of managing a small hospital really well."

Marion Mackey's testimony before the Select Committee is fortuitous as it gives the best possible view of the nighttime London Hospital wards during the period of the Jack the Ripper murders. It is invaluable in evaluating with some certainty D'Onston's alibi and ability to leave without detection. As this suspect's historical details are to an extent ambiguous and incomplete without a definite police conclusion from Chief Inspector Donald Swanson, the importance of credible firsthand accounts given in evidence cannot be gainsaid.

Mackey was examined, and attention paid to the night staffing levels of the hospital.

Your experience of the London Hospital is limited to your experience there in night duty? — Mackey; Yes, as a night sister. — What views do you hold about the work of the nurses, as to whether they were able to perform their duties? — I think there was not sufficient on for night duty; I think the wards were under-nursed. They did the best they could, but it was rather rough nursing in that respect; they could not give as much attention as I should like to have given individually. — Did you mean to say you were deficient in numbers? — Yes, I did not consider I had enough for the wards. I spoke to matron, and I think she generally gave me more (I think I was rather importunate, and so I got rather more) than she considered was necessary for each ward. — And when you got the greater assistance that you wanted, had you sufficient then? — I never had too many. — Now as night sister, how many cases had you under your charge in the ward? — There were calculated to be 400 beds on my side [East Wing]; I was expected to visit all the wards three times, ... There were nine wards I had under my charge; I could only be in one at a time; the other wards were left to do the best they could till they could summon me from another part, if I was wanted.... — It might take some time to find you, might it not? — Yes, it might. — And, therefore, that nurse might be absent from the ward for some time? — She might ... it might take a quarter of an hour to find you? — Perhaps not quite so long. — Or perhaps longer? — Just as it might be; it would take quite that, if I happened to have gone into the nursing home to see a sick nurse, and they did not know I was there. I had charge of the sick room in the nursing home as well as the wards. As sister I went in there to see that they were being properly cared and nursed during the night. — Then you might be in any portion of your wing in the hospital? — Yes, I might be when I was required at the exact other corner of it. — Or possibly they might be searching for you in the other part of the hospital, and you might be in the nurse's sick room? — Yes.... — Do you think that that amount of superintendence, namely, one night sister to each wing of the hospital is sufficient? — If there were a satisfactory staff, an efficient staff of elder nurses it would be quite sufficient; but it makes it extremely heavy when you have probationer nurses who are not experienced, and who, however willing they may be, cannot help you efficiently. — How long was your night duty that you were responsible for? — I went on duty at twenty minutes past nine to preside with the other night sister at the day nurses' supper and register their attendance. I then had my own meal, and started on my first round at ten at night, and I was on duty till seven the next morning. — Who was your colleague; was she a staff nurse? She was a sister, the other night sister. — Have you any idea what standing she had in the hospital? — The first one, I believe, was a certified nurse, when I was there first; afterwards she left, and the one who succeeded, I believe, had not quite finished her two years then. — Then she was not certified? — Not till two years. — And she had charge of the other wing?—Of the other wing.—And she, not a certified nurse, had charge of the wing in which, according to what you say, very likely some of the wards were in charge of probationers under 18 months?—Certainly.—Do you think that a satisfactory system?—No.—Is it not essential that the head of the nursing staff should frequently visit the wards?—It is very desirable.—Do you think that is sufficiently done in the London Hospital?—I do not know anything about the day. I think matron visited about once a month on an average; sometimes, again, twice in one week, and not for some weeks afterwards.—But then she had assistant matrons?—She had assistant matrons. The assistant matron did not visit me in the night.—But that was all the supervision that there was?—She left it to her night sisters, in whom, I suppose, she had very great confidence. We gave her a daily report of everything that occurred.

Matron Luckes was recalled before the Select Committee on July 21, 1890, for further testimony:

I want to ask you about the evidence given by Miss Mackey; she said that she reported to you about what occurred in the night when she was night sister; was that report in writing?—Luckes—Not in writing, except on Sunday morning, and then I get written reports.—What is done with these reports; are they kept?—No; they are only written on Sunday mornings when the night sisters go off duty earlier, and as they are only written once a week there is no object in keeping them.—Who admits the patients at the London Hospital?—Whichever house physician or surgeon is taking in for that particular week; and of course the out-patient physicians and surgeons send up cases to the wards during the afternoon.—There is no delay in the admission of the cases?—There is a receiving room medical officer as well, so that the patients do not wait a moment when they are brought into the hospital.—I think we have been told that your ward maids do not sleep on the premises?—No, they are ordinary strong middle-aged women from Whitechapel.—Does your work get busier in the winter, for instance?—Yes; in the late autumn we feel it heavier: we get a good many more typhoid cases and others; then in the summer months a good many go from Whitechapel to the hop-picking, and that diminishes our number.

Shortly after the murders of Elizabeth Stride and Catherine Eddowes on September 30, 1888, a press report asserted, "The attention that has been paid to the hospitals has been quite as close, but the police have not always found the hospital authorities too eager to assist them. The ethics of medical etiquette appear to stand in the way of full and free investigation among medical students at least, for they are slow to tell what they know or suspect when it may affect one of their number."[40] At another institution shortly after the murder of Mary Kelly, the same paper alleged, "Nurses and doctors were going in and out of a Croydon infirmary at night by scaling gates and walls. They were getting the night watchman to place false information in the official records."[41]

Security at the London Hospital during the Whitechapel murders was dictated through by-laws and standing orders set down by a House Committee, as were all administrative and staffing functions of the institution in the interests of effective patient care. However, as with any growing major and public institution during the late Victorian period, in practice the ideal rarely matched the reality of day-to-day activity. Guidelines were a means for maintaining certain standards for inpatient and outpatient care, safety, statutory requirements, and the retention and training of medical and nursing staff.

At the London Hospital, night shift security was governed by the *London Hospital Standing Orders for Night Porters, 1888*.[42] Section 2 of the order stated, "They shall see that the gates and doors of the Hospital are duly secured by 11 P.M." Section 3 added, "After that hour the Head Night Porter shall register in the night-book the names or particulars of all persons, whether officers, servants, patients, or others, entering or leaving the Hospital." The standing orders for the front gate porter state: "He shall not allow any patient to leave the Hospital without written permission from the House-Governor, nor admit any person contrary to the rules of the Institution." Contemporary illustrations and plans of the London Hospital show a gate lodge on the northern Whitechapel road and railings at the back of the grounds.

If D'Onston did leave and reenter London Hospital on at least three occasions to commit the murders, he would have had to coerce the night and gate porters to record false details and would have needed the cooperation or inattention of nursing staff. He could have taken a route from the grounds that was not under observation, such as the eastern or western sides of the hospital. No record is known of D'Onston leaving at night with the knowledge of night porters detailed in the night register, so he could only have executed the crimes by alerting several staff in some way.

Roslyn D'Onston took some bold chances in making false claims to Scotland Yard. His letters of recommendation from W.T. Stead and his acquaintance with Inspector Roots probably spared him the indignity of contempt charges. He could only have taken the risk in the hope of gaining details of the police investigation that by late 1888 had been restricted to the press. Stead and D'Onston, influenced by American-style journalism, attempted to adopt a tabloid style in hopes of rescuing the failing *Pall Mall Gazette*. But it was not to be. With detailed night nursing records and notes on patients that have not survived, the cross-referencing with Scotland Yard files on the investigation of Jack the Ripper would almost assuredly have drawn the noose around the neck of the patient who attempted it.

In the October 8 and 9 issues, Stead published a series of articles titled "The Police and the Criminals of London." The proprietor of the *Pall Mall Gazette*, liberal Henry Yates Thompson, had according to Inspector Roots's report refused D'Onston and Stead funds to track the murderer. Later, Stead and D'Onston became disillusioned with press sensationalism. After leaving the *Pall Mall Gazette* in 1889, Stead set up the monthly *Review of Reviews* in 1890 and the spiritualist periodical *Borderland* in 1893. Roslyn D'Onston would follow him as a contributor.

The early sexologist Havelock Ellis was a friend of Stead, and in writing to one of his biographers in 1925 said,

> I am interested to hear that you are writing the biography of Stead; it is a large and fine subject; he was a great journalist, one might almost say a great man, and it is all the better that his life should be written by one who can look at him from a little distance, and so perhaps view him more truly. During recent years I have often wished that we had a journalist of his calibre, so honest and so forceful, to deal with the problems which have arisen. At the same time there were few questions on which I entirely agreed with him, and on many I had no sympathy whatever. There was, also, a certain coarseness of texture in his mind which, though I recognized that it was an inevitable part of his great qualities, always rather repelled me.
>
> In reply to your query, I have written nothing about Stead. I knew him personally, but on one side only. When my "Studies in the Psychology of Sex" were prosecuted in 1898, he became interested in them, and he spoke frankly on the question in the Review of Reviews. He would write to me from time to time (sometimes with intervals of years), and now and again would invite me to spend the evening at Smith Square where we would talk in his study till eleven when his daughter would bring him a cup of tea, which was the sign for me to leave and for him to go to bed. The main subject was always sex. He told me that his friends considered him "mad on sex." He did not dispute that opinion. In his life and actions he was undoubtedly a rigid moral Puritan and his strong self-control kept him in the narrow path. But in his interests and emotions he was anything but a Puritan, and in the absence of that stern self-control he would have been quite a debauched person. The mastery of sexuality was a great problem with him. His repressed sexuality was, I consider, the motive force of many of his activities."[43]

From 1888, the liberal *Pall Mall Gazette* was in decline, battered by competition from major newspapers such as the newly established *Star* of T.P. O'Connor, an Irish member of

Parliament. Publicity for *The Times* during the Parnell Special Commission and for conservative daily London papers[44] made it hard to maintain readership, advertisers and viability.

On December 1, 1888, the *Pall Mall Gazette* published an article titled "The Whitechapel Demon's Nationality: And Why He Committed the Murders." Signed only by "One who Thinks he Knows," it proposed a highly original theory on the Whitechapel murders. The December 3, 1888, issue of that newspaper hinted at the name of the contributor. Stead noted, "One who Thinks he Knows"—the contributor in question—is an occultist of some experience. When he was a lad of eighteen he studied necromancy under the late Lord Lytten at Alexandria. It would be odd if the mystical lore of the author of "Zanoni" were to help to unearth Jack the Ripper."[45] These claims were to reappear in the April 1896 issue of *Borderland*. They were in a semiautobiographical article titled "A Modern Magician" by Roslyn D'Onston, the pseudonym of Jack the Ripper suspect Robert Donston Stephenson.

That article has been the cause of further suspicion laid upon D'Onston for the Whitechapel murders. The occult and literary conjectures inserted within it are taken as supposition that he as the killer was eluding capture and tauntingly confessing to the crimes. It rather shows D'Onston's developed thinking on the murders derived from details he sent in the letter to City Police on October 16, 1888. Though he dismissed the murder of Mary Kelly as part of the Ripper series in the article, he nevertheless focused on her killer in statements to Scotland Yard several weeks later. Was this the mind of a serial killer or the fantastic fabrications of a journalist and avowed occultist commissioned by W.T. Stead?

D'Onston begins the article with a theory about the wording of the Goulston Street wall writing. The substitution of the term "Juwes" for the (misspelled) French term "Juives," due to a police transcription error, leads him to the conclusion that the killer was a Frenchman. He adds, "This most important clue to his identity, which 'he who runs may read,' seems to have baffled the combined intellects of all grades of the police. This admits of no question, because we find in all the journals a note from Sir C. Warren to the effect that 'no language or dialogue is known in which the word 'Jews' is spelt 'Juwes.'" With the mistaken detail added that a piece of Eddowes's apron was found at her crime scene in Mitre Square, his source of information on the murders is again indicated as coming from a close reading of the press.

After a long diatribe on the semantics of the French language, scripts and history, D'Onston declares, "On the contrary, in France, the murdering of prostitutes has long been practised, and has been considered to be almost peculiarly a French crime." For D'Onston, now that the "ground for research [is] thus cleared and narrowed, the next question is, what is the motive?" He cautions that "in endeavouring to sift a mystery like this one cannot afford to throw aside any theory, however extravagant, without careful examination, because the truth might, after all, lie in the most unlikely one." The theory has proved unlikely over time, but it does suggest motives for D'Onston to insert himself into the police investigation and illustrates his literary and occult associations. He continued:

> There seems to be no doubt that the murderer, whether mad or not, had a distinct motive in his mutilations; but one possible theory of that motive has never yet been suggested. In the nineteenth Century, with all its enlightenment, it would seem absurd, were it not that superstition dies hard, and some of its votaries do undoubtedly to this day practice unholy rites.
>
> Now, in one of the books by the great modern occultist who wrote under the nom de plume of "Eliphaz Levy," "Le Dogme et Rituel de la Haute Magie," we find the most elaborate directions for working magical spells of all kinds. The second volume has a chapter on Necromancy, or black magic,

which the author justly denounces as a profanation. Black magic employs the agencies of evil spirits and demons, instead of the beneficent spirits directed by the adepts of la haute magie. At the same time he gives the clearest and fullest details of the necessary steps for evocation by this means, and it is in the list of substances prescribed as absolutely necessary to success that we find the link which joins modern French necromancy with the quest of the East-end murderer.

These substances are in themselves horrible, and difficult to procure. They can only be obtained by means of the most appalling crimes, of which murder and mutilation of the dead are the least heinous. Among them are strips of the skin of a suicide, nails from a murderer's gallows, candles made from human fat, the head of a black cat which has been fed forty days on human flesh, the horns of a goat which has been made the instrument of an infamous capital crime, and a preparation made from a certain portion of the body of a harlot. This last point is insisted upon as essential and it was this extraordinary fact that first drew my attention[46] to the possible connection of the murderer with the black art.

Further, in the practice of evocation the sacrifice of human victims was a necessary part of the process, and the profanation of the cross and other emblems usually considered sacred was also enjoined. In this connection it will be well to remember one most extraordinary and unparalleled circumstance in the commission of the Whitechapel murders, and a thing which could not by any possibility have been brought about fortuitously.

Leaving out the last murder, committed indoors, which was most probably not committed by the fiend of whom we speak,[47] we find that the sites of the murders, six in number, form a perfect cross. That is to say, a line ruled from No. 3 to No. 6, on a map having the murder sites marked and numbered, passes exactly through Nos. 1 and 2, while the cross arms are accurately formed by a line from No. 4 to 5. The seventh, or Dorset-street murder, does not fall within either of these lines, and there is nothing to connect it with the others except the mutilations. But the mutilations in this latter case were evidently not made by any one having the practical knowledge of the knife and the position of the respective organs which was exhibited in the other six cases, and also in the mutilated trunk found in the new police-buildings, which was probably the first of the series of murders, and was committed somewhere on the lines of the cross, the body being removed at the time.

Did the murderer, then, designing to offer the mystic number of seven human sacrifices in the form of a cross — a form which he intended to profane — deliberately pick out beforehand on a map the places in which he would offer them to his infernal deity of murder? If not, surely these six coincidences are the most marvellous event of our time.

To those persons to whom this theory may seem somewhat farfetched, we would merely remark that the French book referred to was only published a few years ago; that thousands of copies were sold; that societies have been formed for the study and practice of its teachings and philosophy; and, finally, that within the last twelve months an English edition has been issued. In all things history repeats itself, and the superstitions of yesterday become the creeds of today.

One who Thinks he Knows.[48]

D'Onston's occult explanations of the Whitechapel murders is embellishment on an earlier theory sent in a letter to the press by an anonymous writer. The *Pall Mall Gazette* had reprinted it almost two weeks before D'Onston wrote to the City Police, and it echoes the December 3, 1888, editorial of W.T. Stead on the challenge to Arthur Diosy to predict the next murder by magical astrology.

Suggestions by the public in the morning papers. — The cryptogrammatic dagger. — In examining the chart representing the locality of the Whitechapel murders, says one, it is curious to observe that lines drawn through the spots where the murders were committed assume the exact form of a dagger, the hilt and blade of which pass through the scenes of the sixth, second, first and third murders, the extremities of the guard making the fourth and fifth. Can this possibly afford a clue to the position of the next atrocity?[49]

D'Onston's front-page article was discussed among members of mystical and occult subcultures and drew responses in the form of letters to the editor. Vittoria Cremers, who had developed a Jack the Ripper theory, would later tell crime reporter Bernard O'Donnell how members of the Theosophical Society would gather round Helena Blavatsky to read the article. It would form the basis of mystical and occult Jack the Ripper theories and anecdotes that continued into the next century.

## IS JACK THE RIPPER A FRENCHMAN?

To the Editor of the Pall Mall Gazette
Sir,

I venture to offer you a few remarks upon the singular article which appeared in the Pall Mall Gazette last Saturday upon the Whitechapel murders. Under some circumstances I might comment upon the inferences drawn by your contributor, "One Who Thinks He Knows," from the fact that straight lines, drawn through the point at which the outrages were committed cross one another, but, remembering that I am in a country where Mr. Ignatius Donnelly and his Great Cryptogram[50] are the subjects of serious discussion, I, as a native of a frivolous land, abstain from saying more than that I am myself engaged in preparing a diagram by which I hope to prove that the crimes were really the work of a Unionist who is gradually marking out in the East end of London an exact reproduction of the Union Jack.

Now, Sir, to speak seriously, I do not at all deny that the assassin may be a Frenchman; there are plenty of French assassins in the world, and, though I venture to think that in London English assassins are more plentiful, I am willing to admit the possibility of "Jack the Ripper" being my compatriot. But I say that the arguments by which "One Who Knows" seeks to establish this are utterly baseless and absurd.

Frenchmen may be, as he says "the worst linguists in the world," but if he were a better "linguist" himself he would know that bad "linguists" may know their own language, and in this respect, Frenchmen may be compared favorably with any other people. As to his assertion that they constantly make mistakes in gender, it is simply untrue. There are a few substantives, such as "hotel," "ouvrage," &c., which have a feminine sound to the ear, and as to which some utterly uneducated French people fall into the error of applying to them feminine articles or adjectives; such a person might therefore talk of "une hotel juive," or "une ouvrage juive," but no French man, woman, or child would ever mistake a feminine for a masculine substantive, and the idea that they could, under any circumstances, write Juives for Juifs when using the word as a substantive is enough to make a Frenchman hold his sides with laughter. Perhaps "One Who Thinks He Knows" also thinks that the uneducated Frenchman speaks of femmes when he means hommes!

Your contributor refers for proof of his assertions to the "voluminous correspondence of Napoleon III." As I have not had access to this source of information — and, indeed, though tolerably conversant with the literature of my country, now hear for the first time of its existence — I should be much obliged if "One Who Thinks He Knows" would send you for publication a few extracts from this "voluminous correspondence" containing examples of mistakes in gender. He would be a doing a kindness to a poor French professor, who has always held that Napoleon III did much harm to his country, but who has hitherto held him guiltless of having introduced into its literature a new form of grammatical error.

I remain, Sir, your obedient servant,
A FRENCHMAN
December 4.[51]

## JACK THE RIPPER'S MOTIVE

To the Editor of the Pall Mall Gazette
Sir,

Though the anxiety to solve the Whitechapel mystery is, for the nonce, allayed, if not extinct, it may interest students of human nature to hear of a somewhat similar case in which the murderer, when discovered, was found to be actuated by a less extraordinary motive than that of solving necromantic problems, attributed to the Whitechapel monster by the writer of "Who is the Whitechapel Demon?," published in your issue of the 6th. Inst.[52] ... I have no details of the criminal's modus operandi, as it occurred long before my time; I had in fact forgotten this episode in my grandfather's judicial career until the accounts of the London ghastly tragedies brought to my mind the conviction that should the East end murderer ever be brought to justice, which I do not anticipate, it will be ascertained that his motive has been either a morbid taste of the very same kind, or an exaggerated longing for notoriety, coupled with the love of excitement that feeds on perusing the different versions of his deeds, his intentions, and the means he employs to defeat the combined intellects of the detective administrations of London, which last feat, be it said, might make anybody a little proud.

Esther Delaforce
9 Courthope villa, Wimbledon
December 8.[53]

On December 8, 1888, another article was published in response to the occult theories then gaining wide publicity in an attempt to allay the superstitious fears of the public. Its author was the editor of the periodical *Light*, "M.A. Oxon." This was the pseudonym of Stainton Moses,[54] a spiritualist of note. The article is completely transcribed here for the first time. Mabel Collins, Helena Blavatsky and other members of the Theosophical Society also contributed to the pages of *Light*, which were circulated throughout England, Europe and the United States. It also illustrates the extent to which occult theories about Jack the Ripper had taken hold during the events.

## OCCULT EXPLANATION OF THE WHITECHAPEL MURDERS

There has come to us a booklet entitled The Curse upon Mitre Square, A.D. 1530–1888 (Simpkin, Marshall and Co.), by John Francis Brewer, which is extraordinary reading. It is concerned with the recent Whitechapel atrocities, with which we should have no desire to meddle, for that one's very soul revolts at the thought of them, were it not that in more quarters than one an attempt is being made to connect them with matters that concern us.

In order to be intelligible we must give some account of this little shilling book. Prefixed to it is what purports to be a sketch of Aldgate in the days of Henry VIII, showing from existing books and MSS. the great Church and Monastery as they then existed, the High Altar, the great Court of the Priory, and the " Mitre Court,"[55] where one of these ghastly tragedies was recently enacted.

The scene opens in the year 1530, when the magnificent revenues of the Priory had attracted the cupidity of Henry VIII. Thomas Audley, Speaker of the House of Commons, a creature of the King's, had his wicked eye on this rich prize. The King was in debt to him, and readily assented to confiscation as a means of wiping out his obligation. In what way this was gradually worked out it is not necessary to tell. It is a story of human passion, of a monk entrapped by a designing schemer into sin, of a mind unhinged by the conflict between conscience and determination to carry out his purpose. Mad, at length, with the prolonged conflict, he goes to the altar steps to keep his vigil, and to meet the woman whom a minute later he had murdered and gashed and trampled out of every recognition, save that a physical peculiarity revealed to him, on the suggestion of his tempter, who was watching him, that the object of his lust and the victim of his knife was his own sister. And so he plunged the blood-stained weapon into his own heart and died beside her.

Soon it came to pass that ghosts of the murdered dead haunted the accursed spot. The monk appeared, and always pointed to the spot stained with his sister's blood and his own, uttering strange prophecies of terrible events that must occur there.

We pass two centuries. The Priory has been closed, and its revenues confiscated. The scene is at the Mitre Tavern, where there is a merry-making of young bloods, a richly dressed, dissipated crew, ready for anything. The host suggests an adjournment, when the feast was over, to interview the ghost, who had not ceased in all these years to walk in the hour after midnight. The half-drunken sots assent, sally forth in a furious storm, and see more than they bargained for, or think they do. At any rate, a spectral arm, holding a bloodstained dagger, sobers them too late. The storm raging above strikes the church — the local gossips had it that the spectral hand and dagger did the harm — and buries the roysterers beneath the ruins of an arch exactly on the spot where the foul murder of two centuries before had occurred: on the site of the high altar.

And so we come to Whitechapel of to-day, with its squalid misery, its cheerless life, out of which all light has died, and its unspeakable abominations. What a comment on Christianity and civilisation!

To what, then, does all this melodramatic retrospect conduct us? To this. Measure this spot where the murder of Catherine Eddowes (one of the Whitechapel victims) was committed, and you will find that the piece of ground on which her mutilated body lay is the exact point where the steps of the high altar existed, and where the catastrophe of two centuries later occurred, when the spectral arm and dagger appeared as the ghost of the monk was seen, and the ten gallants perished.

So much The Curse upon Mitre Square for what it is worth. Now for a theorist in the Pall Mall Gazette. It may be remembered that above the hacked body of the Mitre-square victim was scrawled on the wall an inscription to this effect: "The Juwes are the men who will not be blamed for nothing." So it was read. Unfortunately it was at once obliterated. But the writer in the Pall Mall points out that no one would be likely to spell Jews in the way of Juwes. What was written, he guesses, was the French word Juives, the feminine of Juif, and he draws attention to the very lax use of gender among most uneducated Frenchmen.

He believes, therefore, the murderer to be a Frenchman, and he proceeds to suggest a theory as to motive, which is our justification for concerning ourselves with his speculations.

He has come upon Eliphaz Levi's work Le Dogme et Rituel de laHaute Mayie, and draws attention to a chapter in it on Necromancy or black magic. The directions given for evocation by this nefarious means are too horrible to be reproduced. Among them is "a preparation made from a certain portion of the body of a harlot."

Further, in this diabolical rite the offering of human sacrifices was essential, and the profanation of all sacred symbols was enjoined. The inversion of all that was held holy, the contempt of the pure and good, the exaltation of the base, brutal, devilish, was to be aimed at.

Now, it is remarkable that the sites of the Whitechapel murders, six in number, form a perfect cross, not an approximate but an accurate one: i.e., a line ruled straight from the site of murder 3 in Buck's-row to the site of murder 6 in Mitre-square passes directly and exactly through the sites of murders 1 and 2. A line from Hanbury street (murder No. 4) strikes Berner-street (murder No. 5), and forms the arms of the cross. The mutilated trunk found in the new police buildings on the Embankment was probably the first of the series of murders, the body being removed from the scene of murder on some spot on one of the lines of the cross. Did the murderer, desiring to offer up the mystic number of seven human sacrifices, and to profane the sacred emblem of our religion, select his places on a map and deliberately decoy his victims? Or is it all coincidence? If so, a very remarkable one.

So, it seems that what is called superstition is still rife. The two stories we have rapidly summarized are at least indicative of a phase of modern thought. The man who wrote and published them ten years ago would have ended his days in a lunatic asylum.[56]

D'Onston's references in his December 1 article draw attention to the occult source of his theories. Though crime historians regard the details as curiosities, they nevertheless provide some background. In attempting to separate Jack the Ripper lore from streams of Victorian occultism to arrive at D'Onston's true place as a suspect for the Whitechapel murders, examining his stated sources is useful. Given the dis-

**Stainton Moses aka "M.A. Oxen" (standing left), with his family in this Victorian spirit photograph. Moses wrote a rare review on Ripper occult theories late 1888 (courtesy the S.P.R.).**

crepancies in his claims compared to the historic record, D'Onston either misled the reader or was unable to concentrate due to a nervous and debilitating medical condition during the years 1888 and 1889. This applies as well to his other articles and to his statements made to the police. The discrepancies are taken as further circumstantial evidence that he was Jack the Ripper.

D'Onston notes that his black magic theories are derived from a French book that was later translated for English readers. Titled *Le Dogme et Ritual de la Haute Magie*, it was a seminal work of the Victorian and French Occult Revival. It was published as two volumes in 1856 by the French occultist Eliphas Levi, the pseudonym of Alphonse-Louis Constant. Two chapters in the book mention "Necromancy," as D'Onston states, but neither volume contains the specific nefarious recipes that he ascribes to the book. D'Onston further muddles the source, saying that "the French book referred to was only published a few years ago; [...] that thousands of copies were sold ... and, finally, that within the last twelve months an English edition has been issued." The problem with D'Onston's reference is that the book he names had been published in Paris some thirty years previously and was not translated into English until 1896 by Arthur Edward Waite.[57]

The readership of the *Pall Mall Gazette* was probably unaware of the publishing history of Levi's book. Yet D'Onston's erroneous reference is so obvious, once one is aware of it, that we must question D'Onston's motive. It turns out that he was alluding to another work entirely. The book was an early English-language compilation of the works of Eliphas Levi, in fact the first book on the subject. Edited by a young Arthur Waite, *The Mysteries of Magic: A Digest of the Writings of Eliphas Levi* was published in 1886.[58] It contains the information that D'Onston had selectively paraphrased, though the addition of "a preparation made from a certain portion of the body of a harlot" appears to be his elaborate invention.[59] D'Onston carefully avoids attributing the work to Waite as its English translator and compiler and to its publisher, George Redway. By writing "within the last twelve months an English edition has been issued," D'Onston alludes to an accompanying and original text by Waite released the following year in 1887. It contained an unflattering passage on his fictional occult mentor, Lord Bulwer-Lytton. D'Onston was either confused about the dates of Levi's English publications or created a black magic Ripper theory out of religious trends.

Arthur Waite had first learned of Levi's work from quotations found in Helena Blavatsky's *Isis Unveiled* (1877), at a time when he was associated with the Theosophical Society. In 1885 he had suggested to A.P. Sinnett the literary prospects of an English anthology of Levi's French writings. Sinnett recommended Waite to publisher George Redway, with whom he would have a long association and for whom he worked with Welsh supernatural horror novelist Arthur Machen.[60] Waite and Machen as journalists during the Whitechapel murders were aware of W.T. Stead's *Pall Mall Gazette* and of supernatural characterisations of Jack the Ripper, as was *Dracula* author Bram Stoker. Black magic theories on Jack the Ripper were thus publicized further and entered into horror fiction. The portrayal of the murder of Catherine Eddowes in *The Curse of Mitre Square* and the elaborate occult fascinations of Sir Arthur Diosy and Roslyn D'Onston were influential on the supernatural period setting of early horror literature and later developments.

In D'Onston's comment "on Necromancy, or black magic, which the author justly denounces as a profanation," he is not advocating malevolent occultism but condemning it as a cultural and religious trend. In his firm and well-read view, the trend was capable of inspiring the Whitechapel murderer, as W.T. Stead believed. There is no record of D'Onston having entered any occult order in England, Scotland or mainland Europe except in his published claims. D'Onston's use of the name "Roslyn" is thought to be derived from the Templar Rosslyn Chapel. No evidence links him to that tradition apart from the claims of the Romantic author Lord Edward George Bulwer-Lytton.[61]

The Alexandrian Lodge where he is supposed to have had contacts as a pupil of Bulwer-Lytton does not seem to exist. It was probably invented by Stead and developed by D'Onston based on the account of the Earl of Crawford, who, as a member of the aristocracy with similar interests, probably did know Lytton. However, D'Onston did rely on an early Christian Alexandrian Bible literary tradition for the writing of his *The Patristic Gospels* (1904).

D'Onston's last work, *The Patristic Gospels*,[62] was researched from at least 1881. The Revised Version of the Bible and associated critical and ancient biblical texts were his sources.[63] He began his English version of the New Testament with, "The preparation of these Gospels has taken eleven years [c. 1893], most of which time has been one long fight against pain and paralysis; and nothing but the undeniable aid of the Holy Spirit could have enabled them to have been completed single-handed, and without any assistance whatever from anyone."

The golden days of the *Pall Mall Gazette* ended with backlash from the 1885 "Maiden Tribute of Modern Babylon" scandals and ebbing reportage on the Whitechapel murders from December 1888. The newspaper that ran D'Onston's black magic Ripper theory also ran into financial difficulties. In the struggle to maintain subscriptions and readers during fierce competition, Stead commissioned from D'Onston two more editorial features on the early novel by Sir Henry Rider Haggard, *She: A History of Adventure*, first serialized in *The Graphic* from October 1886 to January 1887. *The Graphic*, which also offered coverage and illustrations of the Whitechapel murders, competed with the established *Illustrated London News*. It featured early book releases and positive reviews on works including those of Arthur Edward Waite and the compilations and translations of a young Arthur Machen for the publisher George Redway.

"The Real Origin of 'She'" by "One Who Knew Her"[64] appeared in the *Pall Mall Gazette* on January 3, 1889, signed R.D. "What I Know of Obeeyahism by the Author of the Original of 'She'"[65] appeared on February 15, 1889, and was signed Roslyn D'Onston. These articles served as sources for "African Magic," published in the November 1890 issue of *Lucifer*, the periodical of London's Blavatsky Lodge of the Theosophical Society. It was signed "Tau-triadelta," the nom-de-plume of Robert Donston Stephenson.

The ramifications of D'Onston's articles on *She* and "Obeeyahism"[66] are not crucial in considering him as a credible suspect for the Whitechapel murders apart from the claims made about his views of ritual killing. In these articles, D'Onston referred to a projected full-length work based on the articles, which apparently was never released. However, they were written with a tendency for allusion, as was his December 1, 1888, piece on the Whitechapel murders. The *She* and "Obeeyahism" articles were rather an elaborate press attack on an emerging author (Haggard) and the British political explorations of Africa, which was an issue Stead was to champion in the later years of his life. Sir Henry Rider Haggard, the author of *She*, left a reference to those years in his 1926 memoirs.

> In the winter of 1886, as I remember very much against my own will, I was worried into writing an article about "Fiction" for the *Period Review*. It is almost needless for me to say that for a young

writer who had suddenly come into some kind of fame to spring a dissertation of this kind upon the literary world over his own name was very little short of madness. Such views must necessarily make him enemies, secret or declared, by the hundred. There are two bits of advice which I will offer to the youthful author of the future. Never preach about your trade, and, above all, never criticise other practitioners of that trade, however profoundly you may disagree with them. Heaven knows there are critics enough without your taking a hand in the business. Do your work as well as you can and leave other people to do theirs, and the public to judge between them. Secondly, unless you are absolutely driven to it, as of course may happen sometimes, never enter into a controversy with a newspaper.

To return: this unfortunate article about "Fiction" made me plenty of enemies, and the mere fact of my remarkable success made me plenty more. Through no fault of mine, also, these foes found a very able leader in the person of Mr. Stead, who at that time was the editor of the *Pall Mall Gazette*. I should say, however, that of late years Mr. Stead has quite changed his attitude towards me and has indeed become very complimentary, both with reference to my literary and to my public work. For my part, too, I have long ago forgiven his onslaughts, as I can honestly say I have forgiven everybody else for every harm that they have done, or tried to do me.[67]

In 1890, D'Onston published "African Magic"[68] in the *Journal of the Theosophical Society*. His pseudonym for the article, Tau- triadelta, literally "cross three triangles" in Hebrew and Greek, is a Christian Hermetic reference to the mysteries of the resurrection, holy trinity and redemption of Jesus Christ. The prefix "Tau," which was an Egyptian form of the cross, was a Victorian title of nominal "Bishops" of the French Gnostic (early Alexandrian heretical Christian sect) movement founded in Paris in 1890, the year of D'Onston's first use of the pseudonym. Though the historic records of the French Gnostics and its members have survived, D'Onston is not found amongst them. His use of the Victorian term may indicate rather a tribute to early heretical Christian observances. He had earlier written a cryptic title in Greek denoting a Latin rendition of his name on his 1876 marriage certificate in the style of Erasmus's 1516 Greek New Testament, the first *Textus Receptus* and a referenced source on his *The Patristic Gospels*.

D'Onston's further literary efforts were mostly with the publishing enterprises of W.T. Stead. In 1892, he wrote "Dead or Alive" for Stead's *Review of Reviews*.[69] It was a semiautobiographical short story in the style of period supernatural horror writing, and was reprinted several times, notably in book form in *Real Ghost Stories* (1897). In the July 1896 issue of the spiritualist periodical *Borderland*, Stead introduced "A correspondent, signing himself 'R.D'O.'" D'Onston's article, titled "Elementals," was a response to an 1895 German paper, "Seelenbraute und Vampirismus" ("Soul Brides and Vampirism"), by Franz Hartmann.[70] Hartmann, an associate of Helena Blavatsky and Mabel Collins, founded the German Theosophical Society in 1896. D'Onston's article, published the same year, was an objective discussion of the topic in which he did not resort to fantasy.

D'Onston's minor works include a contribution to an 1893 pamphlet titled *Brief Sketches of the Life of Victoria Woodhull*. He also notes having written scientific essays, but these have not been located. His use of pseudonyms makes it difficult to trace his other writings. The most significant piece that D'Onston wrote for *Borderland* was the semifictional "A Modern Magician: An Autobiography,"[71] from which much background information on his life is gleaned. It was prefaced with Stead's suspicion that D'Onston was Jack the Ripper and a disclaimer of having knowledge of his Scotland Yard attention.

> The writer of the following extraordinary fragment of autobiography has been known to me for many years. He is one of the most remarkable persons I ever met. For more than a year I was under the impression that he was the veritable Jack the Ripper; an impression which I believe was shared by the police, who, at least once had him under arrest; though, as he completely satisfied them, they

liberated him without bringing him into court. He wrote for me, while I was editing the Pall Mall Gazette, two marvellous articles on the Obeahism of West Africa, which I have incorporated with this article. The Magician, who prefers to be known by his Hermetic name of Tautriadelta, and who objects even to be called a magician, will undoubtedly be regarded by most people as Baron Munchausen Redivivus. He has certainly traveled in many lands, and seen very strange scenes.

I cannot, of course, vouch personally for the authenticity of any of his stories of his experiences. He has always insisted that they are literally and exactly true. When he sent me this MS., he wrote about it as follows:

"If you do chop it up, please do it by omitting incidents bodily. The evidence of an eyewitness deprived even of its trivialities is divested of its resemblance. If you leave them as I have written them, people will know, will feel, that they are true. Editing, I grant, may improve them as a literary work, but will entirely destroy their value as evidence, especially to people who know the places and persons." I have therefore printed it as received, merely adding cross-heads.

W.T. Stead[72]

Stead was himself also suspected of being Jack the Ripper during the murders, details that he recorded in a press interview.

As so many confident statements, many of them manifestly absurd, had been made fixing the authorship on the Editor of the *Pall Mall Gazette*, our News Editor sent an interviewer to ask his chief if he could throw any light on this subject. He [W.T. Stead] replied:—

"It is not usual to be interviewed for one's own paper, but, as you say, the circumstances are peculiar. What do you want to know?

"The papers, or at least several of them, say that you..."

"What papers?"

"Truth, for instance, among others."

"Mr. Labouchere [House of Commons radical MP, editor and proprietor of *Truth*] is really too fond of paying me equivocal compliments. It is not so long ago he informed the world that there was a strong prima facie case against me as having committed the Whitechapel murders. Having failed to run me in as Jack the Ripper, he saddles me with the authorship of 'The Bismarck Dynasty.' After all, what does it matter?"[73]

D'Onston's "A Modern Magician: An Autobiography" has a checkered history. Its development and publication, particularly with Stead's preface, perpetuated suspicions that he was Jack the Ripper. An 1887 work with similar title appeared in a review in the January 1888 issue of the Theosophical Society journal as *A Modern Magician: A Romance* by J. Fitzgerald Molloy.[74] After D'Onston's popular article was published in *Borderland*, it was later translated, reprinted, and serialized. The French occult periodical *Le Voile d'Isis* [The Veil of Isis], from 1923 to 1924[75] translated the complete article.[76]

D'Onston's *Patristic Gospels* was mentioned in Stead's *Review of Reviews* in 1904, the year of its release. In 1905, a 1903 edition of Robert Anderson's *The Bible and Modern Criticism*[77] was mentioned in the *Review of Reviews*. Into this world of religious publishing and letters entered Roslyn D'Onston with his *Patristic Gospels* of 1904, released at about the same time as Anderson's *The Bible and Modern Criticism*. Anderson and D'Onston, associated with the Whitechapel murders as senior police official and suspect respectively, were in the thick of the Victorian debate on early modern biblical revisionism. Jack the Ripper to them was the evil symbol of demonic possession, the supernatural antichrist, the dubious redeemer of East End vice and prostitution.

What then, does all this have to do with the legend and police investigation of Jack the Ripper? Everything, if one allows that Victorian perceptions were shaped by the religious viewpoints of suspects, press theories and senior police officers. The material cannot be dismissed as it affects objective attempts to follow the investigation. The Jack the Ripper case was a Scotland Yard milestone saturated with unresolved questions. It was permeated with interpretations of the nature of evil, crime, class distinctions and political reform at the apogee of the Industrial Revolution and waning of the British Empire that formed the roots of the modern era.

Robert Anderson approached religious subjects as he would an unsolved serial murder case, by the rules of evidence. Despite there being none to convict anyone of the Whitechapel murders, he declared it an "ascertained fact" that the murderer was known to Scotland Yard.[78] D'Onston likewise formulated an influential press theory on an occult Jack the Ripper. He took advantage of public debate then raging on the disputed sources of the 1611 King James Version of the Bible as opposed to the Revised Version of 1881. To staunch Royalists and Unionists, as Robert Anderson undoubtedly was, crime and Jack the Ripper intruded in the East End's Garden of Eden, a night dweller of the Gehenna of Jewish immigration.[79]

Anderson wrote:

> The decision should rest with those who have practical experience in dealing with evidence. To allow the critics to adjudicate upon the evidence they have themselves prepared would be quite as stupid and as dangerous as to permit the police to try the prisoners whose cases they bring into court. And yet, this is, speaking generally, the attitude maintained by educated Englishmen towards every question raised by the controversy. It is intellectually as deplorable as that of the Irish Roman Catholic peasant who grovels before his priest and takes the law from his mouth.[80]

Anderson was determined to apply his practical Scotland Yard experience with the rules of evidence to the religious fray that seemed to be undermining the Bible. In a footnote, Anderson expressed his thoughts on the issues.

> Infidelity is a strong term, but not too strong. In an article in The Nineteenth Century for January 1902, Professor Cheyne says that Abraham was a "lunar hero." Having regard to our Lord's references to the Patriarch, this is shockingly profane; and having regard to the recent discoveries of archaeology, it is on other grounds extraordinary. Professor Cheyne would possibly deny that he says this. But he says that Winckler, the German, says it; and he repeats it with approval, calling it "A turning-point in Old Testament study," and commending it to the attention of English scholars. I never knew a receiver of stolen goods who did not resent being called a thief!

Anderson ran a tight moral ship at Scotland Yard[81] during and after the Whitechapel murders. D'Onston's approach to the police could not have been luckier for him and Stead given their wild theories on the occult, "Juwes," and a Welsh doctor suspect with no evidence and the alibi of the London Hospital. CID was as desperate to capture the killer as everyone else. Police statements on Roslyn D'Onston could not have concluded he was Jack the Ripper, though it would have made vivid news copy. Robert Donston Stephenson, however, later concerned himself with other esoteric pursuits and did not develop the Whitechapel theme further. D'Onston died at age 75, on October 9, 1916, at Islington Infirmary. His name was recorded in error as "Roslyn D'Ouston." His occupation was noted as "author," and the cause of death listed as carcinoma of the esophagus and gastronomy. It was left to Vittoria Cremers to raise the ghost and for Stead to tell anyone who would listen that Jack the Ripper was a Jesuit conspiracy.

# 5

## Vittoria Cremers and the Lodger

Baroness Vittoria Cremers did not go to the police with suspicions that her lodger, known as Dr. Roslyn D'Onston, was Jack the Ripper. Nor did her close friend Mabel Collins, pseudonym of popular Victorian novelist and fashion reporter Mrs. Kenningale Cook, his lover.

By August 1890, according to the unpublished O'Donnell manuscript, the two sophisticated women were afraid of meeting the fate of East End prostitutes. They were also exposed in a love-triangle dalliance set amid an untidy and widely broadcast Theosophical Society press scandal. They did not want to disavow their beliefs. They shared a house for "over eighteen months" with D'Onston (Robert Donston Stephenson). They recanted their suspicions. Vittoria Cremers was to remain silent for over forty years.

The explanation in the O'Donnell manuscript, which outlines events "twenty-one months" after the Dorset Street murder, includes belief in reincarnation, enchantments and the alleged use of incriminating letters. These beliefs had persuaded Cremers and Collins to accept their suspect's assurances that the gruesome work of Jack the Ripper had ended with Mary Jane Kelly. The story is supposedly based on a memoir by Cremers that does not seem to exist.

Rather than go to Scotland Yard with their information and the blood-encrusted neckties Cremers is believed to have found locked in Stephenson's trunk, along with whatever material evidence Mabel Collins is reported to have held, they remained mute. This was evidence that author Melvin Harris regarded as "high priority." He based this opinion on the work of author and psychologist Joel Norris with the cited support of FBI profiler Robert Ressler and crime writer Patricia Cornwell.[1] The unpublished O'Donnell manuscript has been viewed as proof of D'Onston's guilt, so it is useful to verify the chronology of events.

Cremers and Collins never went to the police. However, official files released during the 1970s contained statements from D'Onston's visit to Scotland Yard in late December 1888. Cremers and Collins justified their inaction by submission to a resolute faith in the laws of karmic retribution — unlike George Marsh, who declared his suspicions to police on December 24, 1888.

Though Scotland Yard did not regard Roslyn D'Onston as Jack the Ripper, the documented affairs of the Theosophical Society in London are crucial in testing Cremers's allegations. Its history is inextricable for the credibility of Cremers's suspicions and in reviewing D'Onston's modern status as a suspect. The stories in the O'Donnell manuscript are the backdrop to this theory and indicative of the interest taken by Victorian subcultures in the Whitechapel murders.

Cremers, as she preferred to be known, finally confessed, apparently disavowing her beliefs to O'Donnell in the early 1930s. D'Onston and Mabel Collins had died in 1916 and 1927 respectively. Neither is known to have left any supporting statements about Cremers's Jack the Ripper theory. In addition to interviewing her, O'Donnell did further research on D'Onston and produced a 372-page document intended for publication titled "Black Magic and Jack the Ripper or This Man Was Jack the Ripper," now referred to as the O'Donnell manuscript. The manuscript is a blend of fact and fabrication.[2] O'Donnell began his manuscript after receiving a tip from Ted Hayter-Preston, the literary editor of the *Sunday Referee*. He completed it in 1958, and before he died in 1969 he submitted it for consideration to the London publisher Harrap. It was never published, but unbound copies are now in circulation.

Crime author Richard Whittington-Egan first explored D'Onston with access to official files and the O'Donnell manuscript and, along with Stephen Knight, introduced the suspect in the 1970s.[3] Whittington-Egan and Knight discounted D'Onston as Jack the Ripper. Melvin Harris revived the theory with further research in his 1987 book *Jack the Ripper: The Bloody Truth*, and also appeared in the 1988 television special on D'Onston, *The Secret Identity of Jack the Ripper*.

Hayter-Preston picked up the story from Vittoria Cremers in 1913 and the *Sunday Referee*'s poetry editor, Victor Neuburg, who was another of her close friends, as well as a one-time consort of Aleister Crowley and mentor to Welsh poet Dylan Thomas. Crowley and Thomas would go on to write for the *Sunday Referee*, and George R. Sims, a Ripper enthusiast, had done so when it was the *Referee* in the early 1900s. A letter to Sims from Ernest Crawford, dated September 24, 1907, two days after his *Lloyd's Weekly News* article on Jack the Ripper, is the earliest known written account of elements of the theory, even though it was attributed to W.T. Stead. This early appearance of these particular details found later in the O'Donnell manuscript was repeated in print several times, though Melvin Harris reveals that Cremers's reminiscences were "circulating in one form or another from 1902."[4]

George Sims does not appear to be taken in by the conjecture, as he is known to have supported Sir Melville Macnaghten and the official police view of the murders. However, he does mention a "Dr. D." (Most probably suspect Montague Druitt), in his 1913 letter to ex–Special Branch head Chief Inspector John George Littlechild. Crawford seems to have gotten the details in his letter from W.T. Stead or D'Onston himself.

These cross-references explain why for forty-odd years O'Donnell's theory has earned serious consideration. Earlier references to the D'Onston story exist in the writings of Cremers's acquaintances East End–born Betty May, Aleister Crowley and later Jean Overton Fuller. Who was she, and did she know the identity of Jack the Ripper as she so persistently claimed?

While undertaking research for her 1965 book, *The Magical Dilemma of Victor Neuburg*,[5] Jean Overton Fuller received information from a Mrs. Joyce Saunders, the daughter of the artist Olivia Haddon. Cremers, who was also noted as an artist, with Haddon had been interested in the ideas and practices of Aleister Crowley for a time. Mrs. Saunders informed Overton Fuller that she and her family not only knew Cremers well but that her brother Geoffrey Haddon had been an executor of her estate. Saunders claimed that Cremers had destroyed her papers before she died, intending to obliterate her tracks.

Details of Vittoria Cremers's life today remain sketchy apart from the information presented in Melvin Harris's 1994 book *The True Face of Jack the Ripper* and the O'Donnell manuscript. Crowley notes knowing her and her literary and artistic circles. Crucially, Overton Fuller met Vittoria Cremers through their mutual friend Victor Neuburg at about the time Bernard O'Donnell had interviewed Cremers. Overton Fuller also completed an obscure biography on the life of Helena Blavatsky, although it makes no mention of either Cremers or Mabel Collins.

Saunders's personal revelations seem reliable enough as her artist mother, Olivia Haddon, is known to have worked with Vittoria Cremers at the London offices of Aleister Crowley from 1912. Saunders had also rented out her cottages in Branscombe, South Devon, to Cremers and Victor Neuburg after they all fell out with Crowley in 1913. Saunders's brother Geoffrey Haddon was noted as an executor on Cremers's last will, as she told Jean Overton Fuller. There are further traces of Cremers's eventful life, but vital statistics, primary documents and photographs are unavailable. Her Jack the Ripper account was discounted by Overton Fuller, who later supported Walter Sickert on her mother's information and in preference to Cremers's lodger, the veritable Dr. Roslyn D'Onston.

Cremers was born Vittoria Cassini in about 1860 in Pisa, Italy, or London depending on the source. The International Genealogical Index has it listed as Italy and a ship manifest has it as London. She appears to have dropped references to her Italian birth when she obtained British citizenship. Her father is noted as Manrica Vittoris Cassini, possibly an error as Manrico is the male form of the name, and her mother as Agnes Elizabeth Rutherford, though Saunders asserted that her mother was French. Cremers claimed, and several sources affirm, that she was actually the illegitimate daughter of a wealthy Jewish gentleman. Saunders and her family believed that Cremers was referring to a Rothschild, but a check with the Rothschild Archives yielded no confirmation. Saunders relates of the Rothschild in question that "while he made her an allowance she was almost obsessively concerned with not causing him embarrassment by allowing the connection to be known."

Vittoria Cremers first arrived in the U.S. in 1875 at about 15 years of age. Little else is known of her early life until she married, at the age of 26, Baron Louis Cremers on November 25, 1886, in Manhattan, New York. She thus acquired the title of baroness, although she rarely used it. Louis was born in St. Petersburg, Russia, in 1858, the son of Louis Cremers and Anna Struse. The baron was apparently attached to the Diplomatic Corps of the Russian Embassy in Washington. The Cremers's marriage did not go smoothly. Baron Cremers gave scathing press interviews about his wife that cast a poor light on her character. He said she had a tendency to be involved with financial scandals, socialist thinkers and bohemian artists.

The O'Donnell manuscript reported that Cremers found a copy of Mabel Collins' 1885 book *Light on the Path* in a New York bookshop, and it inspired her to join the Theosophical Society (presumably the existing New York or Washington branch) before she left for England sometime in mid–1888. Arriving in London, Cremers discovered the Theosophical Blavatsky Lodge and its Esoteric Section in October 1888. These associations were established at the request of members to consolidate leadership of the Theosophical Society. Internal disruption and bad press resulting from the release of a critical report by the Society for Psychical Research in 1885 had damaged the original London Lodge of the Theosophical Society.

Vittoria Cremers was admitted to the inaugural Esoteric Section of the Blavatsky Lodge in October 1888, at about the same time Roslyn D'Onston's first entered the London Hospital. The O'Donnell manuscript quotes Cremers: "I managed to qualify for entry into the Esoteric Section of the Society of which I was now a fully-fledged member." What is not mentioned in the O'Donnell manuscript is that she was expelled, together with Mabel Collins, in February 1889 for a "serious breach of their pledge," according to an internal memorandum of the Theosophical Society.[6] The memo, issued to members in early 1889, is the only verifiable record that Vittoria Cremers was in London at the time of the Whitechapel murders. It also shows that she had met Mabel Collins while both were members of the Theosophical Society, as O'Donnell had noted.

# LIGHT ON THE PATH.

## A TREATISE

WRITTEN FOR THE PERSONAL USE OF THOSE WHO ARE IGNORANT OF THE EASTERN WISDOM, AND WHO DESIRE TO ENTER WITHIN ITS INFLUENCE.

By Sri: Hilarion.

WRITTEN DOWN BY

M. C.,

A FELLOW OF THE THEOSOPHICAL SOCIETY.

*Work done under Sri: Hilarion.*
*"Light on the Path" begun October, 1884.*
*"Karma" written December 27, 1884.*
*Mabel Cook.*

**The title page of *Light on the Path*, annotated by Mabel (Collins) Cook. The popular Victorian treatise influenced Vittoria Cremers to join the Theosophical Society (courtesy the Theosophical Society).**

William Butler Yeats, the Irish poet and a member of the Dublin Theosophical Lodge, also joined London's Esoteric Section in December 1888. He wrote that Collins was expelled over a "flirtation"[7] and Cremers for gossiping about it. In the O'Donnell manuscript, Cremers indicates the trouble was over, "tantric worship" and "certain sexual black magic rites." Aleister Crowley wrote in 1919, "There is a certain amount of melancholia with delusions of persecution about this verse. Natural, perhaps, to one who was betrayed and robbed by Vittoria Cremers?" Crowley also noted in his 1929 autobiography, "At the critical moment of her mission, Madame Blavatsky had been most foully betrayed by Mabel Collins with the help, according to the stratagems and at the instigation of Cremers, who not only justified, but boasted of her conduct."

Helena Blavatsky's views were also noted in administrative letters to branch presidents on the rivalry and competing personalities of that period, the "Old Lady" herself adding to the turmoil. Though she doesn't mention Cremers directly, the differences with Mabel Collins are made clear. In the O'Donnell manuscript, Cremers is asked by Blavatsky to choose between herself and her friend's indiscretions but by her own account remains stead-fast with Collins.

Cremers commented on D'Onston's *Pall Mall Gazette* article of December 1, 1888, which was later read to members of the Theosophical Society because of interest in the murders and the occult subject expressed in the article. She said, "I was young in years, about twenty-eight, and densely, pathetically ignorant of things occult. The words I heard meant absolutely nothing to me. I was still a newcomer to the Theosophical movement, and so far as the Ripper murders were concerned knew little beyond the shrieking headlines. Such things did not interest me and I did not read the reports. As for black magic, I had never heard of such a thing any more than I knew that the Earl of Crawford and Balcarres was one of the leading occultists of that day."

Cremers claimed that Mabel Collins and other officials of the Theosophical Society were her source for asserting the Earl of Crawford's authorship of the *Pall Mall Gazette* article during Cremers's attendance at its reading in early December 1888. L. Perry Curtis, author of *Jack the Ripper and the London Press*, supported this tenuous attribution to Craw-ford, as did Bernard O'Donnell. However, editor W.T. Stead endorsed D'Onston's authorship with his December 3, 1888, *Pall Mall Gazette* comments, and it was noted in Scotland Yard reports. What is not clear is why Crawford, a close friend of Robert Anderson, would be associated with a Jack the Ripper black magic theory. Lord Lindsay, Earl of Crawford and Balcarres, was indeed a confirmed dabbler in the occult and Theosophy and a collector of rare antiquarian books. He had also written an undated letter to Anderson in which he claimed to have gotten information on the Whitechapel murders from an anonymous woman of his acquaintance.[8]

The December 1 press report, in which D'Onston developed his occult theories, is generally examined with emphasis on "the profanation of the cross and other emblems usually considered sacred." The reference, along with other veiled comments in the article, is taken as a confession of D'Onston's murdering method and motives as he is portrayed in the O'Donnell manuscript. For D'Onston to know anything about the Theosophical Society as assumed, he would have been aware of the mistaken attribution of his article of December 1. From what is known of him, he would not have tolerated the incursion into his reputation. He would certainly not have wasted any opportunity to let Vittoria Cremers or Mabel Collins know the truth of its authorship, which he does not do in the O'Donnell manu-script.

October 1888 also saw the release of Blavatsky's seminal work *The Secret Doctrine*. The early feminist Annie Besant reviewed it in the *Pall Mall Gazette* on April 25, 1889, at the request of Stead. Besant, Blavatsky's right-hand woman, replaced Mabel Collins in 1889. Collins and Cremers remained opposed to Besant's style of leadership for years to come. Stead had approached his friend Besant, a newcomer to spiritualism, to review *The Secret Doctrine*, a weighty and convoluted tome of Theosophical fragments and mystical cosmology. (D'Onston's interest in such topics would have made him the natural choice for a review had he been a member of the Theosophical Society.)

According to the O'Donnell manuscript, Cremers left for America sometime in 1889 after her expulsion from Blavatsky's Theosophical Society. She is said to have returned to England in February 1890 and also spent several weeks in Paris for unspecified business and enjoyment of the fashion shows. Noted also is a meeting with the actress Sarah Bernhardt in France during 1890, a time when Mabel Collins was said to be living with D'Onston in Southsea. Based on O'Donnell's work, Mabel Collins first met D'Onston sometime after writing to him about his articles on Rider Haggard's *She* and the Obeah shamanism of West Africa. Cremers and Collins are shown to have known him only by his alias, as did Bernard O'Donnell.

In a follow-up *Pall Mall Gazette* article on February 15, 1889, signed "Roslyn D'Onston," he continues with "The unexpected and extraordinary amount of interest excited by my article in the Pall Mall Gazette of the 3rd ult., and the numberless letters of inquiry which I have received." These may have included a letter from a susceptible 37-year-old named Mabel Cook, aka Collins, as Cremers contends in the O'Donnell manuscript. Collins said she wrote to him in care of the newspaper, and he replied that he was ill in hospital and would write to her after his release to make an appointment.

The O'Donnell manuscript continues the spotlight on Mabel

The actress Sarah Bernhardt in 1889. Vittoria Cremers admired Bernhardt's performances and was actively involved in New York theater productions.

Collins with, "She paused to light another cigarette, for she was smoking furiously throughout her talk." It might have been an apt description of Helena Blavatsky seen by Vittoria Cremers and others, but Collins is known not to have smoked, considering her frail constitution and vegetarian habits. Bernard O'Donnell is again developing the ghostwritten conversational style of his 1923 *Sunday Express* articles for Betty May. May gave a brief and vivid account of Cremers's Jack the Ripper necktie story derived from Aleister Crowley's unpublished autobiography. She was the first to publish the story lifted from Crowley's work for her 1929 autobiography, *Tiger Woman*, while living at his home, the "Abbey of Thelema" in Italy in the early 1920s. In May's account, the addition that Jack the Ripper attained invisibility seems to derive from the Sergeant Stephen White press story of 1919 as it was developed by Crowley.

By Vittoria Cremers's account, then, Collins met D'Onston sometime after his release from the London Hospital on July 25, 1889, and before August 1890, 21 months after the murder of Mary Kelly. In author Melvin Harris's version of events, closely aligned with the

O'Donnell manuscript, the trio is further seen busy establishing their Pompadour Cosmetique Company. However, any independent evidence that they actually did meet or live together is not known to exist. Cremers is simply correct in her account of when Mabel Collins is supposed to have arranged to meet D'Onston after his release.

Mabel Collins was also sick and indisposed during 1889. A letter by Ellen Hopkins, her half-sister, printed in the spiritualist periodical *Light* on June 15, 1889, read, "Will you allow me to state that my sister, Mabel Collins, is too ill at the moment to be able to speak for herself, but I trust she will be well enough in a few days to furnish you with a reply which will put a very different aspect on the whole affair?" The periodical later expressed in its issue of June 29, 1889, "We have no intention of publishing anything further on the Coues-Collins case, unless a rejoinder is made by Mrs. Cook."

Collins did not respond in *Light* to the affair involving Blavatsky's American rival Dr. Elliott Coues. However, she did take it up in other English publications during 1889, with permission given for Coues to release her ambivalent letters on Blavatsky. Later, in 1910, Collins issued a statement in the *Occult Review* that she was an occasional sufferer of "nervous breakdown, incessant headache, inability to bear anything but subdued light, loss of appetite, extreme weakness and general depression of spirits," not to mention being "a very great sufferer of eczema for twenty years." Mabel Collins was hardly in a position to care for Roslyn D'Onston during 1889 as conjectured.

It is therefore not established when Collins and D'Onston actually began living together nor with Cremers later, if indeed they ever did, because dates are not recorded in any coinciding detail. Cremers simply says in the O'Donnell manuscript that there was a bundle of letters. If this is true, it would suggest that Collins and D'Onston corresponded for some time before they cohabited. They are thought to have begun living together at the earliest in late 1889 or early 1890, and Vittoria Cremers moved in around August 1890.

Mabel Collins is known to have attended many social and artistic events in London while avoiding others. An instance was noted in her correspondence with the artist James McNeill Whistler. He enthusiastically encouraged her to come with Mary "May" Morris, her friend and the daughter of socialist William Morris, to Whistler's famous Sunday breakfasts. So it is conceivable that the bohemian D'Onston also mixed in these circles and had possibly met Collins with Vittoria Cremers. Whether or not they actually lived together and for how long is conjecture based entirely on unsupported claims found in the O'Donnell manuscript. Collins is known to have preferred living alone or with other women after the death of her husband in 1886, and D'Onston makes no bold claim to having resided with her.

If statements in the O'Donnell manuscript are taken literally and compared to available primary sources, a clearer picture emerges of Vittoria Cremers's movements and assertions during this period. Claims that she lived with D'Onston and allegations of murder are sometimes significantly at variance with documented sources and the official police files on the Whitechapel murders.

Cremers records in the O'Donnell manuscript that D'Onston entered into this sub-culture of post–Darwinian religious exiles with the Ripper theory he gave to the police earlier. The main points he told her — about Dr. Morgan Davies, the alleged sodomy of Mary Kelly, and the occult motive for the Whitechapel murders — is consistent with his statements in the official police files but diverges from the facts and medical evidence of the overall case. That she later recounted to O'Donnell the main points of D'Onston's statements to police is a strong indicator that she had met him or at least heard elements of his story from Mabel Collins. O'Donnell died in 1969 at the age of 86, before the official files on the murders were released, so he could not consult them for his manuscript.

A letter in Mabel Collins's hand, dated February 27, 1889, a time she is said to have corresponded with D'Onston, was sent to Clive Holland, a young and later successful author in reply to his query on joining the Theosophical Society. Collins was a past administrator by this date and, along with Vittoria Cremers, had fallen out with Helena Blavatsky.

> Letter to: Clive Holland Esq.
> Eastbury
> Bournemouth
> Feb. 27 [1889]
>
> Dear Sir
>
> I think if you were to write to the Manager of the Theosphical [sic] Publishing Company 7 Duke Street Adelphi W.C. you would get much more information there
> than I can give you, as they have a library and know of all the books on the subject.
> Of course you know of Madame Blavatsky's "Isis Unveiled" and "Secret Doctrine" of
> "Five Years of Theosophy" & of Mr. and Mrs. Sinnett's works. For myself I consider Bulwer-Lytton's "Strange Story" "Zanoni" Georges Sand's "Countess of Rudolstadt" and "Consuelo" Rider Haggard's "She" and Marion Crawford's "Mr. Isaacs" also Edwin Arnold's "Light of Asia" all necessary volumes in a Theosophical library. Of old books the "Bhagavat Gita" and Putanjali Yoga are perhaps the most important. I do not consider any of my novels Theosophical, not even "The Blossom & the Fruit."
>
> Very truly yours,
> Mabel Cook[9]

This letter is germane because it lists some works that a well-read Victorian woman with esoteric interests would consume and discuss with D'Onston and also in the mentoring of Vittoria Cremers. By the time Collins wrote the letter, she and Cremers had fallen out with Blavatsky's Theosophical Society. Neither would relinquish continuing interest in alternate spiritual beliefs throughout the rest of their lives.

Collins, noted for her healing and leadership qualities, had several members follow her after her expulsion. D'Onston appears to have benefited from Collins' nurturing touch and recovered from his illness during the period he is thought to have lived with her. He demonstrates more sober habits in his writing and lifestyle after the supposed association with Mabel Collins and before any suggested Christian conversion after meeting with American spiritualist and early feminist Victoria Woodhull in 1893. Cremers, who made it a mission to expose the mighty, seems not to trust D'Onston at all in the O'Donnell manuscript. Collins is generally reported to have spoken highly of him and his accomplishments. His Jack the Ripper story would have been one of the many tales he told to entertain attentive Victorian ladies.

Mabel Collins' February 27, 1889, letter refers to Mr. and Mrs. Sinnett, who maintained the competing London Lodge of the Theosophical Society. It was the founding English guild, begun on June 27, 1878, but became the subject of allegations of fraud by the Society for Psychical Research in 1885. Collins is known to have retained membership in it before and after it split with the Blavatsky Lodge in 1887.

D'Onston and Cremers would certainly have read Mabel Collins' *The Blossom and the Fruit*, a novel she serialized while she was editor of the Theosophical periodical *Lucifer* between September 1887 and August 1888. It was published as a book in 1890. In her own words, it tells of, "Fleta, who, in her earlier incarnation, took power selfishly into her own hands, became by virtue of that power a black magician: one who has knowledge and uses it for selfish ends." Blavatsky rewrote the final chapters due to what she regarded as scandalous material. The final sentence of Collins's letter — "I do not consider any of my novels Theosophical" — was to become the substance of a libel suit against Blavatsky that she filed in July 1889 and which was brought to court in July 1890.

In an editorial in the August 1890 issue of the New York Theosophical periodical *The Path*, W.Q. Judge, president of the American section and Blavatsky's legal representative, reported that "the plaintiff (Mabel Cook) was ready to proceed and had through her counsel demanded the production of a certain letter written before the suit to people in London. The case was expected on for some days and people were there for the sake of the expected

Mabel Collins in October 1911. She was an active anti-vivisectionist, early feminist, author and fashion reporter. In the account of Vittoria Cremers, Collins resided with Jack the Ripper suspect Roslyn D'Onston.

scandal, but the defendant's attorney's showed the letter beforehand to the plaintiff's counsel, who then came into court and asked the Judge to take the case off the docket, thus confessing the weakness of the charge and bringing the matter to a final conclusion."

According to the O'Donnell manuscript, Vittoria Cremers witnessed these proceedings at the time she was living with D'Onston, which would have drained Collins of funds and ruptured her relationship with Blavatsky irreparably. D'Onston may also have attended the proceedings. It is likely that D'Onston supported Cremers and Collins in their Theosophical struggles with Blavatsky. By the time O'Donnell noted these letters, they had become incriminating evidence.

By February 1889 Mabel Collins' name had dropped off the editorial page of *Lucifer*. She corresponded by cablegram with Blavasky's rival Dr. Elliott Coues throughout 1889 and 1890. He was president of the Washington branch of the Theosophical Society and a former member of the Society for Psychical Research. The result of this fiasco, which Cremers and the

O'Donnell manuscript make some comment on, was publication of more defamatory letters, pamphlets and an article in the New York paper *The Sun* on July 20, 1890, by Coues titled "Blavatsky Unveiled." This began another series of libel suits against *The Sun* after Coues also was expelled from the Theosophical Society in June 1889. Before it came to trial, Madame Blavatsky passed away on May 8, 1891, at 19 Avenue Road, St. Johns Wood. She died of heart disease, rheumatism, Bright's disease and complications from influenza, and her death left the newspaper free from further legal burden.

The branches of the Theosophical Society in London, Europe, India and America saw a great deal of upheaval and dissension. It had been in flux since its formation in New York in September 1875 until Blavatsky's death in London. The public and internal upheaval waxed intensely during the period 1887–91. It coincided with the Whitechapel murders. These Theosophical rivalries caused the formation of splinter groups well into the 20th century when Annie Besant took leadership in opposition to other branches. They had also involved Vittoria Cremers and Mabel Collins.

By August 1890, the time Vittoria Cremers was lodging with Collins and D'Onston in Sherlock Holmes' famous Baker Street, she had been immersed in arcane studies for at least four years, since locating Mabel Collins' spiritual tract *Light on the Path* in New York in 1886. If her account in the O'Donnell manuscript is accepted, she was also aware of the criminal implications of her alleged details and suspicions based on D'Onston's narratives and theories.

D'Onston and W.T. Stead are known to have commented from the sidelines in articles and letters, yet neither joined the Theosophical Society. They remained in peripheral contact with some of its members and were generally sympathetic to its ethos. Cremers, Collins and D'Onston were then in agreement on Blavatsky's brash style. However, as the early Theosophical Society had roots and contacts in British India, its activities were of some concern to English authorities, which raised the stakes of personal and legal squabbles involving its members.

Cremers asked D'Onston to write out his theories to present to Stead. But Cremers is not told in the O'Donnell manuscript that D'Onston had already written a letter to the City Police on October 16, 1888. In the letter he outlined a theory that he later developed in his only Ripper newspaper article, for the *Pall Mall Gazette* on December 1, 1888. The O'Donnell manuscript mentions that he acted as an informant to police on the suspect Dr. Morgan Davies but does not mention his authorship of the *Pall Mall Gazette* article. This he had stated to Inspector Thomas Roots in the summary report of December 26, 1888, and forwarded to Chief Inspector Donald Swanson, who had overall charge of the case.

Cremers was told only that he was "interviewed and released by the police on two occasions." Stead also recorded in *Borderland* (April 1896) that he was "under the impression that he was the veritable Jack the Ripper." Cremers's suspicion of police involvement appears to echo Stead's preface that she either read or O'Donnell had inserted. Stead recalled that the police "at least once had him under arrest."

In the account of these events, Vittoria Cremers does not know that D'Onston had already written a Ripper article for Stead. She now sees that he is not prepared to go public with his Dr. Davies theory. He simply reiterates that "by the time they went to arrest him, he had gone," though it is known that Dr. Morgan Davies continued to reside and work in the East End with the Welsh community. Cremers observes, "the perspiration simply poured from him as he wrote, and he was obviously laboring under some great emotional strain as he scribbled away." As D'Onston's Ripper article was already written and published by that date, her comments appear exaggerated. His documented condition of tremors due to alcoholism and drugs and that he was supposedly under the care of Mabel Collins at the time could account for it. The writer of the O'Donnell manuscript thus piles further unfounded suspicion upon him in expanding Cremers's original story.

It may be assumed that D'Onston's failure to reveal these salient details in the O'Donnell manuscript to Cremers or Collins is evidence that Robert Donston Stephenson was guilty of Jack the Ripper's crimes. However, in effect it undermines Vittoria Cremers's account and O'Donnell's sensational story as circumstantial grounds for the Whitechapel murders. This document, on which the modern assessment of D'Onston as a credible suspect for the Whitechapel murders is based, is then reliant on the hearsay of Vittoria Cremers. Bernard O'Donnell worked only with the suspect's alias and the unpublished manuscript is seriously deficient on important points of documented fact.

Dr. Roslyn D'Onston confesses to Cremers of meeting Dr. Morgan Davies: "Did I ever tell you that I knew Jack the Ripper? Just after the last of the murders I was living in the Whitechapel neighbourhood ... I was taken ill and had to go into hospital. It was there that I met him." However, D'Onston had stated to police on December 26, 1888, that he had met Dr. Davies before the murder of Mary Kelly on November 9, 1888. He had thus reported his suspicions before his second London Hospital admission in 1889. The O'Donnell manuscript is again divergent with police reports on certain crucial points.

Vittoria Cremers's belief that D'Onston was a murdering mutilator is of course a common theme running throughout the O'Donnell manuscript. This belief was apparently shared by Mabel Collins, W.T. Stead and the laborer George Marsh based upon the suspect's own narratives, but not, evidently, by the police. Clearly, D'Onston enjoyed and encouraged shock and suspicion from his witnesses. Chief Inspector Donald Swanson, in daily contact with the City Police regarding the Mitre Square murder of Catherine Eddowes on September 30, 1888, is not known to have made any statement on D'Onston's unsolicited letter to the City Police or Scotland Yard's report. In his summary report dated December 26, Inspector Thomas Roots concluded he was not responsible for the murders. No record of charges or arrest is extant that would support comments by Cremers and by Stead later in 1896, or any other claims D'Onston may have made after.

D'Onston is said to have repeated to Cremers his Dr. Davies story, complete with his obsession about the sodomy of Mary Kelly. He told police in his statement of December 26 that Stead was his source for the medical details, presumably obtained from the suppressed autopsy report or an informant. Dr. Thomas Bond made no mention of sodomy and neither does his assistant Dr. Charles Alfred Hebbert in the rediscovered extra pages of Bond's autopsy report, published in the 1998 *Criminologist* articles of Stephen Gouriet Ryan. Dr. George Bagster Phillips also makes no mention of any sexual assault in the inquest hearing into the death of Mary Kelly held on November 12, 1888.

Based on what is known about Morgan Davies, he would not have tolerated D'Onston's bluster and extravagant claims. Vittoria Cremers is shown in the O'Donnell manuscript to reach the same conclusion as George Marsh in taking the stories as misleading, detracting from his own guilt. In talking of his doctor friend, he is perceived by witnesses as indirectly referring to himself and his knowledge of the crimes. The police disagreed. Any quarrel D'Onston may have had with Dr. Davies can only be guessed at, and it is hard to imagine that the two men were very agreeable.

In a rare work on the life of Mabel Collins, Kim Farnell's *Mystical Vampire: The Life of Mabel Collins* (2005), no new details appear on Vittoria Cremers or the Ripper crimes, as the author sourced details from Melvin Harris and Aleister Crowley's *Confessions*. The book is nevertheless a well researched and detailed biography of Collins. One fresh and relevant point that Farnell does make is on Collins' financial losses beginning in 1891 due to an extreme dip in the American and English paperback markets at a time when D'Onston is said to have bilked her and Cremers of funds. A worldwide depression during the 1890s weakened Collins' earnings as a writer of cheap paperback novels. It affected D'Onston's commissions and Vittoria Cremers's income.

The Pompadour Cosmetique business that they ineptly worked was also affected by the depression, and was liquidated soon after it began. Cremers records in the O'Donnell manuscript, "Beauty parlors as we know them today, were practically non-existent in the nineties, but feminine vanity was by no means lacking, and I felt that the idea might prove a good business proposition. Mabel Collins and I put up the money, and D'Onston provided the recipes from which the various unguents and lotions were prepared. We formed a company named the Pompadour Cosmetique Company, and took premises in Baker Street on the site where Baker Street Tube Station now stands." Cremers goes on to claim that she and Mabel Collins were the first to suspect D'Onston of being Jack the Ripper, sometime after Collins's libel case with Blavatsky in July 1890. She says, "It was a month or so after this scene that an incident happened, fraught with tremendous consequence to all three of us in partnership in the Pompadour Cosmetiques Company. It was Mabel Collins who first aroused suspicion in my mind that D'Onston was Jack the Ripper."

The Board of Trade Companies Registration Office and Files of Dissolved Companies 1855–1976 are retained at the National Archives at Kew in London. Pompadour Cosmetique Ltd, as it is listed in their files, was not incorporated in 1890 as the O'Donnell manuscript assures. "The Certificate of Incorporation for Pompadour Cosmetiques is clearly dated and signed by the Registrar of Joint Stock Companies on 16 October 1891," said the National Archives. Vittoria Cremers's mistake might be explained by her reliance on memory or that of O'Donnell. Later, Melvin Harris researched the company's file previously held at Companies House in London. It had the year 1890 incorrectly noted, according to the archivist. The claim of a partnership thus rests on the hearsay of Cremers and O'Donnell, as the certificate of incorporation does not bear their names. However, a company named Pompadour Cosmetics was operating from 17 Upper Baker Street, Marylebone, N.W. from at least 1890 and had advertisements in *The Women's Penny Paper*. If D'Onston, Cremers and Collins were in partnership at that time, they had not registered the company.

Nevertheless, given that the Pompadour Company was incorporated on October 16, 1891, it can be reasonably presumed that Cremers, Collins and D'Onston were living together as the O'Donnell manuscript assures by this date. Not quite. At the time of the 1891 census conducted in April, Mabel Collins was living under her legal name, Mabel Cook, at 63 York Terrace in London with a servant and her child. D'Onston is listed as a boarder at the Triangle Hotel, Charterhouse Street, St. Sepulchre's, London, under the alias "Roslyn D'Ouston" with the fictional birthplace of Elsham. Where Cremers was located is anyone's guess, but she was certainly not with them as Bernard O'Donnell wrote. As Cremers mentions the "nineties" for cosmetics as a business venture, 1890 was a likely time of their meeting; this was the year D'Onston wrote "African Magic" for the Theosophical Society periodical *Lucifer*.

Vittoria Cremers is also recorded in the O'Donnell manuscript to have seen further evidence of her lodger's murderous inclinations. She reportedly attested, "The sinister throat-cutting gesture he made with his finger seemed to confirm what Mabel Collins had confided to me, and at once my brain began a process of speculation." When she shares her discovery, Mabel Collins replies, "Yes Vittoria, I know he has been married, but he will never talk about his wife. I did not know that he had killed her. He simply said that she had disappeared suddenly — vanished completely, and he had not heard of her in years."

Though the eventual fate of D'Onston's wife Anne Deary is vague and unconfirmed to date, author Chris Scott has researched her alleged murder and her whereabouts. In 2004 he wrote, "There has been much discussion about the fate of Anne Deary, D'Onston's wife and, as it has been theorised that D'Onston actually murdered her, and hers was one of the unidentified bodies found in the Thames, the fate of the lady in question becomes fairly crucial." According to Scott's ongoing research, it would appear that Mabel Collins was incorrect and that she had not been murdered. D'Onston's estranged wife, born in Thorne, Yorkshire, in 1847, was described in the 1891 census as "Annie Stephenson, 16 Douglas Road, South Islington, London, Cook, domestic servant (married)," alive and well.

Before Cremers finally parted ways with Collins and D'Onston sometime in 1892 (as is thought), she claimed to have discovered blood-encrusted neckties in his locked trunk. This legend seems to be derived from the witness statement of George Hutchinson regarding the murder of Mary Kelly. The ties supposedly hid the organs that the Ripper removed from the victims. The anecdote appears in the O'Donnell manuscript. It is an implausible elaboration on D'Onston's original theory. The D'Onston neckties are a later embellishment akin to the famous Gladstone bag supposedly carried by Jack the Ripper.

General observers on Jack the Ripper express generic beliefs and attempt to debunk every instance of occultism and spiritualism as fraudulent or inclined to murder. In contrast, D'Onston cited for support in his July 1896 *Borderland* article the work of author and mystic Anna Kingsford. She was one of the first female doctors in London, having earned her degree in Paris. (Victorian English laws restricted women from medical careers.) She died prematurely on February 22, 1888, at the age of 42. On May 13, 1886, Kingsford delivered "*Pasteur: His Method and Its Results: A Lecture*," in Hampstead for the North London Anti-Vivisection Society, an attack on the effectiveness of Louis Pasteur's rabies vaccine and the use of live animals in producing it. Victorian women like Kingsford who voiced informed concerns were vilified by mainstream medical authorities and, if they were also members of occult subcultures, were easily excised from historical treatments. Anna Kingsford was also a staunch opponent of Helena Blavatsky, a close associate of Mabel Collins and a founding member of the London Lodge of the Theosophical Society.[10]

D'Onston's contact with Blavatsky and her Theosophical Society is otherwise based upon one known submission to the periodical *Lucifer* in November 1890 titled "African Magic." It was signed by 'Tau-triadelta,' the first appearance of the pseudonym. O'Donnell read it apparently before researching D'Onston and hearing Cremers. Melvin Harris regarded the article, which is tentatively and cautiously considered written by Blavatsky in Theosophical circles, as commissioned by Cremers and Collins because D'Onston was short of funds. This cannot be the case, as both Cremers and Collins were expelled in February 1889. Neither makes the claim in the O'Donnell manuscript as neither was in a position to commission for *Lucifer* at that time. Furthermore, *Lucifer* did not pay its contributors. Most probably, D'Onston penned the article on the request of editor W.T. Stead and Madame Blavatsky.

"African Magic" is taken as evidence of D'Onston's capacity for ritual murder. The contextual proof rather points to the view that it was intended as a semi-autobiographical taunt of Blavatsky, as it recounts the killing of a powerful shaman woman by magical means. Cremers says only, "I did not see the article and never bothered to read it till it was brought to my notice years later in 1931. Even if I had read it at the time, I doubt whether I should fully have understood it, and I cer-

Dr. Anna Kingsford was one of the first licensed English female doctors. She was linked with Jack the Ripper when a published letter of her biographer was used by crime reporter Bernard O'Donnell to support the suspect Roslyn D'Onston.

tainly would not have associated the writer with the Ripper crimes which, by the end of 1890 had almost faded from public memory." Yet elsewhere in the O'Donnell manuscript, Cremers says, "I remember too my curiosity when he brought to me the article for Lucifer. I just glanced at the title and then noticed that it was by Tautriadelta." The murder of Francis Coles on February 13, 1891, reignited the ongoing investigation and press reports. So who first linked the writer of "African Magic" with the Ripper crimes? Who brought it to her attention if not Bernard O'Donnell?

In January 1893, Cremers appears on ship manifests as traveling back to New York. Though little is known of what she did during the later part of the 19th century, Melvin Harris suggests that Anthony Comstock's New York Society for the Suppression of Vice employed her as an agent. Aleister Crowley had also noted Cremers's association with Comstock in his autobiography *Confessions*: "She had, at one time, been the paid spy of some blackmailing vigilance society in America, which, under cover of moral indignation, forged false evidence against convenient candidates, implicating them in the white slave traffic, extracting hush money, or prosecuting when the victim was not worth despoiling or refused to pay up, and sometimes by way of "making an example," in order to frighten the next batch whose blood they proposed to suck."

Crowley, who knew Bernard O'Donnell, was also an aspiring journalist. With O'Donnell's citing of Montague Summers, a famous vampirologist and author of *Victorian Ghost Stories* (1933), the O'Donnell manuscript was well placed for the attempted exorcism of Jack the Ripper. What D'Onston began with his occult theory, Vittoria Cremers perpetuated in casting out the satanic archetype of the Whitechapel murderer, her lodger.

In the July 1896 issue of *Borderland*, Stead commissioned D'Onston under the alias "R. D'O" to refute an article by a Dr. Hartmann on vampires. Hartmann was also an associate of Blavatsky when she was alive. He was considered a leading member of the Theosophical Society and was at one time president of its German branch. The tenets of the society attempted to dispel fanciful notions of spiritualism and snake charmers, ideals that had attracted Cremers and Collins. They challenged Stead and D'Onston in their writings and periodical editorials. Dr. Hartmann is also known to have frequented the same circles as Collins and Cremers in association with Blavatsky and Crowley.

Aleister Crowley, in August 1943 wrote an article based on Cremers's account. It began

A portion of Vittoria Cremers's last will, signed on September 15, 1937, two months before she died (courtesy Stewart P. Evans).

as follows: "To acquire a friendly feeling for a system, to render it rapidly familiar, it is prudent to introduce the Star to which the persons of the drama are attached. It is hardly one's first, or even one's hundredth guess, that the Victorian worthy in the case of Jack the Ripper was no less a person than Helena Petrovna Blavatsky."

The remark summarized events of the Theosophical Society at that time which were later developed in Cremers's account and O'Donnell's theory. Crowley's statement, without the necessary historical context, has also been taken as a suggestion that Blavatsky herself may have been Jack the Ripper. Crowley adds, "One theory suggests that he [D'Onston] was loyal to H. P. B. [Helena Petrovka Blavatsky], and thought it essential to fight against the influence of Cremers. This, at any rate, is what she thought, and it made her all the more anxious to get rid of him; judging everybody by herself, she was quite sure he would not hesitate to use the love letters in case of definite breach."

By 1900, Vittoria Cremers was again living in America. She is found listed in the Canadian Theosophical periodical *The Lamp* as one of the directors of the Eclectic Theosophical Society of New York. This splinter group was independent of the leadership squabbles that occurred after Blavatsky's death in 1891 between rivals W.Q. Judge and Annie Besant. *The Lamp* issues of May 15, 1900, and June 15, 1900, state, "The Brooklyn Branch of the Eclectic T.S., meets every Sunday afternoon at 3 o'clock at 130 Underhill Avenue. Mrs. Vittoria Cremers, is secretary."

She returned to England around 1910 and in 1912 joined Crowley's early esoteric order Mysteria Mystica Maxima, the British branch of the German Ordo Templi Orientis. Cremers was its first secretary and treasurer. After falling out with him in 1913, Vittoria went on to live in isolation until her death in Buckinghamshire, England. She signed a last will on September 15, 1937, and she died a childless widow on November 12 of that year, mourned only by a few of her close friends.

# 6

## Hexes, Hoaxes and the Beast

Conspiracy theories were born in the furnace of medieval dichotomy on faith and reason, of fact and fiction. The Victorian analogy for police inquiries and the press portrayal of the Whitechapel murders was then set. As each piece of the puzzle is precisely shaped, rarely does it fit the larger picture, induce an exercise in resolution or provide relevant or conclusive leads. The exposure of historic hoaxes emerging in this cryptic vacuum adds further distractions contrary to the facts of an unsolved serial murder case that perpetuates beliefs in a high profile conspiracy of silence.

The Whitechapel murders serve as both social and criminal history, with the lives of the victims contributing to a study of the period. Scotland Yard was scrutinized as politics were forgotten. Jack the Ripper conspiracy theories derive from a unique set of circumstances. Sensational news reports of Royal Masonic schemes, the 1889 Florence Maybrick trial and Cleveland Street brothel scandal, gothic horror fictions of the 20th century and the emergence of speculative history as a literary subgenre, have added to the mystique.

A conspiracy theory may also be convenient for those who seek to suppress a social truth. Others may create conspiracies, despite facts to the contrary, as a form of protest. Jack the Ripper has come to wear a variety of masks that signify social change and partisan historical conflicts. However, due consideration of the Scotland Yard manhunt for an enigmatic serial killer continues to lead the way through the East End labyrinth.[1]

At the turn of the 20th century and with the death of Queen Victoria, the portrayal of the Whitechapel murders assumed an altered cultural significance. Changing attitudes on class, gender, immigration, and national identity reflected the social nature of evil and crime. The Edwardian period[2] saw marked divergence of Jack the Ripper theories with further blending of fact and fictions. Sir Robert Anderson's extreme theories did not end speculation. Theories about a phantom sexual serial killer persisted alongside senior police memoirs and press statements.

Theories about the Whitechapel murders also shed their pseudo-religious and ritual murder trappings. The release of inconclusive police memoirs and official sources ensured the development of other speculative theories. Increased production of Ripper literature can generally be seen during the 20th century before and after wartime paper shortages. With repeal of the archaic Vagrants and Witchcraft Acts and introduction of the Fraudulent

Mediums Act in 1951, mass production of supernatural and occult literature was encouraged. Gothic horror stories re-emerged widely in the 1970s with Freemasonic conspiracy theories. Jack the Ripper was then open for new depictions during the liberal 1960s and 1970s.

Subsequent theories, though they may have appeared new, were rooted in the past and were embellishments on earlier established legends. They were presented as fact but released in speculative fictional or novelized forms. Primary sources available to early crime historians were press reports. Sometimes they were fabricated, designed to provoke official response, or intended to express partisan editorial positions on crime and the police. The years between 1888 and the First World War also gave rise to confusing semi-official press statements effectively masking the actual events.

Two days after the murder of Annie Chapman on September 8, 1888, *The Star* issued an editorial on the investigation of serial murder cases that was very modern in outlook. It is largely due to enterprising Victorian journalists that the sources on the Whitechapel murders today are as complete as they are, especially with transcripts of inquest testimony, witness reports and suspect arrests.

## THE POLICE AND THE PRESS

The police, justly or unjustly, come in for a large share of the blame of these undiscovered crimes. It is true that Whitechapel is densely populated and difficult to cover, but it is also true that under anything like intelligent police management such a quartette of openly committed murders could hardly have occurred. One thing is absolutely certain, and that is that murderers will always escape with the ease that now characterizes their escape in London until the police authorities adopt a different attitude towards the Press. They treat the reporters of the newspapers, who are simply news-gatherers for the great mass of the people, with a snobbery that would be beneath contempt were it not senseless to an almost criminal degree. On Saturday they shut the reporters out of the mortuary; they shut them out of the house where the murder was done; the constable at the mortuary door lied to them; some of the inspectors at the offices seemed to wilfully mislead them; they denied information which would have done no harm to make public, and the withholding of which only tended to increase the public uneasiness over the affair.

Now if the people of London wish murderers detected they must have all this changed. In New York, where the escape of a murderer is as rare as it is common here, the reporters are far more active agents in ferreting out crime than the detectives. They are no more numerous or more intelligent than the reporters of London, but they are given every facility and opportunity to get all the facts, and no part of any case is hidden from them unless the detectives' plan makes it necessary to keep it a secret. The consequence is that a large number of sharp and experienced eyes are focussed upon every point of a case, a number of different theories develop which the reporters themselves follow up, and instances in which the detection of a criminal is due to a newspaper reporter are simply too common to create any particular comment.

Reporters are not prying individuals simply endeavouring to gratify their own curiosity. They are direct agents of the people who have a right to the news and a right to know what their paid servants the police and detectives are doing to earn the bread and butter for which the people are taxed. No properly accredited reporter[3] ever wishes to know or print anything that will thwart the ends of justice, but he does desire and is fully entitled to the fullest scope in examining all the details of the case. The sooner the police authorities appreciate and act on this the sooner the Whitechapel fiend will be captured and human life in London rendered a little more safe.[4]

It is not known why Sir Robert Anderson, after his 1901 retirement as Metropolitan Police Assistant Commissioner, would place on public record without proof that the murderer was detained and that Scotland Yard knew the identity of Jack the Ripper. It remains unclear why he would make such confident statements, now known to be at odds with his confidential official reports and other statements of investigating police. These influential and open statements were made without cause, except, perhaps, to deflate liberal press theories and disarm adversaries during periods of political upheaval.

Anderson single-handedly generated more conspiracy theories on Jack the Ripper than has any other author. It should also be noted that it is not Anderson's conservative affiliations or cultural and religious perspectives on crime that are a historical millstone on Jack the Ripper. It is his at least inadvertent evasions of Scotland Yard's investigation of the Whitechapel murders that are of direct concern. They have led to unfounded conspiracy theories and intrigues that submerge the facts of the case in late Victorian political partiality.

At the beginning of the new century the retired Anderson had become a self-appointed bulwark of the dying embers of the British Empire. Jack the Ripper, he believed, in his cage must remain. No one at the time of Anderson's remarks faulted Scotland Yard for its adequate and laudable efforts to protect the law-abiding community of the East End.

It could be said that his successor as Assistant Commissioner, Sir Melville Macnaghten, was also a factor in the failure to capture and bring to justice Jack the Ripper. But Macnaghten also qualified his official and public statements with the proviso that no firm evidence was brought upon any suspect. The marginalia in a copy of Anderson's memoirs by ex–Chief Inspector Donald Swanson,[5] taken as support for Anderson's Polish Jew theory, differ in detail with Macnaghten's 1894 memo naming the same suspect, Kosminski. The Swanson Marginalia and the Macnaghten Memorandum are not as mutually supportive as commonly believed because by 1894 no other related official reports are known to exist. None corroborate their views at a time that all three senior police officers were active at New Scotland Yard, Anderson as Metropolitan Police Assistant Commissioner and head of CID, Macnaghten as Chief Constable and Swanson as a Chief Inspector of CID.

The roots for developing dichotomy in facts and fiction on the portrayal of the Whitechapel murders of course lay in social reform, class hypocrisy and excesses of the late Victorian period from 1888 onwards. Though the conservative press kept up pretenses until they were unsustainable, the liberal press was asking why it took the murder of innocent women of the East End to expose squalid conditions of dire misery and poverty in the midst of the greatest metropolis of the British Empire. Leading the way of social reform on the back of the East End murders was a letter to the editor of *The Star* by George Bernard Shaw. An extract follows.

> Private enterprise has succeeded where socialism failed. While we conventional Social Democrats were wasting our time on education, agitation, and organization, some independent genius has taken the matter in hand, and by simply murdering and disembowelling four women, converted the proprietary press to an inept sort of communism. The moral is not a pretty one, and the Insurrectionists, the Dynamitards, the Invincibles, and the extreme left of the Anarchist party will not be slow to draw it. "Humanity, political science, economics, and religion," they will say, "are all rot; the one argument that touches your lady and gentleman is the knife."[6]

T.P. O'Connor, an Irish MP in the House of Commons, wrote a preamble to Shaw's letter. It was inconvenient for the conservatives in power during the murders of Jack the Ripper, as the following extract shows.

> But we willingly give Mr. Shaw the opportunity of ventilating his ideas; first, because we are in favor of free discussion; and secondly, because though we may not accept his remedies, we sympathize largely with the protest he makes against the fashion in which some of our contemporaries have treated the Whitechapel murders. His revolt against the gush and the cant which are now appearing in certain aristocratic journals, is timely and called for. These journals, which are now calling upon the West [London] to do its duty to the East, are the very journals, as Mr. Shaw points out, which but a few months ago were applauding Sir Charles Warren as warmly and enthusiastically as though

he were another Mr. Balfour. In the House of Commons, and still more in the drawing-rooms of the West-end, gilded youths and Primrose matrons were pluming their feathers on the spirited way in which the mob had been taught to conduct itself; and after the triumphant reply of Mr. Matthews in the House of Commons, and the splendid majority — largely made up of men calling themselves Liberals — all the reactionaries were congratulating themselves on the excellent results of a policy of coercion in London, as well as in Ireland.[7] On these gratulations come four hideous and squalid tragedies, and at once the same society, that was exultant with class triumph, has grown pale with class terror, and follows with babbling, childish, unctuous proposals — as much a remedy for the state of things revealed as the buns of the French lady for the starvation of the French revolutionaries. We may ask why it required these murders to call attention to the state of the poor at all? The deaths of these unhappy women certainly call aloud for vengeance, and the officials through whose incompetence such things are possible, will be called by-and-bye to a heavy account.[8]

Victorian socialists and religious progressives seemed to agree on the portrayal of Jack the Ripper as an avenger of dire East End conditions. This had its roots in the Fellowship of the New Life movement, founded in 1883.[9] The Fabian Society[10] was born of the New Life movement in 1884 and included such luminaries as George Bernard Shaw, Annie Besant and science fiction author H.G. Wells. Soon after, in 1913, a novel by Marie Belloc Lowndes, *The Lodger*, was published.

Sir Melville Macnaghten, had noted reading Lowndes's novel in his memoirs:

Only last autumn I was very much interested in a book entitled The Lodger which set forth in vivid colors what the Whitechapel murderer's life might have been while dwelling in London lodgings. The talented authoress portrayed him as a religious enthusiast, gone crazy over the belief that he was predestined to slaughter a certain number of unfortunate women, and that he had been confined in a criminal lunatic asylum and had escaped therefrom. I do not think that there was anything of religious mania about the real Simon Pure, nor do I believe that he had ever been detained in an asylum, nor lived in lodgings.[11]

The response to Anderson's remarks on Jack the Ripper, including his admission to writing the 1887 "Parnellism and Crime" articles for *The Times*, was swift from politicians, immigration representatives and journalists.[12] It was reported that "Dr. Forbes Winslow issued the following with reference to the "Jack the Ripper" murders, interest in which was revived by the published statements of Sir Robert Anderson and Mr. George Kebbell."[13] Kebbell was the solicitor of a "poor demented Irish [medical] student," William Grant. Kebbell stated in the *Pall Mall Gazette* on April 15, 1910, that Anderson was mistaken and that his client, now dead, was Jack the Ripper. Grant is generally known by his alias, "Grainger," which

***The Lodger: A Story of the London Fog*** was released in 1927, and is loosely based on Jack the Ripper. Directed by Alfred Hitchcock (courtesy ITV Global Entertainment).

was published in the *Pall Mall Gazette*. The *Gazette* was the only source to use it. The court record shows the suspect was named Grant.

Dr. Forbes Winslow was a specialist in insanity who had swamped Scotland Yard with "opinions that the murderer is a homicidal lunatic" after the murder of Mary Kelly on November 9, 1888. He was also prepared to place his services at the government's disposal.[14] A letter he wrote to the *Pall Mall Gazette* was published on April 19, 1910. It disputed Anderson and Kebbell, and took up the cause of Grant's defense. Contrary to Kebbell's claims, Grant was alive.

Grant was first mentioned as a Ripper suspect in the *Pall Mall Gazette* of May 7, 1895, which included a rare interview with Chief Inspector Donald Swanson: "Mr. Swanson believed the crimes to have been the work of a man who is now dead." The report goes on to outline the investigation of Grant's antecedents in relation to the Whitechapel murders and notes that he was brought to the attention of the Royal Irish Constabulary as he was "known to associate with loose women, and had been frequently stripped and robbed by them." Grant was charged and convicted to ten years' penal servitude for feloniously wounding Alice Graham near Buck's Row. Though Buck's Row was the scene of the first Ripper murder seven years previously, no evidence to support Grant as a suspect for the Whitechapel murders could be proved.

Nevertheless, the 1895 report also noted that "there is one person whom the police believe to have actually seen the Whitechapel murderer with a woman a few minutes before that woman's dissected body was found in the street. That person is stated to have identified Grant as the man he then saw. But obviously identification after so cursory a glance, and after the lapse of so long an interval, could not be reliable; and the inquiries were at length pulled up in a cul-de-sac. We have not given this statement with any view of holding a brief against Grant."[15] The woman's dissected body was that of Catherine Eddowes, murdered on September 30, 1888, and the witness, Joseph Lawende, could not attest to the accuracy of his sighting of a man with the victim minutes before.

There was always some room for the lighter side of Jack the Ripper during the Edwardian period. The *Penny Illustrated Paper*, affectionately known as *P.I.P.*, ran a regular political satire feature. In 1910 one was titled, "Private and Confidential. Some Unauthorized Peeps Into the Letter-Bags of the Week":

To Inspector Dew, Canada, From Dr. Forbes Winslow, Hampstead.

Dear Inspector,

Pardon my taking this opportunity of crowing over you. You and I are interested in criminals. You think you are very clever in your search for Crippen. My great interest in life is "Jack the Ripper," who is a kind of a bee in my bonnet, and whom for many years I have been tracking.

But note this difference between us. With all your good fortune you will only capture one Crippen, while through a long and honorable career I have tracked down at least fifty real and original Jack the Rippers, and could lay my hands on a dozen at the present moment if only the absurd police would arrest them. Come and see me when you get back. I believe I have again located John. —Yours, with best wishes, FORBES WINSLOW.[16]

To Sir Henry Smith, Ex-Commissioner of [City] Police, From Sir Robert Anderson, K.C.B., Late Head Of Criminal Investigation Department.

Dear Smith, —

Your volume of reminiscences is very interesting, especially where you explain how the police didn't capture Jack the Ripper.

But take warning. We Scotland Yard men have given some hard knocks in our time, and the people we dealt with have still a little kick in them.

Keep to Ripper stories, and the worse you will do will be to make Dr. Forbes Winslow rush into print. Don't tell your other doings, as you may get into a mess like I did when I told the secret history of the Parnell Commission.— Yours truly, R. ANDERSON.[17]

The P.I.P. also covered serious crime subjects for a general readership. It reported the murder of Mrs. Charlton and compared details with those of the Whitechapel murders. The report is a useful outline of the official police view on the motive at the time. It shows hardening of assumptions that the Whitechapel murderer was motivated by sexual perversion two decades after the events. The real prospect that Jack the Ripper had targeted prostitutes as ready victims or killed for personal or public shock value contradicts the sexual characterization that pervades factual and fictional portrayals of the murders. As shown below, the *P.I.P.* reports suggest that confusion about the motive of Jack the Ripper resulted in vague theories.

It should be understood that, in extreme cases, the sadistic, or masochistic, act is usually unaccompanied by any desire to indulge the normal sexual instinct. The sadist begins by finding pleasure in tantalising and annoying, this propensity being, as a rule, accompanied with more or less normal sexual desire. But as the impulse to injure becomes more acute so the individual becomes less passionate, until actual sexual passion is replaced by an uncontrollable mania to stab, to strangle, to kill, and, finally, to mutilate.

It is this apparent absence of actual passion which has caused such general misinterpretation of the motives which impel sexual maniacs to crime. The police, until the matter was made clear to them by those who had made a special study of the sexual forms of mania, were wont to confess that they were utterly at a loss to discover the motives which impelled the notorious Jack the Ripper to committal of his frightful deeds.

By some he was declared to be a moral imbecile; but imbecile is scarcely the term one would use for a man who defied all the efforts and vigilance exerted to capture him with such consummate skill; on the contrary, it was his mental ability which aided him to accomplish and then to escape the penalty.

The revulsion of feeling which almost invariably follows the gratification of a maniacal passion expressed itself in him, not in any hysterical display of remorse, as is usually the case with degenerates of this description, but in a kind of bravado which prompted him to leave behind some intimation that the crime had been committed by him.

The case of Jack the Ripper is cited merely to show to what awful extremes the sexual pervert may go. And it is the brutal manner of the murder of Mrs. Charlton which would suggest the probability that the crime was done in a similar transport of uncontrollable frenzy on the part of the murderer.[18]

If the inundation of Scotland Yard with theories from sleuths such as Forbes Winslow was not enough (Winslow was one of the first to propose that Jack the Ripper was a high society gentleman), the management of police reports was intensely consuming. As ex–Chief Inspector Frederick George Abberline, in charge of East End detective inquiries on the murders, recalled in a 1903 press interview "We made out no fewer than 1,600 sets of papers respecting our investigations."[19] Correspondence with the Home Office was equally daunting. With the advent of technological advances such as the telegraph, Jack the Ripper theories were promoted at an ever-advancing rate.[20]

While the House of Commons in 1910 was hotly debating censure of Anderson for his unauthorized public disclosures and threatening to suspend his police pension, crime journalist and author George R. Sims, a friend of Macnaghten, was receiving intriguing letters on Jack the Ripper via regular post. The letters were in response to Sims's article on the Whitechapel murders for a section in the *Lloyd's Weekly News* titled "My Criminal Museum."[21]

They confirmed that as a new face of Jack the Ripper was emerging, alternative theories and suspicions had darkly developed simultaneously.

One of the letters to Sims dated September 24, 1907, by Ernest Crawford, printed two days after his article on Jack the Ripper, reflects on previous theories and the statements to police given by Dr. Roslyn D'Onston — but from the point of view of past *Pall Mall Gazette* editor W.T. Stead. It is the earliest known written account that contains elements of the story of Vittoria Cremers. Apart from the 1888 police statements and the *Pall Mall Gazette* article of D'Onston's "inventions," the letter otherwise indicates that originally they were Stead's theories.

These fictional elements were found later in various print versions that had reemerged in the 1958 O'Donnell manuscript. Sims does not appear to be taken by the conjectures of Crawford's letter, as he is known to have favored Macnaghten's and the general police view that the killer had committed suicide. Sims later requested details on a "Dr. D," generally assumed to be suspect Montague Druitt, noted in a 1913 letter from ex–Special Branch head Chief Inspector John George Littlechild. It is possible that the reference was to Dr. D'Onston, of whom Littlechild had not heard, as his comments six years later suggest.

Sept 24th 1907
2, Rosehill Terrace,
Larkhall, Bath.

Dear Sir,

I was much interested in your theories respecting the identity of Jack the Ripper in your recent article in Lloyd's. The map called to my mind a curious theory of the crimes which was held by an acquaintance of mine, a man well known in reform movements and as an editor of magazines and Journals who is now leaping into fame as an inventor. Mr. S as I will call him, told me that he believed that the outrages were instigated by the Jesuits who had reasons for getting foreign detectives into the London service, (you remember that the importation of foreign detectives was talked of at the time), the miscreant never passed through the cordon of police because in the center of the district was a Jesuit college in which he took refuge after his deeds. The Jesuits, according to Mr. S., left the sign of the cross on all their work and sure enough lines drawn from the points in your map make a fairly regular cross. I am afraid Mr. S's theory must be regarded as a wild speculation but it is curious nevertheless. I am not aware that there is any Jesuit religious house in that particular locality. Another theory by the same gentleman is more plausible; you remember that the cut in the throat of the victims gave the investigators the idea that the murderer was left handed. Mr. S. thought that the Ripper had induced the women to allow connection from behind, a very convenient position for concealing his purpose and using the knife effectively. I see you make no mention of the Ripper letters which caused so much sensation at the time. I do not think that they had any connection with the crimes and probably you are of the same opinion.

You are welcome to use any matter in this letter I have only marked the envelope "private" to save it from being opened by a lady clerk or amanuensis.

I am Sir,
Yours Faithfully,
Ernest Crawford.[22]

The details in the letter from Ernest Crawford to George Sims of "Mr. S." are without doubt attributable to W.T. Stead. The reference "Mr. S. thought that the Ripper had induced the women to allow connection from behind" was noted in the statement made to Scotland Yard on December 26, 1888, by D'Onston. He added further references to Stead and submitted a letter on his behalf to Inspector Thomas Roots. D'Onston stated, "I was positively informed by the Editor of the '*Pall Mall Gazette*' that the murdered woman last operated on had been sodomized."[23] Though no medical evidence existed for Stead's sensational conjecture, the reference and theory do not appear in any other known source. Further mention of Jesuits and foreign detectives, a conspiracy theory also found with the Victorian Theosophical Society in London, was one of Stead's stories on Jack the Ripper. He published a religious extremist theory at least as early as September 19, 1888, in his newspaper. Stead also wrote a scathing attack on Italian Catholicism after retiring from the *Pall Mall Gazette*, titled *The Pope and the New Era*.[24]

Apart from police memoirs, detective fiction[25] was another genre that grew from the Whitechapel murders in the early 1900s. Some found subversive political intrigues in the spy novels of Joseph Conrad[26] and William Le Queux. Fiction about Jack the Ripper at the time served as commentary on the seeming official reticence of Scotland Yard and the Home Office. What could not be said openly on the police investigation of Jack the Ripper could always be fictionalized or fabricated.

In the author's note to *The Secret Agent*,[27] Joseph Conrad referred to a work of Sir Robert Anderson as a source for the novel:

> I came upon a book which as far as I know had never attained any prominence, the rather summary recollections of an Assistant Commissioner of Police, an obviously able man with a strong religious strain in his character who was appointed to his post at the time of the dynamite outrages in London, away back in the eighties. The book was fairly interesting, very discreet of course; and I have by now forgotten the bulk of its contents. It contained no revelations, it ran over the surface agreeably, and that was all. I won't even try to explain why I should have been arrested by a little passage of about seven lines, in which the author (I believe his name was Anderson) reproduced a short dialogue held in the Lobby of the House of Commons after some unexpected anarchist outrage, with the Home Secretary. I think it was Sir William Harcourt then. He was very much irritated and the official was very apologetic. The phrase, among the three which passed between them, that struck me most was Sir W. Harcourt's angry sally: "All that's very well. But your idea of secrecy over there seems to consist of keeping the Home Secretary in the dark." Characteristic enough of Sir W. Harcourt's temper but not much in itself. There must have been, however, some sort of atmosphere in the whole incident because all of a sudden I felt myself stimulated.

NEW STORY OF "JACK THE RIPPER"
RASPUTIN DOCUMENT CHALLENGED
SPECIAL TO "EMPIRE NEWS"

> In his book, "Things I Know," published this week — see page eight — Mr. William Le Queux claims to have revealed the actual identity of Jack the Ripper. He cites a Rasputin manuscript to the effect that the amazing criminal who terrorized London was a mad Russian doctor sent here by the Secret Police to annoy and baffle Scotland Yard.
>
> He gives the name of this doctor as Alexander Pedachenko, who, when in London, lived in Westmorland-road, Walworth. The "revelation" has opened up controversy, and it can be said that the evidence in favor of the Russian doctor theory is not convincingly strong. The theory is directly challenged by an Empire News student of criminology, who writes: "Every head of police knows that Jack the Ripper died in Morris Plains Lunatic Asylum in 1902."[28]
>
> And in favor of the Russian doctor theory Sir Robert Anderson, who was [Assistant] Commissioner of the Police at the time, always maintained the view that the murders were the work of a medical man.[29]

In the wake of police ambiguity on Jack the Ripper, press theories were simply made up. Senior police assurances did not clear up matters, and general interest in the Whitechapel murders remained a mystery. William Le Queux, an Anglo-French journalist and author of spy novels, had with his theory of the Russian Pedachenko stayed influential until the release of official files discounted his claim. The "Empire News student of criminology" cited in the extract has not been identified. Bernard O'Donnell was known to write for the *Empire News* and had, of course, an interest in Jack the Ripper, so it is conceivable that he challenged Le Queux's autobiography.

Two years later, O'Donnell was developing a story on Jack the Ripper and the blood-encrusted neckties supposedly found in a tin box of the British occultist Aleister Crowley. An acquaintance of Crowley, a sometime criminal and artist's model named Betty May Sedgewick,[30] had stayed with her husband Raoul Loveday at Crowley's "Abbey of Thelema," a house in Sicily. Loveday died there. Sedgewick apparently blamed Crowley for her husband's death and gave retaliatory interviews to an outraged British press.

Betty May claimed to have read Crowley's unpublished autobiography with the D'Onston Ripper story, but the real source for the account was Vittoria Cremers while in England in the early 1900s.

Aleister Crowley[31] was a product of late Victorian society and the issue of wealthy puritanical parents. He led a protected upper-class life but took an interest in the Whitechapel murders from an early age. Crowley was merely a lad of 13 in 1888. The earliest mention of his attention to the crimes is with the stories of Vittoria Cremers, whom he met in about 1912.[32] In one of the last articles he wrote,[33] Crowley claimed to have known Bernard O'Donnell and Ripper suspect Roslyn D'Onston. In this piece he also expanded on Cremers's theories and drew on his earlier Jack the Ripper newspaper articles.[34]

O'Donnell confirmed knowing Crowley and both were associated with the same literature and press establishments. As Crowley's 1943 article is close in content to O'Donnell's, it is likely that the crime reporter had access to Crowley's unpublished 1929 notes in the early 1930s, before the complete autobiography with the Ripper reference was published in 1969. However, it is not clear if he knew D'Onston, as he claimed. Cremers had reignited Crowley's fascination with her dramatic story about a suspect brought to the attention of Scotland Yard. On May 24, 1922, Crowley approached the publisher of D'Onston's 1904 *Patristic Gospels*, Grant Richards, with proposals for his autobiography and a novel, *The Diary of a Drug Fiend*.[35] Neither mentioned any discussion of D'Onston as Jack the Ripper.

Crime author Richard Whittington-Egan noted a supporting entry by Crowley in his copy of Betty May's 1929 autobiography, *Tiger Woman*.[36] As May claimed she had read Crowley's unpublished autobiography and the Ripper story during the early 1920s, thus she would be the first to publish Cremers's story. Her account was also serialized earlier,[37] apparently ghostwritten by O'Donnell as he noted details about the D'Onston theory. Crowley intended to release his version of Cremers's story but could not include the Ripper section in the 1929 edition.

**Betty May first published the Jack the Ripper story of Vittoria Cremers in serialized articles in 1925 (ghost-written by crime reporter Bernard O'Donnell). They were collated and published in her 1929 autobiography, *Tiger Woman*.**

Aleister Crowley's mother, a strict religious puritan, reportedly dubbed him "the Beast" (courtesy the O.T.O).

The complete six volumes of *The Confessions of Aleister Crowley* were published in 1969 though he had the Ripper story by 1929 and developed it until 1943. Betty May was likely to have met Cremers and alerted her to Crowley's intended release of her Jack the Ripper story. It is these early versions of the story of Cremers, Crowley, and Betty May that O'Donnell would later collate and expand for his unpublished manuscript completed in 1958. They become the secondary sources on Roslyn D'Onston as a suspect for the Whitechapel murders.

Vittoria Cremers was linked with Crowley during the Edwardian period and became a member of his early occult order, Mysteria Mystica Maxima (M.M.M.), the British branch of the German Ordo Templi Orientis (O.T.O) cofounded by Theodor Reuss. Cremers was the M.M.M.'s first secretary and treasurer. She fell out with Crowley over alleged embezzlement of funds, an accusation for which he had printed up wanted posters. The notice included the only known sketch of Cremers as she appears to have destroyed her personal papers and photographs.[38] The M.M.M. had offices at 93 Regent Street and later at 33 Avenue Studios and 76 Fulham Road, South Kensington. In 1912 Cremers met there artists Olivia Haddon and Nina Hamnett, poet Victor Neuburg and Ted Hayter-Preston, journalist and literary editor later for the *Sunday Referee*. Hayter-Preston had tipped off O'Donnell about Cremers's Jack the Ripper story in about 1929 and probably introduced her to him. Nina Hamnett would later attend the social breakfast parties where Walter Sickert would tell his Jack the Ripper lodger story. Sculptor Jacob Epstein, who fashioned Betty May and a lewd statue of Oscar Wilde in France, joined them. Aleister Crowley, who idolized Wilde, was the star to which the dramatist personae gravitated at either Paris or London's Café Royal.[39]

When Crowley wrote to Cremers in 1913 after she left his association for New York, he confirmed the thefts but added, "The stereos of Book 4 were sent to N[ew] Y[ork] in cartons with your written articles some little time before you came over. I am sorry to hear you have been so ill, and hope you are now quite well again and ready to return to duty." On the same day he wrote to Cremers, September 4, 1913, he also enlarged on the issue of missing stereos of his manuscript to an unknown American correspondent:

> I am very sorry to have been away when you came to England, as I very much wanted to see you about various things. In particular the question of those stereos. They were sent over to America at the request of Mrs. Cremers before she left America, and I understood from her that you would

undertake her work while she was over helping us. I need hardly say that we had no wish to involve you in any expense and would gladly have refunded you any sums which you might have dispensed on our account.... At present I am faced with the alternative of having these valuable plates destroyed and I hope that you will take delivery at once and save them. As soon as I come over to America I will see about having the book published though I should certainly be very much obliged if you would try and get a publisher to issue it. I think he would be likely to do so, as he would only be put to the cost of printing from the plates, and as I should be quite prepared to forego any royalties until he himself has recouped his expenses.[40]

On vacation in the American South during the winter of 1917, Crowley began a novel called *Moonchild*. It was completed the following spring in New York but not published until 1929.[41] It gave vivid descriptions of a character named Cremers. In his autobiography Crowley gave further details on the novel. "Most of the characters are real people whom I have known and many of the incidents are taken from experience."[42] However, Moonchild was prefaced with a diplomatic disclaimer. "Need I add that, as the book itself demonstrates beyond all doubt, all persons and incidents are purely the figments of a disordered imagination?" Crowley's novel is set in the Edwardian period and is a rare insight into Cremers's personality.

> Her squat stubborn figure was clad in rusty-black clothes, a man's except for the skirt; it was surmounted by a head of unusual size, and still more unusual shape, for the back of the skull was entirely flat, and the left frontal lobe much more developed than the right; one could have thought that it had been deliberately knocked out of shape, since nature, fond, it may be, of freaks, rarely pushes asymmetry to such a point. There would have been more than idle speculation in such a theory; for she was the child of hate, and her mother had in vain attempted every violence against her before her birth.
> The face was wrinkled parchment, yellow and hard; it was framed in short, thick hair, dirty white in color; and her expression denoted that the utmost cunning and capacity were at the command of her rapacious instincts. But her poverty was no indication that they had served her; and those primitive qualities had in fact been swallowed up in the results of their disappointment. For in her eye raved bitter a hate of all things, born of the selfish envy which regarded the happiness of any other person as an outrage and affront upon her. Every thought in her mind was a curse — against God, against man, against love, or beauty, against life itself. She was a combination of the witch-burner with the witch; an incarnation of the spirit of Puritanism, from its sourness to its sexual degeneracy and perversion.[43]

Crowley also recorded her manner of speech:

> Now, look 'e here. We gotta get these guys. An' we gotta get them where they live. You been hitting at their strong point. Now I tell you something. That girl she live five years with Lavinia King, durn her! I see that bright daughter of Terpsichore on'y five minutes, but she didn't leave one moral hangin' on me, no, sir. Now see here, big chief, you been beatin' the water for them fish, an', natural, off they goes. For the land's sake! Look 'e here, I gotta look after this business. An' all I need is just one hook an' line, an' a pailful o' bait, an' ef I don' land her, never trus' me no more. Ain't I somebody, all ways? Didn' I down ole Blavatzsky [sic]? Sure I did. An' ain't this like eatin' pie after that?[44]

In 1923, alarmist articles appeared in the tabloid press about the horrors of a debauched lifestyle and the dangers of Crowley's brand of black magic as seen by Betty May in Italy.[45] Crowley was becoming somewhat of a bugbear to conservative English society, and Cremers's Jack the Ripper story was useful ammunition in the war of words. The death of Betty May's husband on Crowley's Italian commune and other accusations of impropriety made Betty May an instant celebrity. The papers took up her cause and investigated her claims for possible submission to New Scotland Yard and the Home Office.[46] Crowley had been brought to the attention of the police previously for alleged pornographic and other offences.[47] However, as Crowley was a Cambridge scholar recruited to wartime British secret service who had family diplomatic connections to ex–Prime Minister Lord Salisbury, nothing came of the uproar. Later in the 1930s, the dirt was dredged up again with a press scare featuring Jack the Ripper, Bernard O'Donnell, and Roslyn D'Onston.

Crowley's autobiography added further descriptions of Vittoria Cremers and his version of her Jack the Ripper account. He also counted the number of Ripper victims as seven, the same as in D'Onston's December 1, 1888, *Pall Mall Gazette* article, which he likely read. The account is also notable as a close rendering of what Bernard O'Donnell would develop. It shows that the theory of D'Onston as Jack the Ripper was originally based on a blend of Cremers's anecdotal sources and the supernatural extrapolations of Crowley and O'Donnell. It was a dramatic story, provided commentary on the feuds of the Theosophical Society, and it implicated rivals in a serial murder case with a suspect brought to the attention of Scotland Yard. Crowley noted his recollections with the following brief extracts, which in their unpublished form were available to Bernard O'Donnell and Jean Overton Fuller.

Aleister Crowley in a photograph taken at Trinity College, Cambridge. His fascination with Jack the Ripper grew after he met Vittoria Cremers in 1912 (courtesy the O.T.O.).

Laylah had spent some weeks in New York with "Two Little Brides." I had given her introductions to various correspondents of mine in the city; people interested in my work. One of these demands attention, both for her own sake as one of the most remarkable characters I have ever known and for the influence of her intervention on my affairs.

Her name was Vittoria Cremers. She claimed to be the bastard of a wealthy English Jew and to have married a knavish Austrian baron. She was an intimate friend of Mabel Collins, authoress of "*The Blossom and the Fruit,*" the novel which has left so deep a mark upon my early ideas about Magick. In 1912 she was in her fifties. Her face was stern and square, with terribly intense eyes from which glared an expression of indescribable pain and hopeless horror. Her hair was bobbed and dirty white, her dress severely masculine save the single concession of a short straight skirt. Her figure was sturdy and her gait determined though awkward. Laylah found her in a miserable room on 176th Street [New York] or thereabouts. Pitifully poor, she had not been able to buy "*Liber 777*" and had therefore worked week after week copying in the Astor Library. She impressed Laylah as an ernest seeker and a practical business woman. She professed the utmost devotion to me and proposed to come to England and put the work of the Order on a sound basis. I thought the idea was excellent, paid her passage to England and established her as a manageress. Technically, I digress; but I cannot refrain from telling her favorite story. She boasted of her virginity and of the intimacy of her relations with Mabel Collins, with whom she lived a long time. Mabel had however divided her favors with a very strange man whose career had been extraordinary. He had been an officer in a cavalry regiment, a doctor, and I know not how many other things in his time. He was now in desperate poverty and depended entirely on Mabel Collins for his daily bread. This man claimed to be an advanced Magician, boasting of many mysterious powers and even occasionally demonstrating the same.

At this time London was agog with the exploits of Jack the Ripper. One theory of the motive of the murderer was that he was performing an Operation to obtain the Supreme Black Magical Power.

The seven women had to be killed so that their seven bodies formed a "Calvary cross of seven points" with its head to the west. The theory was that after killing the third or the fourth, I forget which, the murderer acquired the power of invisibility, and this was confirmed by the fact that in one case a policeman heard the shrieks of the dying woman and reached her before life was extinct, yet she lay in a *cul-de-sac*, with no possible exit save to the street; and the policeman saw no signs of the assassin, thought he was patrolling outside, expressly on the lookout.[48]

Miss Collins' friend took great interest in these murders. He discussed them with her and Cremers on several occasions. He gave them imitations of how the murderer might have accomplished his task without arousing the suspicion of his victims until the last moment. Cremers objected that his escape must have been a risky matter, because of his habit of devouring certain portions of the ladies before leaving them. What about the blood on his collar and shirt? The lecturer demonstrated that any gentleman in evening dress had merely to turn up the collar of a light overcoat to conceal any traces of his supper.

Time passed! Mabel tired of her friend, but did not dare to get rid of him because he had a packet of compromising letters written by her. Cremers offered to steal these from him. In the man's bedroom was a tin uniform case which he kept under the bed to which he attached it by cords. Neither of the women had ever seen this open and Cremers suspected that he kept these letters in it. She got him out of the way for a day by a forged telegram, entered the room, untied the cords and drew the box from under the bed. To her surprise it was very light, as if empty. She proceeded nevertheless to pick the lock and open it. There were no letters; there was nothing in the box, but seven white evening dress ties, all stiff and black with clotted blood!

...I left a book of signed cheques in her [Cremers] charge; I allowed her access to my private papers. I gave no sign that I saw how she was corrupting the loyalty of Laylah and making mischief all round. Presently, at the end of 1913, she got influenza. I went to visit her unexpectedly; there, on the table by her bed, was a memorandum showing unmistakably that she had embezzled large sums of money by fraudulent manipulation of the aforesaid cheques. I failed to conceal from her that I had seen and understood, but I continued to act towards her with unvarying kindness and continued to trust her absolutely. It was too much for her! She had hated me from the first, as she had hated Blavatsky, and vowed to ruin me as she had ruined my great predecessor; and now, when she had robbed me and betrayed me at every turn, I had not turned a hair. The consciousness that her hate was impotent was too much for her to endure. She developed an attack of meningitis and was violently insane for six weeks, at the end of which time she melted away to hide her shame in Wales, where she supposed sensibly enough that she would find sympathetic society in thieves and traitors after her own heart.[49] I understand in fact that she is still there.[50]

O'Donnell interviewed Cremers in about 1930 when a spate of Jack the Ripper newspaper articles, books and police memoirs emerged. It was conjectured that she recorded her account in a series of diaries or memoirs from 1888 to 1891 and gave them to O'Donnell. No proof of this exists. From O'Donnell's unpublished manuscript, it is clear that he collated anecdotal accounts on D'Onston as the Ripper. He enlarged upon Cremers's, May's and Crowley's earlier versions of the theory. This era also saw the release of notable books on Jack the Ripper by Leonard Matters in 1929, Edward T. Woodhall in 1935, and William Stewart in 1939.

Meanwhile, the Receiver for the Metropolitan Police District and Metropolitan Police Courts from 1919 and at the Home Office from 1905 to 1918, Sir J.F. Moylan, issued details about the case. He gave further official background to the Whitechapel murders derived from previous police accounts.

The dynamite campaign practically ceased after 1885, but 1887, the Jubilee year, was full of anxieties for the C.I.D. and its special branch. Next year, 1888, came the series of fiendish murders in Whitechapel popularly attributed to "Jack the Ripper," a name that first appeared as the signature to a bogus letter which was treated as possibly authentic and given undue publicity by Scotland Yard. Notwithstanding the peculiar character of these murders, both as regards locality and victims, there was a general scare, many believing that Satan, or perhaps Cain, was revisiting the Earth. Feeling ran very high against Scotland Yard and the C.I.D. for their failure to lay hands on the murderer, who, it is now certain, escaped justice by committing suicide at the end of 1888.

Interviews of retired police officers who had Ripper stories were especially sought after. Pierre Girouard, a retired officer of the French police, appeared to support the concerns of Sir Robert Anderson about the legal restrictions on British police in detaining a suspect. In a 1929 article Girouard blended several Jack the Ripper theories.[51] He recounted the story of Vittoria Cremers and claimed to have met her, but with significant variations from other accounts: "She reported her discovery to the society of which she was a member, or rather to the chiefs of this society whose address you will not find in any telephone directory, and which has been disbanded since, but whose members probably belong to other organizations." Author Melvin Harris believed Girouard is referring to Anthony Comstock's Society for the Suppression of Vice, but as she was in London during the murders, it likely refers to the Theosophical Society.

After a summary of Cremers's D'Onston story, Girouard reveals that the suspect is Norwegian seaman Fogelma, who believed he was Jack the Ripper. Fogelma's story had been published in the *Empire News* on October 23, 1923, with Le Queux's theories on Pedachenko. Girouard concluded his article: "Personally, I think that the Baroness's [Cremers] tale is perfectly true. The CID story is that the murderer committed suicide and that his body was found in the Thames, but that may have been put out simply to allay public alarm. The police cannot always make public what they know and what they do not know. If Scotland Yard had been given a little more rope in the time of the outrages, I have no doubt that they would have narrowed down their investigations and ultimately caught the guilty party."

During the early 1930s, Aleister Crowley was the subject of highly publicized press attacks, lawsuits, and bankruptcy proceedings. A proposed lecture at Oxford University on Gilles de Rais was banned and in 1933, he began action in the Vacation Court, Chancery Division, against publisher Constable and Co. Ltd and others. It was dubbed the "black magic libel case." The lawsuit involved the book *The Laughing Torso*, by artist Nina Hamnett.[52] She was a close friend of Vittoria Cremers, Walter Sickert, and Betty May, who was summoned as a witness with testimony that included writing of her 1929 book, *Tiger Woman: My Story*, which contained her Ripper account. Crowley lost the case but acrimony smouldered. It was during this time that O'Donnell interviewed both Cremers and Crowley while conducting further research on Roslyn D'Onston. The question arises: Did Cremers agree to press interviews and to give O'Donnell her story in retaliation to both Crowley and D'Onston's memory with the support of Nina Hamnett and Betty May?

In 1935, Crowley again became embroiled over a rejected article with the managing editor of the *Sunday Referee*, Mark Goulden, and its literary editor, Ted Hayter-Preston, who had told O'Donnell about Cremers's Jack the Ripper story. This episode also resulted in a suit by Crowley for alleged breach of contract, and it prompted even more news items about Jack the Ripper. Hayter Preston, who had also been associated with Crowley's M.M.M. from 1912, remarked to Goulden on the court steps, "I wish I had nothing to do with this ghastly case. Didn't you see that Crowley was trying to put a 'hex' on the judge in court and now that he has lost the case he'll put a curse on us."[53]

In a review of a 1930 biography on Crowley by P.R. Stephenson,[54] Victor Neuburg, who had become poetry editor for the *Sunday Referee*, suggested that press vilification of Crowley was an expression of English "mob rule." If Crowley could be promoted as larger than life by awkward tabloid machinery, what could they do with Jack the Ripper? Neuburg wrote:

At one time we knew Aleister Crowley pretty well, as is plain from this book; and though in some respects he was perhaps "not quite nice to know," as the slang phrase goes, we do not think that it is quite fair to charge him with murder, cannibalism, black magical practices, moral aberrations, treachery, druggery; as is the custom among the cunninger and more degraded jackals of Fleet Street. We know something of journalists, but we know very few members of the newspaper craft who would not sell themselves for twenty guineas down if it were quite "safe."[55]

Author Jean Overton Fuller had met Cremers in the early 1930s and recorded the social occasion where the hostess introduced them.

"You may find her rather frightening. She is very downright. This is her seventieth birthday and she hasn't been out of her own house and grounds for ten years." A young man whom I had not seen before, but who was apparently a reporter on the Sunday Graphic, said, "Do you think I could ask her to give me a story about Jack the Ripper?"... She was dressed in black, and had white hair which she wore cut short.... The young man from the Sunday Graphic came down the stairs and said to Cremers, "Might I have a few words conversation with you alone, before you go?" Astonished, she asked, "Why do you wish to speak with me alone?" He murmured something about Jack the Ripper. She drew herself up to her full height, looking even more imperious and threatening, and said, "Why do you wish to speak with me about Jack the Ripper?" He faltered something about "an interesting story." In a tone of inconceivable disgust, she asked, "Are you a newspaper reporter?" One could have thought she had said sewer-rat. Vicky [Victor Neuburg] had at first looked as puzzled as Cremers, but as he took in the situation a smile of delicious mischief broke out upon his face. He said, "Dear Cremers, you're at the mercy of the press!" He left her to it; and to my surprise she stepped back into Cyril Moore's room with her pursuer.[56]

The Jack the Ripper witch-hunt during this period was a captivating press story. Senior police statements that the killer had died or been incarcerated as a lunatic did not allay speculation and conspiracy theories. They did not solve the Whitechapel murders, the active investigation ceasing in 1892. Reminiscences by Scotland Yard officers on the Jack the Ripper investigation were becoming a genre in their own right. Jack the Ripper was all but developing into a fictional character.[57]

Bernard O'Donnell, however, was a respected Fleet Street crime reporter. He reported on cases heard at London's Central Criminal Court and the Old Bailey, and worked for over 25 years at the conservative *Empire News*, among others. His son Peter, author of the popular Modesty Blaise detective novels, retained his father's Jack the Ripper manuscript although his widow burned most of his papers. Peter O'Donnell produced the original for author Melvin Harris's works on Roslyn D'Onston, of which several copies have survived. Bernard appears to have been reserved about his life, so complete biographical details are scarce apart from the surviving works he left behind after his death in 1969 at the age of 86.

Bernard O'Donnell was a fairly prolific author and journalist. He wrote popular history books for American readers on the English court system. The *Harvard Law Review* noted that he worked as the "night news editor, Kemsley Newspapers" and was a reporter for the Sunday *Empire News*.[58] His most notable books were *The Old Bailey and its Trials, Cavalcade of Justice, The World's Worst Women, The Trials of Mr. Justice Avory, Crimes That Made News, Should Women Hang*, and *The World's Strangest Murders*.[59–65] His unpublished Jack the Ripper manuscript was begun in 1930, completed in 1958, and bore the title *Black Magic and Jack the Ripper (or alternatively) This Man Was Jack the Ripper*.

Donald McCormick, his fellow journalist, had published his influential *The Identity of Jack the Ripper* in 1959. If O'Donnell's work was published at the same time, it would have influenced later developments on the historical assessment of Jack the Ripper and the Whitechapel murders. O'Donnell was an experienced crime reporter with police contacts and an understanding of the state of research on the Whitechapel murders at that time. Crime authors Robin Odell and Richard Whittington-Egan both knew O'Donnell, and though they regarded him as an earnest reporter and personable character, they were not convinced of his conclusions on Jack the Ripper.

O'Donnell was also a personal confidant of Chief Constable Frederick Porter Wensley of New Scotland Yard. In 1931, Wensley published *Detective Days*,[66] a memoir about his period of service between early 1888 and 1929. *Time* magazine gave him a glowing but slightly exaggerated review on his retirement.

Aged 64, Chief Constable Wensley has been on the Force for 42 years. He joined it as an ordinary "bobby." He has left his mark upon the Chinese dens of Limehouse. the anarchists' haunts and crime slums of Shoreditch, Hackney and Wapping. There he learned to be fearless while carrying no gun (London "bobbies," the world's best, are forbidden firearms). From the very first he saw excitement. In 1888 the Whitechapel District of London was being terrorized by the murders of "Jack the Ripper." Suddenly in a great crowd of people a child or a young girl would be found murdered and mutilated with a knife. No one ever saw "Jack." The C. I. D. and Policeman Wensley gradually caught his accomplices but "Jack the Ripper" never was found. Timid English women still stiffen and pale when strange men address them in Whitechapel.[67]

Bernard O'Donnell began his unpublished manuscript with Wensley's account of the East End, which does not appear in *Detective Days*. Wensley endorsed O'Donnell's theory, indicating the esteem in which O'Donnell was held by senior New Scotland Yard officials. O'Donnell wrote:

To appreciate the extraordinary immunity from detection which Jack the Ripper enjoyed throughout his orgy of crime, it will be as well to set the scene of his activities in the Whitechapel area as it was in the year 1888.

To this end I cannot do better than quote my friend the late Fred Wensley, ex–Chief Constable of the Metropolitan Police Force, who at the time of the Ripper murders was a young police officer stationed at Leman Street Police Station, in the very heart of the murder area. He was also actively engaged in the investigations into the various crimes as they were committed.

We were discussing my story of the Ripper crimes in the garden of his home at Southgate, whither he retired after retirement from the Force. He agreed that mine was the only solution of the mystery which stood up to all the facts as he knew them, and I invited him to describe Whitechapel and its poverty-stricken inhabitants.

"Drab people, living drab lives, amid drab surroundings," was how he put it, and who should know better than this man who was on the spot at the time, engaged on daily or nightly patrol of the area in the course of duty.

"Whitechapel and its environs was little more than a warren of ill-lit narrow courts and dingy alleyways with a couple of main roads running through from East to West," he went on. "The pubs were open day and night, far into the early hours of the morning. There were no cinemas in those days at which the poor devils who lived there could seek temporary respite from their sordid surroundings; there was no wireless to relieve the tedium of their uneventful lives. Brawls, 'knifings,' robberies, and cries of 'murder' were of nightly occurrence; so frequent indeed that those who heard them took little or no notice. Their main relaxation was to creep from the shadows of their hovels in the labyrinth of musty courts into the garish lights of the gin palaces where they could obtain a 'half-quartern and two out' for a modest 2½d.

"Street lamps were few and far between, and the dim flicker of light they shed added an even more sinister aspect to the neighbourhood. Street fights were numerous among men and women alike in this web of squalor where vice of all kinds could not help but flourish..."

Such was the picture of Whitechapel drawn for me by the first man ever to rise from the ranks to become Chief Constable of the Metropolitan Police[68]; and, while Hitler's minions have demolished many of the fetid slums which disfigured this part of London, it still remains a district of narrow courts and dingy alleyways though the sinister atmosphere of seventy years ago has long since departed.[69]

The unpublished manuscript of Bernard O'Donnell as it was in 1958 consists of ten chapters and is summarized by Stewart P. Evans as follows:

Chapter One — "This Man Was Jack the Ripper."
Consists of 82 pages and includes accounts of the murders of Emma Smith, Martha Turner [Tabram], Nicholls [sic], Chapman, Stride, Eddowes, Kelly, Jackson, McKenzie and Coles. Sources he used included the Daily Telegraph, Pall Mall Gazette and The Times. He includes Arthur Diosy and "Our Society" and Ingleby Oddie. The black magic theme is introduced and D'Onston appears as early as page 56.

Chapter Two — "Ripper Theories Exploded."
Consists of 36 pages and includes the stories of Sir Robert Anderson, Major Arthur Griffiths, Sir Melville Macnaghten, Sir Basil Thomson, and Sir Charles Warren. It goes into the theories of Forbes Winslow, William Le Queux, Klosowski, R. J. Lees and the "Spiritualistic Circle," "Jill the Ripper" as per William Stewart, and "Mr. Stanley" Leonard Matters' theory.

Chapter Three — "The Ripper and Black Magic."
Consists of 24 pages where O'Donnell introduces the black magic theme. It includes the Pall Mall Gazette article and misidentifies the author as Lord Crawford [D'Onston's authorship would not be revealed until the publication of the official material], black magic, candles, the Hermetic Order of the Golden Dawn, Eliphas Levi, Necromancy, the significance of the Cross, The Patristic Gospels, Aleister Crowley, Wynn Westcott, Diosy again, the Order of the Silver Star, Madame Helena Petrova Blavatsky, Montague Summers, the Dagger, Hayter Preston, the Sunday Referee, Lucifer, the Theosophical Society and Mabel Collins.

Chapter Four — "Mrs. Cremers's Own Story."
Consists of 15 pages where O'Donnell gives the well-known Cremers's story of D'Onston, which includes Blavatsky, Mabel Collins, Archibald Keightley, Lucifer, Mrs. Heilman, the Southsea story, Rider Haggard, the Pompadour Cosmetique Company, African Magic and black magic.

Chapter Five — "The Story of Roslyn D'Onston."
Consists of 32 pages and includes Black Magic and Jack the Ripper, the Pall Mall Gazette, the "Real Origins of She," Slave Trade, Bulwer-Lytton, Obeeyah, Sube, Stead, The Lucifer article, Zanoni, Tautriadelta, Cremers, necromancy, The Patristic Gospels, Borderland, the Hermetic Lodge of Alexandria, Dr. Allan, Karl Hoffmann, the Pentagram, the dopple-ganger, the Evil Eye, Mr. Jacob of Simla, etc.

Chapter Six — "D'Onston the Man."
Consists of 44 pages and includes Baker Street, D'Onston, Collins, Cremers and the Pompadour Cosmetique Company, Black Magic, Blavatsky, Bulwer-Lytton, Zanoni, Borderland, Dweller on the Threshold, Eliphas Levi, Symbol of Solomon, California, Garibaldi, Pall Mall Gazette, the Evil Eye, Southsea, the story of Ada, Lucifer, origin from a yeoman family, Tautriadelta, Jack the Ripper, black magic candles, the East London Advertiser, Sir Max Pemberton, Pentagram, prostitutes, Keightley, A. P. Sinnett, the Theosophical Society, Tantrik Worship, D'Onston's family, the black ties story, Crowley, Betty May, Equinox, the Order of the Silver Star, etc.

Chapter Seven — "I Knew the Ripper."
Consists of 27 pages and includes Baker Street, the black ties, Jack the Ripper, Miller's Court, the Chinaman, the London Hospital, left handed man, Major Arthur Griffiths and Mysteries of Police and Crime, selected sites of murder, D'Onston's description of the murders, witchcraft, alchemy and black magic, Chapman, Eddowes, Nicholls, The Times, Triangle, D'Onston confession, W. T. Stead, Theosophist, the tin deed box and Mabel Collins' letters, the Pompadour Cosmetique Company, Mrs. Heilman, Marylebone Court, Montague Place, D'Onston in court.

Chapter Eight — "Black Magic and the Ripper Crimes."
Consists of 35 pages and includes Huysman, the Pall Mall Gazette, Satanism and Black Magic, the Empire News, Jack the Ripper, Eliphas Levi, the Book of Job, De Givery, Witchcraft Magic and Alchemy, Lucifer, the Sunday Graphic, Dennis Wheatley, Porter Baptisa, goat, crucifix, the Beast 666, Crowley, the Abbey of Thelema, the scarlet woman, the Number Five, Pentagram, Nicholls, Chapman, Cremers, Stride, Eddowes and Kelly, Borderland, Hermetic Lodge of Alexandria, Bulwer-Lytton, Societas Rosicrucian in Anglia, Dr. Wynn Westcott, forty days, etc.

Chapter Nine — "D'Onston and the Ripper."
Consists of 25 pages and includes Lord Crawford, D'Onston, Eliphas Levi, Pentagram, De Givery,

Diosy, Sir Max Pemberton, Borderland, the harlot, Lucifer, the Borderland picture of D'Onston, Jack the Ripper, W. T. Stead, Tautriadelta, triangle, Ada, black magic, Collins, Cremers, the Dopple-Ganger, Bulwer-Lytton, the murder sites, Bucks Row, Commercial Road, Hanbury Street, the London Hospital, Stride, Berner Street, Eddowes, Mitre Square, Obeeyah, the Pall Mall Gazette, Transcendental Magic, the harlot, Dr. Frederick Gordon Brown, candles, devil worship, Forbes, Inspector Reid, Inspector Helson, etc.

Chapter Ten—"A Last Glimpse of D'Onston."

Consists of 52 pages and includes Black Magic, Whitechapel, Fritz Harmann, Jack the Ripper, Murder and Its Motives, Miss Tennyson Jesse, Peter Kuerten, George Joseph Smith, Vacher, Ada, the Beast 666, the Book of Revelations, Crowley, the number five, the Abbey of Thelema, Bucks Row, Eddowes, Mitre Square, cross, Roslyn D'Onston, Eliphas Levi, Nicholls, Mary Kelly, paranoia, Kraepelin, Berner Street, Diemschutz, Chapman, Borderland, Bulwer-Lytton, Cremers, Lucifer, forensic science laboratory, Scotland Yard, Dr. Forbes Winslow, the Finger Print Bureau, scene of the crime, California, Chinaman, the Gold Rush, Dr. [sic] Wynne Baxter, *Pall Mall Gazette*, talismans, Dr. Bagster Phillips, O'Donnell evidence summing up the facts, D'Onston The Patristic Gospels, Grant Richards, Somerset House, W. T. Stead, Mabel Collins, Baroness Vittoria Cremers, Karl Hoffmann, Mr. Jacob of Simla, The Times, Garibaldi, Jack the Ripper, British Medical Association, British Museum Reading Room, General Medical Council, Montague Place, Pompadour Cosmetique Company, Mrs. Heilman, Irene Osgood, the Evil Eye, etc.

Clearly, for Bernard O'Donnell, the Whitechapel murders were a criminal study and captivating story. However, for Crowley and Cremers, the issue had always been more personal. It is another example of a speculative portrayal of Jack the Ripper as scapegoat, with hearsay inspiring conspiracy theories. The theories become far removed over time from the police investigation.

Crowley's 1943 and final Jack the Ripper article is thus an apology and defense of the beliefs of Blavatsky and D'Onston as he saw them against the slanders of Vittoria Cremers. Crowley alters the number of victims from seven (as he had previously stated) to five. He was enlarging on the notion that the killer wanted to form a pentagram, not a cross, over East End London. Horror writer Robert Bloch developed the black magic theme with a short story, "Yours Truly, Jack the Ripper"[70] also written in 1943. The motif was later used in the 2001 movie *From Hell*, starring Johnny Depp and Heather Graham, which made use of the pentagram design in a fictional plot.

The second author after O'Donnell to fully examine D'Onston and the black magic motif was Richard Whittington-Egan. A true crime writer, he had early access to the O'Donnell manuscript through contacts with crime publisher Joe Gaute. Whittington-Egan was also one of the first researchers, along with Stephen Knight, to view official Scotland Yard files on the Jack the Ripper case during the 1970s. The discovery of police statements relating to Roslyn D'Onston created a credible suspect for the Ripper's crimes. Knight's appraisal of D'Onston[71] was an abrupt dismissal of his standing as a viable suspect in favor of his anti–Royal Masonic conspiracy theory that continued to inform the historic view of the Whitechapel murders.

When the official files were released in the late 1970s, crime historians were able to seek facts about the Whitechapel murders. D'Onston was now confirmed as a police suspect. His statements to Scotland Yard were on record, emphasizing the value of reports in understanding of the investigation. D'Onston's police file continues to remain part of the corpus of known official primary sources on the Whitechapel murders for these reasons. O'Donnell submitted his manuscript to Harrap before he died in 1969.[72] Whittington-Egan made the following notes on O'Donnell's manuscript for his definitive 1975 work, *A Casebook on Jack the Ripper*.

"D'ONSTON INVESTIGATED— O'Donnell's investigations into D'Onston.
page 158/ Second article in Pall Mall Gazette (1889. Feb.15th) The African Magic article in Lucifer (Nov. 1890)
page 162/ The She article in Pall Mall Gazette (1889. January 3rd)
page 167/168 The Borderland article (1896. April) & what Stead wrote!!!

From the PMG articles it became obvious that D'Onston not only believed in black magic, but also practised it.
page 164/ The Lucifer article was signed TAUTRIADELTA. (p. 207)

The clue of the ties / p. 226 [Mrs. Cremers died in 1937]

D'Onston born c. 1841
Sir Edward Bulwer Lyton. [sic]

(Chapter X p. 31. Visit to Grant Richards.
(Chapter X p. 45–50 The Patristic Gospels

## O'DONNELL'S CROWNING ACHIEVEMENT....

The decipherment of Tautriadelta. Not its literal meaning but its mystic significance.

## THE LITERARY QUEST

The quest for D'Onston proved almost as will-o'-the-wispish as that for the Ripper himself. However, diligence, patience & tenacity yielded a small dividend of clues.
First of all there were D'Onston's published writings. O'Donnell discovered five articles.

Two in the Pall Mall Gazette —
(p.158) January 3rd, 1889 —"The Real Original of "She" by One Who Knew Her." signed R.D.— was not signed "D'O." (as p. 149. It was signed R.D. p. )
(p. 162) February 15th 1889 — Second article on African Experiences signed Roslyn D'Onston.
(p. 164) One in Lucifer on "African Magic" in November 1890 (+ page 156) signed Tautriadelta.
(p. 167) One in W. T. Stead's magazine the Borderland in April 1896. Signed Tautriadelta. (gives biographical data)

And in a book, The Patristic Gospels, published in 1904, which O'Donnell ran to earth in the Reading Room at the British Museum.
[Sees Grant Richards]
The P.M.G. articles made it obvious that D'Onston not only believed in black magic, but practised it. [as already written on first page]

[Footnote. Mabel Collins was Mrs. Cook, the widow of Dr. Kenningdale Cook who had used her as a spiritualist medium, the phenomena later being recorded in a book written by him. (p. 142)]

## SOMERSET HOUSE

Chapt. X p. 33 — 36. Somerset House.
If he was 22 when he first met Bulwer-Lytton in 1863 or thereabouts he must have been born c. 1841.

I searched the registers from 1836 to 1845, inclusive looking under D'Onston, Roslyn, Rosslyn & Ross. [& concentrating especially for anyone having those names in the Yorkshire area, because Mrs. Cremers had mentioned that Mabel Collins had an idea that he belonged to the Rosslyn family, but had adopted Roslyn with a single s as his christian name. Yorkshire came into it because in D'Onston's article in the Borderland he refers to himself as an "obstinate Yorkshireman."]
Drew a blank.

I pursued the same process with the registries of deaths from 1904 to 1930.
Another blank.

Grant Richards had mentioned to O'Donnell that D'Onston had said that he intended to go & live in France, so perhaps he did so, & died abroad. Or, of course, the strong possibility that he was using a completely FALSE NAME.

## ADA INQUEST / COURT ACTION

Chapter X
p. 36–37. O'Donnell tried to trace through a report of the inquest on Ada, but without knowing a surname it proved a hopeless task.

There had been an action brought by D'Onston against Mabel Collins for the recovery of some letters. The case had come up at Marylebone some time in the early 90's. The most rigorous search failed to disclose any mention of it in any newspaper.

## MEDICAL REGISTERS

Chapter X

p. 37–39 D'Onston claimed to be a doctor of medicine. O'Donnell checked with the British Medical Association & with the General Medical Council. There was no Dr. D'Onston.

One interesting small point. In the catalogue of authors at the B. M reading room someone has inserted in ink beside the author of The Patristic Gospels printed name the letters "M.D." Since there is no mention of Roslyn Donston's medical status on the title page of the work, it can only be assumed, said the Superintendent of the Reading Room that it was D'Onston himself who interpolated the "M.D." in the catalogue on some later occasion.

## FACTS ESTABLISHED

Chapter X

see p. But, whatever, Bernard O'Donnell had succeeded in establishing a number of indisputable facts. 1. A man calling himself Roslyn D'Onston & Tautriadelta existed in [blank space]

(p.6)

Fred Wensley, who B. O'D. knew well, sitting in the garden of his home at Southgate, agreed that B'O'D's was "the only solution of the mystery which stood up to all the facts as he knew them."

(p.36–38) Arthur Diosy.
p. 47/Black magic progression.
p. 50. Black magic & Mitre Square. and p. 52 and p. 55. p.56
p. 80. Black magicians.
p. 119 –121 Black magic general.
p. 122. Profanation and page 131
p.123–126 Black magic general.
p.127. Eliphas Levi quote.
p.128–136 Black magic general.
p.155. Cleanliness & magic.
p. 157. A black magician?
p. 194. The magical significance of the triangle.
p. 212 Ripper victims all harlots — magical significance.

## THE EVIDENCE OF THE TIES...

Pages 226–233 and p.246 Betty May / Aleister Crowley

p. 245. D'Onston claims police had him in twice for questioning — but had to let him go. O'Donnell discounts the 'confiding surgeon' story.

p. 251. Why Mrs. Cremers did not go to the police."[73]

The East End suffered heavily from World War II bombing, and of course this included widespread destruction of historical archives, among them official police sources on the Whitechapel murders — notably the City of London Police records on the murder of Catherine Eddowes. In addition, routine disposal of paper files to make space at New Scotland Yard meant a great loss of records. Research was therefore an arduous task. Crosschecks with primary sources were not always possible.[74] Authors and journalists Donald McCormick and Nigel Morland, for example, concocted fictional tabloid stories about the Ripper.

The ensuing Cold War brought about further conjectures of Jack the Ripper as the demonized personage of rogue social and political systems.[75] In considering the long history of Ripper conspiracies and theories, it is useful to separate threads and sources. Is the theory an attempt to evaluate historically the police investigation on the Whitechapel murders? Or does it seek to disparage or to condone social movements, implicating associations, subcultures, or tenuous suspects in a serious crime? Does the name "Jack the Ripper" simply encourage discourse? Or is the story an attempt to capitalize on readers' interest in popular historical works and studies under the banner of the unsolved crimes of Jack the Ripper?

Author Stephen Knight during the liberal 1970s adopted the Victorian serial killer as a comparative case study in politicized criminal policy. The enigmatic Jack the Ripper came to symbolize an assortment of social and pseudo-religious ills. Worthy as such issues are, they never reflected the East End autumn of 1888.

Though dismissed as a credible theory, Knight's story has lived on in fictions based on the Ripper case, particularly in movie treatments. However, fictional versions of Whitechapel cannot by definition be complete historic views of actual events. Reliance on primary sources is indispensable, as is a fair and unbiased reading of these sources, which engenders sensitivity to the Victorian partialities that produced them.

## THE TERRIBLE SCANDALS IN "HIGH LIFE"

We are exceedingly glad that the horrible scandal which Reynolds's Newspaper was the first to bring under the notice of the general public has at last come more prominently forward through the proceedings at Bow-street Police-court. The police have been deliberately employed in attempting to hush up the whole matter. If they had displayed as much activity in their endeavours to discover the Whitechapel murderer, "Jack the Ripper," in all probability he would now have met with his deserts. But in the latter case it was merely the lives of unfortunate women that were at stake, while in the former the reputations of several of the nobility and others moving in the highest spheres of society that were endangered. Hence Mr. Monro, the chief of police, in all likelihood with the sanction and approval of Mr. Matthews, the Home Secretary, did his uttermost to keep the hideous doings at Cleveland-street from the knowledge of the public.

These right-about-face movements in both cases are solely attributable to the influence of public opinion. As, under a Tory Government, the police are given to understand that persons of high degree are not to be interfered with in their amusements, however brutal and bestial. The whole matter will doubtless be brought before Parliament by Mr. Labouchere, or some other member in whom the people have faith and confidence, and henceforth the Home Secretary or his myrmidons, the Police Commissioners, will find it more difficult than hitherto allowing great culprits to escape and smaller ones to be punished.

The existence among us of a Sodomite institution is a matter of a far more serious nature than his lordship, judging by the way in which he gave his evidence, would seem to think. The most severe measures the law will admit of should be resorted to in order to stamp out practices of an unnatural and revolting shape too hideous even to mention.[76]

As time went on, the commercial value of Jack the Ripper stories as a genre became established. The result was a new deluge of publications, literary hoaxes, and the introduction to the case of forensic technologies and serial killer profiling. However, in a case as cold as the Whitechapel murders, modern forensics consistently proves to be less useful than one might hope.

It is fitting that Whittington-Egan prefaced his influential 1975 book, *A Casebook on Jack the Ripper*, with these words:

It is, surely, the phantasmagoric quality of the creature who, lacking a known patronym, has been allocated the adjectival substantive Jack the Ripper, that compels the unabating and perfervid interest. Had the Ripper, fleet-footed, insubstantial Jack, been "buckled," his trial embalmed between the appropriate blood-red covers of a volume in the exemplary Notable British Trials series, his psychopathology expatiated upon in a learned introductory essay, the case would, no doubt, be gathering dust upon the crammed shelves of the systematic criminologists. But he was not. It is not.[77]

The efforts of early crime authors, such as Whittington-Egan, Donald Rumbelow, Robin Odell, and Colin Wilson, to document and assess sources from the police investigation of Jack the Ripper formed the bedrock of further study. In 1973, the first authoritative bibliography was published. *Jack the Ripper: A Bibliography and Review of the Literature*,[78] was compiled by Alexander Kelly, a pseudonymous former Scotland Yard librarian, introduced by Colin Wilson and professionally prepared by the Association of Assistant Librarians.[79]

On the centenary of the Whitechapel murders and with the official files finally deposited at the Public Record Office, a shift in perspective emerged that would propel Jack the Ripper into the 21st century. The appearance of anonymous packages containing police material long thought lost added to the suspense and renewed fervour that the identity of Jack the Ripper was perhaps in reach. The medical notes of Mary Kelly prepared by Scotland Yard police surgeon Dr. Thomas Bond was a useful source addition. The material that had gone missing with the neglect of Metropolitan Police and City of London Police archives and records was slowly restored.[80] Some suspects' files, for instance, are now missing, but the copies retained by researchers of the 1970s and 1980s were compiled.[81]

There is another tradition of Jack the Ripper mentions in official and unofficial Scotland Yard histories and police memoirs. Written as background to the historic growth of the Metropolitan Police with some discussion on the early formation of its Special Branch, they add inconclusive, incomplete or borrowed details on Jack the Ripper. However, they are useful sources on the investigation and on Scotland Yard methods in the Victorian period. The most notable of the background studies are the works of Bernard Porter, Douglas G. Browne, Margaret Prothero, and K.R.M. Short.

One of the remarkable discoveries of the centenary, which has since been relegated to the conspiracy theories outbox, was the unpublished memoir of James Monro. He was Metropolitan Police Commissioner from November 1888 to 1890 and a founder of the British secret service. Christopher Monro, grandson of James, wrote to authors Robin Odell and Colin Wilson after reading their 1987 book *Jack the Ripper: Summing Up and Verdict*.[82] Previous correspondence with Odell during the period 1967-68 had suggested that James Monro was Jack the Ripper. Christopher Monro further told Odell he believed his grandfather "came up against an official conspiracy of silence imposed by blackmail over the Ripper case, which, with other shenanigans, soured him of police work." Monro's letter to Odell "conjectured that his grandfather had allowed a carefully edited memoir to pass to junior members of the family while reserving a second version, dealing with the Ripper case alone, and possibly including details of the Cleveland Street affair, for the eyes only of his elder son." Christopher Monro believed that his grandfather knew the identity of Jack the Ripper and that the case was "a very hot potato."[83]

Christopher Monro told researchers Martin Howells and Keith Skinner, authors of the 1987 *The Ripper Legacy*,[84] that he "believed that his grandfather had written a confidential memoir about the murders, which had been passed down through the family." Howells and Skinner "traced a surviving member of the Monro family in Edinburgh and saw a document written by James Monro in 1903 for the benefit of his children." There was no mention of the Whitechapel murders. There was however, a detailed background to Monro's covert work during the reign of Jack the Ripper, and it is a rare and informed primary source on the late Victorian secret service arrangements of the Home Office.

Howells and Skinner wrote of James Monro that "he had to know more about both investigations than he was prepared to say." They believed he was the source of Macnaghten's private information on Montague John Druitt. The authors suggested that Druitt was the murderer known as Jack the Ripper, and that he was mixed up with the 1889 Cleveland Street brothel scandal and a member of a mystical secret society implicated in the murders, the Cambridge Apostles.[85]

On September 22, 1888, the Home Secretary, Henry Matthews, sent a memo to his Principal Private Secretary, Evelyn Ruggles-Brise, asking that he "stimulate the Police about Whitechapel murders. Absente Anderson, Monro might be willing to give a hint to the C.I.D. people if needed."[86] This memo has produced numerous conspiracy theories about high-level subterfuge in the Whitechapel murders. Monro had resigned his post as Metropolitan Police Assistant Commissioner and head of CID in August 1888. Anderson replaced him, but the memo supports the assertion that at that early date the Whitechapel murders were investigated at a high level within Scotland Yard. Monro had taken up the confidential post under the Home Office internal criminal department as head of the first permanent British secret service unit, established in early 1888. Matthews thus backed the special department Monro formed to assist CID and the divisional police investigation of the Whitechapel murders.

This was a common, albeit informal, Victorian police arrangement for hard-to-solve crimes occurring in London. The absence of Anderson, who was on holiday, was reason enough for the experienced Monro to direct CID. The memo also notes that the Home Office allocated attention and resources to the early Whitechapel murders. Despite Monro's other pressing duties, it shows how effectively Scotland Yard reorganized its priorities in the absence of its assistant commissioner and other East End senior divisional detectives. It is not known what Monro may have gleaned from CID on the murders at that time, but he was appointed Metropolitan Police Commissioner in November 1888, on the resignation of Sir Charles Warren. He continued the hunt for Jack the Ripper until he resigned in 1890 under political pressures over police management and inequitable pension rules.

With the release of the official Whitechapel files to researchers in the late 1970s came also a gaggle of works on suspects both credible and not credible. Nevertheless, these works at least gave an unprecedented insight into the police investigation, Home Office and Foreign Office documentation. Then in 1988, the centenary of the murders, press releases and publicity renewed interest. The renewed scholarly interest in the crimes and Victorian East End London was tempered by some who warned against exploiting the murder and mutilation of women. A local pub changed its name to the "Jack the Ripper," but eventually changed it back to "The Ten Bells"—as it was in Mary Kelly's day.

Then along came a book to rule them all, *Jack the Ripper: The Bloody Truth*,[87] by BBC researcher Melvin Harris. Harris in his 1987 work effectively demolished major Jack the Ripper fables of the time which influenced numerous nonfiction books on the subject. Harris first challenged, in his 1989 *The Ripper File*, the veracity of Anderson's historical claims on Jack the Ripper contrary to the influential theories of authors Paul Begg and Martin Fido on an insane Jewish suspect. He had also introduced Vittoria Cremers and was later to resurrect D'Onston as a credible suspect with further supporting documentation in three Ripper books.[88]

Harris first encountered D'Onston while examining the "Dead or Alive" chapter in *More Ghost Stories* for his 1986 book, *Sorry—You've Been Duped*.[89] The article had been included in W.T. Stead's special New Year's Extra Number of the 1892 *Review of Reviews*. D'Onston's Victorian supernatural story was then reprinted in the 1897 book *Real Ghost*

*Stories* and republished during the 20th century as definitive proof of ghost activity and the existence of an afterlife. The exposure of paranormal and mystery claims had first sparked Harris's interest in the Whitechapel murders.

Richard Whittington-Egan suggested that D'Onston seemed a viable suspect worthy of further research, having noted his place in official files with Stephen Knight for their 1975 Ripper books. After examining D'Onston as a suspect, Whittington-Egan and Knight rejected him as Jack the Ripper, but Harris pursued D'Onston with the confidence and citations of 1980s FBI serial killer profiling. (Crime novelist Patricia Cornwell would later develop with modern forensics the weak suspect Walter Sickert on a nod from retired Metropolitan Police Deputy Assistant Commissioner John Grieve, in 2001.)[90]

Melvin Harris was not a criminologist or crime historian but an author skilled in literary research and the exposure of media and historical hoaxes. By 1994 and his third book on D'Onston, he had developed his Jack the Ripper theory with additional secondary sources found in the O'Donnell manuscript. However, he had not included a detail first referenced in Whittington-Egan's 1975 book. Harris had noted on his sources for D'Onston that "his indictment is based on solid evidence, without recourse to faked documents or journalist's inventions."[91] Yet in 1989 he had cause to suspect elements of O'Donnell's manuscript were fabricated. He had advised prolific British author Colin Wilson of the discrepancies in a review letter he sent on the impending paperback updated edition of *Jack the Ripper: Summing Up and Verdict*.

Harris remained true to the sources of indictment on D'Onston, despite his untenable position as a suspect for the Whitechapel murders, by dropping the reference attributed to D'Onston and quoted in O'Donnell's manuscript: "'I became obsessed with the idea that the revelation of the Doppel-ganger phenomenon would make me an instrument of the Gods; henceforth, on occasion, I would destroy to save; I would become as Hermes, son of God... For they who would slay and save must be armed with a strong and perfect will, defying and penetrating with no uncertain force. This Herpe, the sword that destroyeth the Harlot, by whose aid the Hero overcometh and the Savior is able to deliver.'" It is a reference that O'Donnell regarded as "a powerful piece of self-indictment on D'Onston's part, it shows him as prepared to destroy in order to save; it portrays him as a Harlot killer." The relevant extracts on the O'Donnell manuscript in Harris's letter to Colin Wilson follow:

By now you should have received a copy of my "Ripper File." It is a shorter work than I at first planned. In fact I had to lose 3 chapters, plus notes and bibliography, so that Allen's could keep the price down! Now that you have it I should give you some corrections for your "Summing up and verdict" book — in case you want to revise prior to paperbacking. So here goes:—

"Black Jack" chapter; p217, the December "Pall Mall" piece was D'Onston's not the Earl of Crawford's. In fact the Earl wrote nothing at all for the "Gazette." Oddly enough Crowley correctly identified the piece as D'Onston's though he clearly hadn't read it, and asserted that it was signed "Tau Tria Delta," which it wasn't.

Page 221. D'Onston did not claim to have studied chemistry at the University of Giessen under Dr. Allen Liebig. There was no Dr. Allen Liebig. What we have here is a muddle created when O'Donnell was transcribing his notes. What D'Onston actually wrote was "...I was studying chemistry under Dr. Allan (who was for many years Baron Liebig's assistant at the great laboratory at the University of Giessen)." The Dr. Allan in question was the Scot James Allan from Edinburgh. He was Baron Justus Liebig's pupil at Giessen and when Liebig shifted his laboratory to Munich (1852) Allan went with him.

Page 221. The quote beginning [sic] "I became obsessed by the idea..." is not from D'Onston. It was faked by O'Donnell.[92]

Harris found that Bernard O'Donnell, in the long traditions of invented Jack the Ripper sources by authors such as McCormick before release of official files, had prepared the passage on "harlots" from unrelated text in *Borderland*. D'Onston had written his semi-autobiographical article "A Modern Magician," for the April 1896 issue of *Borderland*, which O'Donnell had located. He then turned his attention to a letter in the same issue written by Dr. Maitland on the Theosophist Anna Kingsford. O'Donnell extracted sections of the letter, inserted the word "harlot" and added the opening words for the passage that the O'Donnell manuscript attributed to D'Onston.

Harris added in the letter to Colin Wilson details of his ongoing research on D'Onston and the O'Donnell manuscript.

Page 227. "The address was a humble..." and all that follows — the Walter Mitty line etc. has to be abandoned. As I've shown his family was wealthy and influential. His father was apart from being a mill owner, the City Treasurer of Hull. Ordinance Survey maps show his family's house and grounds to be huge. Possibly the largest house in the whole of North Hull. His father's declaration in the 1861 census confirms D'Onston's service with the Southern Army of Garibaldi. There is completely independent evidence of his travels and searches in India, and this was published in "Borderland" for July 1896 and July 1897. The fact of his application for the Police Orphanage post gives credence to his medical diplomas. Roots knew of them and an interviewing board would certainly have insisted on examining them, especially not directly equated with British qualifications. In short I have unearthed lots of bits and pieces (some of which I have not yet published) which provide independent support for many of the accounts given by D'Onston. And the search still goes on.

P228. O'Donnell's attempt to decipher "Tautriadelta" is a non-starter. What he conjectures is negated by D'Onston's article in the December "Gazette." But O'Donnell had been misinformed about the articles authorship so he had no real clues to work with. So goodbye Pentagram; come back Cross.

Harris's work on a police Ripper suspect began during the centenary. It was driven by a "Master Profile" he had developed based on 1980s FBI investigations of serial killers. Harris noted in 1994: "My first [1987] book on the murders was planned to end with this profile, leaving the killer as a faceless anonymous blur. But, with a deadline limiting extensive research, a rejected suspect suddenly grew in significance. No published author had ever taken Roslyn D'Onston seriously; the man had long been since dismissed out of hand as a Walter Mitty character. This dismissal arose from blunders made in 1975."[93]

Earlier in the same section, Harris confirmed his motive for relentlessly pursuing D'Onston: "My first verdict on the Whitechapel mystery was an open one. None of the contending theories stood up to close scrutiny, so the killer was probably someone unknown and unsuspected. Study of FBI material on serial killers led to a slight alteration in emphasis: the killer could have been suspected at one time but may well have been able to give a convincing display of total innocence. Then, using the documents of the time and coupling these with our present-day understanding of the serial sexual killer, I was able to draw up a comprehensive profile of the man."

D'Onston fitted the profile at least as well as George Hutchinson, the witness at the crime scene of the murder of Mary Kelly. Hutchinson is also tentatively considered as a suspect for the way he insinuated himself into the police investigation. The problem was that while Harris was investigating D'Onston, an FBI profile prepared on Jack the Ripper[94] alternatively endorsed an insane suspect type, suggested by authors Paul Begg and Martin Fido, who appeared equally viable.[95] The centenary profiling considerations of Jack the Ripper as a "serial sexual killer" preceded the theories of crime novelist Patricia Cornwell[96] on Walter Sickert by nearly twenty years. With similar inconclusive results, Cornwell's discovery was preceded in 1993 by graphologist Marie Bernard.[97] Criminal profiling of a cold case such as the Whitechapel murders with fragmentary case files is not a reliable guide to the killer.

Hasty conclusions on Jack the Ripper have been the bane of the subject and Harris, an otherwise reliable and insightful researcher, relied on fieldwork at times that was not sound. An example of the myopia that can plague the topic particularly with ill-considered suspect bias may be found in his third book on D'Onston (published in 1994): "In 1890, the Westminster Gazette raised the specter of the Ripper once more. In its July report it claimed that the police had gained advance information about the killer's intentions. A new cycle of horror was about to begin. Cremers read this and decided to mention it to D'Onston to gauge his reaction. But he was one step ahead of her. At the office, he waved the very paper at her while ridiculing the report."[98] The only problem with this entry is that the *Westminster Gazette*, established by George Newnes, was not launched until January 31, 1893.[99]

The tendency for innovation in the study of the Whitechapel murders has been countered by the commentary of dispassionate and objective crime historians. It is, however, in the dichotomy of facts and fictions that conspiracy theories and hoaxes take root in proportion to the dearth of primary and incomplete historic sources. The height of innovation on the murders, with which author Melvin Harris was intimately associated, was the production and release of the alleged "Diary of Jack the Ripper." Adherents to the 1992–93 literary sham claimed that Victorian aristocrat James Maybrick was Jack the Ripper.

The diary is supposed to have been written by James Maybrick as a deathbed confession, but it is a literary fiction and hoax. It achieved notoriety because it was brought to the attention of the House of Commons,[100] New Scotland Yard and one of the most established and traditional of UK literary agencies.

The New Scotland Yard investigation of the Maybrick Diary hoax could not find clues within its pages to solve the Whitechapel murders. Melvin Harris and a host of informed crime historians discounted it as a prank. Experts and analysts on serial killers gave it serious consideration. The Maybrick Diary has entered the annals of misinformation on Jack the Ripper and accordingly is not considered a reliable historic source. Rather, it is widely regarded as an opportunistic attempt to capitalize on scant documentation on the case.

## HOW THE SUNDAY TIMES WON A LEGAL BATTLE TO EXPOSE THE FAKE

The Sunday Times first established that the "diary" of Jack the Ripper was a fake three months ago, after it was offered exclusive serialisation rights for £75,000.

The newspaper told the publisher of the findings of its investigation and wanted to warn the public that there was a danger the Ripper's forged confessions could become the biggest international fraud in the book world since the "discovery" of the Hitler diaries. The proposed print run of 250,000 copies and the worldwide sale of television and newspaper rights meant it was worth at least £4m.[101]

*The Sunday Times* to its credit withdrew from the deal. However, the "diary" was published. Though its value as a source on the unsolved crimes of Jack the Ripper was in doubt from the start, it would not be the only hoax. With the "Hitler Diaries," the British National Archives experienced similar embarassment.

## FORGERIES REVEALED IN THE NATIONAL ARCHIVES

It all began with a letter uncovered nine years ago addressed by a duke to "Dear Mr. Hitler." One of the most extraordinary academic detective stories of modern times ended yesterday when the National

Archives, the official custodian of Britain's history, admitted that it had been the victim of a master forger.

The public records office, which holds the written record of the British state going back 800 years, said its reputation had been compromised by the discovery that 29 documents from 12 separate files were all forgeries inserted into its records.

Sir Max Hastings, an expert on the second world war, said: "It is hard to imagine actions more damaging to the cause of preserving the nation's heritage than wilfully forging documents designed to alter our historical record."

John Fox, a historian specialising in Nazi Germany, said the National Archives' statement casts doubt on the veracity of documents in other collections.[102]

Melvin Harris took up the cause of exposing the Maybrick diary as the hoax it was. In 1996, Harris published an article titled "The Maybrick Will: The Crucial Key to a Shabby Hoax,"[103] which outlined results of several years' research. It drew ready responses from crime historians, notably Keith Skinner as the following extracts note.

> I do not, however, intend to debate Melvin Harris's observations on Alexander MacDougall's representation of James Maybrick's Will. Paul Feldman will defend his interpretation of the existing Will in his forthcoming book "Jack the Ripper — The Final Chapter." My own position is that, evidentially, there are unresolved historical peculiarities surrounding the circumstances under which the Will was signed — and this, curiously, is reflected in the text of the Journal. The easy explanation, of course, is that, as this information was in the public domain, so it has just been creatively woven into the Journal. I can accept that, but this implies a certain degree of required and acquired knowledge of the Maybrick Case. A certain amount of thought and preparation in order to slip in an arcane, esoteric detail. And yet I keep on being told that this Journal is an "amateurish fake"; "a crude forgery": something which was "knocked together" as a practical joke to play on Michael Barrett!
>
> What puzzles me, then, is Melvin Harris's need to devote so much time and discussion to James Maybrick's Will, when, apparently, he is cognizant of the identities of the people who are meant to have created the Journal. In December 1994, the Evening Standard quoted Melvin Harris as claiming: "The identities of the three people involved in the forgery will soon be made known."[104]

Skinner added,

> Melvin Harris has written that "every hoax contaminates the fields of honest research." I support that view, though not wholly, as it makes no allowance for the valuable historical data which may be discovered in the process of researching the hoax. Also, the idea for the hoax might have been inspired by an old tradition which, in itself, merits further research — as with the genesis of Joseph Sickert's original story. If Mr. Harris, therefore, could just identify for us who actually is involved in this collusion, and provide the supporting proof, then it will probably banish James Maybrick's candidature as "Jack the Ripper" to the realms of fiction.[105]

Harris did not in the end prove the identity or identities of the faker of the Maybrick Diary, but he was vindicated with success in relegating it to the realms of Ripper fabrication, as *The Sunday Times* had initially done. While Harris was pointing out discrepancies in the handwriting of the document, he was also writing to author Donald McCormick. He asked some pertinent questions on a verse found only in McCormick's 1959 book, *The Identity of Jack the Ripper*, yet discernible in the text of the Maybrick diary. McCormick responded to Harris as they were in correspondence for some time over other literary matters and discrepancies. However, the plain issue of scientific testing of paper and ink of the manuscript continued to remain contentious, inconclusive, and elusive.

14 March, 1995

Dear Melvin Harris,

Many thanks for your letter and for your good wishes.

I would like to help you regarding the "Eight little whores" poem, but unfortunately my Ripper papers were disposed of a long time ago. The most detailed references to it are contained in my updated book, "The Identity of Jack the Ripper," published by John Long in 1970. Pages 103–105. However, I agree with your suggestion that "it is the work of a very clever man who enjoys his quiet fun." I should certainly accept that viewpoint. For one thing the poet was either a friend of very many prostitutes and/or someone who knew about the peccadilloes of the leading statesmen of the day, viz. his reference to Gladstone. Incidentally, I once wrote a book, "The Private Life of Mr. Gladstone," published by Frederick Muller.

If you want to smell out a possible author for this poem, you might consider James Kenneth Stephen, a cousin of Virginia Woolf and Vanessa Bell. I learned a lot about him when I was researching my book, "The Cambridge Apostles," published by Robert Royce in 1985. Stephen was an Apostle and he is best remembered for the two small volumes of verse and parody, "Lapsus Calami" and "Quo Musa Tendis." He was appointed tutor to the Duke of Clarence, the eldest son of the Prince of Wales (later King Edward VII) and was devoted to him. Study Stephen carefully and you will find that he might even have been the Ripper.

3 Oct 1997

Dear Mr. McCormick,

Since last writing to you on the subject of the "Eight little whores" poem things have worsened and got out of hand. You are the only person who can remedy this. You see, those verses were used by the fakers of the Liverpool "Jack the Ripper" Diary. They took them as an inspiration for sections of that Diary. This is so clear that even the present owners of the Diary accept it. If you look at the enclosed photocopy you will see that a new book on the Diary makes great play of this use of the poem.

In short a bogus poem is being used to seemingly validate a bogus Diary. In my last book of 1994 I wrote of this Diary:—"Unfortunately every hoax contaminates the fields of honest research, even if it is exposed. Like the Clarence hoax this one will not die overnight. Its time-wasting stupidities will linger on to dog historians for years to come." And my forecast has come true.

You are now in a unique position of being able to stop this contamination spreading any further. We both know that this poem is a 20th Century concoction, reflecting the PC Spicer story of Henage Court; a story that did not emerge until 1931. And its lines were unknown until it appeared in your book in 1959. All the world needs from you is a simple statement that you accept that the poem is bogus. That, on its own, will put an end to this wretched state of affairs and give historians a chance to investigate, free from the need to combat this time-wasting nonsense.

I am not asking you to name the faker of this poem. It is enough for you just to acknowledge its real status. I know that there are a number of writers who are prepared to savage your reputation the moment you are gone. But I am not one of them. I am concerned with this one issue only and it would reflect well on your reputation if you would now make the statement I am asking for.

Yours sincerely
Melvin Harris

Harris gave further details of the outcome of his correspondence with McCormick on this key detail making up the forgery.

I put it to McCormick that these verses had no antiquity; they were unknown before appearing in his book, IN 1959. While the reference to Henage Court showed that the writer had drawn on the PC Spicer story, which did not reach print UNTIL MARCH 1931. In short it was not a Victorian piece, but a 20th Century concoction. Again, at no time did I ask him to name the faker. But I asked him to acknowledge it as a MODERN fake and stated that I would be content to describe it as being the work of a "very clever man who enjoys his quiet fun." McCormick accepted that formula AND WITHOUT ANY BLUSTER OR EQUIVOCATION ADMITTED THAT IT WAS A FAKE AND WAS INDEED INSPIRED BY THE SPICER STORY; A STORY THAT HE DISCOVERED IN A BUNDLE OF OLD PRESS CLIPPINGS AND THEN USED IN CONSTRUCTING HIS BOOK. [Harris's emphasis]

In truth it was McCormick who FIRST made the Spicer story known to Ripperologists. Until 1959 it had stayed forgotten in the newspaper archives. (As early as 1979 he had told me that the starting point for almost all of his books lay in the Kemsley Newspaper library which had masses of cuttings going back to early Victorian days. Other newspapers, he advised, held similar archives. They saved him a journey and a search at Colindale.)

Finally in October 1997 I wrote to him and asked him to stop the fooling and write a candid letter fit for publication. Sadly the reply that came back read "I have an ulcer on my right eye and have great difficulty in writing at present. Please let the matter drop." I did and there was never to be a further chance. Within a short while I learned that he was dead.

But his legacy lives on. Fortunately for the truth one fragment of that legacy gives the lie to the false Diary provenance that tries to place it back in the 1940's. Not a chance. McCormick's poem is reflected in the Diary text. Both Feldman and Shirley Harrison agree on that. That poem did not exist until 1958, when it was composed and did not appear in print until 1959. And that is the rock on which the flimsy Ark of Provenance perishes.[106]

One of the earliest mentions linking Jack the Ripper with the Florence Maybrick murder case in sequence was an extract from the popular 1957 crime book, *This Friendless Lady* by Nigel Morland,[107] released by Frederick Muller, also the publisher of McCormick's *The Private Life of Mr. Gladstone*. Melvin Harris commented:

> With the catalyst providing the inspiration, the material basis for the hoax itself is easy to come by, for the hoaxers present us with nothing that is new or obscure. Simply list the names found in the diary; list the relationships and the basic chronology and you will find just how sparse this diary information is. Just: Michael, Thomas , Edwin and William; Bobo and Gladys; Davidson, Lowry and Smith; Dr. Hopper; the nickname "Bunny"; and St. James's Church — and there you have all the real Maybrick material that is embodied in the diary. You can find all these items and their significances, in assorted writings on the case, but you can find them all, together, in just one popular book: Nigel Morland's "This Friendless Lady."

Nigel Morland, who later became founding editor of *The Criminologist*, was born Carl Van Bienal in 1905 and died in 1986. He wrote an article on the Maybricks for *MacKill's Mystery Magazine* in 1954 titled "The Innocence of Florence Maybrick."[108] However, there was an even earlier link of Jack the Ripper with the Maybrick murder case. It was depicted in an illustrated edition of *St. Stephen's Review* in 1889 titled, "Whitechapel at Whitehall."[109] The illustration suggested duplicity of the Home Secretary, Henry Matthews, in that he had previously issued a royal pardon for accomplices of Jack the Ripper but had refused clemency for the American-born Florence Maybrick.

In 1983 appeared a novelized history of the wartime exploits of stage illusionist and magician Jasper Maskelyne. He had served in a counterintelligence capacity during the Second World War. Prime Minister Winston Churchill had employed artists, writers, occultists, actors, and stage magicians in the military to confuse and mislead the Nazis. The novel, *The War Magician*,[110] was based on Maskelyne's scrapbook[111] and his 1949 memoir, *Magic: Top Secret*.[112]

The memoir was ghostwritten by an author represented by the literary agency that would later, in 1992, arrange publication of the "Diary of Jack the Ripper."[113] That author was Frank S. Stuart, who had a long history of popular and ghostwritten works to his name. Is it then possible that Stuart had fabricated the original Maybrick diary during the 1950 or 1960s? That it was drawn from the works of McCormick and Morland and, never released, left to gather dust in storage? This theory could explain the diary's appearance of having been written in one sitting. However, would Stuart have had the interest in Maybrick and Jack the Ripper to expend time and effort on its production to satisfy the credulous?

The diary managed to intrigue, deceive, and confound Jack the Ripper serial killer analysts and general readers with a deceptively simple formula that imitated Victorian style. It was also a feature developed and employed with British wartime counterintelligence.[114]

As questions on the Maybrick Diary are vexed ones of ownership, provenance, and authorship, perhaps a novel approach in contextually defining the document in the corpus of Jack the Ripper literary traditions would be to examine contractual arrangements of ghostwritten works in the post war period. Richard Stokes, a military historian and magician, has made publicly available[115] his research attempts to expose the alleged fabrications in Maskelyne's 1949 memoirs. In the course of those inquiries, Stokes spoke to Alistair Maskelyne, son of Jasper, who indicated that his father's memoirs were ghostwritten. In October 2004, Stokes contacted Random House, the current owners of Maskelyne's publisher Stanley Paul. The archive librarian there found the contract for *Magic: Top Secret*, and said it was "signed by Jasper Maskelyne on June 23rd, 1947." The librarian said the contract did not include a second writer.

The librarian stated that Stanley Paul had solely employed Maskelyne as the author and that the literary agent was noted as Rupert Crew. Stokes claims he then spoke with Doreen Montgomery of Rupert Crew Literary Agency. He noted that the conversation included the recollection of Alistair Maskelyne that his father's memoirs were ghostwritten.

Ghostwriter Frank S. Stuart, who may have authored the Maybrick diary in the 1950s.

Montgomery is reported as saying, "The agreement with a ghost-writer is done through the agent, not the publisher. The celebrity signs with the publisher, but they make separate arrangements with their collaborator and these terms are sorted out with their agent. Such an arrangement would not show up in the publisher's contract." She reportedly said that Frank S. Stuart had ghostwritten several books for the agency and that he may have been responsible for an earlier Maskelyne memoir, *White Magic*, published before the war. According to Montgomery's reported comments, Frank Stuart was a reputable and conscientious writer. In the course of the reported phone conversation, Montgomery is quoted as saying that as the literary agent for the Jack the Ripper "diary," "I don't understand what the fuss was. They looked genuine to me."

Frank S. Stuart was commissioned to ghostwrite Maskelyne's memoirs. According to Stokes, he used similar techniques of invented facts, dubious provenance, and untraceable chronologies, as McCormick had. As contemporaries, Stuart, Morland and McCormick may have known of one another's work. They had at their disposal, the Kemsley newspaper archives, a boon to journalists with little time or inclination for effective historic research on crime and military subjects.

Few biographical details are known about Stuart, who was born in 1904. In 1937, he authored the purported nonfiction account *Vagabond: Reminiscences of a Tramp, Recorded by F. S. Stuart*, with echoes of the late 1800s Tichborne case. In 1935, he completed *Memoirs of a Royal Detective*, the reminiscences of Special Branch Detective Inspector Herbert T. Fitch.[116] Stuart wrote of the commission, "When Mr. Fitch had almost completed this book, he was found dead in his study chair. Sheets of the story still littered his desk. So that his tale of these unique experiences should not be wasted, I was asked to conclude the task."[117]

What is curious about Stuart's commission to complete Inspector Fitch's memoirs was that he was a young and relatively unknown author. He had no established contacts with police or official archives, as the following extracts indicate. Though he may have been researching the growth of Special Branch for use in Fitch's memoir, his approach appears to indicate otherwise. Nevertheless, his published queries confirm his interest in Scotland Yard and its cases, which of course included the Ripper murders.

> THE HISTORY OF NEW SCOTLAND YARD.— I would be grateful if your readers could tell me when the Special Branch of New Scotland Yard was formed, and anything especially pertaining to the formation.
> I am preparing a book on the history of the Special Branch. Where could I obtain information which would help me in this? New Scotland Yard tell me that they are unable to give information. Frank S. Stuart.[118]

> THE HISTORY OF NEW SCOTLAND YARD (clxviii. 78).— The Special Branch of the C.I.D. was formed in 1884 to combat the Irish-American dynamite campaign of 1883–1885. Mr. Stuart should study the only authoritative history of the Metropolitan Police yet published, or likely to be: "Scotland Yard and the Metropolitan Police," by Sir John Moylan, C.B., C.B.E., Receiver for the Metropolitan Police District (Putnam's "Whitehall Series," revised and enlarged edition, June 1934). If Mr. Stuart cannot get information from the "Yard" (and I am not surprised that they have refused) surely he would be well-advised to give up his idea? It would be impossible to write anything approaching an adequate record of the Special Branch without official help. As it is, there are far too many books purporting to lay bare the secrets of Scotland Yard.
> A. R. L. M.[119]

Frank Stuart's book on the history of the Metropolitan Police Special Branch was not realized. He continued writing press articles and works on a variety of subjects, among them novelized military accounts with occult and stage magic references, crime fiction, and travelogues using stylistic techniques similar to those of Morland and McCormick. His last known work, published in 1954, was, *A Seal's World: An Account of the First Three Years in the Life of a Harp Seal*. His best-known book of 1949, *The City of Bees*, was only surpassed by his one true literary work, the 1951 Shakespearian novel, *Remember Me*, for the publisher Stanley Paul. The novel demonstrated Stuart's skill as an author. It demonstrates his ability to have produced the "Diary of Jack the Ripper" if called for. Perhaps Frank Stanley Stuart fabricated the original manuscript of the diary and perhaps he did not. Either way, the Maybrick Diary stands as a testament to the convoluted postwar contractual arrangements of ghostwriters.

Back in 1892, Robert Anderson gave an interview to *Cassell's Saturday Journal* almost two weeks after Inspector Abberline was approached. Anderson was reported as saying, "I sometimes think myself an unfortunate man ... for between twelve and one of the morning of the day I took up my position here the first Whitechapel murder occurred."

The mention of this appalling sequence of still undiscovered crimes leads to the production of certain ghastly photographs.

"There," says the Assistant Commissioner, "there is my answer to people who come with fads and theories about these murders. It is impossible to believe they were acts of a sane man — they were those of a maniac revelling in blood."[120]

### Robert Anderson had the widespread support of experts and specialists in insanity:

Professor Ordrenaux, of Columbia College Law school, author of standard works on the legal bearings of insanity, and for nine years state commissioner of lunacy for New York, gives this opinion: "The murderer is a lunatic, of course. There is no doubt of that. His very cleverness in eluding the police might be a proof of it. The devilish cunning and resource of some maniacs is marvellous. The question is, what frightful nightmare of madness is this that possesses him? When he is caught he will speak out; he won't hesitate to give reasons as far as he is able.

Meanwhile, we can only guess. But cases of the kind have not been so rare that we need guess at random. The vampires of the middle ages that haunted the cemeteries and dug up the bodies of women to tear the flesh from their bones were doubtless madmen of his calibre. They were a very real terror to their time, not at all creatures of an excited fancy. At times their peculiar madness became fairly epidemic on the continent of Europe. The reason why the psychology of the middle ages presents many more such cases than our day is that then they ran unhindered, while nowadays such lunatics would be very soon arrested.

"Science may ridicule the idea of demoniacal possession. Those who deny that there is anything but matter will see no proof to the contrary. Proof expires with the conditions of matter you are examining, and when you drop the subject as a mental and take it up as a moral question you tread on uncertain ground in a sense. It is true that you cannot find a demon with a microscope or figure it out by tables of logarithms: and yet it is not irrational to suppose that a distance evil agency does dominate the human mind under circumstances when it is overthrown to the last degree and has lost its personal and subjective identity. When insanity, originating in a perversion of the sexual instinct, passes beyond bounds within which it can be explained on conditions of physical deterioration, it is permissible to recognize a superhuman cause as the controlling power in the domination of human conduct. This is demoniacal possession. Granted that the only foundation for belief in it is the utterly inhuman and illogical conduct of the victim, yet if he alone of ten thousand lunatics similarly affected goes this length, we shall have to assume either that he is a being differently formed, which we cannot do, or that some new agency is discovered in his case, as in that of this London murderer. Here is where 'possession of an evil spirit' steps in to supply the explanation. It seems to me as admissible in this last emergency as the law of gravitation. Nobody sees it, yet nobody doubts it. We all see its results.

"The law of blood atonement is written on the constitution of the human mind, and when utterly perverted by a sense of intolerable wrong makes of the man such an ogre as this slayer of women. There are many kinds of vampirism, but they all cluster around this one idea of motiveless mutilation of dead bodies. No one would do the deeds of this monster unless dominated by the law of blood atonement mingled with an evil principle that then takes the form of demoniacal possession.

"The law must furnish by punishment some motive for the man to resist. The taking possession of a mind is a gradual process, a consequence of wilful sin against nature's law, or weak yielding. The whole subject opens up such a wide field of metaphysical study and religious suggestion that you cannot answer any question in one word, yes or no. It is yes up to a certain point and no beyond it."[121]

# 7

# Whitechapel Secret Service

Sir Charles Warren, Metropolitan Police Commissioner during the Whitechapel events, quit under political pressure[1] as the Ripper's last victim, Mary Jane Kelly, was murdered on November 9, 1888. Warren, unlike his senior police colleagues in later years, did not leave a detailed public record of Jack the Ripper theories. However, he did note an official statement for the attention of both the Home and Foreign Office on secret societies. It has fueled conspiracy theories and historic beliefs since the official files were released during the late 1970s.

Warren's rank in regular Freemasonry has also led to conjecture on a conspiracy to murder destitute East End prostitutes — a plot supposedly hatched at the top level of the ruling classes, not excluding the Royal Family. There is no evidence to support such imaginative views. The mutilations create an impression of a serial killer who is sophisticated and clever, yet a maniac who escaped the joint efforts of Victorian London's Metropolitan and City Police forces, Scotland Yard's Criminal Investigation Department and its Special Branch.

Compared to modern serial killers, Jack the Ripper worked in a very small part of the East End. He escaped detection, yet he came to the attention of a vigilant and well-organized police structure. It is precisely because the best detectives were employed on the Whitechapel murders that the case became such a baffling mystery.

At the height of the Whitechapel murders, responding to a dispatch to the Foreign Office from Sir A. Paget, the British ambassador to Vienna, on October 13, 1888, Sir Charles Warren discussed a European suspect associated with anarchists who had been brought to the attention of Scotland Yard. He included an opinion on a motive for the murders: "As Mr. Matthews [the Home Secretary] is aware I have for some time past inclined to the idea that the murders may possibly be done by a secret society, as the only logical solution of the question, but I would not understand this being done by a socialist because the last murders were obviously done by someone desiring to bring discredit on the Jews and socialists or Jewish socialists."[2]

Warren's statement is in marked contrast to that of his Assistant Commissioner and head of CID, Robert Anderson. Later in 1910, Anderson formulated and published a semi-official theory that Jack the Ripper was a "low-class Polish Jew." He noted that Scotland

Yard officials arrived at that position sometime after the murders ceased.[3] Anderson also went further than Warren in saying that the identity of Jack the Ripper was definitely an "ascertained fact" known to the police. Chief Constable Melville Macnaghten named Kosminski as a suspect but preferred Druitt as more likely. Kosminski was also cited by Chief Inspector Donald Swanson in his copy of Anderson's memoirs. The "local and insane Jewish suspect" theory has become entrenched with the blessing of modern criminal profiling. But is this what happened and does it really reflect the continued police inquiries?

During 1888, Scotland Yard experienced a great deal of reorganization. The Whitechapel murders occurred at this critical time in English politics.

## THE CHANGES AT SCOTLAND YARD

Mr. James Monro, C.B., late chief of the Criminal Investigation Department at Scotland Yard, has received an important appointment at the Home Office and assumed the duties of his new post yesterday. Colonel Wilkinson has been appointed assistant to Mr. Monro, and both gentlemen were busily engaged at the Home Office during the day. The unofficial announcement of Mr. Monro's appointment has, says the Central News, caused considerable surprise at Scotland Yard and in official circles generally, and much curiosity is felt as to the duties connected with his new post. On this point the authorities absolutely refuse to give any information, but there is reason to believe that Mr. Monro's work will be of a character similar to that formerly performed by Mr. Jenkinson.[4] Mr. Robert Anderson, the new chief of the Criminal Investigation Department, has formally taken over the duties of his office. It is persistently rumored that Sir Charles Warren will shortly retire from Scotland Yard, and that he will be appointed to succeed Sir Hercules Robinson as her Majesty's High Commissioner in South Africa.[5]

"Secret society" as a modern term connotes occult associations, Freemasonic orders, or other such groups.

However, in the Victorian period, the term applied to any association that was private, cultural, clandestine or covert. It included the occult, Freemasonry, mystical groups, political groups, gentlemen's clubs, sororities and terrorist groups. The Invincibles, an Irish Republican and military arm that committed the Phoenix Park murders in 1882, had stimulated the Victorian debate on secret societies. A contemporary view of the phenomenon was outlined in *The Times* in 1883.

## A SECRET SOCIETY

From their very nature secret societies are difficult of treatment, as well from a literary as from a social or political point of view. It is only when, by some accident or by some great effort, a secret society is unmasked that the public get access to the inner life and organization of its members. We now know something of nearly all the European secret societies. The Society of the Holy Vehm is medieval in its position, but in more modern times the Illuminati in Bavaria, the United Irishmen in Ireland, the Philadelphians in France, the Tugendbund in Germany, the Carbonari in Italy, the Communeros in Spain, the Hetairia in Greece, the United Sclavonians, and the more modern Nihilists in Russia have all left their marks upon history. During the last 15 years England has felt the influence of the Irish Republican Brotherhood, alias Fenians, in her political history, and the Communists of Paris have left a memory not easily wiped out from the minds of the French.[6]

Official files on the Whitechapel murders note that the Chief Commissioner of the Metropolitan Police and both the Home and Foreign Office believed secret societies might be implicated. But how far was a clandestine motive for the crimes of Jack the Ripper regarded as credible and how high up in the chain of command was it considered? Why would a political extremist secret society repeatedly murder and mutilate innocent civilians? That Jack the Ripper was bent on committing crimes of a perverse sexual nature and deviant bloodlust may seem the obvious conclusion. But does it reflect the lines of inquiry that Scotland Yard actually pursued?

With the resignation of Warren and appointment of James Monro as Metropolitan Police Commissioner in late 1888, the Whitechapel murders investigation diverged with new lines of inquiry as more details were collated and sifted. Robert Anderson commissioned a fresh medical report from Central Office police surgeon Dr. Thomas Bond. Details previously leaked to the press and aired at inquests were curtailed. The police on the ground continued their usual investigation and vigilance as the press hounded them for copy. The conspiracy of Jack the Ripper was born too late to officially turn back until a change of government on August 15, 1892.[7] The resulting political imbroglio peppered with ambiguous police statements had done more to inspire conspiracy theories than the murders themselves.

A background to how the Scotland Yard investigation of a serial killer affected Victorian politics was noted in a series of press reports titled "Old World News by Cable" by the London correspondent of *The New York Times*. Signing himself "H.F.," Harold Frederic had covered English affairs since 1884 and had explained the Whitechapel murders for an American readership.

> On the resumption later of the Government, Ireland will be the chief topic of interest and discussion, no matter what the outcome of the Parnell Commission be, as he and his lawyers firmly believe it will be, to discredit the Times and its allies, the session will be very stormy and, perhaps, productive of real results.
>
> But a more tangible danger to the Ministry, curiously enough, is to be found in what all the civilized world knows now as the Whitechapel murders. If it should happen when Parliament meets that the strange assassin is still undiscovered, or if more of these horrible murders be committed and the perpetrator is tracked by outsiders, there would be a storm of indignation let loose in St. Stephen's under which certainly Mr. Matthews and very possibly his associates would go down.
>
> It seems odd enough to an American mind to wreck an imperial Government because an abnormal sort of criminal killed some women in the slums and escaped detection, but this is one of the risks of a system which gives executive powers to certain members of the majority party in Parliament and places their tenure of office at the mercy of a yea and nay vote. The House of Commons does not like or respect its police, and the Home Secretary is responsible for the police. It is to be remembered that the first time the present Government was beaten it was on a case where a constable arrested a girl named Cass on a charge of street-walking.[8] The Government did not resign on this rebuff any more than it did last summer, when it was beaten on army resolution, but unless the Whitechapel scandal is cleared up before November and the Government unloads Mr. Matthews he is likely to be condemned by a majority so heavy as to discredit and destroy the whole Ministry.[9]

Frederic followed up on the state of English affairs with a report soon after the murder of Mary Kelly on November 9, 1888.

> The Tory Government's compact with Germany jointly to occupy the East African coast grows in unpopularity with discussion. [Prime Minister] Lord Salisbury's declaration that the English liability is limited to naval action reassures nobody, for Berlin is seething with plans for raising a volunteer infantry force to co-operate with the combined fleets, and a favorite scheme is to enlist the Sikhs and Maharattas for this purpose. It is, indeed, stated that the agent of the German East African Company has already started for Bombay to begin this work. Questions on this point will be asked in Parliament next week, and the matter bids fair to assume large political importance.
>
> So, too, does the subject of the new Whitechapel murders. On the occasion of the last two previous butcheries by this strange assassin on the closing day of September, I pointed out the probability that this would give the Ministry serious trouble in Parliament. The latest atrocity has made this a certainty. On Monday Davis, one of the South London Tory members, will raise the question on a motion to adjourn the House and a resolution attacking both Matthews and Warren will be moved. There will be a big debate during the evening and the division is regarded by some members of the Government with apprehension. Urgent telegraphic whips have been sent to the Irish members who are still in Ireland, begging them to come over in time for this division, the effect of which may be to upset the Ministry or at least to sorely damage it. London Tory members will vote almost solidly

against Matthews, for their constituents are all up in arms against the existing police inefficiency. This is very characteristic of London, which reads of Clanricarde's turning out into the wintry blasts thousands of helpless [Irish] tenants without concern, but is willing to wreck a Ministry because some street-walker in the slums has been murdered by a mysterious lunatic.[10]

Jack the Ripper came to personify Victorian fears of imminent change. Though the murders were a local concern, the international fever they engendered was symptomatic of Victorian global developments. Social outrage over the plight of the poor and sympathy for the victims intensified these feelings. Jack the Ripper embodied malign competitiveness and the sea change of the Industrial Revolution with its heightening of class and gender inequities. American, European, English and other press agencies observed the events in the heart of the British Empire with sustained interest.

### DEMOCRATIC SCHEMES COMING FORWARD IN ENGLAND

"Legislation grows increasingly difficult every year," sighed Lord Salisbury three weeks ago. The present condition of affairs in English politics makes very clear the cause of his complaint, and it is no less perplexing to the Prime Minister than it is interesting to the world at large. While history may not declare the present Ministers of England the most intelligent that ever administered the Government, it should do them justice to state that their position has been unusually trying. Home rule is not the chief difficulty. It is merely one of special forms taken by a much wider movement whose advance is bothering all the conservative thinkers of the country without any prospect of its being stopped. This is the ever-increasing demand for popular rule in all things, for doing away with class lines, and, as a result, for the abolition of several great social systems, which, to the conservative English mind, are vital elements in the very life of the nation itself. Among these are the abolition of hereditary rights in legislation and the disestablishment of the Church of England. Home rule simply leads the line, the other great questions standing in abeyance until the first great point is gained.

The fact is that the masses in England, like those in all the Continental countries, in varying degrees, are learning not only that they have rights ungranted, but also that through the general extension of the elective franchise in 1884–6 they have the power to obtain them. Democracy, to use Lord [Salisbury] Rosebery's phrase, is getting on its legs. It is the universal tendency of the time, and shrewd statesmen recognize that they can no more combat it by legislation than they can arrest Atlantic tides by a breakwater of red tape.[11]

With affairs strained in government and the reorganization of Scotland Yard during the Whitechapel murders, the concern to the press and electorate was immense. Officials desperate to find the killer inevitably suspected peripheral persons and extreme secret societies. The murder of Elizabeth Stride on September 30, 1888, for instance, had occurred beside the Berner Street International Working Men's Educational Club, one of the East End branches of European and Russian Jewish socialist movements. The transfer of large numbers of police into the criminal slums of Whitechapel from other divisions was legitimized with the murders.

Though extreme anarchist groups from Russia and the European continent found asylum under Britain's immigration regime, they would not jeopardize their sanctuary on English soil. Anarchists were documented as violently active in London, but later than the Whitechapel murders. They had been kept under surveillance since the 1887 Trafalgar Square socialist riots where Sir Charles Warren sent in mounted police to quell the disturbances. Agents of the German secret service had a distinct motive to discredit Jewish socialists during the Whitechapel murders, as Warren suggested. Prussian detectives found it difficult to apprehend wanted anarchists in England. The socialist news sheet of William Morris, *Commonweal,* claimed that German spies were infiltrating East End clubs during 1888. Theodor Reuss, a journalist with the Central News Agency, was named as an infiltrator of the German government and likely attended the Berner Street meetings.

There is, however, no direct evidence, despite Warren's official hints to the Home and Foreign Office, that the Scotland Yard investigation of East End Jewish socialists was fruitful. Stride was officially declared one of the Ripper's victim count but it is not certain that she was. It seems that in contrast to the murders of Catherine Eddowes, Mary Ann Nichols and Annie Chapman, Stride's murder was committed by another hand. Eddowes was killed 45 minutes after Stride. The "double event" of the night of September 30, 1888, included the discovery in Goulston Street of a piece of Eddowes's bloodstained apron beneath wall writing that read, "The Juwes are the Men who will not be Blamed for Nothing." Warren did not believe that Jews or socialists were responsible for the murders.

In a series of articles released in 1895, *Scotland Yard: Its Mysteries and Methods*,[12] retired Detective Sergeant Patrick McIntyre,[13] a Special Branch veteran familiar with the East End and the Whitechapel murders investigation, gave an account of the Berner Street murder.

A number of Englishmen who had been mixed up with the socialist movement, and were dissatisfied with it, appeared on the scene at the "Autonomie Club" soon after its establishment. This band included men like Charles Mowbray, David Nicholl, Tom Cantwell, and H.B. Samuels. They began to form groups of English Anarchists, and it became our duty to pay a little attention to the new departure. All through the summer the members of these groups were to be heard in Hyde Park on Sundays preaching the new doctrine to the casual stroller. At this time the Commonweal newspaper served as their chief organ, and one of the groups met at a small room in the City-road where the paper was published. The groups were chiefly to be found in North, North-East, and East London.

One group held meetings in Berner-street, Whitechapel. Concerts and dancing took place here on Saturday nights, and while one of these was taking place, during the time of the Jack the Ripper scare, an extraordinary event took place just outside the Anarchists' meeting place. At the very moment when these people were indulging in festivity in an upstairs room, the "Ripper" was cruelly murdering an unfortunate in the courtway adjoining. It is worth noting that no kind of suspicion fell upon the Anarchists in this connection; no one believed for a moment that the anonymous stabber was one of their confraternity. And here I can say that I am certain that, though the Anarchists talked wildly and advocated schemes that seemed utterly impractical to the ordinary observer, they were all quiet and peaceful men, well disposed to their fellow-creatures in general. I had a good deal of experience among all sections of the East-end Anarchists, and, according to my observation, in spite of their tenets, they were a good-hearted and sympathetic class of the community.[14]

Domestic political terrorism in Victorian England was the responsibility of the Home Office and assigned to the Metropolitan Police Special Branch headed by Chief Inspector John Littlechild, and Assistant Commissioner and head of Scotland Yard CID, Robert Anderson. Jack the Ripper's crimes were regarded as serious affairs of state bearing on the reputation of Scotland Yard. Inquiries had considered the Whitechapel murders as opportunities for East End extremists. The murders had galvanized the official machine in the slums of Whitechapel.

On April 19, 1910, the Secretary of State for the Home Office, Winston Churchill, was asked in the House of Commons a question about Anderson's *Blackwood's Magazine* articles in which he stated his theory on the Whitechapel murders. Had Churchill's "attention been called to the revelations published by Sir Robert Anderson with regard to what are generally known as the Jack the Ripper murders; [had] he obtained the sanction of the Home Office or Scotland Yard authorities to such publication, and, if not, whether any and, if so, what steps can be taken with regard to it?" Churchill replied, "Sir Robert Anderson neither asked for nor received any sanction to the publication, but the matter appears to me of minor importance in comparison with others that arise in connection with the same series of articles."[15]

So minor were Anderson's leaks on Jack the Ripper compared to his writing the 1887 "Parnellism and Crime," articles for *The Times* that by 1932, an official history of the newspaper had thoroughly expunged any mention of his involvement. Authors in support of an insane Jewish suspect have followed suit with Churchill in partly absolving Anderson of publishing allegations against duly elected Ministers of the Crown despite contrary historic material. Nevertheless, it was not Anderson's only professional indiscretion. *The Times: Past Present and Future* wrote:

In the winter of 1885–86, to the general consternation, came the announcement of Mr. Gladstone's adoption of Home Rule for Ireland and The Times at once constituted itself the center of resistance, encouraged the Whig Lord Hartinglon and the Radical Joseph Chamberlain to come out against their leader, and was greatly responsible for the formation of the Liberal Unionist party. The Home Rule Bill was defeated in the Commons in 1886; but the efforts of the paper did not relax, and the second Home Rule Bill was thrown out by the Lords in 1893. Meanwhile, the staff of The Times was strengthened by the coming of a very able, very well-informed and very trenchant writer, John Woulfe Flanagan, whose articles entitled "Parnellism and Crime" revived the downrightness and vehemence of The Times in former days. These articles began in March, 1887; and that year and the two following years made up the troubled period in which the publication of a forged letter attributed to Parnell and other attacks on Irish leaders for countenancing and abetting crime led to the Parnell Commission. The findings of that Commission established the truth of a great part of the charges made by The Times, while showing also that in that period of fierce political passions and of widespread corruption and intrigue it had been the victim of contaminated sources of information.[16]

According to testimony of Richard Pigott, the forger of the letter, at sittings of the Special Commission in early 1889, the contaminated sources that *The Times* complained of were government agencies.[17] As admitted in one form or another on the publication of the 1910 *Blackwood's Magazine* articles, Sir Robert Anderson had supplied the intelligence and drafts. He was officially active in 1887 as Secretary to the Prison Commissioners. Unofficially, he was employed as a political crime advisor and spy handler for the secret internal criminal department of the Home Office headed by James Monro.

On resumption of the parliamentary debate of April 21, 1910, Mr. MacVeagh, MP, in his speech said,

I would ask the Government to tell us plainly — I asked the question the other day, but could not get any information — whether there is any Home Office Minute on record forbidding the writing of articles by Government officials, whether still in the public service or in receipt of pensions. What was the fate of Sir Charles Warren, a Commissioner of Police, who wrote much less serious articles in "Murray's Magazine"?[18] He was censured and retired from office because he wrote an article on the administration of Scotland Yard. Anderson did infinitely worse than Warren; and yet Anderson was loaded with honors, while Warren was hunted from the public service. I think Sir Charles Warren has just reason to complain of the manner in which he was treated by the Home Office and by the Government.[19]

Winston Churchill gave further details on the potential implications of Anderson's late disclosures.

That is the extent of the first charge against Sir R. Anderson, which rests upon his own voluntary confession. As to that, if it had been known at the time, if the Government of the day had done its duty, and if the Government of the day had followed the ordinary course which would be adhered to in a case of this character, there could be no doubt whatever that Sir R. Anderson would have been dismissed at once. The Treasury Rule, made in 1875, and republished in 1884, was to the effect that "no official information is to be communicated to public journals without the sanction of the responsible heads of the Departments, and any gentleman infringing this regulation renders himself liable to instant dismissal."[20]

To dispel Anderson's professional and clearly partisan indiscretions, supporters of his Jewish suspect theory claim that he later tried to correct the record regarding the 1887 *Parnellism and Crime* articles.[21] Anderson's supporters propose that, if the details in *The Times* articles were correct, then his 1910 comments on the identity of Jack the Ripper are also likely to be sound. However, according to the 1888–89 Special Commission, they were not. It is said that any questioning of them was political bias. Anderson was no politician and, as a civil servant, was bound by the same Treasury rules on public official disclosures that had contributed to the resignation of Warren after the release of his 1888 *Murray's Magazine* articles on police matters. Accordingly, the Jack the Ripper case was assumed an entirely separate issue from the political violence and rhetoric of the late Victorian period.

In a letter to *The Times* dated April 25, 1910, and not published until April 30, Anderson had more to say on his official engagements. He responded to comments by Arthur Balfour in the House of Commons, who was Chief Secretary for Ireland and the Prime Minister's nephew in the Salisbury Tory government from 1887 to 1892. Anderson had intended the statement to be inserted in his memoirs. He said:

> On April 21st [1910] my misdeeds were made the ground of an attack upon me in the House of Commons. I thereupon prepared a full statement of what I had to say in my defense; and this I intended to publish in the present volume. But after the MS. had gone to the printer it was urged upon me that I was thus about to cumber these pages with matter which had entirely ceased to interest the public. Accordingly I recalled it, and decided to content myself with reproducing the above letter to The Times [12 April 1910], and also the following [21 March 1889], which was written twenty-one years ago, when I was attacked upon practically the same grounds as in the debate of last April. Part of it could not be more germane to these recent charges if it were written with special reference to them."[22]

## SIR ROBERT ANDERSON AND MR. BALFOUR
## TO THE EDITOR OF THE TIMES.

Sir,—When I wrote the letter which appeared in The Times of Friday last I intended it to be my last word for the present on the subject of Thursday's debate. But Mr. Balfour's speech, which I had not read, forces me to appeal to you for a further hearing. The fact that in Mr. O'Connor's philippic I was merely a foil for an attack upon the Unionist Administration of the Parnell era makes Mr. Balfour's words about me seem all the more strange. Surely he cannot have realized that he was joining in condemning an absent man who had not been heard in his own defense, though he had appealed for a hearing in terms of studied respect and deference.

Here are the facts about the genesis of my Times articles. In April, 1887, in conversation with a friend with whom I had formerly been in close touch officially about such matters, I mentioned the dynamite plots then hatching in America in view of the approaching "Jubilee celebrations" in London. This led to a suggestion that the danger might be averted by action such as had succeeded on former occasions—namely, by a public exposure of the conspiracy.[23] My friend was then connected with one of our leading publishing firms, and the proposal was that I should write a short pamphlet for publication by that firm. I acted on that suggestion; but they hesitated to publish it anonymously, and so the matter dropped. After an interval, however, he urged me to let him offer it to The Times, but this I refused to authorize. But, as the days went by, the danger was becoming increasingly imminent and grave, and I allowed him to take the manuscript and use it at his discretion. The Times wished to publish it, but required the name of the author; and this again brought matters to a full stop. Finally, however, in response to a further appeal from him, I left myself in his hands on this point also. It is fortunate, perhaps, that I have preserved his letters. The result was that my MS was "edited" in the form in which it ultimately appeared as three separate articles in The Times.

I need not repeat for the tenth time that this was the only help I gave The Times in their public-spirited campaign against the Parnellite movement; and my purpose was not to "help The Times" at all, but to thwart the most infamous and dangerous conspiracy with which we have had to cope within living memory. Mr. O'Connor's statement that I slandered Parnell is itself a wanton slander. I challenge him to find in the whole literature on this subject a kindlier or more generous estimate of

Parnell's character and conduct than that which is contained in my book on the Home Rule movement.[24]

People may wonder why I did not say all this before last Thursday. When I saw my hurriedly-penned letter in print in The Times of the 12th I felt that it was inadequate, and I wished to supplement it. But a trusted friend (his name, if I might give it, would satisfy any one that I was entitled to yield to his judgement) advised me that, having by that letter placed myself at the disposal of the Prime Minister, I could not with propriety break silence again pending the debate in Parliament. But I now lay the facts before the public to enable them to judge of my conduct. And as for the charge of violating a rule of the Civil Service,[25] I can only plead that I had no knowledge of the existence of such a rule; that what I did was done in wholly extraordinary circumstances; and that my lapse might be condoned in view of the great public benefits which resulted from it. And yet this is the only foundation for the bitter attack that has been made upon me.[26]

But I am forgetting the Le Caron papers. Though the answer I gave to that charge 21 years ago was accepted even by Sir William Harcourt,[27] I suppose I must now go into the whole matter again. But I cannot ask you to allow me a page of The Times in which to refute them. Mr. Monro's amazing letter[28] I will deal with hereafter, repeating in detail my former words. To me it is an echo of a most painful incident, which, on the eve of his resigning the Chief Commissionership of Police, broke up a close friendship of several years. I cannot doubt that Mr. Balfour supposed I knew of that letter, and that I had no answer to it, for he would presume that a man with my record would be treated with ordinary courtesy. And I venture to hope that, when he finds that I have been denied even common justice, his generosity will lead him to undo the injury he has inflicted on me — it is the only injury which the debate has done me.[29]

I am, Sir, your obedient servant,
April 25. ROBERT ANDERSON.[30]

In 1889 Henry Matthews, the Home Secretary during the Whitechapel murders, was questioned in the House of Commons about the treatment of Warren and Anderson according to the rules on disclosure. He responded:

But I had to look at that letter upon the challenge of the right hon. Gentleman in the strict light of the prison discipline and prison rules, and the prison rule on the subject I will read with the permission of the House. It was circulated by the Prisons Department some years ago. It is a rule prohibiting the publication of books relating to the department. It was issued on July 22nd, 1879, and is to the effect that the attention of the Secretary of State has been called to the question of allowing the publication by officials of books relating to the department, and he desires that no officer shall publish any work relating to the department unless the sanction of the Secretary of State has been previously obtained. I may add that the rule was a consequence of a Treasury regulation of some years before which was directed against publications of this kind.

The Treasury issued an order in which they stated that their attention had been called to the fact that official information had been communicated to the public Press by officials, and the rule was made to prevent the publication of official secrets from official sources of information. I think that rule was very properly enforced by the head of the department for this purpose also, to prevent discussions in the public Press of matters connected with the department by officials of the department, a matter which I think is equally to be deprecated with the disclosure of official secrets. Though originally aimed at disclosure of official secrets, I think the rule ought to be applied to the public discussion of matters on which controversy takes place within the department. I hope that nothing I may say will be taken as minimizing the rule in the slightest degree.[31]

There appears to be no consistent pattern of official secrets requirements[32] in this period that would allow an effective check of police or political statements on Jack the Ripper, apart from the Treasury Rule of 1875 (republished in 1884). Anderson admitted that he had met the real danger of extremists.[33] The Treasury Rule as quoted by Home Secretary Matthews was not without ambiguity, as it was applied and enforced arbitrarily. The resolution was not retrospective or applicable with the Home Secretary Winston Churchill in 1910 weighing Anderson's indiscretions. Jack the Ripper, it would seem, had escaped notice amid the administrative confusion.

An official remark made openly was then acceptable to reveal, with the discretion of the Home Secretary. If Jack the Ripper had been captured and deemed insane under English common law, any later public disclosures by senior police officials would have been, on paper at least, prohibited. Anderson's unproved theories seem intended to avert conditions that led to the widespread Whitechapel murders scare. Comments were made as to shifting the electoral grounds for increased legislative powers granted to police, as Anderson had advocated.[34]

Anderson was, in effect, promoting a change of English criminal law with Jack the Ripper as a case study. Scotland Yard may have known the identity of Jack the Ripper without evidence to convict as Anderson indicated, but it did not follow that the killer was a Polish Jew. There was no senior police consensus. However, that is not to say that Anderson's opinions on reform, derived of official experience, were not without merit.[35]

So what in theory could and could not civil servants officially divulge about Jack the Ripper during this period, and how, in practice, did it actually work? It is clear from Churchill's answer in the House of Commons that details on Jack the Ripper by a senior police official were regarded as official secrets, as might be expected of a high-profile unsolved serial murder case. Anderson, responding to questions from Sir William Harcourt in the House of Commons, supplied an overview of the arrangements. They concern the retention and nature of official documents and disclosures of privileged information to the press. His March 20, 1889, letter to *The Times* was reprinted in Anderson's 1910 memoirs, of which extracts follow.

## SIR W. HARCOURT AND MR. ANDERSON
## TO THE EDITOR OF THE TIMES

Sir,—It is an excellent rule that Civil servants of the Crown, when publicly attacked, should leave their defense in the hands of their Parliamentary chiefs. I have always observed that rule, and I have no intention of departing from it. But when acts done by me wholly outside the sphere of my official position are assigned as proof that I am unworthy of the office I have the honor to hold under Her Majesty's warrant, I must not shelter myself behind the Secretary of State, for whose generous defense of me in Parliament to-day I am most deeply grateful. It is my privilege, as it is clearly my duty, to put myself right with the public immediately.

I have already intimated that my action in relation to Major Le Caron's [a British spy] evidence was wholly apart from my official position as Assistant Commissioner of Police. It rose from the fact that in former years, in an entirely unofficial position, I rendered advice and assistance to the 1880 Government in matters relating to political crime. A complete explanation of my conduct would involve such an appeal to documents and details as would amount to a disclosure of the secret service arrangements of that period. To me, personally, the disclosure would be intensely gratifying. It would, moreover, supply a missing chapter of uncommon interest in the political history of recent years. But Sir W. Harcourt knows me well enough to feel assured that I would not, except under compulsion, say anything to embarrass ex–Ministers of the Crown who admitted me in any measure to their confidence. Whether it is generous of him to take advantage of this in attacking me as he has done I will not discuss. It is not in keeping with the kindness I have hitherto experienced at his hands.

The suggestion that I should have pleaded privilege for these manuscripts as being official documents claims notice. I might, of course, have set up such a plea, but the following facts will make it clear that I could not have sustained it without prevaricating to the verge of falsehood. The letters in question do not come within the definition contained in the Official Secrets Bill now before Parliament. They were never "filed" in a public department. I kept them at my private residence. When Sir W. Harcourt once took me to task for acting in this way with reference to my informants, I immediately asked him to relieve me of my share in the secret service work of the Home Office. His reply, which now lies before me, reads strangely when compared with his present utterances.

Nor had I personally, in relation to such matters, any official position of a kind to lend an official character to the documents in question. If sometimes, through over-zeal, I placed myself "in evidence" in any way, I was reminded that I had "no official position whatever," when I asked for a salary from public funds, I was told it was impossible because I had "no official position." So entirely unofficial were my relations with the Secretary of State and the Irish Government that no intimation of them was ever given to the head of the department in which I had then recently become a "Civil servant," and the most sustained and scrupulous care was taken to conceal from Her Majesty's Treasury the fact that I had any engagements outside that department. But now, because I happen to be in the line of fire between the two front benches in Parliament, it is contended that I had an official position all the time!

But, it is urged, these letters were paid for by the Government. This is an ad captandum argument to which I could give a complete reply if I were relieved from the honorable obligations to reticence which now restrain me. I will only remark that giving back letters to informants is not an uncommon practice. And this discussion may do good if certain parties on both sides of the Atlantic should learn from it that they may give information to Her Majesty's Government, and receive remuneration for doing so, with the certainty that their secret will be as well kept as Le Caron's was, and that, if they like to make the condition, their communications shall be treated as strictly unofficial documents and be returned to them at any time they wish to claim them.

As regards Sir W. Harcourt's criticisms upon the discharge of my official duties my mouth is closed. But I want to emphasize, and I am prepared to substantiate on oath, the fact asserted by Mr. Matthews that neither the "Assistant Commissioner of Police" nor the department which he controls has given help to The Times in the presentation of their case before the Commission.

I am, &c.,
R. ANDERSON.
March 20.[36]

With this open letter on official matters Anderson transgressed the Treasury Rule in 1889, shortly after Warren, his Chief Commissioner, resigned while the Jack the Ripper investigation was active. He denied knowing the rule in 1910 in reply to Arthur Balfour. Or he had forgotten, or he was simply not cognizant of the rules on disclosure of direct concern to the departments he headed. If he could be mistaken on the rules that applied to his tenure as Her Majesty's civil servant, perhaps he was also mistaken about an "insane Polish Jew" as a suspect for the Whitechapel murders.

However, the problem for the Tory administration and the Assistant Commissioner of the Metropolitan Police during the murders was that the spy Henri Le Caron (alias of Thomas Miller Beach), had already testified at the Special Commission. He had been in receipt of Secret Service monies and had passed on sensitive documents to the government. This had prompted Sir William Harcourt, a previous Home Secretary, to question Anderson's professional propriety. As a civil servant, Anderson had erred in not referring official matters to the Home Office for prior approval.

The question became, what did the gov-

Henri Le Caron, alias Thomas Miller Beach, was a British spy who for 25 years infiltrated U.S. Fenian secret societies. Robert Anderson was his handler.

ernment know of Anderson's indiscretions under the heat of violence and hostile threats, and did he receive the sanction of the Home Office? Republican terror was met with Royalist terror and vice versa during the period. Civilians were caught in the crossfire. Further details emerged at the resumption of the Special Commission in early 1889: "The Attorney General (to witness)[Le Caron]: All these documents I have been referring to were sent over to England to the British Government after you had taken a copy of them? Yes; they have never been in my possession since. Witness said that all the documents to which he had referred were sent by him to the British Government after he had taken copies of them."[37]

On April 21, 1910, the debate in the House of Commons resumed with an opening speech by the past editor of the *Star* and *Sun* newspapers, Irish MP T.P. O'Connor. During his speech O'Connor said of Anderson's 1887 *Times* articles on "Parnellism and Crime:

> In order to give the popular impression which these articles created, I will read an extract from a speech made by a warden in one of the colleges in Oxford, and he was an Irishman. He said:—"And so they had not only a Home Rule League, which undergraduates of advanced views had been earnestly pressed to join, but also, as he understood, an Oxford branch of the National League, with a nonconformist minister for its president, which had not yet taken any active part in organising outrage so far as he knew, but which might yet succeed in attracting the attention of the Parnell Inquiry Commission. (Laughter.) They had already had visits from Mr. George. Mr. Hyndman, Mr. Davitt and Mr. Dillon, and his impression was that if the Whitechapel murderer could be identified, he would be invited to lecture by a club he could name."[38]

The speech mentioned by O'Connor was given by the Warden of Merton College, Oxford, George C. Brodrick. (This family's surname is also spelled Broderick.) It was brought to the attention of the Parnell Special Commission in late 1888 for contempt of court based on the Whitechapel murders remark. Liberal Unionist Broderick was also the uncle of St. John Broderick, Financial Secretary of the War Department in the House of Commons. He was associated with Conservative MP Henry R. Farquharson, who in 1891 had his own Jack the Ripper story on suspect Montague Druitt.[39] The hint that socialists and Irish leaders were implicated in the murders of Jack the Ripper was thus made the substance of an official state inquiry into alleged criminal dealings of secret societies in early 1889. In a chapter of his memoirs titled "Appearance before the Special Commission," Brodrick fully explained the affair and his statement on Jack the Ripper, as the following extracts show.

> But I am here anticipating the course of events, and must recur to a little episode which rudely disturbed my quiet life during the Winter of 1888-89, and attracted some public attention. This episode arose, under circumstances which require explanation, out of the violent controversy which raged over the publication of the celebrated articles on "Parnellism and Crime" by the Times newspaper. It will be remembered that some of these articles contained what purported to be facsimiles of letters signed by Mr. Parnell and other Nationalist leaders, which letters were said to show complicity with the Phoenix Park murders and other crimes. Of course, these accusations were furiously resented by the Home Rule members, and Mr. Parnell at last took up the challenge of the Times by instituting an action for libel,[40] but in the meantime a Special Commission was appointed by Parliament to inquire into all the questions, including that of the letters, which had been raised in the obnoxious articles.
>
> Of this Commission Sir James Hannen was President, with Mr. Justice Day and Mr. Justice (now Lord Justice) A. L. Smith for his colleagues. It sat for several months in 1888 and 1889, with the result that its report had been quoted ever since by Home Rulers as an acquittal on the smaller issues, and by Unionists as a conviction on the larger issue.
>
> It happened that while the Special Commission was sitting, I had taken the chief part in founding a society called the "Oxford University Unionist League," and had become its President. In an address delivered at the first meeting of this body on December 1, 1888, I frankly admitted that I had long hesitated to do anything which might seem like encouraging political agitation among the

younger members of the University. I stated that, in my opinion, the University, as a place of education and learning, was not a suitable arena for politics, and that, if it were, it would seldom be well for undergraduates to mix themselves up prematurely with political controversy. I justified my departure from academical neutrality partly on the ground that the country was in the throes of a great national crisis, making it the duty of all patriotic citizens to stand together shoulder to shoulder, in presence of a common enemy and of an overwhelming danger; partly on the ground that unscrupulous efforts had been made in Oxford itself "to enlist recruits in the service of the National League a body which is now on its trial for crimes which shock humanity." "The Irish Question," I said, "has ceased to be a question of mere party politics it has ceased to be a merely political question, and has become mainly a moral question. The Liberals, headed by Mr. Gladstone, have entered into an open alliance with men who receive their instructions and draw their pay from the foreign enemies of Great Britain, who have declared war against Civil Government itself, and who defy the supremacy of the law. We Unionists might almost say of them in the language of Scripture: 'Our princes are rebellious, and have become the companions of thieves.' There is but one answer to such an alliance. It is the formation of a counter-alliance that is, of a National Party and I know of no reason why the formation of such a party embracing Conservatives and Liberal Unionists, should not begin at Oxford."

I have ventured to quote this passage, not only as containing an early forecast of the present Unionist Coalition, then in the clouds, but also as throwing light upon another paragraph in the same address, upon which a motion for contempt of Court was actually founded. The full text of that paragraph, abridged in the report of the London papers, is given in the affidavit which I submitted to the Court, and which I reproduce on a later page of this chapter.

On December 14, 1888, an application was made by the Attorney-General before the Commission against Mr. William O'Brien, described as the proprietor of United Ireland, for a contempt of Court, alleged to have been committed by the publication of an article in that paper. This article, read in Court, was represented to convey not only libellous reflections on the conduct of the prosecution, but gross imputations on the impartiality of the Court itself. Before the President had expressed any opinion upon it, Mr. Reid, Q.C., as counsel for Mr. Dillon, Mr. Harrington, and other Irish members of Parliament, started up and made a similar application against myself, founded on a passage, carefully divorced from its context, in the condensed Times report of "what purports to be" the address delivered by me on December 1. This passage he declared to be "a clear comparison of Mr. Davitt and Mr. Dillon with an infamous criminal."

## Below is Brodrick's affidavit submitted to the Special Commission:

In answer to the application made to this Honorable Court by Mr. Reid, Q.C., on the 14th day of December [1888] last, I George Charles Brodrick, make oath and say as follows:

1. I desire respectfully to state that I do not disavow the substance of the words cited by Mr. Reid, but that I do repudiate, most strongly and most indignantly, the construction which is sought to force upon them. I deny absolutely that in the passage cited I said anything constituting or resembling a "contempt of Court," either by showing disrespect towards the Special Commission for which no man entertains a higher respect than I do or by commenting directly or indirectly on its proceedings, or by prejudging any one of the issues now before the Commission.

2. I respectfully submit for the consideration of the Court the circumstances under which I spoke and the passage cited. I was addressing a private assembly, mainly composed of Oxford undergraduates, and my one object in the introductory paragraph to which exception is taken, was to ridicule, in a spirit of good-humoured banter, the love of innovation and of sensational notoriety-hunting prevalent in a certain school of young Oxford politicians. This is self-evident on the face of the paragraph itself, which I here subjoin, and the whole of which, as the Court will see, is conceived in that spirit:

And first I would point out that our main object is defensive. That is more than our opponents can say. Their policy and tactics are essentially aggressive, and this strange to say gives them a great advantage, specially in appealing to young Oxford minds. Some of you may remember the old Parliamentary squib in which the Radical reformers are described as framing a motion, "to abolish the sun and the moon," and if such a measure were proposed by Mr. Gladstone, I do believe that it would be easier to get up an association in Oxford to support the abolition of those ancient institutions than it would be to rouse enthusiasm in favor of maintaining them. And so we have not only a Home Rule League, which undergraduates of advanced views have been earnestly pressed to join, but also, as I understand, an Oxford branch of the National League, with a Nonconformist minister for its president, which has not yet taken any very active part in organising outrage, so far as I know, but which may yet succeed in attracting the attention of the Parnell Inquiry Commission. We have also already had visits from Mr. H. George, Mr. Hyndman, Mr. Davitt, Mr. Dillon, and Mr. Healy, and my impression is that if the Whitechapel murderer could be identified, he would be invited to lecture by an Oxford club which I could name if I thought proper.[41]

3. There are three allusions of the same character in this paragraph. I would ask whether the first is to be construed seriously as attributing to Mr. Gladstone an intention to move for the abolition of the heavenly bodies? If not, is the second to be construed seriously as attributing to an Oxford branch of the National League the design of organising outrage, and thus coming within the cognisance of the Commission? If not, is the last to be construed seriously as purporting to associate and compare, in respect of criminality, gentlemen represented before the Commission and not only these, but Mr. Henry George and Mr. Hyndman with the most atrocious of unknown murderers? The very extravagance of the supposed parallel is enough to rebut so absurd a construction. However, since it has been gravely urged, I hasten to admit that if such had been the real purport of the allusion, I should have been guilty of a grievous impropriety and injustice towards the gentlemen named, including Mr. H. George and Mr. Hyndman, as well as those represented before the Commission. But I can assure the Court, and I can assure these gentlemen if they care to accept my assurance that no such idea ever crossed my mind. The single idea present to my mind was the idea of notoriety, and not that of criminality. Having named several gentlemen notorious for their advocacy of extreme opinions on various subjects, all of whom had been invited to lecture at Oxford, I suggested, by way of climax and reductio ad absurdum, the invitation of the Whitechapel murderer, simply as the most notorious personage that occurred to me. Perhaps it was not the most felicitous illustration which could have been chosen, but I am certain that no man who heard me understood me for one moment to associate Irish Nationalists with the Whitechapel murderer in point of criminality, and I maintain that no rational man reading the passage would put so preposterous a construction upon it.

4. The rest of the speech referred to in the summons has been greatly abridged in the Times report, which embodies but one-third of the original. It contains strong expressions of political convictions, which I believe that I share with the whole Unionist party, and strong reflections on the revolutionary movement in Ireland; but I submit that it contains no expression of opinion upon the subject matter of the present inquiry, nor any statement imputing criminality to Mr. Reid's clients, or calculated to prejudice in the smallest degree the conduct of these proceedings. Not only had I no such intention, but I abstained throughout from touching upon topics which might appear to fall within the jurisdiction of this Commission, acknowledging, as I do, that it is the duty of every fair-minded man to suspend his judgement on all matters which are now sub judice.

5. This is my explanation, and I leave it with entire confidence in the hands of the Court. If I have erred unwittingly, I beg to express my sincerest regret. But I submit to the Court as a matter of reason and common-sense that my words, fairly interpreted, were perfectly innocent. Were it necessary or relevant, I should be prepared to contend that I did not overstep the legitimate bounds of political discussion. But this is not the question before the Commission. The question before the Commission is exclusively one of "contempt of Court." Now I submit once more to the Court, that I said not a word that can possibly be construed to show disrespect for its authority, or to comment directly on its proceedings, or to prejudge any one of the issues now pending before it. I therefore appeal to the Court, most respectfully, but most earnestly, to acquit me honorably of an offence which, I declare on my honor, was as remote from my thoughts as it is repugnant to my character.

GEORGE C. BRODRICK.

### Brodrick commented on the affidavit:

So ended this frivolous and vindictive attempt to damage the Unionist cause through me, as though I had any claim to be treated as a standard-bearer of the party. On the same day, and on a later occasion, Sir James Hannen, whom I knew personally, expressed a wish to discuss the matter privately with me, but I firmly declined, and, on his pressing me, told him plainly that I feared I could not do so, without being guilty of a real contempt of Court. It is needless to say that, while I received a shower of condolences and congratulations from the Unionist and even non–Unionist friends, I was vilified for some weeks by the Home Rule press. Out of many sympathetic letters I select that of Lord Bramwell, as expressing the deliberate judgement of an eminently judicial mind:

17 CADOGAN PLACE,
Jan. 25, 1889.
Dear Mr. Brodrick,

I have read the speech, and for the first time rightly understood and known what it was that you said. I am utterly surprised that any one could have considered it a contempt of Court, or any imputation on the Home Rulers. And, as to saying that you liken them to the Whitechapel murderer, it is preposterous. You say that in Oxford there are people with extravagant notions, and in particular one club which would give a hearing to the Whitechapel murderer. So far from saying that the Home Rulers are murderers, you by implication say that they are not. For you say that certain persons had been to Oxford, and that even the murderer would be invited by one club. Besides, George and Hyndman are not Home Rulers, or at least not notorious as such. It really was outrageous to charge this as a contempt. I thought Reid ungracious, and, to say the truth, I thought Hannen cold. I cannot but think now that he ought to have severely denounced the proceeding. I have the highest regard and respect for him. He is the perfection of a judicial character. I wonder if he apprehended the matter rightly.

Very truly yours,
BRAMWELL[42]

It is not clear why Sir James Hannen, who presided over the Parnell Special Commission, would want to speak to Brodrick privately. Scotland Yard had actively investigated a tip implicating the Irish Nationalist Party in the Whitechapel murders from at least the murder of Mary Kelly on November 9, 1888. The surviving crime index of CID has two abridged entries with reference numbers to files that are no longer available, as paper files were routinely purged for space.

Page 339: Crime — General
Whitechapel Murder suggested complicity of Irish Party [93867]
Whitechapel Murder Medical aspect [93305 / 179022][43]

The "Crime Index" ledger books were not dated at Scotland Yard chiefly to protect the information from falling into the wrong hands in the event of their loss. However, in this case, the entries can be correctly dated from the attached reference number of one entry for which there exist official crosschecks. The entries were recorded sequentially down the page. One Whitechapel murder is noted in both entries, and Scotland Yard reviewed the medical aspect in the murders of Mary Kelly and Rose Mylett of December 20. Late 1888 therefore seems to be when police investigated the Irish Party on suggested complicity.

Chief Inspector Donald Swanson noted a reference to the medical aspect file marked as "93305" in a report on the murder of Rose Mylett dated January 18, 1889.

I beg to submit Correspondence No. 93305/11 from the General Registry which sets forth how Mr. Bond was employed as an expert to examine and report upon the surgical reports of the four murders, ending with Mitre Square, but in these cases he did not examine the bodies. The final body, which he examined was that of Mary Janet Kelly, but so far as I am aware, the examination was with the consent of Dr. Phillips, who was called by Police, and the reports do not show that the Coroner's consent was asked for or necessary. Mr. Bond did not give evidence before the Coroner.[44]

Though Dr. Bond's medical report on prior Whitechapel murders for Scotland Yard was dated November 10, 1888, and referenced within a Home Office file,[45] correspondence included reports from Anderson bearing the crime index reference number 93305/11a. They showed that Bond was commissioned on the Whitechapel murders from October 25, 1888, after consultations with Sir Charles Warren on the medical aspect of the case. Anderson had returned on October 6 from a holiday break and Warren had made his remarks to the Foreign Office on suggested complicity of secret societies on October 13, 1888.

Anderson did not notify the Home Office officially of Dr. Bond's initial engagement until November 13, 1888. The crime index entry titled "Whitechapel Murder suggested complicity of the Irish Party," was noted prior to Dr. Bond's report on the murders ending

**File cover of the special medical report by Dr. Thomas Bond, commissioned by Anderson, bearing the Scotland Yard crime index reference number 93305. It reads, "Whitechapel murders. Result of Post Mortem examination of body of woman found in Dorset St." (courtesy Stewart P. Evans).**

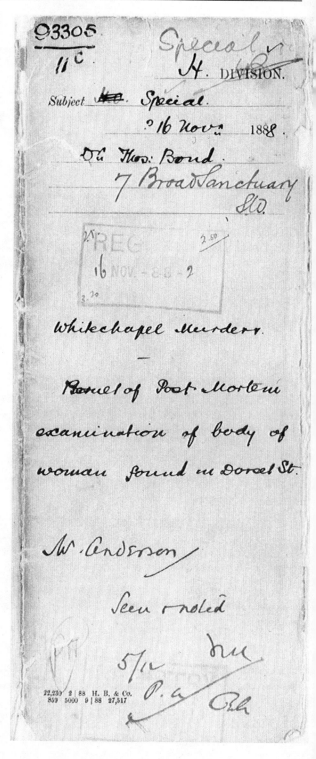

with the fifth, Mary Kelly. Scotland Yard, it appears, had considered alleged Fenian involvement earlier, when Americans were also under suspicion and Francis Tumblety was arrested as a suspect. The suspicions and victim count had been set on the early morning of November 9, 1888, according to the crime index and Dr. Bond's known reports.

George Brodrick was eventually cleared of contempt of court. He had convinced the Special Commission that his reference to the Whitechapel murderer was intended as a joke. The Unionist sense of humor at the expense of socialists and Irish Nationalists was not to last long. Sir Charles Russell, counsel for Parnell and Irish MPs, proved that the incriminating letters supposedly written by Parnell and others that were published in *The Times* alongside Anderson's 1887 articles were blatant forgeries. The Attorney General had known that they were suspect as early as December 1888 based on a letter sent to him by Pigott, which he was forced to admit in the House of Commons.

This incident confirms the gossip and political currency that Jack the Ripper was encouraging within official circles. The real issue for a study of the Whitechapel murders is that such partisan gossip entered official documents that have been relied upon as primary sources.

It is also worth noting that in this period, as Brodrick pointed out on political conflicts as moral issues, many focused on a religious war pitting good against evil.

Sir Robert Anderson, was active after retirement as an author on crime, prisons and police matters. His writing influenced government policy makers who framed legislation about the management of habitual criminals and political crimes. Despite his advancing years, he appears to have retained powers of reasoning as evident with his writing. However, it is not plainly discernable why he would make, in hindsight and over some years, contradictory statements on the status, incarcerated or otherwise, of Jack the Ripper.[46] In 1910, aged 69, Anderson published in *Blackwood's Magazine* articles on the Ripper, and admitted involvement with *The Times*'s 1887 "Parnellism and Crime" series. At this time, criminal aliens were a political concern as England was approaching World War I. The resurgence of Irish Republican dissent was back on the agenda. It then seems likely, as Anderson did not produce facts to support his theories on a Jewish Ripper when asked by the Jewish press, that he had used the Jack the Ripper case simply to illustrate a conservative point — an informed commentary on what he saw as the alarming trends in the immigration policies and crime of the time.

In 1911, Anderson wrote an article titled "The Problem of the Criminal Alien"[47] in response to the "Siege of Sidney Street," an event that had been sparked by Jewish refugees and had involved Home Secretary Winston Churchill. Anderson's Whitechapel murder theories found support with Macnaghten's 1894 report naming Kosminski and in Swanson's marginalia. Jack the Ripper was judged a "low class Polish Jew" who had been identified by a witness and "caged in an asylum." Anderson was at liberty at this stage to expand upon press reports on East End immigration and police investigative reports of 1888. In similar fashion, he would expand upon details in the "Parnellism and Crime" articles.

The social and political context of Anderson's Jack the Ripper theories of 1910 conveyed an entrenched racial prejudice of the time. The perception influenced his certainties, which lacked proof that the suspect was a poor immigrant and Polish Jew. Anderson traditionally made press statements at important junctures in the entry and debate of legislation in the Houses of Commons and Lords. His "Parnellism and Crime" articles were for instance released on the appointment of Arthur Balfour as Irish chief secretary. They were introduced with the Crimes Bill, which effectively made illegal, political secret societies in England and Ireland. The articles and bill had implicated the Irish Party in criminal association, seditious political speeches and free press that led to the conviction of 86 members of the opposition benches. The Whitechapel murders were to prove effective in deepening Conservative smears on a coalition with Liberals. They promoted perceptions of an electorate threatened by murderers and foreign criminals on the basis of minority extremist acts and the Ripper murders.[48]

Anderson had likewise introduced his 1910 Jewish Jack the Ripper theory during the long-term efforts of Lord Salisbury in the House of Lords to establish the Aliens Bill.[49] It is clear that Victorian England's ruling classes were becoming more insular and isolated during the Whitechapel murders, clinging desperately to a recalcitrant Tory administration and House of Lords. The threats of immigrant poverty, serious rebellion of commoners and socialist agitation were also big issues on the European continent. In England, they contributed to the formation of the Labor Party. Politics fed into the international press coverage of Jack the Ripper, demonized as the foreigner who endangered the English-speaking free world. These were historic events that had a bearing on the electorate's perceptions of police and criminal investigations of East End refugees.[50]

Crime historian Donald Rumbelow has given a vivid impression of the conditions prevailing at the time:

> In 1909 nearly two million Londoners were officially classed as poor or very poor. Most of them lived in the East End. For centuries the City of London's stringent corporate and guild restrictions had forced new labor to live and work on the open marshland outside the City wall . Immigrants fleeing continental persecutions, notably the seventeenth Century Huguenots, settled in East London. Steadily the number of immigrants increased. By the end of the nineteenth Century the brickfields and the pleasant weavers' houses had become rack-rented ghettos.
>
> At the time of the Jack the Ripper murders in 1888 there had been the serious risk of riots in London's East End as it was popularly believed that only a Jew could have committed such murders. Anti-Jewish feeling became anti-alienism and vice-versa. A foreign news editor said of the East End at the time that just by watching the eyes of passing Englishmen as they saw the Jewish girls in their Sunday finery, with golden rings on their fingers, sitting outside in the street, already you could "discern the look — which is already half indicative of the pogrom." He went on, "A pogrom in Brick Lane, in the crossroads of Commercial Road can be a more bloody and terrible affair than one in the Baltic."[51]

Did Anderson have other plausible reasons for promoting a fairy tale theory of the Whitechapel murders apart from criminal reform? If the comments on Jack the Ripper by an ex–Assistant Commissioner of the Metropolitan Police are taken at face value, maybe an answer lay in his veiled comments. His sense of urgency perhaps rested in protecting the workings and methods of his old department, Scotland Yard's CID, and as head of its secret service arrangements acting with discretion of the Home Office.

Anderson wrote in his 1910 memoirs, "Scotland Yard can boast that not even the subordinate officers of the department will tell tales out of school, and it would ill become me to violate the unwritten rule of the service ... no public benefit would result from such a course, and the traditions of my old department would suffer." He added, "The outside working of the machine is public property, and may here be explained, for the knowledge may possibly be both interesting and useful to the public. But if any one takes up these pages in expectation of learning the secrets of the department, he may throw them down at once. For I cannot speak too highly of the sense of honor which prevails, not only among the officers, but among the pensioned officers, of the C.I.D. in regard to all matters of which they have official knowledge."[52]

In pointing to all official matters, which included the unsolved Whitechapel murders case, Anderson wrote of not violating the "unwritten rules" and the "traditions" of his old department. These statements — clear and unambiguous — may seem odd to modern ears, as they seem to imply an undue degree of personal discretion. If they were made today by an official of equal rank they would likely attract the sanction of civil libertarians and Members of Parliament calling for dismissal — as did the House of Commons in 1910 when Anderson's *Blackwood's Magazine* articles were brought to the attention of the Home Secretary Winston Churchill. Yet, Anderson had summed up the working operations of early Special Branch, CID and its sense of internal honor.

In 1888, Britain's secret service lacked effective legislative accountability. There was also official vagueness on the retention of confidential files. The informal handling of documentation, public disclosure and disinformation by civil servants was governed at the discretion of the Home Secretary and at the will of the police official. Anderson had described the Metropolitan Police as the "outside working of the machine," though Special Branch had independently developed a more detailed system of managing information.

References to Jack the Ripper investigated as a political criminal add further complexities to the case. A sufficient history of Victorian English secret service arrangements, with their clearly partisan and rigid seclusion at senior levels, does not exist.[53] However, practical and evolving domestic security arrangements were effective in the conflicted political climate. They met the real danger but with the passage of time, sparse details were not entirely useful in showing the investigation of Jack the Ripper. Though some primary sources on secret service inquiries in the Whitechapel murders have survived, they are officially closed in perpetuity.[54]

The Metropolitan Police Special Branch, as it was known in 1888, was recruited at the height of the Whitechapel murders. It acted on information that indicated Jack the Ripper was an extremist associated with a political secret society — the ultimate conspiracy theory on the Whitechapel murders, no doubt.[55] But what evidence is there to support it, apart from the CID crime index entries implicating the Irish Party?

Special Branch, a division of Scotland Yard CID, was originally formed as a temporary task force within the Home Office to combat Irish Republican activity and high-level assassination attempts during the early 1880s on English soil. It used the resources of the Metropolitan Police except for its finances, a separation in statutory functions that annoyed Sir Charles Warren. After 1887 it was reorganized. It was permanently established[56] in 1888 with funds passed on debate through Parliament as the Secret Service Vote. The funds pledged were £40,000[57] during the Whitechapel murders. Unlike the Metropolitan Police, Special Branch was exempt from detailed accounting in the House of Commons. Detailed accounts of the secret service expenditure were kept in Special Branch index ledgers retained at Scotland Yard with references to files begun in 1888.[58] They were also used in maintaining a select system of paid informers.

> Hon. Members on the other side of the House would remember the numerous occasions on which O'Donovan Rossa [early Irish dynamiter] had been abused in the House. It was said to be perfectly monstrous that O'Donovan Rossa should be receiving money here, there and everywhere for the purpose of dynamite to destroy the Government of England. Now, he [Labouchere, MP in the House of Commons] was prepared to assert, without fear of the Government being able to show that he was wrong — he was prepared to assert that Secret Service money was, at that very time, actually being given to O'Donovan Rossa, and that the funds which hon. Gentlemen sitting on the Benches opposite complained of being given to O'Donovan Rossa were supplemented by contributions from the Secret Service Fund by Her Majesty's Government themselves.[59]

Ministers were dipping into secret service money for party purposes and electioneering. The extent of misuse moved the Auditor General during 1888 to introduce a certificate system for ministers. They had to declare that monies were properly spent without giving specific details. Ministers of the Crown were then required to sign and declare the following: "I hereby certify that the amount actually expended by me or under my direction for Secret Service in the year ending March 1, 18___ was so much, and that the balance in my hands was so much; and I further solemnly declare that the whole sum so expended has been paid for purposes to which, in my belief, Parliament intended that Secret Service money may be allowed, and that no part of the sum has been paid for any service which has been or could properly have been provided for by an ordinary public department."[60]

Anderson's 1910 memoirs noted,

In this country we know nothing of Secret Service in the Continental sense of the term. In England the duties thus designated are such as any competent police force would discharge. But with us the expenditure of public money must be open, and subject to audit. In the annual Estimates, therefore, a specified amount is taken for Secret Service; and, as regards this fund, the controlling authority must accept a certificate under the hand of a Secretary of State that it is expended for purposes authorized by the statute in that behalf. Were it not for this no Government could obtain information about conspiracies against the State.[61]

The Special Branch in the late Victorian period employed about 30 men. Details were devoted to Fenian and anarchist extremism, port watch, and protection of the Royal Family, important politicians and visiting dignitaries. Chief Inspector John George Littlechild, a specialist in Irish extremist plots, was its head, working under vague statutory and legislative requirements. He was technically responsible to the Home Office, Metropolitan Police Commissioner and, to the Assistant Commissioner (Crime), Scotland Yard. The Foreign Office also had its own secret service system that was responsible to the Permanent Under Secretary and directed to work with Scotland Yard. Little else is known of the early British secret service, and scant historical source material is available for a full evaluation of its functions in the period, particularly on the Whitechapel murders.

Special Branch collated and acted upon information gathered in reports from its special detectives. Details were also sent from UK provincial police, Metropolitan Police divisional superintendents and detectives, Dublin Castle, the Royal Irish Constabulary, the City of London Police and overseas police departments and detective agencies such as Pinkerton in the U.S. The early Metropolitan Police Special Branch was a centralized, organized, highly confidential and remarkably successful unit for the period. Experienced detectives John Littlechild, James Monro and Adolphus Williamson, its founding members, developed its system of surveillance, reporting and filing. It was effective with serious crime, preventing extremist plots, disseminating misinformation, and averting danger, and in infiltrating subversive movements and secret societies.

Special Branch was also called upon to investigate other serious crimes and to shadow suspects in cases deemed impenetrable to the detective department of CID. "Scotland Yard CID" has often been substituted in referring to Special Branch in contemporary press reports, parliamentary debates, and records of officers cross-examined in courts of law to protect official sources and prevent open disclosure. The Dr. Thomas Neill Cream murder case, for instance, was investigated by Special Branch detectives along with other high-profile investigations of the period. James Monro, as Assistant Commissioner of the Metropolitan Police, gave details in his 1903 unpublished memoirs of the investigation of the 1887–88 Lambeth dynamiters. He described how information from H Division detectives was passed on to Special Branch: "the police of H. in Whitechapel division reported to me the presence within their jurisdiction of a man they could not account for. He seemed to have nothing to do and all that he did was to visit a man living at (I forget the street) who was very ill and who also seemed a stranger. The Secret Department at Scotland Yard took over the case from the local police and shadowed the visitor of the sick man."[62]

The extreme nature of the Whitechapel murders were consequently brought to the attention of Special Branch. Its interest in the case is known historically through fragmentary documentation. Complete primary sources of its investigation have been lost, destroyed, purged or classified indefinitely. There is also the ethical consideration not to reveal detectives' and informants' names, though the surviving incomplete records are very old.

What, then, was really at stake for the police and political investigation of the White-chapel murders that would make Anderson revive, without proof, misleading theories in 1910? He referred to Jack the Ripper in articles admitting his involvement with "Parnellism and Crime" that almost cost him his pension.[63] The central issue that emerges from the ambiguity of senior police statements rests upon the question of the killer's escape, death or supposed incarceration. No one could reasonably fault Scotland Yard in its strained efforts to capture Jack the Ripper and contain the associated killing spree if he had simply escaped. They would be wanting for evidence if it was alternatively claimed that the identity was known and the killer incarcerated in one of Her Majesty's asylums.

*The Times* during the Whitechapel murders and Parnell Special Commission was running a few plots of its own. The conservative newspaper employed private detective agencies in its case before the Commission. Indeed, Scotland Yard had preferred to use the Pinkerton Detective Agency for investigations in the U.S. than to work directly with American police forces. In the prevailing climate of counterintelligence, subterfuge, competing national spies and highly paid double agents, Jack the Ripper was a welcome distraction for *The Times.*

Irish Parliamentary members were often sent private detectives as plants for *The Times.* According to the Chief Constable's Special Branch ledger entries with reports from Chief Inspector Littlechild and Detective Sergeant McIntyre, the Clan-na-Gael in the U.S. employed private detectives to shadow Michael Davitt, who they thought was getting too close to the truth. The Westminster Detective Agency employed by *The Times* and run by Matthew O'Brien and a Captain Webb had also attempted to entrap Parnell and Labouchere. O'Brien was later recommended by Patrick Egan to Parnell and Labouchere while sending reports to a Major Gosselin who was sending reports to the Irish Chief Secretary Arthur Balfour and the ear of Salisbury the Prime Minister.

O'Brien, a failed Dublin lawyer, had drawn on his past contacts with Home Office spymaster Sir Edward Jenkinson who, along with another informer, James McDermott, he would later blackmail. O'Brien it was who had planted the false details on Inspector Moser's American trip to entrap Labouchere in a libel suit. According to a letter sent to Earl Spencer, Jenkinson arrived in London on October 20, 1888, and the next morning went to the offices of solicitor George Lewis where he heard details on the forged Pigott letter. The Westminster Detective Agency was hired during October 1888. Another cheap private detective agency on the Strand, Le Grand & Co., was employed by the Whitechapel Vigilance Committee to catch the Ripper. In early 1889 it had pressured Lewis for engagement as it, too, was employed by *The Times.* There was money to be made during the Whitechapel murders thanks to the Secret Service Vote and *The Times*'s desire for evidence to present before the Special Commission.

In June 1889, Melville Macnaghten joined the Metropolitan Police as Assistant Chief Constable of CID, Scotland Yard under the direction of Chief Constable Adolphus "Dolly" Williamson. He was further installed as the confidential assistant to the Metropolitan Police Assistant Commissioner, Robert Anderson.[64] When Williamson died, on December 9, 1889, Macnaghten took over his post as Chief Constable and held it until promoted to Anderson's position in 1903. By 1893–94, most of the veterans from the Ripper era at Scotland Yard had either retired or died, leaving only Anderson, Swanson and Macnaghten under Chief Commissioner Sir Edward Bradford.

James Monro, deeply involved with the permanent establishment of Special Branch from 1887 and the building of New Scotland Yard, had retired on June 12, 1890. Monro disagreed with the Home Secretary on police pensions and on what he regarded as political duplicity in the management and control of the Metropolitan Police. He retired to India to establish a charitable medical mission and returned to England in 1905. Monro denied in 1910 that he gave Anderson permission, as Anderson claimed, to publish the "Parnellism and Crime" articles in *The Times* in 1887. Chief Inspector John Littlechild, active head of Britain's secret service from 1883, resigned on April 10, 1893.

Scotland Yard's Chief Constable kept the responsibility for the recording, filing and maintenance of Special Branch files and index ledgers.[65] They were available to Monro, Macnaghten, Swanson, Anderson, Littlechild and the Home Secretary. Anderson, Swanson and Macnaghten were therefore aware of the contents of Special Branch files on the Whitechapel murders investigation.

Anderson's statements on Jack the Ripper have been examined, with Swanson reiterating and supporting him with his set of later marginalia. But what of the one official report, the cornerstone of the "insane Jewish suspect" theory, the so-called Macnaghten Memorandum? How does that compare with Anderson's ambiguous and vague public statements? Other police officers active during the Ripper investigation strongly denied the claims, remained silent or furnished theories of their own. Though a few accepted that Jack the Ripper had escaped, this certainly shows that no consensus existed in Scotland Yard, as Anderson intimated. Unless the Ripper was detained by a special, top secret act without going through official channels, only a few ministers and bureaucrats would know the suspect's identity, as Anderson and Swanson seem to suggest. This is a convoluted senior police position on the Whitechapel murders, as time has proven and has been previously stated. It does not explain why the suspect, if caught, escaped formal justice as insane, as has been claimed. Or why details were not officially released rather than hinted at in the press and in memoirs.

By 1893, the official mood had eased somewhat. The Whitechapel murders scare was seemingly over, and there had been a change of government in late 1892. The British electorate had ousted Salisbury's Tory administration in favor of Gladstone's Liberal Party with its Irish Nationalist supporters. Jack the Ripper had, by press handling and the politics of crime, contributed to the downfall of the government. Macnaghten wrote in his memoirs: "I incline to the belief that the individual who held up London in terror resided with his own people; that he absented himself from home at certain times, and that he committed suicide on or about the 10th of November 1888, after he had knocked out a Commissioner of Police and very nearly settled the hash of one of Her Majesty's principal Secretaries of State."[66]

Though the politics of the "Autumn of Terror" was apparently over, the witch-hunt for the Whitechapel murderer remained enthralling. Every theory devised by amateur detectives, politicians, journalists, and the police was discussed. *The Times*, humbled by the financial losses of staging the Parnell Special Commission, was most conciliatory in its coverage of the new regime.

> Last night, in Willis's Rooms, Mr. T. P. O'Connor, M.P., was entertained to dinner by way of commemorating the completion of his 26th year of journalism and his entrance upon his latest journalistic enterprise, the editorship of the Sun. Mr. Asquith, the Home Secretary, who was announced to preside, was unable to be present; and, in his absence, the chair was occupied by Mr. R. T. Reid, Q.C., M.P., while among those present were members not only of the Irish Nationalist party, but also of the Gladstonian and the Conservative party.... Mr. Lockwood, Q.C., M.P., and Mr. Cust, M.P.,

also spoke in terms of appreciation of the journalistic qualities of Mr. O'Connor, who feelingly responded, and said he tried to do full justice to the abilities and to the success of even his strongest political opponents, among whom he recognized men of the highest political genius. Mr. Dillon, M.P., toasted the health of the chairman, and said that, though he and the guest of the evening came to this country as strangers in a strange land, they soon learnt to recognize the kindly qualities of the English race. The gathering was entirely non-political.[67]

Early in 1894, T.P. O'Connor's new enterprise, the *Sun* newspaper, boasted that it had finally solved the mystery of Jack the Ripper. Chief Inspector Chisholm, Inspector Race and P.S. McCarthy of CID had investigated a suspect for unrelated offences in 1891. The new political climate was conducive to police officers airing grievances, expanding on theories, and telling stories on their part in the hunt for Jack the Ripper. The *Sun* serialized a number of investigative reports on its suspect, Thomas Hayne Cutbush, who happened to have the same surname as the Executive Superintendent of Scotland Yard during the Whitechapel murders, Charles Henry Cutbush. Macnaghten confirmed the name, which seemed to be known to the *Sun*, though it never named Thomas Cutbush. It was a ploy that O'Connor had successfully used at the height of the Whitechapel murders for scoring political points by analogy. When his *Star* newspaper, established in early 1888, published a story on the suicide of the nephew of Home Secretary Henry Matthews, it was based on no evidence but the similarity of surnames: "A Reputed Nephew of the Home Secretary Does All He Can to Die.— Mr. Lumley Matthews, a gentleman who is said to be a nephew of the Home Secretary, is lying in University Hospital with two severe gashes and another great wound in his throat caused by his tearing open one of the cuts with his hands."[68]

The five serialized *Sun* articles, released beginning on February 13, 1894, prompted an official response by Scotland Yard. The final, complete and official document, the Macnaghten Memorandum, dated February 23, 1894, was aimed at refuting "the sensational story in 'the Sun.'" The articles claimed that Thomas Cutbush, a lunatic detained at Her Majesty's pleasure in Broadmoor Asylum on charges of stabbing and attempting to stab two women in Kennington, was Jack the Ripper. Macnaghten's report was retained in the official files of Scotland Yard apparently in readiness for questions in the House of Commons to Home Secretary Henry Asquith. As the opening parliamentary session of 1894 was taken up by other business of the new administration, questions on the *Sun*'s exposure of Jack the Ripper were not thought important. However, the Macnaghten Memorandum has established itself as vital in naming three alleged police suspects believed "more likely than Cutbush" to have been the Whitechapel murderer.

The most likely candidate to have brought up the matter of the *Sun*'s Jack the Ripper story in the House of Commons was the Radical MP Henry Labouchere. He was the editor of *Truth* and was interviewed by the *Sun* shortly after the articles appeared on 19 February 19, 1894, as Macnaghten was framing his report. The new administration supported Labouchere on moves to abolish the House of Lords to enable passing of Home Rule legislation, and the Radical MP could not be drawn out by the *Sun* on the issue. He rather candidly gave his own theories on Jack the Ripper and opinion of the Cutbush articles in this rare interview.

EXTRA SPECIAL
JACK THE RIPPER

## A TALK WITH MR. LABOUCHERE
## WHAT HE THINKS OF THE CHAIN OF EVIDENCE

A Sun representative called on Saturday on Mr. Labouchere to elicit his views as to what steps ought to be taken in order to bring the House of Lords to a political end, but the member for Northampton declined to be drawn on the subject.

"I don't like the system of interviews," he said; "they are very well for newspapers that want 'copy,' but they are nuisances, not only to the interviewed, but also to the public, except in very rare cases. The thing has been overdone."

In vain The Sun representative endeavoured to convince Mr. Labouchere that he might be one of the exceptional cases. He was civil but uncommunicative; but The Sun representative was determined not to be beaten, so he asked him in an incidental fashion whether he had read The Sun revelations respecting the identity of Jack the Ripper? Yes, Mr. Labouchere had. "And what do you think of them?" softly asked The Sun representative.

The subject seemed to interest the member for Northampton. "I once had a lot of papers," he said, "proving conclusively that Jack was a Spanish sailor. The murders were all committed when the vessel in which the sailor navigated was in the London Docks. He died at Aden and the murders ceased. He might have been this sailor, and equally he might not."

"But now, I suppose," said The Sun representative, "you have given up the sailor and believe in the lunatic at Broadmoor?"

"I neither believe nor disbelieve in either," said Mr. Labouchere, slowly puffing his eternal cigarette; "hundreds of men might have been Jack, only one man was. What has The Sun shown? That a man of nasty habits and of homicidal tendencies lived in London while these murders were being committed. This man was employed in the neighbourhood of Whitechapel, and resided within a short walk of it. He was accustomed to sleep late in the daytime, to go out in the evening, and to return home in the small hours. He was fond of medical questions and often made anatomical drawings. He stabbed some girls in the back, and, tried to cut a relative's throat, was arrested for the offence, when he turned out to be so much of a lunatic that he could not plead, and was sent to the Broadmoor asylum. All this does not show that he committed the crimes set down to 'Jack the Ripper.'"

"But look at all the coincidences," said The Sun representative; "his return home with bloodstained clothes, his knife presumedly such a one as Jack must have used, the distorted countenance, and the fact that the police find clothes evidently washed with turpentine in his room."

"What of all that?" said Mr. Labouchere. "Who testifies to the bloody clothes and the distorted countenance? A relative. No evidence of this sort is of value until it has been subjected to the test of cross-examination. There is a natural tendency to exaggerate it all involving a murder on the part of witnesses. They improve on facts, and then they stick to their improvements. To distrust your own witnesses is the best rule in these sort of investigations. As for the knife, a great many sorts of knives would have enabled Jack to effect his purpose. As for the clothes, many people clean their clothes with turpentine because they are dirty not because they are covered with the blood of victims. Evidently the police [illegible] think that your lunatic was Jack, [illegible] they would have sought to prove [illegible] to get the reward."

"So my lunatic, as you call him," said The Sun representative, "hinted to many that he was Jack."

"And that," answered Mr. Labouchere, "is the strong proof to my mind that he is not. Your lunatic, too, fancied that he had some malady, and took remedies for it. Is a man a murderer because he is a malade [illegible]?"

The Sun representative was not to be talked down in this sweeping fashion. He referred to the vast number of coincidences, and asked Mr. Labouchere whether he considered that no murder could be proved by a number of circumstantial proofs, all leading to one conclusion.

"Of course, it can," replied Mr. Labouchere, "murders, indeed, generally proved by circumstantial evidence, for which a man intends to murder another, [illegible] to be hanged; he does it secretly, but not in the presence of witnesses. Your Broadmoor lunatic may have been Jack, [illegible] I for all that you know. Jack very probably was the sort of man as the lunatic. But this, I should fancy, might be said of many inhabitants of this metropolis. But when you have to prove the commission of a murder by an individual, you must show, [illegible] that he might have committed it, but [illegible] there is no other hypothesis for an [illegible] effect but one. This you have not done. I read through attentively all the proofs and suggestions of The Sun, for they interested me. The conclusion that I arrived at was that The Sun had made out [illegible] case for public investigation."

"Then you recommend public investigation?" asked The Sun representative.

"Yes; if I were Mr. Asquith I should select a clever officer to look into the matter. He would do so carefully, for I suppose that the reward still remains [illegible]."

"And now, Mr. Labouchere, how about the Lords?"

"I have already told you that I decline to be interviewed on any subject whatever."

The Sun representative withdrew, feeling that he had managed to get an interview out of this very recalcitrant and most dogmatic M. P.[69]

Inserted with the *Sun* interview of Labouchere calling for Asquith to conduct a public inquiry on claims that the identity of Jack the Ripper was known were a few replies from readers of note also clamoring for results. Someone at Scotland Yard and in government was reading the *Sun* with measured concern.

## A COMMITTEE OF EXPERTS

"A Liberal" writes:— I have read with interest your thrilling account of the discovery and also of the career of the ruffian known to the world as "Jack the Ripper." The story which you have given to us with so much dramatic power seems to me to establish the identity of the miscreant beyond all possible doubt. Sir, is it not clear that the matter ought not to be left where it stands? Surely some action by the Home Office is necessary. What have the police authorities to say? It reflects no credit on Scotland Yard that the detection of this infamous scoundrel should be left to the enterprise of The Sun. If Scotland Yard still entertains a doubt, let Mr. Asquith appoint a committee of experts to examine into and sift the mass of evidence which you have gathered with so much labor.

"Pall Mall, W.," writes: There is so much of circumstantiality about your story of the Whitechapel tragedies, and so clear evidence that you have kept back many of the most important facts bearing upon your inquiry that I have slowly come to the conclusion that you have, at least, made out a very good case for official investigation.

In a lengthy letter to the editor of the *Sun*, a Mr. H.D. Thatcher, of Kennington Park-road, S.E., wrote, "After reading your story of 'Jack the Ripper,' I must give you a description of my 'Jack.'" Thatcher goes on to give details that sound like Thomas Cutbush, but he says, "On one occasion he had communicated with the Public Prosecutor; also several M.P.'s, among them Mr. Labouchere, who was going to bring a Bill before the House to prevent doctors dispensing their own prescriptions." It seems that accounts sent to the editor of the *Sun* naming Labouchere as a recipient of letters from Cutbush also prompted a representative of the paper to obtain an interview from the man himself.

That was the genesis of the Macnaghten Memorandum: an official policy brief commissioned by Scotland Yard officials and held in readiness for a public inquiry to Home Secretary Asquith. Since its publication in 1965, it has been the primary historical source for three police suspects, Kosminski, Druitt and Ostrog, against whom other evidence is lacking.[70] The document was available to the Chief Commissioner of the Metropolitan Police, Sir Edward Bradford, to Anderson, and to Chief Inspector Donald Swanson of Scotland Yard, CID. Anderson and Swanson, who supervised the overall investigation from September 1888, were actively engaged in the Whitechapel murders inquiries. By early 1894, Macnaghten had arrived at an official Scotland Yard position on the crimes for CID's political masters at the Home Office but was careful to qualify his statements: "No one ever saw the Whitechapel murderer, many homicidal maniacs were suspected, but no shadow of proof could be thrown on any one."[71] Inspector Frederick Abberline, in charge of East End detective inquiries, confirmed in 1903 that a report was made to the Home Office about a medical student, as Druitt was presumed to be, who was found drowned in the Thames, but he noted that Scotland Yard did not regard it as final. Abberline added, "No; the identity of the diabolical individual has yet to be established, notwithstanding the people who have produced these rumors and who pretend to know the state of the official mind."[72]

What had prompted Scotland Yard to respond so quickly to sensational press reports on Jack the Ripper in early 1894? Neither Scotland Yard nor the Home Office were easily distracted by public opinion, let alone a newspaper run by an Irish MP with theories. Scotland Yard and the Home Secretary had all the extant facts on the Whitechapel murders. What was it about a potential public inquiry on Jack the Ripper that prompted the establishment to official reactions? The answer: Events which galvanized Anderson later to claim definite police knowledge about a serial killer.

In 1913, a letter on Jack the Ripper[73] was sent to the journalist and author George Sims by John George Littlechild, retired Chief Inspector and head of Special Branch from 1883 to 1893. Now working as a private investigator and consultant with the London branch of Pinkerton Detective Agency, Littlechild was still bound by official rules on release of sensitive details of political crime. In the letter, Littlechild introduced Francis Tumblety as "among the suspects." News of Dr. Tumblety's complicity in the Whitechapel murders was not reported in England, but the U.S. press was awash with reports on Tumblety, the extraordinary Irish-American herbalist.

> Police Superintendent Campbell of Brooklyn has been investigating a little of the life of Dr. Tumblety, now under arrest in London on suspicion of being "Jack the Ripper." ... He was a man who delighted in notoriety, but those in Brooklyn who know him think the notoriety he is getting as the suspected slayer of the unfortunate women in Whitechapel is certainly undesirable. No one in Brooklyn believes that he is the murderer or that he knows aught about it.[74]

Numerous cases of Irish-Americans visiting England were reported, and some were found in the official files as suspects in the Whitechapel murders. As the murders ran concurrently with the Parnell Special Commission, which drew visitors to London, police vigilance and public relations were strained. The following press interview described the atmosphere during the murders from an Irish-American point of view.

## BRITISH BULLDOZERS
## OUTRAGEOUS TREATMENT OF SEVERAL AMERICAN CITIZENS

Hounded by Scotland Yard Detectives While Visiting Ireland — Unpleasant Experiences Across the Water

"If a citizen of the United States who belongs to the class known as 'Irish-Americans' goes abroad for a few months' recreation there is, in the language of the cable correspondents, signs of increased activity at Scotland Yard."

Thus spake Dr. Thomas O'Reilly yesterday, and he knew whereof he spoke. The doctor had been rather conspicuous in matters of Irish relief, not to say "agitation," for years. The chances are that from the day he left St. Louis, which was June 11 [1888], until last Wednesday, October 3, when he returned, he never was completely beyond the surveillance of a detective system which is said to cost the British government not less than L100,000, or a full half million American dollars each month. Dr. O'Reilly, seated in his sanctum last night, said:

"I am only one of many. I got off the ship at Liverpool, rosted up, spent a few days at Chester and Lemington, and then went to London. Naturally I had letters of introduction to the Irish members of parliament. These I naturally presented to them. The first thing I know (and of this, to tell the truth, I was informed by Englishmen that I had not) was that I was being followed daily from the Hotel Metropole, where I was stopping, to such places as I might go, and back again. It was am uncanny feeling to be 'shadowed,' but I did not fully feel it until I got to Dublin, where British surveillance of 'Irish-Americans' has been brought to a science that would put to the blush the exploits of Claude or Vidocq [Famous French detectives]. I was invited to the mansion of Dr. Kenny, on Rutland square, to meet, among other distinguished Nationals, John Dillon. Two men lurked in my shadow both from and to the Imperial hotel, on O'Connell street, where I stopped during my stay. On September 20 a complimentary dinner was given me at the Imperial by Michael Davitt. I made a speech, which was printed in the Freeman's Journal the next morning. The next day I visited the hospitals of

Dublin, particularly that of Meath, where I was a student. By the papers of the next day I learned that during my tour I had been dutifully attended by two of 'Balfour's Uhlans.'"

William P. Smyth of this city, who met Dr. O'Reilly in Dublin and returned with him on the steamer Servia, was seen at the Plantors' house last night, and informed the reporter that he had conferred with Senator Vest by letter on the subject of police interference with American citizens in Ireland. He related the particulars of his own case, which has been referred to in a general way by some of the American and Irish papers, and expressed his determination to submit a sworn statement for the personal consideration of President Cleveland. It appears that shortly after Mr. Smyth arrived in Dublin, in last July, Inspector Sheridan, one of the castle detectives, was detailed to call upon him at the Gresham hotel to obtain information as to the object of his visit, its scope, duration, etc., and to ply him with interrogatories that were calculated to make his blood boil with rage. He promptly denounced the action of the castle authorities for subjecting him to such treatment and reminded the detective that he had rights there as a citizen of the United States which neither he nor any officer of the British government could afford to ignore. Mr. Smyth produced his passport and the detective withdrew.

Colonel McCaskill, the United States consul in Dublin, on learning the particulars, addressed a letter to the chief commissioner of police protesting against such a course. The reply pleaded ignorance of the affair and asked for the name of the detective. Mr. Smyth thereupon addressed a letter to Chief Commissioner [sic] Mallon, giving Sheridan's name and a free expression of his own sentiments on the matter. In the meantime the question was raised by one of the Irish members in the house of commons, and in the course of the debate that ensued the administration was strongly denounced for such aggressive interference with the rights of American citizens in Ireland. Balfour replied in behalf of the government, and with his characteristic mendacity denied that any citizen of the United States had been terrorized by the castle authorities in Ireland or that any correspondence had passed between the American consul and the commissioner of police on the subject. The latter's letter, with the consul's protest and Mr. Smyth's letter attached, was promptly forwarded to one of the Irish members, who was only too glad to use it in scoring another point against Mr. Balfour's reputation for veracity. Mr. Smyth feels justly indignant over his treatment. He says that while in other cases the police subject the person's movements to surveillance only, they charged on him at his hotel with a modest demand for a sketch of his life, with an illustrated diagram showing his political connections in the United States.

Congressman John J. O'Neill received a letter from Mr. Smyth from Dublin on the subject, and expresses his determination to unite with Senator Vest in bringing the matter before the president. As they are both warm personal friends of the gallant "suspect," it is safe to say the matter will be thoroughly sifted by the government.—*Chicago Times*.[75]

Reports on Tumblety's alleged complicity in the Whitechapel murders began to surface with cable transmissions sent by London correspondents to the U.S. press beginning around November 17, 1888: "Dr. Francis Tumblety, who, according to a cable dispatch, was arrested in London on suspicion of being concerned in the Whitechapel murders and held on another charge for trial under the special law passed after the 'Modern Babylon' exposures, is known in nearly every large city in this country."[76] The *San Francisco Chronicle* dateline on the Tumblety/Jack the Ripper story was: "THE NEW YORK WORLD CABLE SERVICE; COPYRIGHTED, 1888 — SPECIAL TO THE CHRONICLE."

LONDON, November 17. Another arrest was a man who gave the name of Dr. Kumblety [sic] of New York. The police could not hold him on suspicion of the Whitechapel crimes, but he will be committed for trial at the Central Criminal Court under the special law passed soon after the Modern Babylon exposures.[77] The police say this is the man's right name, as proved by letters in his possession; that he is from New York, and that he has been in the habit of crossing the ocean twice a year for several years.[78]

It was followed the next day by *The New York World* newspaper with:

A special London despatch to THE WORLD yesterday morning announced the arrest of a man in connection with the Whitechapel crimes, who gave his name as Dr. Kumblety, of New York. He could not be held on suspicion, but the police succeeded in getting him held under the special law passed soon after the "Modern Babylon" exposures.[79]

With similar variations the news was spread throughout the U.S. It did not enter the British press until late December 1888. Two reports alluded to an American suspect without naming him. It was a strong reason why Francis Tumblety had not historically surfaced as a suspect in the Whitechapel murders until 1993. Until then, English press accounts were the chief primary sources for crime historians researching Jack the Ripper and the Whitechapel murders, along with release of official files during the 1970s. Special Branch files, which of course noted interest in the movements of suspected Irish-Americans, were not available. As the days unfolded, further details emerged in American newspapers on the fantastic and eccentric Dr. Tumblety, each elaborating and adding details to the story.

## THE SAME TUMBLETY
## THE ARREST IN LONDON NOT HIS FIRST EXPERIENCE

The Dr. Tumblety who was arrested in London a few days ago on suspicion of complicity in the Whitechapel murders, and who when proved innocent of that charge was held for trial in the Central Criminal Court under the special law covering the offences disclosed in the late "Modern Babylon" scandal, will be remembered by any number of Brooklynites and New-Yorkers as Dr. Blackburn, the Indian herb doctor. He is the fellow who in 1861 burst upon the people of Brooklyn as a sort of modern Count of Monte Cristo. He was of striking personal appearance, being considerably over six feet in height, of graceful and powerful build, with strongly marked features, beautifully clear complexion, a sweeping mustache, and jet black hair. He went dashing about the streets mounted on a handsome light chestnut horse, and dressed in the costliest and most elaborate riding costumes, and soon had a stream of customers at his office and laboratory on Fulton-street, near the City Hall. In these rides he was invariably accompanied by a valet as handsomely apparelled and horsed as himself, and a brace of superb English greyhounds. He boarded with a Mrs. Foster, at 95 Fulton-street, then a fashionable quarter of the city, and cut a wide swath in the affections of the feminine lodgers.

After a few months he dropped out of sight as suddenly and as mysteriously as he had appeared and was next heard of as being implicated in the famous "yellow fever importation" and "black bag" plots that the rebel sympathizers tried to develop in New-York during the civil war. It was at this time that his relation to the celebrated Blackburn family of Kentucky became known, and he thereafter went by his real name instead of his curious assumed name, Tumblety. His interest in the two previously-mentioned plots was, luckily for him, so slight that he was allowed to go unpunished, while several of his associates did not get off so easily. For several years after this he kept pretty well out of the public gaze, and then suddenly took up his herb-doctoring business with its attendant swagger again. He visited both this city and Brooklyn at about semi-yearly intervals and became a member of several questionable clubs. He dropped out of sight some 10 years ago, and the first that has been heard of him since is the news of his arrest and imprisonment in London.[80]

## SOMETHING ABOUT DR. TUMBLETY

SAN FRANCISCO, Nov. 22.— Chief of Police Crowley has lately been in correspondence with officials of Scotland Yard, London, regarding Dr. Tumblety, who is at present under arrest on suspicion of being implicated in the Whitechapel murders. The Chief, in pursuing his investigations, discovered that the doctor still had quite a balance in the Hibernia Bank, which he left there when he disappeared from this city, and which has never been drawn upon. Mr. Smythe of that institution says that he first met the doctor in Toronto, where he was practicing medicine in July, 1858. He next met him in this city, at the Occidental Hotel, in March or April, 1870. Tumblety rented an office at 20 Montgomery-street, where he remained until September 1870, and then disappeared as suddenly as he came. In 1871 the doctor turned up in New York. On Oct. 29 Chief Crowley sent a dispatch to the London detectives, informing them that he could furnish specimens of Tumblety's handwriting, and to-day he received an answer to send the papers at once.[81]

Chief Crowley sent a dispatch to London detectives on October 29, 1888, regarding specimens of Tumblety's handwriting held at the Hibernia Bank. This suggests that Tumblety was suspected of the Whitechapel murders sometime before that date. *The Brooklyn Daily Eagle* later expanded on one of the "questionable clubs" he attended, as noted in *The New York Times*.

Dr. Gloucester had had many predecessors in the art of ministering to a body diseased through the medium of "yarbs," and prominent among them was the famous Dr. Tumblety, who, in the early sixties, had an office and laboratory on Fulton street, near Nassau. Tumblety described himself in those days as the "Indian herb doctor," and by judicious and extensive advertising managed to make a handsome income. He believed in keeping himself constantly before the public in the literal sense of the word, and it was his custom to spend a great portion of each day in promenading up and down Fulton street, accompanied by a fine greyhound. He was of a striking personal appearance and wore long hair and an immense hat. He was last heard of a couple of years ago in New York, where for a time he was under suspicion on account of his supposed connection with the advanced branch of the Irish national party.[82]

One of the earliest U.S. newspapers to have disseminated reports on the complicity of Tumblety with the Whitechapel murders was his old nemesis *The New York Times*. It was closely followed by *The Chicago Tribune* and other associated smaller and independent newspapers in America and around the world, except England. It was a pattern that had emerged previously with press rumors on Dr. Francis Tumblety, which he encouraged at times as a form of advertising for his herbal products. Back in 1865, Tumblety was still fending off press-engineered innuendoes when he wrote a letter in his defense to the *Washington Star*. It was reprinted with some poetic licence in *The New York Times* and *The Chicago Tribune*.

KIRKWOOD HOUSE. WASHINGTON, D.C., June 8 1865
To the Editor of the Washington Star:

After three weeks' imprisonment in the Old Capitol prison in this city, I have been unconditionally and honorably released from confinement by direction of the Secretary of War, there being no evidence whatever to connect me with the yellow fever or assassination plot, with which some of the Northern journals have charged me of having some knowledge.

My arrest appears to have grown out of a statement made in a low, licentious sheet published in New York, to the effect that Dr. Blackburn, who has figured so unenviably in the hellish yellow fever plot, was no other than myself. In reply to this statement I would most respectfully say to an ever generous public, that I do not know this fiend in human form named Dr. Blackburn, nor have I ever seen him in my life. For the truth of this assertion I can bring hundreds of distinguished persons throughout the United States to vouch for my veracity, and, if necessary, can produce certificates from an innumerable number of gentlemen in high official positions.

While in imprisonment I noticed in some of the New York and other Northern papers, a paragraph setting forth that the villain, Harrold,[83] who now stands charged with being one of the conspirators in the atrocious assassination plot, was at one time in my employ. This, too, is false in every particular; and I am at a loss to see how it originated, or to trace it to its origin. For the past five years I have had one man in my employment, and he is yet with me, his character being beyond reproach. I never saw Harrold to my knowledge and I have no desire to see him.

Another paper has gone so far as to inform the public that I was an intimate acquaintance of Booth's; but this, too, is news to me, as I never spoke to him in my life, or any of his family.

I do hope that the papers which so industriously circulated these reports connecting me with these damnable deeds, to the very great injury of my name and reputation, will do me the justice to publish my release, and the fact of my having been entirely exonerated by the authorities here, who, after a diligent investigation, could obtain no evidence that would in the least tarnish my fair reputation.

I feel it but due to the authorities here to state that while in the Old Capitol I was treated with the utmost kindness and consideration, and was placed in the same quarters assigned to Governor Vance, Governor Brown, Hon. Lamar and others of note.

With these few remarks in justice to myself, I will close by submitting them to the public.

Respectfully
Dr. F. Tumblety[84]

The dirt on this Irish American suspect was emerging unabated. The good doctor apparently had a history of strained relations with the press, as this report put it:

Sixteen or seventeen years since Tumblety had some difficulty with Editor Ralston, of Frank Leslie's Weekly. The outcome of this trouble was a full exposure of his doings in Nova Scotia and also in this city. Some days after this exposure the Doctor met Editor Ralston in the barroom of the Fifth Avenue Hotel. Mr. Ralston was at the time chatting with Supervisor Briggs and Central Office Detective Timothy J. Golden. Tumblety assaulted Ralston and a lively fight was the result, in which the editor came off first best. Tumblety afterward wanted Mr. Ralston to fight a duel, but the latter said that the fellow was really not worth fighting with. Detective Golden arrested Tumblety for assault, but Ralston declined to make any complaint and the prisoner was let go. This occurred about 1872.[85]

Tumblety also furnished an interview for *The New York World* in early 1889:

"My arrest came about in this way ... I happened to be there when these Whitechapel murders attracted the attention of the whole world, and, in the company with thousands of other people, I went down to the Whitechapel district. I was not dressed in a way to attract attention, I thought, though it afterwards turned out that I did. I was interested by the excitement and the crowds and the queer scenes and sights, and did not know that all the time I was being followed by English detectives."
"Why did they follow you?"
"My guilt was very plain to the English mind. Someone had said that Jack the Ripper was an American, and everybody believed that statement. Then it is the universal belief among the lower classes that all Americans wear slouch hats; therefore, Jack the Ripper, must wear a slouch hat. Now, I happened to have on a slouch hat, and this, together with the fact that I was an American, was enough for the police. It established my guilt beyond any question."[86]

Crime historian and author Stewart P. Evans remarked on the interview that "Tumblety confirmed that he was actually arrested as a Whitechapel suspect, rather than for the misdemeanours of gross indecency with which he was eventually charged. This is enlightening, for it would seem that the London police were sanguine of obtaining a confession from Tumblety, probably the only way in which they could prove his guilt (if indeed he was guilty) as there was no witness to any of the murders."[87]

In Tumblety's interview, he promised the reporter that he would prepare a pamphlet on the history of his life, which would refute the charges made against him. The pamphlet was produced in 1889 but only alluded to his treatment at the hands of the press. Instead, it added further details on his Irish Nationalist sympathies:

Now let me say a word about the attacks which certain American newspapers recently made upon me, attacks that were as unfounded as the onslaught made on the great Irish leader.[88] While I was not in a position to defend myself, these papers continued their foul slanders, but my friends will readily see, from the foregoing pages and from the testimonials that follow, how utterly base and wholly groundless these aspersions were. Like Parnell, I have emerged from the battle entirely unscathed with my social and professional standing unimpaired. It is gratifying to recall the pleasure with which my friends welcomed me to my native land. I treasure their tributes among the dearest things in my possession. I subjoin some of the letters which I received.[89]

Tumblety by his own admission confirmed Littlechild's information that police had suspected and arrested him for the Whitechapel murders. He also freely confirmed his Irish Nationalist sympathies and associations. The English part of the American suspect affair went on with press revelations and parliamentary theories linking the Jack the Ripper investigation with the Parnell Special Commission. It has since muddied the waters somewhat with regard to the presence of Scotland Yard detectives in the United States at the time. As the nature of Scotland Yard inquiries across the Atlantic were officially veiled, beliefs that the Whitechapel murderer was followed by detectives in America remain as nebulous and ambiguous as the senior police statements on Jack the Ripper which were made in later years.

## THE SEARCH FOR THE WHITECHAPEL MURDERER
## DETECTIVES ON THE OUTLOOK IN NEW YORK

Inspector Andrews, of Scotland Yard, has arrived in New York from Montreal. It is generally believed that he has received orders from England to commence his search in this city for the Whitechapel murderer. Mr. Andrews is reported to have said that there are half a dozen English detectives, two clerks, and one inspector employed in America in the same chase. Ten days ago Andrews brought hither from England Roland Gideon Israel Barnet, charged with helping to wreck the Central Bank, Toronto, and since his arrival he has received orders which will keep him in America for some time. The supposed inaction of the Whitechapel murderer for a considerable period and the fact that a man suspected of knowing a good deal about this series of crimes left England for this side of the Atlantic three weeks ago, has, says the "Telegraph" correspondent, produced the impression that Jack the Ripper is in that country.[90]

On March 22, 1889, *The Times* reported a House of Commons debate in which Irish MP Timothy Healy asked Home Secretary Matthews "whether Inspector Andrews, an officer from Scotland-yard, had visited America since the passing of the Special Commission Act; and whether his business there was connected with the charges and allegations made before the Royal Commission. Mr. Matthews replied that the answer to the first paragraph is in the affirmative; to the second in the negative."

A 1928 reference added, "The murders ceased, I think, with the Miller Court one, and I am the more disposed to this view because, though the fact was kept a close secret at the time, I know that one of Scotland Yard's best men, Inspector Andrews, was sent specially to America in December, 1888, in search of the Whitechapel fiend on the strength of important information, the nature of which was never disclosed. Nothing, however, came of it, and the Inspector's mission was a failure."[91] In 1938 Walter Dew, a CID officer attached to H Division in 1888, also noted that Andrews was assigned to the Whitechapel murders along with Inspectors Abberline and Moore.[92]

There is an assumption that the late 1888 U.S. trip of Inspector Andrews was in search of Francis Tumblety, regarded as "among the suspects" by ex–Chief Inspector Littlechild in the 1913 letter to Sims. Though he is not officially referred to as the object of Andrews's visit, the idea has been quashed by correspondence between Scotland Yard and the Home Office[93] indicating Andrews was due in America before Tumblety left England. It is concluded that Andrews could not have been on a search for Jack the Ripper along with his other duties. However, this does not preclude Scotland Yard interest in the U.S. on the Whitechapel murderer. Inspector Andrews, or other detectives delegated by Scotland Yard to the U.S., could have been investigating suspicions of Irish Party complicity noted in the CID crime index data on the murder of Mary Kelly.

As Scotland Yard detectives were known to be in the U.S. in late 1888, it seems likely that if they were on the hunt for Jack the Ripper, they would have acted on certain details. The full extent of that information, sent in codes, was never disclosed as the matter came under duties of Special Branch and the Home and Foreign Offices. Some official telegrams were intercepted and decoded by Irish Nationalists and found to discuss matters related to the ongoing Special Commission. Anderson transmitted a request for the writing samples that Crowley had collected. The nature of the request is not known to have relevance to the Whitechapel murders investigation. Rather, it is conjectured that the handwriting samples were for comparison to the Jack the Ripper letters, which have not been proved and were not regarded by Scotland Yard at that time as having come from the killer.

When the news of Tumblety's arrest reached this city, Chief of Police Crowley recollected that the suspected man formerly lived here, and he took the necessary steps to learn all about his career in this city. He found that Tumblety arrived here in the early part of 1870 and took rooms at the Occidental Hotel. He opened an office at 20 Montgomery Street, but remained in the city only a few months, leaving in September of the same year. While here he opened an account with the Hibernia Bank and left a considerable amount to his credit in that institution when he went away. This account has never been closed and the bank still has the money in its vaults. After he left Tumblety had some correspondence with the bank officials.

As soon as Chief Crowley learned these facts he cabled to the London police that specimens of Tumblety's handwriting could be secured if they wanted them. Yesterday morning the following cablegram was received:

London (England) Thursday November 22 — P. Crowley, Chief of Police San Francisco Ca.: Thanks. Send handwriting and all details you can of Tumblety. ANDERSON, Scotland Yard.

The chief will have the correspondence photographed and will send it at once to London together with all the information he has been able to gather concerning Tumblety.[94]

All this correspondence between the San Francisco Police and Scotland Yard would of course have been added to the "large dossier" on Tumblety referred to by Littlechild, which seems not to have survived. The sensitive nature of the correspondence, despite its partial press publication, indicates that a Special Branch file on Tumblety was kept. The fund held at the Hibernian Bank, established on Irish Nationalist principles, was considerable and presumably included proceeds from the sale of Tumblety's herbal products and consultations. According to press reports the funds were not drawn out by the end of 1888. However, a fund for the legal defense of Parnell at the 1888–89 Special Commission had been formed with contributions from several continents, and accounts of the Land League were scrutinized for links with extremists. In that event, Anderson would have been particularly keen on the financial details offered by Crowley with specimen handwriting of an associate member of the New York branch of the Irish National Party — a good reason, in fact, for detectives to shadow Tumblety in the East End as an Irish Nationalist and a suspect for the Whitechapel murders. Anderson's interest in Tumblety's financial dealings with the Hibernia Bank would have indicated that Scotland Yard was involved in proceedings of the Parnell Special Commission, which the government was eager to keep under wraps.

Jack the Ripper neither died nor was incarcerated in England, but rather escaped abroad, beyond the reach of Scotland Yard and the Home Office. Given the political situation at the time, the internal investigation became shelved as highly confidential. Needless to say that this is the stuff of conspiracy theories. However, it has some support in the suppressed secret service files. It is at least an alternative and credible historic position to that offered superficially by Anderson, Macnaghten and Swanson, and it explains their reticence. There was a line of Special Branch detective inquiries that all three senior police officials directed and thus were in a position to know.[95]

In Littlechild's 1913 letter to Sims, he added, "I knew Major Griffiths[96] for many years. He probably got his information from Anderson who only 'thought he knew.'" Griffiths was the first to publish Macnaghten's theories on Jack the Ripper without naming suspects. Anderson's claims, however, were also challenged by Dublin Castle on Fenian matters, as he had noted them for posterity. In the 1910 book *Irish Conspiracies*, journalist Frederick Bussy, working from memoranda by Inspector John Mallon, gave another point of view.[97] Mallon was head of G Division, Dublin Castle detectives on the Phoenix Park case and during the Whitechapel murders. He later rose to Assistant Commissioner of the Dublin Metropolitan Police.

I have some further notes that may interest Sir Robert Anderson, and, in any case, they go to show how very difficult it is to discriminate between the genuine, meaningful Irish conspiracy and the meretricious dodges of the quick-wits who batten on the ready credulity of the amateurs who are after personal glory and are ever ready to absorb, and pay for special knowledge of, fancy pot-house plots, so long as they are imparted with a sufficiency of thick, guttural accent and the slouch hat is shabby and the eye blood-shot enough — details that are easily and satisfactorily acquired by artists of this kidney. I want it to be clearly understood that I have no knowledge of the special circumstances herein set out. I give them because Mallon seems to know all about them, because I believe that Sir Robert Anderson, among others, has frequently been deceived, and because my principal object in writing this book is to make things plain, in so far as I am able, and to dispel fallacies.[98]

So to what, then, could Littlechild be alluding to George Sims, journalist and contact of Sir Melville Macnaghten? Comments that may have found press release. As Tumblety seems to have had Irish Nationalist contacts and given financially to the cause, Littlechild would be suspecting an associate of the Irish Nationalist drive with a dossier known to Anderson. To Littlechild, Jack the Ripper was not a poor, insane Polish Jew, nor a suicidal medical student found floating in the Thames, nor a Russian doctor, but an Irish-American with a deviant sexual malady. If the evidence for any of these suspicions was remotely sustainable, it was sufficient for the attention of Scotland Yard.

"If this letter," wrote the London correspondent for *The New York Times* on November 4, 1888, "were to reflect merely the topic uppermost in Londoners' minds to-day it would deal exclusively with the fog. It is, to my knowledge, more than four years since such absolute Cimmerian darkness has before fallen on the metropolis. In what in more favored latitudes is known as the daytime at 11 o'clock to-day it was literally black. Not even the vaguest outlines of houses on the other side of a narrow street could be distinguished. No street lamps were lighted, and the only guides to the confused mass of traffic in the thoroughfares were the lamps in the hansom cabs. The fog lifted slightly later in the day, but the whole experience was one which not only engrossed present attention, but will be remembered for a long time. Of course such a reign of midnight at noon is a veritable thieves' paradise, and nervous people are all expecting to hear that the fiend of Whitechapel has seized the opportunity for another of his butcheries."[99]

Jack the Ripper, or so it was believed, had taken his chances again on the early morning of November 9, 1888, with the horrific murder and mutilation of Mary Kelly in her room. Local crowds expecting the annual Lord Mayor's Day were gathered in Miller's Court, outside 26 Dorset Street, Spitalfields, Kelly's residence, and the area was reportedly crammed. "Among those who visited the locality were two officials of the Royal Irish Constabulary, a prominent Post Office official, and two or three members of Parliament."[100] Kelly was a young woman aged around 25, apparently of Irish descent. Scotland Yard acted quickly and in a matter of days issued an official announcement.

The Times 12 Nov 1888

The following notice of pardon to accomplices who may give information leading to conviction, has been issued by Sir C. Warren:—

MURDER.—PARDON.—Whereas on November 8 or 9, in Miller-court, Dorset-street, Spitalfields, Mary Janet Kelly was murdered by some person or persons unknown: the Secretary of State will advise the grant of Her Majesty's gracious pardon to any accomplice, not being a person who contrived or actually committed the murder, who shall give such information and evidence as shall lead to the discovery and conviction of the person or persons who committed the murder.

CHARLES WARREN, the Commissioner of Police of the Metropolis.

Metropolitan Police-office, 4, Whitehall-place,

S.W., Nov. 10, 1888.

On the November 23, 1888, Secretary of State Henry Matthews, elaborated in the House of Commons: "I should be quite prepared to offer a pardon in the earlier Whitechapel murders if the information before me had suggested that such an offer would assist in the detection of the murderer. In the case of Kelly there were certain circumstances which were wanting in the earlier cases, and which made it more probable that there were other persons who, at any rate after the crime, had assisted the murderer."[101] Detective Inspector Henry Cox of the City of London Police in 1906 gave more details of the ongoing investigation in this press extract: "We had many people under observation while the murders were being perpetrated, but it was not until the discovery of the body of Mary Kelly had been made that we seemed to get upon the trail."[102]

It is not clear what the Home Secretary was referring to in "certain circumstances which were wanting in the earlier cases." No evidence exists in known police reports to prove one way or another what that information might be — perhaps about persons who had assisted the murderer after the crime? Whatever it was, it was strong enough to gain assurance of a royal pardon in the event that Jack the Ripper was apprehended and convicted, or perhaps to allay the fears of an electorate that was clamoring for results. Sir Charles Warren had in the meantime resigned and James Monro now held the post of Commissioner of the Metropolitan Police. However, there were some unusual circumstances in the procedures adopted in the aftermath of the Kelly murder. Despite continued police surveillance on the streets of East End London, her murder was regarded as the last in the series.

The standard procedure of the Home Office, though it was not a legal requirement, requested the coroner to submit inquest depositions to the Director of Public Prosecutions (DPP) and, if necessary, to the House of Commons.[103] There was no need to have an accused at the inquest stage, as an inquest was not a criminal trial. The unsolved status of the Whitechapel murders was recorded with the DPP as such. These were yearly statements, and there exists an anomaly for the murders of Mary Kelly and Catherine Eddowes. The director of public prosecution returns for the relevant Whitechapel murder inquiries and inquests are as follows[104]:

> DPP 1888: Includes entries on Emma Smith, Martha Tabram, Mary Ann Nichols, Annie Chapman and Elizabeth Stride.
> DPP 1889: Includes entries on Rose Mylett,[105] application by E.K. Larkins,[106] Alice McKenzie,[107] Elizabeth Jackson and Pinchen St. murder.
> DPP 1890: Has no inquest entries but includes an application by a J.E. Harris, solicitor, Leadenhall Street on information relating to the Whitechapel murders.[108]
> DPP 1891: Entry on the charging of Thomas Sadler for the murder of Francis Coles and his discharge.

There are no further entries after 1891; nor is there any record of the coroner's submission to the DPP of depositions on the inquests of Eddowes and Kelly. The absence of an entry for Eddowes might be explained by the murder occurring in the City Police district, though the 1887 Coroners Act request of the Home Office seems to apply. These anomalies may not be significant under informal Victorian arrangements but are worth noting.

However, in view of the confidential nature that seems to have prevailed in the deepening police investigations of Stride, Eddowes and Kelly, it is odd that details of the inquests of Eddowes and Kelly were not recorded or submitted by the coroner to the DPP as usual. Though the Kelly inquest was shorter than prior inquests, which led to conjectures of an official cover-up, the request for depositions noted with the DPP were not formally part of the inquest proceedings. Nevertheless, the main details of the inquests of Eddowes and Kelly were reported widely in the press.

The absence may also be explained with pending police inquiries prompted with information referred to by the Home Secretary granting a royal pardon in hope of securing the confession and arrest of a suspect. Anderson had commissioned fresh medical reports from Central Office police surgeon Dr. Thomas Bond, and this is likely why the inquest of Mary Kelly, which Bond did not attend, was shortened with depositions not sent to the DPP. Coroners were granted powers as magistrates under the Coroners Acts, as were the commissioners under Police Acts, as noted in Anderson's memoirs.[109] Though public inquests were independent and conducted at the discretion of the coroner, the Attorney General had the final say if they progressed to a trial, or he could order another inquest if coroners failed their duties. A requirement for coroners to send inquest depositions was mandatory if the DPP notified the coroner that he was undertaking criminal proceedings.[110] This did not happen in the Whitechapel murders. The situation indicated that Scotland Yard was pursuing fresh leads but, without clear witnesses or clues, there was no firm evidence to prosecute.

In 1956, author Douglas G. Browne in a history of Scotland Yard gave previously unknown details of a further line of inquiry tendered to Special Branch on the Whitechapel murders. Browne is known to have consulted official Scotland Yard files[111] before much of the archival material was lost, purged for lack of space or deposited at the Public Record Office. It has not been corroborated largely due to the sensitivity implied in the information. It has also been dismissed as yet another unsupported conspiracy theory in need of attention. Browne's note has posed awkward questions on prevailing Jack the Ripper suspects and official senior police positions. Hence it has been widely omitted from standard texts[112] on the Whitechapel murders in favor of suspects disclosed in Macnaghten's 1894 policy briefing report.

Browne noted, "According to Sir Basil Thompson, 'in the belief of the police he was a man who committed suicide in the Thames at the end of 1888,' and who 'had been at some time a medical student.'" This is what Macnaghten, Thompson's predecessor as Assistant Commissioner, established about M.J. Druitt. Sir Basil was also the head of Britain's wartime intelligence. After his retirement in 1921, he made further incongruent remarks on Jack the Ripper.[113]

Browne included a crucial detail that does not exist in any other available reference. "A third head of the C.I.D., Sir Melville Macnaghten, appears to identify the Ripper with the leader of a plot to assassinate Mr. Balfour at the Irish Office. Where experts disagree, there is a fine opening for fancy." Macnaghten did not record this theory in any other of his known works, yet Browne had seen its official documentary source. Browne concludes, "There were eight of these crimes in nine months; but at the most five of them, and perhaps only four, were the work of the maniac."[114]

That Jack the Ripper was linked by the secret service with a seditious Fenian military secret society, the Invincibles, a group charged with assassination plots, remains a sensitive issue. It is a historical legacy of the Whitechapel murder victims. It is also an alternative position noted by Macnaghten that Browne saw in Scotland Yard files as they existed in 1956, three years before the rediscovery of the Aberconway draft of the Macnaghten Memorandum and later with the official version. Early Fenians had declared war on the Royal Family, government, dignitaries, officials and commercial interests, as it emerged at the 1888–89 Special Commission in an attempt to implicate the Irish Party.

The Irish Republican Brotherhood later splintered, and its inner circle was called the Invincibles. Terrorist acts were accepted by British legal authorities as politically motivated and treasonable rather than common crimes, a distinction which altered the legality of convictions. Though civilian casualties did occur during the 1880s campaigns on English and Irish soil, giving authorities reason to cast a wide net, the Invincibles charged with the 1882 Phoenix Park murders of the previous Chief Secretary of Ireland did not advocate assassination of innocent civilians.

However, by 1888, with dynamite outrages muted, conspirators detained and Special Branch reorganized, the loss of English civilian life was a potential threat considered in splintered Republican groups. Atrocities in eastern Ireland and forced evictions further galvanized the Republican movement, putting the Vatican into the arms of the Tory Party. Scotland Yard had viewed the Whitechapel murders as a plot to create havoc in the metropolis and to undermine the Conservative government after the failure of Home Rule debate and during the Special Commission. It noticed that the mutilation of Ripper victims was performed using similar surgical knives as in the Phoenix Park murders.[115]

If Jack the Ripper was identified with a leader of a plot to murder Balfour, as Macnaghten noted, the serial killer was thus disloyal to standard political and militant Irish efforts in his drive to assassinate casual East End prostitutes — unless the Whitechapel murders became part of the policy implicating Irish MPs with violent criminal acts in association with Republican secret societies. It is not known where the source of the entry noted in the Scotland Yard crime index on suggested complicity in a Whitechapel murder of the Irish Party originated, though it can be dated. The dangerous prospects of London in the period 1887–92 prompted official disinformation, press distortion and political propaganda.

Browne noted that Macnaghten recorded a Balfour theory in his capacity as the "third head of the CID," a post he took up in 1903 and held until 1913, when he retired. It was the year his journalist contact, George Sims, received a letter on Jack the Ripper from John G. Littlechild. As the retired Anderson was unexpectedly promoting Scotland Yard Jack the Ripper press theories from early in the new century,[116] it seems plausible that what Browne saw was a document Macnaghten framed as a senior police brief for the House of Commons after 1903. Parliament was then concerned with Irish Republican agitation and possible collusion with Germany and Russia. So the matter of Balfour's assassination attempt linked with the Whitechapel murders investigation may have come up.

The document said that Macnaghten "appears to identify the Ripper with the leader of a plot to assassinate Mr. Balfour at the Irish Office." This refers to the post of Chief Secretary of Ireland between 1887 and 1892. Macnaghten had cited secret service files about an investigation to prepare his Balfour statement. As he had joined the Metropolitan Police in 1889, he had noted another Scotland Yard report broadly concurrent with the 1894 memoranda that named Cutbush, Kosminski, Druitt and Ostrog, indicating that files had also existed on those suspects. Likewise, the Littlechild suspicions of Tumblety were broadly akin to the police investigation of a Ripper linked with a plot to assassinate Balfour because Tumblety had Irish Nationalist sympathies and a Special Branch dossier. The common thread running through all these statements is the assurance that the suspect's disorders and sexual deviances were a matter of record. This position was later favored with forensic profiling and criminal science based on fragmentary case files, press reports and conflicting findings from autopsies.

One of the significant problems in attempting to corroborate Macnaghten's Balfour statement is in determining firstly which of the known assassination plots it refers to, if any. Several targeted the Chief Secretary of Ireland during Salisbury's Tory administration and the period of the Whitechapel murders. James Monro's tenures as Metropolitan Police Commissioner and Assistant Commissioner covered assassination plots with inquiries filed. They were available to Macnaghten from 1889 as Assistant Chief Constable of Scotland Yard. As the Whitechapel murders were contemporaneous with the Special Commission, it is probable that Scotland Yard had details on Jack the Ripper from an American source during surveillance and infiltration of Irish Republican secret societies. The suggested complicity of the Irish Party in the murder of Mary Kelly became part of that investigation.

"Bloody Balfour," as he came to be called, went on to become Britain's Prime Minister and was the architect of the Balfour Treaty establishing a Jewish homeland in Israel. Little mention is made of the assassination attempts during the Whitechapel murders or in alleging any perpetrators in his biographies. A more complete account of the plots is preserved in period and provincial press reports. Of course, inquiries were also documented in Special Branch files. There is a reasonably full 1903 biography that recounts the danger at the start of Balfour's tenure (1887 to 1892).

When Mr. Balfour took up the Irish Secretaryship, the position was one of no little personal danger. The assassination of Lord Frederick Cavendish, and the reckless, inflammatory language used by the Irish members and the Irish press, engendered a feeling of anxiety among his friends regarding his safety. Night and day, wherever he traveled, it was considered necessary that he should have a bodyguard of two detectives. His London residence in Carlton House Terrace was so near Westminster that he made a rule of walking home at the close of the House, and as he crossed the Palace Yard with his long, swinging stride, two figures emerged from under one of the archways and followed him at a distance of twenty paces. He gave no sign of having noticed them, and they went their way with a studied appearance of casually walking in the same direction; but as a matter of fact, they were keenly on the alert, keeping watch and ward over the tall, spare figure that preceded them. And not only in London and Dublin was this friendly surveillance exercised, but even during his holidays, when he retired to a quiet village on the Firth of Forth for a month's golfing, a small posse of police in plain clothes accompanied him, guarding his lodgings by night, and following him about the golf links by day.

On the occasion of his visit to Manchester, in December 1887, to address a great meeting of his constituents in the Free Trade Hall, the police arrangements were of a character without precedent in that city. Not only was a considerable force of men kept on duty near the door of the hall, but the approaches by several streets were protected by double lines of barriers for some hundreds of yards along the center of the roadway. These precautions were not rendered necessary by the mere magnitude of the crowds, but were due to the authorities having received warning that an attempt might be made on the life of Mr. Balfour during his stay in Manchester, and it was even deemed necessary not only to guard his progress through the streets, but that he should sleep in the civic residence at the Town Hall. It was on this occasion that he gave a solemn warning to the Irish Members. "Mere abuse," he said, "could be treated with contempt; but when it comes to open advocacy of crime, when men come over here and speak softly to the English people, go back to Ireland and urge the excitable peasantry of that country to resist the law, then, I say to them, you have passed the bounds of political discussion; then, I say, you have ceased to be politicians, and you have become criminals, and as criminals I shall proceed against you."[117]

Balfour's political rhetoric became the substance for the Special Commission. The evidence was in allegations of the Pigott letter and "Parnellism and Crime" articles. It was during the following year in the autumn of 1888 that claims before the Special Commission would compete for press attention with the Whitechapel murders. In 1889 the Commission vindicated the Irish National Parliamentary Movement of criminal dealings with exposure of the forged Pigott letter.[118] Though danger of extremist outrages was real and officially considered imminent, somebody was playing off Irish MPs and their Liberal supporters against the Tory Party. Salibury's government, responsible for the capture of Jack the Ripper, was dealing with events that started to gather momentum in Queen Victoria's 1887 jubilee year.

> LONDON, June 15.— The Central News issues the following: "A dynamite plot, to be carried out during the celebration of the Queen's jubilee, has been discovered. The police are reticent about it. The details will probably be made known to-night."
>
> The following is from an official source: "Information has been received in London which leaves no doubt that dynamiters have arranged to commit an outrage or a series of outrages during the jubilee week, but the authorities have full knowledge of the conspiracy and those engaged in it and are confident that they will defeat the plotters. For months past reports of the movements of prominent plotters abroad and their probable accomplices in England have been received in London almost daily. The chief ports have been watched during the same period in view of the arrival of certain suspects without previous notice having been received from the British agents abroad. The movements of Patrick Casey and his associates in Paris, who have been very active lately, have been closely followed by special detectives, and others outside of the ring are also known to have been watched. Rossa's complaint to the New York police on June 3 was absurd. He requires little watching. Others in New York and elsewhere are more important and are constantly being shadowed and reported upon."[119]

The press reported wild rumors and traded on political panic and alleged threats in London. Misdirection and propaganda in Irish, English and American newspapers confused the historic issues of the time. Partisan bias and rhetoric is a major issue for crime historians on suggestions of radical complicity in the Whitechapel murders which are found in official police reports and later secondary sources.

IT WAS A HOAX.

Reported Attempt on the life of Hon A. J. Balfour.

A brief sensation was caused to-day by a report that yesterday evening an attempt on the life of the Right Hon. A.J. Balfour, Chief Secretary for Ireland, was discovered and frustrated. In the mail at the Oxford street branch of the Post Office there was a small box addressed to Mr. Balfour.

The mail clerk thought the package was peculiar and suspicious looking and he obtained permission to have it opened. It was found to contain a small phial, filled with what was thought to be an explosive compound, connected with springs attached to the bottle. Careful investigation to-day has, however, shown that the whole thing was a hoax. The box was a jeweler's scarf pin box and the small bottle inside was filled with a brown powder made up probably, of pulverized coffee.[120]

As the threats grew, so was the political rhetoric adjusted to suit. A speech by Mr. Chamberlain, MP, in Scotland, printed in *The New York Times*, summed up the fears.

> "When I refer to assassinations, a man here says 'Take care of yourself.' Has the time come when we dare not discuss political matters in this country without being threatened with assassination? (Great cheering.) This is the spirit of the parties in the convention in Chicago. I am sorry to know that they have any representatives in Scotland. (Cries of 'They are not Scotsmen.') That convention, besides being attended by delegates honestly in sympathy with Ireland, had delegates of a different stamp — apostles of outrage and murder, who have paid the outrage mongers of England. Mr. Redmond, the delegate of the Irish Parliamentary party, explicitly declared before the convention that it was the aim of that party to effect the entire separation of Ireland from England, and that their policy was to make the Government of Ireland impossible. This they seek to effect by the most immoral conspiracy ever devised in a civilized land — by contending for liberty to violate every law, human and divine. Do you think it infamous to restrain these men? (Cheers) Mr. Parnell threatened in the House of Commons, under the specious guise of a warning, that if the Coercion bill were passed there would be a renewal of outrages, dynamite explosions, and attempts to assassinate our statesmen. This grim suggestion may prove the death warrant of some of us. (Cries of 'No!' 'Shame!') Well, what happens

to individuals is not of much consequence; the danger is to the Commonwealth. For the first time in English history our foes have sympathizers within our ancient fortress. Their plan of attack finds encouragement from those who ought to be the strongest defenders of our citadel. This makes our task more arduous. But we will not shrink: we will not abate one jot, we will not yield to threats from whatever quarter they come, but we will endeavour to hand down unimpaired to our children the unity, strength, and honor of the mighty empire our forefathers bequeathed us."

*The New York Times* added:

Mr. Chamberlain's speech excites all parties. The Unionists consider it a declaration of war to the knife with the Separatists. The Gladstonians charge Mr. Chamberlain with slandering and vilifying his former colleagues by the insinuation that they sympathize with the perpetrators of outages in Ireland. It is asserted that during his tour through Scotland Mr. Chamberlain will be attended by a private guard.[121]

Chamberlain later that year withdrew from the Unionist Party over the Proclamation of the Land League, which effectively made political secret societies illegal and censored the formerly free Irish press. Irish MPs' speeches were subject to police surveillance, and 86 ministers were imprisoned, diminishing opposition numbers in the House of Commons.

The first alleged assassination attempt on Balfour was hatched as part of the Jubilee Plot of 1887. A trial was held, based on charges of possession of dynamite, at the Old Bailey on February 1, 1888. The trial, and the prior inquest on the surprise natural death of Cohen, one of the alleged plotters, featured the appearance of James Monro, Metropolitan Police Assistant Commissioner. He pointed out that a *Daily News* press clipping for a speech Balfour was to give in Birmingham was found on a suspected dynamiter. Chief Inspector John Littlechild, head of Special Branch, said a Smith & Wesson revolver was believed to be the weapon of choice. As the suspect had difficulty reading and writing, the claim was dropped. However, the dynamite was real enough and the conspirators were sentenced to severe servitude. It would later emerge that it was possibly an entrapment attempt.

The plot, supposedly engineered by an Irish-American political secret society called Clan-na-Gael, was shrouded in secrecy as it matured in Lambeth and Islington. However, the accused of East London were convicted and locked up, so were unable to commit the Whitechapel murders. The assumed leader of the plot though, a Joseph Moroney alias "Melville," did escape to the European Continent and then to the U.S. He was later accused of complicity in the 1889 Cronin murder.[122] The *Irish Times* printed further details of the desperate men caught up in the revolutionary fever of the period.

(PRESS ASSOCIATION TELEGRAM)

Captain Melville, whose name was introduced at the inquest on Cohen, the dynamitard who died in London, is well known in Liverpool, where he stayed for nine days about nine months ago. He seemed well supplied with funds and paid a considerable sum as balance of an account in connection with the defense of Cunningham and Burton, who were convicted of attempting to blow up the tower of the House of Commons. At the time Melville's visit there were also in Liverpool eleven other members of the Clan-na-Gael, among them being one of the leaders named Quinn. They were betrayed, however, by one of their associates, and the police made a raid upon a number of houses, and seized some documents and arms. This so startled the dynamitards that they made a hasty departure to Belgium, and thence to New York. Associated with Cunningham and Burton was a well-known dynamitard named Lyons. While staying in London previous to the dynamite explosions Lyons passed himself off as a Jew. He also frequently went about disguised as a female. In this attire he was known to have been near the crypt at Westminster at the time of the explosion, and it is believed that he concealed some of the dynamite about his garments. The police nearly succeeded in capturing him, but he managed, with the assistance of London confederates, to escape to Brussels. He then went to Havre, and lately sailed for New York. For some time the police have lost sight of him, but the revelations in connection with Cohen have again brought his name before the authorities. Some people in Liverpool have read a description of the dead man, and they say there is a remarkable similarity between him and Lyons.[123]

While Balfour was giving constituency speeches during 1887 and the press reported the strained affairs on the British mainland, "Lord Salisbury, Mr. Matthews, the Home Secretary, and Sir Charles Warren, Commissioner of the Metropolitan Police, held a conference ... in reference to the condition of the unemployed people of London and the means to be employed to prevent socialist riots Lord Mayor's day, Nov 9."[124] After the Christmas holiday break of 1887, hostilities and rumors resumed.

### HIS LIFE IN DANGER

Assassins Watching the Steps of Ireland's Chief Secretary.
[New York Tribune Cable]

LONDON, Jan. 17.— Official anxiety about Mr. Balfour has of late much increased. The police authorities say that he is in greater danger of assassination than ever Mr. Forster was, whose repeated escapes were nothing short of miraculous. This opinion is based not upon the general hatred shown to Mr. Balfour by the Irish leaders and their English allies, but upon specific information which the police believe is absolutely accurate. Plot after plot to murder the Chief Secretary has been formed and frustrated. The Invincibles are steadily at work. They believed that they had a chance when Mr. Balfour spoke lately at Manchester, and an attempt would certainly have been made had not the police insisted on his sleeping in the town-hall, which is also the police headquarters. The assassins thought that was rather too hot a place to venture into. The precautions now taken at Dublin are greater than ever before. The Viceregal Lodge, where the Chief Secretary lives, and Phoenix Park, in which the lodge stands, swarm with the detectives, and he is never allowed to take a step alone. His custom is, as his enemies well know, to walk every morning from the lodge to the gate of the park. At the gate a carriage is waiting, and he drives to the Castle with a strong escort. During the drive, during the day at the Castle, during the return, and all night long at the lodge he is surrounded by every safeguard which the wit of the police can devise, and it is needless to say that the experience of the Irish police in such matters is extensive.

Thus goes on a sort of duel between the assassins and the police, with the life of the ruler of Ireland at stake. Much more than Mr. Balfour's life is at stake. The triumph of the assassins would ring the death knell of home rule. None know it better than the Home-Rule leaders. None have more cause to pray for his safety. Yet none so bitterly revile him, heedless of the fact that every insult and calumny heaped upon him furnishes so many more provocations and pretexts to his would be murderers.[125]

That Balfour was the target of the Invincibles, implicated in association with Jack the Ripper on the statement of Macnaghten, remains a vexed question. Opposing claims were expressed on the subterfuge of the period that have not been clarified until recently. Early in April 1887, barely a month after release of the "Parnellism and Crime" articles, a spokesman for the Invincibles gave a press interview.

### AN "INVINCIBLES" OPINION.

The Freeman's Journal to-day publishes an interview with Thomas Doyle, a ticket-of-leave Invincible, who states that he knew as much about the working of that body as any member outside the Dublin Four. Tim Kelly was his right-hand man. There was unquestionably no connection with the Land League. If any existed he would have known it. There was very little money disbursed. Any that there was Number One[126] supplied. He believes it came from America. There was no connection directly or indirectly between the Irish party and the Invincibles, or any understanding between them. He is of opinion that the Times was hoaxed.[127]

Sensational assassination press reports had increased after the trial of the Jubilee plotters in early 1888 and also grew with the impending Special Commission.

Patrick Tynan, the alleged "Number One" of the Invincibles in the uniform of the 13th Middlesex (Queen's Westminster) Volunteers. Portrait in *The Graphic* 21 April 1883 from a photograph handed to informer James Carey at the Phoenix Park murders trial. Carey had identified Tynan and Melville Macnaghten linked Jack the Ripper with the leader of a plot to assassinate Arthur Balfour.

## OUR LONDON LETTER

By Our Special Wire
Belfast News-Letter Office, 189. Fleet Street. E.C., Monday Night.

In the general dearth of exciting news we have been treated to-day to the startling rumor that Mr. Balfour's personal safety is seriously imperilled by the remnant of the Dublin Invincibles. The statement was as true twelve months ago as it is now. This story on the face of it points to a certain improvement for the better in assassination circles. The time was, and not so very long ago, when the enemies of British statesmen discharging their duty to their Queen and country hailed from over the Atlantic but rigid enforcement of the law against the hired agents of Fenian anarchy has cut off the supply of criminal conspirators from the United States. Nobody, not even the hard-up purveyor of sensation, now thinks of attributing to Americans the intention of violent intervention in domestic politics, though Mr. Morley used to tell us in the House of Commons we should always have such foreign forces to reckon with until we allowed the noisy majority in Ireland its own reckless way. The remnant of the Dublin Invincibles is a fairly descriptive and suggestive phrase, though even here, where there is still a great deal of incurable ignorance with regard to Irish affairs, it does not serve to create a bogey capable of impressing the simplest natures. The remnant of the Dublin Invincibles is now considerably reduced in numbers. Those who constitute it are well known to the authorities of Dublin Castle; therefore, Mr. Balfour need have no dread of them. It is true that wherever he goes he is accompanied by a brace of detectives just as Sir George Trevelyan and Mr. Gladstone themselves were before they cast in their lot with Mr. Parnell. This is no doubt a prudent precautionary measure to take. In times of great political excitement all our public men are in more or less danger from the excitable portion of the community, but there are just now no grave apprehensions for the personal safety of the Chief Secretary, and those who give circulation to rumors to the contrary do a great deal of mischief.[128]

## ALLEGED PLOT TO MURDER MR. BALFOUR

The sensational piece of news printed in to-days's "People" respecting an alleged plot for the murder of Mr. Balfour will probably form the subject of a question or questions in the House. It is thought a safe prognostication that in case the Government should be interrogated on the subject it will not be by their own supporters. Should Parliamentary notice be taken of the newspaper paragraph, which it is remarked, is so far entirely without corroboration of any kind, it will be most likely by the Opposition. The mere allegation of a conspiracy for the assassination of the Chief Secretary sets rumor at large, and though no detailed information can be obtained, and even though the police authorities go the length of professing entire ignorance of any plot or movement of the kind asserted, we have a variety of reports in circulation concerning it. According to one of these Mr. Balfour is "shadowed" by desperadoes both in London and in Dublin, his movements are dogged, he is followed on his journeys between the Castle and the Irish Office, and tracked in his social exits and entrances, but his personal safety has hitherto been ensured by the vigilance of the detectives who form his bodyguard. Mr. Balfour, it seems, is at present the only member of the Ministry so attended, but it is an error to publish that he is protected by only two detectives. As a matter of fact the whole force told off at the opening of the session for attendance on those Ministers it was thought advisable to safeguard having been withdrawn from duty as regards the Prime Minister, the Home Secretary, and the Chancellor of the Exchequer, have been attached to the following of the Chief Secretary, who while in London at all events, is constantly watched by from half a dozen to a dozen men. The impression respecting the alleged murder plot is that while there is no overwhelming improbability in the story, it is wise to treat it with reserve in the absence of confirmation, which the police authorities here either cannot or will not give.[129]

On March 19, 1888, the Prime Minister, Lord Salisbury, called a highly confidential meeting between Irish Chief Secretary Arthur Balfour, Home Secretary Henry Matthews and Special Branch head and Assistant Metropolitan Police Commissioner James Monro. The Commissioner of the Metropolitan Police, Sir Charles Warren was excluded from the meeting. He wrote shortly after to the Home Secretary that "Monro as Secret Agent has no information of any special danger ... for months now we have had no information of any definite character."[130] What was discussed at Salisbury's meeting is unknown. Shortly after it, a government select committee framed the terms of the Parnell Special Commission. In May 1888, another assassination attempt on Balfour's life was allegedly planned in Paris.

The "Central News" has been supplied with the following from a high official source:—"Disappointed at the failure of the recent dynamite plot and the capture of their agents, the Clan na Gael in America have lately promoted new schemes of outrage in the hope again to attract the subscriptions as well as to clear the leaders from accusations, known to be well-founded, of having embezzled a large proportion of the funds entrusted to them. As the authorities had reason to fear that these fresh plots would be directed to a repetition of the Phoenix Park tragedy, they took measures to watch the movements of the Irish Land League official who escaped to America to avoid arrest for that crime. Some short time since the notorious Thomas Brennan, formerly secretary to the league, was found to be in communication with John S. Walsh and other dangerous agents of the conspiracy. Walsh thereupon disappeared from his home announcing that he was going to join Brennan in Omaha. As a matter of fact, he took a steamer for France. There he was lost sight of for a while, but ultimately he was met in Paris, and followed to an obscure hotel, where he has been lodging under a false name. This man, who was formerly one of the salaried organizers of the Land League, was denounced by Carey as one of the chief promoters of the Phoenix Park murder. A warrant issued for his arrest was executed in France in 1883, under the Extradition Treaty with that country, but the French Government refused to give him up. He has always advocated schemes of assassination, and there is no reasonable doubt that his mission to Europe is connected with some desperate plot of the kind. Walsh's appearance has considerably changed since the year of the Phoenix Park murder. He is a man of about 60 years of age, nearly six feet high, with very square shoulders, and erect bearing. His thick hair and his large moustache have become white."[131]

THOSE ALLEGED ASSASSINS

Special Cable Dispatch to the Tribune

LONDON, June 5.—A high Government official is authority for the statement that Walsh, whose conspiracy was broken up in Paris, really came over here to carry out the assassination of Balfour. This is the last report made by the police officials of Scotland Yard to the Irish Secretary. The police officials were called upon to give the evidence upon which they based this charge. They gave the whole history of the case from the time Walsh left New York. This plot, which has already been described, was first sent to Scotland Yard by an American detective agency. It is now believed that it was planned to kill Balfour in St. James' Park. The Irish Office is near this park, and it had been Balfour's habit to walk through the park on the way to and from the office. He never was accompanied by more than one officer. The police here profess to be well pleased with breaking up the plot and scaring off its planners. The present plan of the Scotland Yard officials is to frighten away all conspirators instead of inveigling them into places where they can be arrested.[132]

John Walsh gave an interview to *The Chicago Daily Tribune* in reply to the claims and disputed the rumors. He gave further details on the alleged American Irish plots on English soil in 1888, and provided background to the factional infighting. However, what if any information was transmitted from an American detective agency to Scotland Yard is not known.

## WALSH AND THE CLAN-NA-GAEL

The Irish Patriot Speaks of His European Experiences — Treachery in the Order.

NEW YORK, June 18.— John Walsh, who is called the boldest and clearest-headed man in the Clan-na-Gael, said last night: "I am not a dynamiter. I have never advocated the use of the explosive. I don't believe in helping Ireland in that way. I had been in Omaha to get work — for I am a laboring man — and, not successful went to Antwerp and wrote to the man in England who owed me money to come over and settle, and he did. I then went to Paris, but had not been in the city a day until the detectives were so thick around me that they almost ran over each other. McKenna I never knew before I met him on a train one day, and we were together because he spoke English. One day a detective brought me a letter from the prefecture of police commanding me to call on him the next day. I went and was asked my reason for being in Paris. I gave it, and when the Prefect told me I could go one of the men blurted out in English: 'You are a liar, Walsh, for you are a conspirator. You came over here to kill Balfour and you have failed. I have been sent here to tell it to your teeth.' We wrangled a while and he asked me some questions which I refused to answer because he called me a liar. When I went to Havre I was followed by detectives, who staid on the steamer until she sailed."

Walsh does not say what he proposes to do now and claims not to know where McKenna is. Walsh's return and the failure of the mission that many expected of him have set the Clan-na-Gael all agog. Certain members of this society declare that Walsh did not go to England to kill Balfour, but they refuse to say what he went for. There are intimations that the journey was in some way connected with the liberating of Dr. Gallagher of Green Point, now serving a life sentence. There are some who say that the failure on Walsh's part to carry out his mission, whatever it may have been, will mean the disruption of the Clan-na-Gael in this country.

This is the third time in two years that such missions have failed. It is said there is treachery within the order, and it is probable that an investigation will be made. Since 1882 a faction fight has been going on, and with all the money collected there has been but one success. That was the rescue of the prisoners at Freemantle, Australia, in 1885. The success of that adventure was due to Walsh. It is now said that such missions are no longer possible, as the British Government keeps all the men under surveillance. Walsh is about the only man who would attempt such a mission. He does not know what fear is. He fled from England in 1883 because Carey, the informer, said he was implicated in the Phoenix Park murders, and since then he has done all he could to make the Clan-na-Gael a success here, but treachery in the ranks, it is believed, has made secrecy no longer possible.

It is said that there are two men in Brooklyn who are suspected of having been bought by the English Government, and that Walsh's failure is due to them. It is thought his return is for the purpose of raising a storm which will bring out some startling disclosures.[133]

The indications were that by this time, Special Branch and the British Government had infiltrated the American Clan-na-Gael to such an extent that they were directing its functions with a system of paid informers and spies. The chances for planning dynamite attacks were curtailed by 1888, and Irish Republican extremists were considering other options. Some of these ideas were the suggested misinformation of British government agencies complicating the historical record on Jack the Ripper.

On August 11, 1888, Queen Victoria recorded in her personal journal a meeting with the Prime Minister: "OSBORNE. 11 Aug. 1888.— A very hot night, but the day cooler than yesterday. Saw Lord Salisbury and talked with him of many things, of Germany, Russia, Ireland, but he was sorry to say the Government had had notice from America of a plot to kill Mr. Balfour, which is terrible, and he has to be well watched."[134] What is significant about Her Majesty's entry is that the details on the assassination plot appear to have been sent directly to the government, perhaps a foreign diplomatic dispatch that would naturally have been passed on to the Foreign Office, Home Office and Special Branch. However, Scotland Yard had also a constant stream of direct information from Pinkerton and other detective agencies in the U.S., and the Queen's journal entry seems at variance with that procedure. It may simply be that the government was taking credit for vigilance on a potential plot to assassinate the Irish Chief Secretary. Or, it may indicate that the Prime Minister knew the identity of the Irish extremist suspected of the Whitechapel murders who was associated with Balfour's potential demise. As the first Ripper murders were mere weeks away, this particular plot seems to be the Macnaghten reference recorded by author Douglas Browne. However, what is of some historical concern is that the ailing Queen Victoria was notified after a full year when several plots on the life of Balfour were already hatched in America to the knowledge of the government. It is a reflection of the vague constitutional arrangements between Parliament and the Monarchy during Victoria's reign.

On the same day of the Queen's journal entry, the *Birmingham Daily Post* confirmed the danger:

Queen Victoria took an active interest in the Whitechapel murders. She noted in her journal on August 11, 1888, a meeting with Prime Minister Salisbury informing her of a plot on the life of his nephew Chief Secretary of Ireland Arthur Balfour. Melville Macnaghten associated the leader of the plot with Jack the Ripper (photograph by Alexander Bassano).

Yesterday Mr. Balfour, Chief Secretary for Ireland, having arrived from London in Dublin, had interviews at Dublin Castle with the Attorney-General, Sir West Ridgway (Under-Secretary), and the principal officials. He remained transacting official business at the Castle till after seven o'clock. During the day the Chief Secretary received several telegrams concerning the inquest on Dr. Ridley. It is understood that the allegations concerning the doings in Tullamore Prison engross a great deal of his attention, if their investigation is not the immediate object of his visit to Ireland. Mr. Balfour will, it is stated, if circumstances permit, return to London on Tuesday evening. Extreme precautions are taken for his safety. Two Scotland Yard detectives traveled with him from London, and two Dublin detectives joined them at Holyhead. Yesterday Mr. Balfour had an interview with his Excellency the Lord-Lieutenant at the Viceregal Lodge.[135]

The "Special Commission to Inquire into Allegations Against Certain Members of Parliament and Others," its full title, meanwhile had opened: "A preliminary meeting of the Commission Court was held on September 17, 1888. The first sitting of the Commission for the purpose of the Inquiry took place on October 22, 1888, the last on November 22, 1889."[136] On its September opening, which 60 journalists attended, The *New York Times* fatefully remarked, "Unless to-day's signs are all misleading, this special commission which the Tories have invented and created to injure Parnell and his cause is destined to prove their Frankenstein."[137]

The last parliamentary sitting before the autumn recess was on August 13. It resumed on November 6, 1888, broadly covering the period of the murders. After the Jack the Ripper murders ended towards the end of 1888, another attempt to assassinate Balfour had been reported. This final attempt, which could also be linked to the event referred to by Macnaghten, began to surface in the press during December 1888 and continued into the following year.

### BALFOUR'S BODY GUARD

London, Jan. 7.— The number of policemen detailed to protect Mr. Balfour has been increased, in consequence of a report that the Invincibles are planning to murder him.[138]

Some years later, there were more dynamite plots in London, alleged efforts of a collusion of socialist anarchists and Irish Republicans. A representative of the Associated Press "made some inquiries at Scotland Yard as to the methods pursued in shadowing the plotters and as to how it happened that the authorities were so well informed of the plans of the plotters in advance. It was stated that the work had been done in the United States by the Pinkerton agency who had for years forwarded every week the fullest reports of every meeting of any revolutionary body in the United States, particularly in Chicago and New York. The espionage maintained on gatherings in those cities is remarkably complete. There is a full file in Scotland Yard on all resolutions, documents, etc., pertaining to the gatherings and full descriptions of members and their actions."[139]

In 2002, the Metropolitan Police Special Branch index books from the Victorian era were rediscovered in the back of a New Scotland Yard cupboard. Their survival indicates that the paper files to which they refer were purged for filing space though some are said to exist. This was perhaps sometime before 1956, when Browne saw Macnaghten's Balfour report, as he does not mention seeing the investigative files. It was Macnaghten's job as Chief Constable of Scotland Yard to maintain the elaborate filing system of Special Branch. The files and index books were also available to Robert Anderson, who is noted as disbursing various amounts of secret service monies to informers. Chief Inspector John Littlechild and Chief Inspector Donald Swanson were also noted making reports on investigations.

The undated entries in Special Branch index books show that it was conducting an investigation and collating divisional police reports and other details on the Whitechapel murders from 1888, the year the filing system commenced, to 1892, when the first volume of the Chief Constable's accounts register was completed. The abridged entries of the Chief Constable's CID register marked "Special Branch" and covering the period 1888 through about 1892, indicate that an extreme Irish Republican was suspected as Jack the Ripper and associated with a plot to assassinate Balfour based on details from a U.S. detective agency. The register also contains, for instance, the investigation of an Irish suspect thought to be involved with the Whitechapel murders, one of many brought to the attention of Scotland Yard. The undated abridged entries noted sequentially for the suspect were:

McGrath, William — suspicious Irishman at 57 Bedford Gardens.
McGrath, William — said to be connected to Whitechapel murders.[140]

The indications according to the Special Branch files are that the Irish Republican suspected and associated with a plot to murder Balfour was not Francis Tumblety, even though he was publicly implicated in the Whitechapel murders on his own admission and was regarded by Littlechild in 1913 as "among the suspects." However, the index books of Special Branch, held indefinitely as a matter of official protocol, support Browne's 1956 mention that Macnaghten had noted an alternative official theory — a report drawn from a covert investigation that suspected "Jack the Ripper" of being an associate of a political secret society with a plot to murder the Chief Secretary of Ireland. This new information corroborates the published reference of Browne and the Scotland Yard crime index on the suggested complicity of the Irish Party in a Whitechapel murder. It questions the validity of the standard theories of Anderson, Macnaghten and Swanson on the direction of the police investigation of Jack the Ripper.

Compared to the official suspects and established theories touted for well over a century, it confirms that Macnaghten, Anderson and Swanson had closed ranks on the Special Branch inquiries of Jack the Ripper. Their vague and ambiguous details have proved misleading to a study of police history generally and the Whitechapel murders investigation specifi-cally. Their reasons, of course, are obvious, given the political climate of the period. James Monro and John Littlechild, however, made entirely different choices to the latter-day certainties of Robert Anderson. The political gambits of the period appear to have contributed to their decisions to retire from Scotland Yard at the height of their distinguished police careers.

Though an alternative Special Branch inquiry on Jack the Ripper can be validated with available primary sources, it does not necessarily mean that the murders were a political plot. In a climate of official misinformation that seeped into reports and suspicions on the Whitechapel murders, a serial killer of destitute East End prostitutes driven by Anglo-Irish hostile relations may not have been the reality. Official face-saving on an unsolved series of enigmatic murders may simply reflect the truth. A historical vacuum has expressed itself in conspiracy theories about corruption in high places at the expense of the lower classes.

Then there were those who took neither side or traded with both. Detective Sergeant Patrick McIntyre described them as, "the cutest of the cute [who] may fall a victim to one of those clever men who trade on the outskirts of political movements."[141] He also said, "the hand of the spy, or agent-provocateur, is clearly visible. These people see their opportunity when any Government is in a perturbed state of mind. They sense the 'flowing tide that leads to fortune.' Their intrigues produce conspiracies. There is this difference between a detective and an agent-provocateur — that, whereas the former is paid by salary and has no interest in increasing crime, the latter is paid by results, and has to depend on the rise and fall of the 'crime' thermometer. What does the 'provocating agent' do when he finds the prevailing danger is diminishing in quantity? He manufactures more 'danger'!"[142]

Macnaghten's Balfour Ripper statement was also available for the government in associating the Irish Party of Parnell with Fenian extremists. The Conservative government was responsible for catching Jack the Ripper and for the protection of London's citizens — and thus under pressure, which would bring about its downfall in 1892 — so it considered that the ends would justify the means in maintaining power and the empire. Anderson's involvements in the "Parnellism and Crime" articles are the example. However, the information on Jack the Ripper was never used in that way, nor did Irish extremists boast of having committed the murders and outwitting Scotland Yard.

Nevertheless, ambiguous police and governmental statements on Jack the Ripper by those who knew about Macnaghten's Balfour position and the Special Branch inquiries on the Whitechapel murders have an alternative interpretation. The system of informers paid from secret service monies brought with it the risk of agent provocateurs. That is, a motive emerged that Jack the Ripper played off official factions and was a by-product of a system in place to contain him. It was a situation that left exposed high-level executive and police arrangements in legal cross-examination.

> The damaging admissions at Eunis of Callinan, the informer, have greatly excited Fenian circles in this city and Paris, and a suspicion prevails among them that certain blatant Fenians in America have for years been in the pay of the British Government. Callinan admitted that he planned the raid on Farmer Sexton's house in order to deliver his companions over to the police, and that all his expenses were paid by the government. The question naturally arises, were the parties who have planned the dynamite outrages in England of recent years also paid by the government? It is certainly strange that all the dynamiters hailing from America were captured, promptly convicted and sent to prison, a number for life terms. It is true that the testimony of the Brooklyn informer, Jim McDermott, secured the conviction of a number of them, but the belief now prevails that "Red Jim" had assistants in America. Fenians both in London and in Paris disclaim any knowledge of intended outrages and say that if any are perpetrated they will be committed by paid plotters of the Callinan stripe at the instigation of the government for the purpose of injuring the Home Rule cause and creating a reaction in favor of its coercion policy.[143]

In May of 1889, a gruesome murder was committed on Dr. Patrick Cronin, a Clan-Na-Gael member, a staunch opponent of the direction the group was taking in Chicago. Cronin was assassinated and reports of the crime spread by cable to England and around the world. Pinkerton Detective Agency was commissioned to investigate the matter in tandem with the Chicago police. Macnaghten was due to join the Metropolitan Police the following month. It is possible that this American event had alerted Scotland Yard to a Balfour source for Jack the Ripper. To some contemporary commentators, events were converging to the extreme.

> The mystery surrounding the murder of Dr. Cronin at Chicago excites keen interest throughout Great Britain and Ireland. It has usurped the position of the Pigott affair and is discussed with nearly as much avidity. Opinions regarding the Cronin murder are as various as the different political parties. Some hold that certain leaders of the Clan-na-Gael at Chicago were the instigators of the crime, while others believe that a woman was at the bottom of it. Others still profess to see in this affair a conspiracy similar to that alleged in the Times-Parnell case. Neither Mr. Parnell, Michael Davitt, nor Mr. O'Brien has the slightest doubt that Alexander Sullivan is innocent of any connection either directly or indirectly with Cronin's death. A prominent lawyer and leader in the Irish circle where the conspiracy theory exist this afternoon said: "The developments in the Parnell case, especially those which led to the flight and suicide of Pigott, created a strong feeling against the Tory government for the part they played in the Irish leader's trial, and made many friends among former enemies for the home rule movement. Among them may be mentioned Sir Thomas Farrer. The government has never ceased to blame the police department for the miserable failure on the part of the witnesses which the detectives brought before the Parnell commission. A glance at the affairs of the London Metropolitan police since the inception of the Nationalist movement will undoubtedly show some strange and startling facts since Mr. Matthews' assumption of the home office, note what has followed: "Mr. Monro, who was chief of the detective department, was removed by Sir Charles Warren, for obvious reasons which were, in my opinion, questionable acts of his detectives in regard to the dynamiters, especially the retention of 'Jim' McDermott, of Brooklyn, in the detective bureau. E.G. Jenkinson, assistant to the Irish Under Secretary for police and crime, was appointed in Mr. Monro's place, the latter being transferred to a created bureau in Mr. Matthews' office with 'Jim' McDermott as his protégé. The dynamite outrages ceased as the latter person could find no more dupes to send to prison for life. Then came the Whitechapel murders one after another until Sir Charles Warren was compelled by public feeling to resign the office of chief of the Metropolitan police, the failure of the police to capture the murderer being placed at his door. Mr. Monro was immediately, despite a strong feeling

against him, installed as Sir Charles' successor, and the Whitechapel murders ceased, and have to some passed almost into oblivion. 'The London Times, Home Secretary Matthews, and Attorney General Webster, were led to believe by this same police department that such startling evidence could be produced against Mr. Parnell and other Irish leaders, that the Irish home-rule movement would not only be squelched, but that Mr. Parnell himself would be sent into oblivion with such a character that no man would wish to assume. The witnesses brought forward by detectives, from Pigott down, have failed miserably, and wrought ruin to both the government and the Times. The Parnell case has, with the exception of the verdict of the judges, drawn to a close. A great meeting of representative Irish-Americans is about to be held in Philadelphia, and something must be done to blacken the Irish character in the eyes of the world. What so fitting for such a foul purpose than to show that conspirators and murderers existed among respected leaders of the Irish people in America who would not hesitate to remove friends of Ireland who antagonized personal desires. A police department that would stoop to employing a man like Jim McDermott, who sent several personal friends to terms of life imprisonment, and concocted with dupes to murder others with dynamite, succeeding by a mistake of the police in more than one case, would not hesitate to perpetrate such a crime as the Cronin murder to accomplish a purpose.'"[144]

Jim "Red" McDermott had his fingers in several pies, not least of all the internal criminal investigation department of the Home Office, for which he had been an informer for the previous Liberal government coalition. He also had close dealings with Dublin Castle and the secret service of Ireland. His Irish Fenian contacts over decades were of great interest to English authorities, but he was more devoted to money and luxuries than to any patriotic sentiment. His description, it is conjectured, may have matched that given of the witness in the Kelly murder, Mary Ann Cox. Several of his letters to important Fenian leaders are known to have survived. However, official documentation on his activities for the British government is lacking. He was on the payroll beginning in 1882 of the first unofficial "spymaster-general" for the Home Office, Sir Edward Jenkinson. This was when Anderson was retained as a political crime advisor. McDermott was associated with a man, also a worker for Jenkinson, called Dawson but whose real name was H. Llewellyn White.[145] Both men were known to have frequented East End public bars and were based in Soho. There is no direct evidence to link McDermott with Jack the Ripper, but if there was, it would be interesting due to his knowledge of both sides of the political equation.

As an agent provocateur, McDermott was in a position to blackmail the previous Liberal administration, which had availed itself of his services. His information on Gladstone and an Irish Party coalition that previously held the support of the Tory Party and Henry Matthews was of interest to the Special Commission. The absence of official files on his dealings with Fenians and the British government add to the murky background. Essentially a man of sophisticated cruelty, he had a history of arranging violent events for money. He would inform and act for remuneration from both Irish Republicans and the secret service. In September 1889, McDermott gave rare press interviews. Some extracts follow.

### A TALK WITH "RED JIM"
The Notorious McDermott Tells a Great Story

### SPECIAL CABLE DISPATCH TO THE TRIBUNE
[Copyright, 1889, by James Gordon Bennett]

LONDON, Sept. 1—"Red Jim" McDermott, who made his home in Brooklyn for many years, who had been denounced as an informer by Irishmen all over the world, whose death in various shapes has been announced nearly a dozen times, and for information of whose whereabouts Henry Labouchere offered £50 during the sitting of the Parnell commission, left London today on an early morning train. He had been in London a week. He took no pains to seclude himself, and last night informed a

Herald correspondent that he was afraid of no one and that the heaviest weapon he carried was a latchkey. This he carried in his trousers pocket attached to a silver chain, after the English fashion.

McDermott never looked more prosperous nor more contented than last night while he sat at one of the small tables with which the smoking room of one of London's principal hotels is lavishly furnished. He was one of a party of six. Five of these were Americans. The sixth might have been a native of Scotland or the north of Ireland, but he had little brogue. Excepting his upper lip his face was smoothly shaven. He wore a small, sandy mustache. His hair, also sandy, was cut reasonably close and was plentiful. His face was fresh colored rather than florid. His attire smacked of the world of sport. It was of Scotch goods, a rather biggish check, and was fashionably made. In his scarf he wore a large cameo pin. On his head was a brown derby hat. His age would be guessed at from 40 to 45. His movements were quick and his air youthful rather than middle-aged, though his manner was perfectly composed.

## RED JIM'S STORY

Then he told something that will interest many American readers. He may at one time have been in fear of assassination. He is no longer. He snaps his fingers at those who threaten him. He denies most vehemently that he was ever in the pay of Scotland Yard and while on the topic said: "Why, I don't know where it is, except that it is in London. I have been hounded as a British spy when I never was one; when I supposed to be getting money from the British Government I was broke, sometimes without a pound to my name. I was driven from pillar to post, a man without a country, but in spite of all I have today all the money I want. I have none to throw away, but plenty for comfort and a little for luxury. Since I left America and was arrested on this side and thrown into Walton jail at Liverpool—the same place Mrs. Maybrick was in—I have talked to several Americans, but when they went home and said they had talked with Jim McDermott they were not believed.

## A MAN WITHOUT A COUNTRY

"I was without a country at the time. I felt rather desperate and I said to myself; 'I'll go to the only free country on earth,' and I went to England. There a man is safe, and my sympathies today are English. They say I betrayed the secrets of Irish societies and am accountable for the imprisonment of Dr. Gallagher and others. I say they lie. I have not belonged to an Irish society since 1863, I was a Fenian, but that was the only Irish society I ever belonged to. I belonged to none of their societies in America and the only secret organization I belong to today is the Masonic order. How could I steal and sell secrets of societies or organizations to which I never belonged. I was arrested in 1883 upon landing in England from America. I was in jail for six weeks. All my papers were taken from me, but they were all returned to me. It was after I was liberated that I began my wanderings.

"I have told myself it was not worth while saying anything, as my enemies would always have the last word. I mean people on the other side of the water. Now take O'Donovan-Rossa, for instance. I see that a man named Cassidy has brought suit against him, and that Rossa denied he had ever received a check from me for the defense fund. He was shown the face of the check drawn by me and made payable to him. He said: 'Look at the back of it,' and on the back of it was his own indorsement. Then he claimed the check was given to him personally by me. Now, do I look like a man who would give Rossa £50! I gave him that money for the defense fund, and when he says I did not he lies.

"When it became matter of general belief that I was in the pay of the British government I received a number of letters from men offering to sell information. Some of these were simply baits, but some were bona fide. I did not answer one of them but turned them over to the proper authorities. What use they made of them I don't know, but unless I am mistaken those letters are at the bottom of the enmity now entertained by one set of English politicians towards another, both of whom were friends until lately. Unlike the average Irishman McDermott is for the government, and displays a pretty intimate knowledge of British politics. In talking of Labouchere's offer of £50 for information of his whereabouts McDermott said he did not want and would not take the money, but he would like somebody to get it out of "Labby," as he called him. He was in London, he said, when the offer was made and did not try in any way to conceal himself. He even asked a friend, a Frenchman, if he did not want to make £50, at the same time showing him the printed offer. His friend refused on the ground that it might harm him. Perhaps the information that there is more than one Irishman in the States who writes to McDermott and keeps him posted will not be uninteresting.[146]

## RED JIM MCDERMOTT TALKS

He Says Parnell Must Soon Step Down and OUT—O'Reilly's Accounts

## SPECIAL CABLE DISPATCH TO THE TRIBUNE

[Copyright, 1890, by James Gordon Bennet]

LONDON, Jan. 24 — Red Jim McDermott is in high feather. After considerable search Labouchere found him, only to be told his address could always have been obtained from the Herald correspondent. Labouchere and McDermott have been in conference several days, but so far they have only been "flirting," as McDermott styles it. McDermott was pounced upon tonight by a raft of correspondents, and the manner in which he handled them was amusing. McDermott warns the persons connected with the so-called "new movement" in New York, directed by Rossa and St. Clair, that the British Government is well posted regarding all they do and the secret society is no secret to the office in Whitehall. He says the physical force party is in the ascendant, and asks what has become of the funds of which O'Reilly is treasurer. He maintains they are $50,000 short, and the league dare not call a convention to audit the books. McDermott further says Parnell must step down and out inside of two months, not on account of the Shea divorce proceedings, but on account of something more serious.[147]

## PARNELL MUST STEP DOWN AND OUT

"Red Jim" McDermott Makes Some Sensational Insinuations — The Irish Party.

NEW YORK, Feb. 17 — Reduced to monologue here is the substance of what "Red Jim" McDermott said in a talk in London with a New York correspondent, whose letter fills over a column in the World of today:

"I was in Auckland, New Zealand, when I read in some American newspapers sent to me that I was dead. I was in Berlin some months afterwards when I saw by more American newspapers that I had been in New York. I assure you solemnly that I have never been in America since I left it, and I never expect to go there again. I went from Berlin to an American diplomatic official in Norway to whom my letters have been addressed for many years. While there I saw copies of an advertisement which Mr. Labouchere put in the English, French, and German journals, asking for my address. I answered the advertisement by writing to an agent of Mr. Labouchere in London, telling him where I could be found. I received in reply a letter telling me to go to another city, where I would find a letters awaiting me addressed so and so. I went to that city, found the letter, came to England, and have been in communication with Mr. Labouchere for the last ten days. What my business is with Mr. Labouchere I propose to keep to myself. I have been able, since I have been going here, to find out what is going on in the under current of Irish politics, and you may quote me as saying that it is the opinion of the staunchest followers of Mr. Parnell that he must step down and out as the leader of the Irish party before Parliament has been in session two months — perhaps much sooner than that. I assure you that the expenses of the Parnell Commission have crippled the resources of the Irish party so badly that they are at their wits' ends. A great deal of the money is gone that cannot be accounted for."[148]

## DAVITT'S COMING DISCLOSURES
## IRISHMEN INTERESTED IN THE EXPOSURE OF MC'DERMOTT'S PLOTTINGS

A good many Irishmen in this city and Brooklyn were glad to read in The Times yesterday the announcement that Michael Davitt proposed to print in his paper, the Labor World of Dublin, a complete expose of the plots concocted in Ireland and America by "Red Jim" McDermott.

Ex-Assemblyman David H. Healy said that the British Government had only itself to blame for the forthcoming exposures, as the cues from which the information was obtained would never have been furnished to the Irish Nationalists but for the evidence brought out in the Parnell investigation which the Government instituted. "Davitt is a man of undoubted determination and honesty," said Healy, "and no Irishman will doubt the truth of the exposures he proposes. McDermott was certainly a spy and a secret agent of England. It has always been her policy to use such methods, and so thoroughly is her secret service organized that I don't think such a thing as a secret Irish society, here or elsewhere, is now possible, for the British Government is almost immediately informed of everything that transpires."

The assertion of Michael Davitt that the British Consul General in this city supplied McDermott with funds to carry on his plottings was met with an unqualified denial at the office of the British Consul yesterday.

"Sir Edward M. Archibald was the British Consul in 1882," said Mr. R. Hoare, an employee of the consulate, "and at that time, it is well known, there was a well organized Irish dynamite and assassination party, whose movements required the closest watching on the part of our Government, and this the then Consul General doubtless did. Any action taken by any of our officials was in the line of detecting and preventing outrages and plots."[149]

THE DYNAMITE PRISONERS
INTERVIEW WITH AN INFORMER
STRANGE STATEMENTS

The London correspondent of the New York Sun had an interview last week with "Red Jim" McDermott, the Irish informer who gave evidence at the last dynamite trial. McDermott, who was armed with a revolver, said he had received warning that two men had been sent from New York to murder him. "This is the first time," he said, "that I have carried a weapon, but I am in fear of my life. Nevertheless I have sent that letter to the Home Office, and have been to-day to Scotland Yard and lodged a description of the two assassins of whom I know. I am waiting now for them to appear, and when they do they will either kill me or go to a police-station. If they attack me I shall defend myself, and while I shall only use this revolver for self-protection, if a bullet lodges in a fatal part it will be their lookout and not mine. I have also had interviews with Mr. Davitt, who told me that if I would give up certain documents that he said I had in my possession he would liberate the dynamite prisoners now in Chatham prison. He would publish in his newspaper, the Labor World, a circumstantial report of my death that would rid me of the assassins who have been following me for years, and thus allow me to end my life in peace. Davitt said that these papers would doubtless incriminate Sir William Harcourt and Lord Spencer, but that he did not care if they incriminated Gladstone himself. What he wanted, he said, was to secure the liberation of the dynamite prisoners; and in a letter to me he says that I put those men there, and am keeping them there. His letter is a distinctly threatening one; but I have the Government and the police on my side, and I am going to see this thing through."

The correspondent called upon Mr. Davitt, who laughed heartily at McDermott's story of the two assassins. However, said Mr. Davitt, there is a movement on foot for the liberation of some of the dynamite prisoners. I have now documents to prove that the dynamite was put into the hands of a lot of poor, irresponsible, unintelligent Irish by men in the employ of the enemy in New York and Glasgow, for the sole purpose of getting money out of the Secret Service Fund. The Home Secretary has promised to look into the case early this autumn, and I confidently expect the liberation of many of these dynamite prisoners. However dastardly the crime may be of any man who wilfully used dynamite for the destruction of his fellow men, it is less than that of Government agents who, for the purpose of getting at the Secret Service Fund, decoy underwitted and ignorant men into such a crime. As for Jim McDermott, he has been outwitted, clever scoundrel as he was, and when the time comes I shall have something to say about him. I know all about him, where he has been, what he has been doing, and where his money comes from. He likes to believe that his movements are developed in mystery, and that he is continually followed by hidden foes. Why, I have known where he has been in London and the vicinity for the last three months, but his miserable carcase is not worth a moment's thought. As for papers compromising Sir William Harcourt or Earl Spencer, that is ridiculous. When I tell what I know about the men who duped the poor fellows who are now in Chatham Prison, there will be some interesting disclosures. Until the time is ripe, however, I shall have nothing further to say. I cannot prejudice our cause by publishing it too soon."[150]

Mr. Davitt throws doubt on McDermott's alleged visit to America. In the opening paragraph of his letter to the Freeman's Journal he says:

"Red Jim" McDermott has lost nothing of his braggart assurance by the wear and tear to which his career has put one of his chief characteristics. He abstracts a sheet of note paper from the Victoria Hotel, London, or gets some of his boon companions to do it for him, and thinks he can make the public believe that he is residing in a respectable house by dating his letter from the place. He sends a letter to some brother spy in New York, to be posted there for him in the hope of inducing people in Dublin to believe that he can visit the United States. These tricks may deceive the chiefs of the Secret Service of the Home Office into the belief that he is still of use to them, but no one else will be taken in by this too transparent dodge.

Mr. Davitt challenges McDermott to sue him for libel, in either England or Ireland, in order that Mr. Davitt may have an opportunity to bring forward his proofs against "Red Jim" in legal form.[151]

And so it continued until the change of government in August 1892, with further Whitechapel murders mistakenly attributed to the "Jack the Ripper" of 1888. One of the last decisions made by Home Secretary Henry Matthews and Irish Chief Secretary Arthur

Balfour was the release of Callen, the dynamiter suspected of involvement with the Jubilee Plot who was convicted in February 1888.

## TALK OF ST. STEPHEN'S

House of Commons, Wednesday.
[From Our Own Correspondent.]

Most of the Opposition journals are in a great state over Mr. Balfour's surrender on the question of dynamiters. The "Times," which was eager for the most rigid inquiry into the iniquity of Mr. Asquith, drops the whole business like a hot coal. It was bad enough to be told that Mr. Matthews had ordered the release of Callen, but it is simply staggering to learn, on the authority of Mr. Balfour, that the late Home Secretary was in favor of liberating Egan too. The only Tory paper which stands to its guns is the "St. James's Gazette," which still demands the head of Mr. Matthews, and hints not obscurely that Mr. Balfour deserves to lose his own. The "St. James's" says that the public have a right to know whether both parties have been "playing fast and loose with the administration of justice," and declares that the whole matter must be threshed out on Sir Frederick Milner's amendment and the amendment which "Mr. Chamberlain and the Liberal Unionists are believed to be contemplating." I imagine that Mr. Chamberlain's contemplation in this direction has not survived Mr. Balfour's speech last night. Nor is it very probable that Sir Frederick Milner will persevere with a notion which must seriously embarrass his leaders. Mr. Matthews is not here to speak for himself, but it is evident that his colleagues are anxious to hear the last of a very unprofitable subject. It is worthy of remark, however, that the release of Callen is still a mystery. When did Mr. Matthews take so strong an interest in this dynamiter whose existence had been forgotten even by the most fervid amnesty advocate. It is suggested that the late Home Secretary may have discovered that the conviction of Callen was one of the games of Jim McDermott, whose exploits as an informer have been more than once exposed by Mr. Davitt. It has been hinted that the reasons for Callen's release would be a great shock to people who believe in the justice of Irish informers. At any rate, Mr. Matthews decided that Callen could not be kept in prison any longer, and the embarrassment of his colleagues suggests that the result of the scrutiny demanded by the "St. James's Gazette" might reach the proportions of an official scandal.[152]

The Whitechapel murders were unique in some regards and lacked a consistent motive. The case was affected by Victorian social mores and politics of crime, poverty, beliefs, imperialism, and prostitution. The question of who Jack the Ripper really was has for over a century effectively masked historic events with conspiracy theories mixed and generated from ambiguous senior police assertions. The available evidence shows that while Scotland Yard CID was covertly seeking a Ripper linked with extremist and political secret societies, an insane local Londoner or immigrant inhabiting the East End was overtly suspected. Medical examinations by police surgeons, a marked feature of the investigation due to the nature of the wounds, guided police inquiries.

The problem with the Whitechapel murders, compared to other cases of serial killers, is that they appear to have been committed by someone who had some form of anatomical knowledge. On that point, however, the police surgeons widely disagreed. Perhaps the murder weapon gave the mistaken impression of medical expertise. That Jack the Ripper's weapon was similar to those used in the Phoenix Park murders is generally agreed upon; there is medical consensus on the type of knife used for the wounds and organ extractions. Victorian police had considered extremists as responsible for the Whitechapel murders of 1888–91 with special reviews on the "medical aspect." Scotland Yard may have known the identity of Jack the Ripper, as Anderson asserted, but he was not proven to be any of those subsequently named.

It would seem then that some senior police officials had an inkling of the Ripper's identity or associations and that the Home Secretary had confirming details related to the murder of Mary Kelly. That knowledge, without substantial proof, was not conducive to popular confidence in the government. Jack the Ripper added to the political machinations of the late Victorian period with mayhem and madness. He may even have been a renegade agent provocateur, a monster created by the system of entrapment in place to contain him.

What is clear, however, despite inconclusive and ambiguous reports, is that Special Branch searched, based on details from an American detective agency, for a killer linked with a plot to assassinate the Chief Secretary of Ireland, Arthur Balfour. Jack the Ripper was pursued as an extreme separatist, sympathizer or provocateur according to Special Branch files. It is possible the killer was an embarrassing by-product of internal government policies. It was reason enough for Anderson, Macnaghten and Swanson to close ranks as senior Scotland Yard officers. Anderson, Macnaghten and Swanson may have believed in the relative truth of an "insane Polish Jew" as a suspect for the murders. However, these allegations cannot be corroborated. As senior police officials, they were in a position to know of an alternative pending inquiry by the Special Branch on Jack the Ripper, as Macnaghten and Littlechild further noted.

The Whitechapel murders did contribute to bringing down a government, as Macnaghten had also intimated. They were likely the official "hot potato," in the words attributed to James Monro. This contributed to his retirement as Commissioner of the Metropolitan Police. The crimes were enmeshed with the political and social fever of the period. Whoever Jack the Ripper was, the fair-minded editorial of the *Liverpool Mercury* on Irish statesman Charles Stewart Parnell summed up events with precision.

> They took care, in making it, that the accused [parliamentary] members should have all the odds against them — that, even when they had established the character they give to the letters and shown their own innocence of all complicity in crimes, they should still have to bear some odium for the folly or viciousness of stupid or malevolent persons who, in two continents, may have advocated or perpetrated offences. The mass of people are not usually close readers and analyzers of current events. It is a very simple and natural proposition that the leader of a great movement enlisting the sympathies of perhaps ten millions of those of his race cannot hold himself responsible for every act of indiscretion of villainy that may spring out of it. We do not hold Mr. Gladstone responsible for the acts and utterances of every Liberal and Radical in the United Kingdom. Nor do we think of saddling upon Lord Salisbury the freaks of the baser sort of Tories.... People do not see so clearly when events are swimming before them; it is in the next generation, after the passion has subsided, that history can be studied discriminately.... Mr. Parnell does not pretend that the half million of men enrolled in the Land League were all free from turpitude, or that scores or hundreds of peasants outside its ranks did not commit crime and outrage. His case is that he committed no outrage himself; that he was not privy to any committed; that he never counselled or approved of outrages; and that the documents professing to link him with conspiracies abhorrent to law are forgeries.... Is any generous or honorable man entitled to reproach him, after such a trial, for failing to prevent some of the vast and mercurial forces he endeavoured to control from breaking the laws of the realm which are particularly directed to the protection of life and property?[153]

The murders were not characteristic of the local population or repeated without measured actions. However, for this unsolved serial murder case, nothing can be resolved unless proven with a reasonable degree of certainty and with less ambiguity than is present in its senior police statements. The Whitechapel case gave rise to advances in criminal technologies and presaged the modern cult of the celebrity sexual serial killer. But were the evil deeds and escapes of Jack the Ripper really ordinary in execution?

Scotland Yard, divisional detectives and the uniformed ranks of 1888–91 certainly did not think or act so. These included men like ex–Detective Sergeant Patrick McIntyre, an Irishman whom Anderson demoted after a distinguished service career for the courage of his public convictions. Macnaghten thought highly of him, mentions him in his memoirs, and was on good terms with his supervisor, Littlechild. McIntyre died shortly after writing the following lines and before he could publish his full account of the years covering the Whitechapel murders.

> I now take leave of my readers with the hope that my tale has given them some insight into the making of our complicated detective system. My narrative, as it has dealt with the political department of Scotland Yard has naturally had a stronger political flavour than detective reminiscences have had as a rule. The main point, which I may claim to have established beyond all possible doubt, is that the agent provocateur is at work in free England. This has been denied, and by many is disbelieved to-day, but I challenge anyone to maintain the non-existence of this creature after perusing these recollections. Englishmen should think over the matter seriously, and I shall not be surprised if they finally come to a determination to suppress, without delay, all crime-provokers and those in high places who encourage them.[154]

# Chapter Notes

Some notes contain codes to the location of sources held at the British Archives. An initial abbreviation (list below) indicate where they are held. The detailed letters and numbers that follow indicate the reference files. Folio numbers are indicated by "f." or "ff." Hansard transcripts are historic collections of British Parliamentary debates widely available as print and online editions. Abbreviations used: CLRO Corporation of London Records Office; GB London Hospital Medical College; GLRO Greater London Record Office (now London Metropolitan Archives); HC House of Commons (Hansard); HL House of Lords (Hansard); HO Home Office (UK National Archives); LH Royal London Hospital Museum & Archives; MC London Hospital Medical College; MEPO Metropolitan Police (UK National Archives); PRO Public Record Office (now UK National Archives)

## Chapter 1

1. The full title was *Napoleon's Book of Fate and Oraculum*, and it was in use by all classes of Victorian London. It was a manuscript discovered in 1801 by a French military expedition in Egypt that Napoleon had translated. The explorer Sir Richard Burton described the English version as "a specimen of the old Eastern superstition presented to Europe in a modern and simple form." *Napoleon's Book of Fate* contained sections about "Dreams and Their Interpretation"; "Weather Omens"; "Astrological Miscellany and Important Advice"; "Chiromancy or Fortune Telling by the Hand"; "Celestial Palmistry"; "Observations on Moles in Men and Women"; "Temper and Disposition of Any Person"; "The Art of Face Reading"; and "Lucky Days," among others. Richard Deacon (the pen name of Ripper author Donald McCormick), published a work on Napoleon's oracle titled *The Book of Fate: Its Origins and Uses* (London: Frederick Muller, 1976).

2. *The Star*, October 29, 1888; *Daily Telegraph*, October 30, 1888.

3. White was adept at conjuring tricks himself. In a notice on his retirement in the *East London Observer*, October 16, 1900, it was said that "many a thief who considered himself an expert in palming has had reason to regret that Mr. White was a professor in the art of legerdemain."

4. *The Times*, June 9, June 16, June 24, 1884. The relevant section of the Vagrancy Act of 1824 stated, "Every person professing to tell fortunes or using any subtle craft, means or device to deceive and impose on any of Her Majesty's subjects shall be deemed a rogue and vagabond."

5. The trial of Helen Duncan in 1944, regarded as the last English conviction under the Witchcraft Act of 1735, was not the sole grounds for the repeal of the act and replacement with the Fraudulent Mediums Act. The Duncan case was one of many that brought legal change for mediums. Spiritualist associations had fought a long campaign that began in the Victorian period. Sir Arthur Conan Doyle, who had an interest in Jack the Ripper, as a spiritualist led a delegation to the Home Secretary in 1930 urging change in the law.

6. Gerald Gardner, *Witchcraft Today* (London: Rider, 1954).

7. According to a 2002 briefing report for the Public Petitions Committee of the Scottish Parliament, "The Witchcraft Act 1735 was originally formulated to eradicate the belief in witches and its introduction meant that from 1735 onwards an individual could no longer be tried as a witch. It was, however, possible to be prosecuted for pretending to 'exercise or use any kind of witchcraft, sorcery, enchantment or conjuration, or undertake to tell fortunes.' Supposed contact with spirits fell into this category."

8. HO 144/221/A49301C, ff. 116–18.

9. HO 144/221/A49301C, f 147. For further reading on the 1887 American exhibit in London of William F. "Buffalo Bill" Cody see Louis S. Warren, "Buffalo Bill Meets Dracula: William F. Cody, Bram Stoker, and the Frontiers of Racial Decay," *The American Historical Review*, October 2002, http://www.historycooperative.org/journals/ahr/107.4/ah04 02001124.html (accessed March 27, 2011).

10. David Mayall, *Gypsy-Travellers in Nineteenth-Century Society* (Cambridge: Cambridge University Press, 1988). David Mayall, *English Gypsies and State Policies* (Hatfield: Gypsy Research Centre, University of Hertfordshire Press, 1995).

11. The term "gypsy" is derived from "Egyptians." A historical variant spelling is "gipsy."

12. *Evening News*, October 9, 1888.

13. For further details on Inspector Edmund Reid, see Stewart P. Evans and Nicholas Connell, *The Man Who Hunted Jack the Ripper: Edmund Reid and the Police Perspective* (Stroud, UK: Amberley Publishing, 2009).

14. There is a legal obligation for a person in some way related to a victim to identify the deceased with a written statement to the Coroner's Office. Mary Malcolm's testimony therefore took precedence until disproved by that of Stride's estranged partner Michael Kidney. Dave Yost with Stewart P. Evans, "The Identification of Liz Stride," *Ripper Notes,*

March 2000. For further reading see Dave Yost, *Elizabeth Stride and Jack the Ripper: The Life and Death of the Reputed Third Victim* (Jefferson, NC: McFarland, 2008).

15. Elizabeth Stride had charged Michael Kidney for assault but failed to appear at court. Stride herself was also a regular at the court in the role of defendant, charged on several occasions with being drunk and disorderly. Philip Sugden, *The Complete History of Jack the Ripper* (London: Robinson, 2002). Thames Magistrate's Court Register, April 6, 1887, GLRO, PS/TH/A1/8.

16. *Daily Telegraph*, October 4, 1888.

17. *Echo*, October 3, 1888.

18. The large correspondence required vetting and filing, which ate up valuable police time and resources. As is the case today, letters from psychics especially burdened the investigation. For the best coverage on the extent of public letters on Jack the Ripper of a supernatural nature and others sent to the Metropolitan and City Police, see S.P. Evans and K. Skinner, *Jack the Ripper: Letters from Hell* (Stroud, UK: Sutton Publishing, 2004). For a full list of letters to the City Police see S.P. Evans and D. Rumbelow, *Jack the Ripper: Scotland Yard Investigates* (Stroud, UK: Sutton Publishing, 2006).

19. *Daily Telegraph*, October 4, 1888.

20. *Daily Telegraph*, October 4, 1888.

21. *Star*, October 8, 1888.

22. *Pall Mall Gazette*, October 3, 1888. Stead also had "positively idiotic" suggestions about the Whitechapel murders published in his newspaper during the investigation. In this issue, a theory of the "cryptogrammatic dagger," the apparent cross shape formed when locations of the murder sites were placed on a map, was printed. The idea was later developed in the *Pall Mall Gazette* of December 1, 1888, by contributor and Ripper suspect Roslyn D'Onston.

23. *Echo*, October 5, 1888.

24. *Evening News*, November 10, 1888.

25. The victim was an unknown woman whose torso was discovered under a railway arch in Pinchin Street, St. Georges-in-the-East, on September 10, 1889. Though not regarded as a Ripper murder, it was included in the official files on the Whitechapel murders and remains unsolved.

26. *The Times*, September 12, 1889.

27. For further reading on the convoluted connections of the 1889 Maybrick case with the Jack the Ripper murders see Shirley Harrison and Michael Barrett (narrative and commentary), *The Diary of Jack the Ripper* (London: Smith Gryphon, 1993); Seth Linder, Keith Skinner, and Caroline Morris, *The Ripper Diary: The Inside Story* (Stroud, UK: Sutton Publishing, 2003); Melvin Harris, *The Maybrick Hoax: A Guide Through the Labyrinth*, http://www.casebook.org/dissertations/maybrick_diary/mhguide.html.

28. *Glasgow Herald*, September 25, 1891.

29. In November 2004, the Ghost Club hosted a series of lectures on the perceived supernatural aspects of the Whitechapel murders. A lecture, "The Ghosts of Jack the Ripper," by Philip Hutchinson, fully examined reported sightings and the works of authors Elliott O'Donnell, Peter Underwood and others. Though studies of Ripper ghost sightings generally tend to focus on later oral traditions and modern psychic investigations, this chapter presents a review of period accounts from a Victorian point of view. Early spiritualist periodicals such as *The Medium and Daybreak* gave reports of contact with the spirit of Mary Ann Nichols and received descriptions of Jack the Ripper. These obscure reports were quoted and spread in the mainstream press. *The Medium and Daybreak* was a spiritualist weekly established in 1869 by James Burns and later published as *The Medium* after absorbing the provincial paper the *Daybreak*. It had the largest circulation of any spiritualist weekly and was published until 1895 when Burns died.

30. *Evening News*, 10 October 1888. This story on the London Spiritualist Alliance cannot be confirmed with official files, but it is an early source for press claims that Scotland Yard used a psychic in its efforts to find Jack the Ripper.

However, psychic Robert Lees kept a diary in which he mentioned approaching the police. The diary entries are dated October 2, 3, and 4, 1888, and thus predate this news item. Lees's story was not reported until 1895. It seems to indicate differences in method and class distinctions among Victorian London's spiritualist subcultures that competed for the attentions of Scotland Yard on the murders. Lees was also a journalist and friend of W.T. Stead, perhaps indicating a close alliance between spiritualist and occult associations and the liberal press which later developed Ripper legends.

31. *Pall Mall Gazette*, May 19, 1892. The City of London Police also received countless letters from the public offering psychic solutions and aid. For further details see Appendix 2 in Stewart Evans and Donald Rumbelow, *Jack the Ripper: Scotland Yard Investigates* (Stroud, UK: Sutton, 2006).

32. F.J. Gould, *The Life-Story of a Humanist* (London: Watts, 1923).

33. The Society for Psychical Research (SPR) was formed in London in 1882 by spiritualists wanting to study evidence for survival after death and claims on the paranormal in a systematic and scientific way. Its members included Sir Arthur Conan Doyle, Arthur Balfour, George R. Sims, and Edmund Gurney. Balfour was interested in the subject beginning in 1882 and became president of the SPR in 1893. He presented papers on after-death survival. He also served as prime minister of Britain from 1902 to 1905. Educated at Trinity College, Cambridge, he devoted himself to philosophical studies for many years.

34. S.P. Evans and K. Skinner, *Letters from Hell* (Stroud, UK: Sutton, 2004). Entries found in Lees's diary are the only evidence that he was involved with the Whitechapel murders: "Tues, 2 Oct 1888 Offered services to police to follow up East End murders—called a fool and a lunatic. Got trace of a man from the spot in Berner Street. Wed, 3 Oct 1888 Went to City police again—called a madman and fool. Thurs, 4 Oct 1888 Went to Scotland Yard—same result but promised to write to me." It is fortunate that these diary entries have survived. However, they were almost due to a fire in the 1970s. A young Paul J. Gaunt, current editor of *Psypioneer*, recognized their historical significance and rescued them. For further background details on Lees, see the research of Stephen Butt and Jennifer Pegg (now Shelden) at http://www.rjlees.co.uk.

35. Stephen Knight, *Jack the Ripper: The Final Solution* (London: Harrap, 1976. Reprint, London: Treasure House, 1984). Stephen Knight was one of the first authors to contribute original historic research to the case upon the public release of official files. His theories are now largely discounted but have survived in novels and movies.

36. D.J. West, "The Identity of 'Jack the Ripper': An Examination of an Alleged Psychic Solution," *Journal of the Society for Psychical Research*, Vol. 35, July-August, 1949; S.P. Evans, *Ripper Notes*, Issue 21, January 2005; P. Begg, *Jack the Ripper: The Facts* (London: Robson Books, 2006), p. 392.

37. The Home Office and New Scotland Yard letters for Donald West's 1948–49 Ripper inquiry are not known to have survived as originals but have been preserved as photocopies. They are reproduced courtesy of Donald West, Stewart P. Evans and the Society for Psychical Research archives.

38. Robert Lees probably didn't know the identity of Jack the Ripper, but according to the recent research of Stephen Butt he may well have acted as one of Queen Victoria's mediums. For further reading on Victoria's supernatural beliefs see Chapter 38, "Seances and Services" in Christopher Hibbert, *Queen Victoria: A Personal History* (New York: HarperCollins, 2001).

39. Cynthia Legh, *Light*, Autumn 1970. This spiritualist periodical was first published in London on January 8, 1881, by the Eclectic Publishing Co., Ltd. It was later transferred to the London Spiritualist Association, which approached Scotland Yard with details on Jack the Ripper in early October 1888. It is regarded as the oldest psychic journal in the world and used experienced journalists from its inception.

40. Melvin Harris, *Jack the Ripper: The Bloody Truth* (London: Columbus Books, 1987); Harris, *The True Face of Jack the Ripper* (London: Michael O'Mara Books, 1994).

41. Thomas E.A. Stowell, "Jack the Ripper: A Solution?" *Criminologist,* Vol. 5, No. 18 (1970).

42. S.P. Evans and K. Skinner, *Jack the Ripper: Letters from Hell* (Stroud, UK: Sutton Publishing, 2004).

43. Lees confirmed the story in *Illustrated Leicester Chronicle,* November 23, 1929. Brackenbury's report appeared in the May 1931 issue of the *Journal of the Society for Psychical Research.*

44. Bernard O'Donnell, unpublished Jack the Ripper manuscript begun in the early 1930s and completed in 1958. For further details see Chapters 5 and 6.

45. Frederick P. Wensley, *Detective Days* (London: Cassell, 1931).

46. Edwin T. Woodhall, *Crime and the Supernatural* (London: John Long, 1935).

47. *The Times,* October 20, 1888.

48. *Sunday Referee,* December 2, 1888.

49. *Pall Mall Gazette,* December 3, 1888.

50. The earl of Crawford wrote an undated letter to Anderson introducing an unknown woman who claimed to have details on the Whitechapel murders. See Chapter 3.

51. Sir Robert Anderson, *The Lighter Side of My Official Life* (London: Hodder & Stoughton, 1910).

52. Sir Robert Anderson, *The Coming Prince* (London: Hodder & Stoughton, 1895).

53. Sir Robert Anderson, *The Lighter Side of My Official Life* (London: Hodder & Stoughton, 1910).

54. Sir Robert Anderson, *Redemption Truths* (Grand Rapids, MI: Kregel Publications, 1980).

55. Sir Melville Macnaghten, *Days of My Years* (London: Edward Arnold, 1914).

56. *Boston Investigator,* July 12, 1893.

57. *East London Advertiser,* September 27, 1919.

58. *The Peoples Journal,* September 27, 1919.

59. *Zanesville Signal,* July 15, 1928.

60. M. Howells and K. Skinner, *The Ripper Legacy: The Life and Death of Jack the Ripper* (London: Sidgwick & Jackson, 1988).

## Chapter 2

1. The Ripper murders were part of a series of eleven unsolved East End prostitute murders between April 3, 1888, and February 13, 1891. The police officially called them the Whitechapel murders. Evidence indicates that the Ripper murders were as few as three and as many as six. The name "Jack the Ripper" was coined in letters sent anonymously to the Central News Agency, but the letters are not confirmed to have come from the killer. They are believed to be hoaxes penned by a journalist. Stewart P. Evans and Keith Skinner, *The Ultimate Jack the Ripper Sourcebook: An Illustrated Encyclopedia* (London: Constable & Robinson, 2001).

2. The Whitechapel murders created a panic that spread throughout London and into the provinces. Sir Robert Anderson attempted to allay public fears but to no avail. It eventually became clear to Scotland Yard that the killer targeted destitute prostitutes in the East End. This led to theories that the killer was a local resident.

3. S.P. Evans and D. Rumbelow, *Jack the Ripper: Scotland Yard Investigates* (Stroud, UK: Sutton Publishing, 2006).

4. Newspaper and journal reports are major primary sources for the study and examination of the Whitechapel murders. Numerous books have drawn extensively on historical accounts of the crimes in attempts to reconstruct the events. However, news reports can be and often are fabricated, distorted, or exaggerated. Contemporary legends, social beliefs, literary hoaxes and conspiracy theories complicate any investigation when not checked against official sources. It is important also to note that some inquest transcripts and witness interviews preserve details that have not

otherwise survived. The researcher must use caution is required when considering press reports. Where possible, police and official reports take precedence.

5. Historian Philip Priestley, in *Victorian Prison Lives: English Prison Biography 1830–1914* (London: Methuen, 1985), writes, "The prostitute was the typical woman prisoner of the later nineteenth century, committed to prison in such numbers as to make possible a remarkable survey of 16,000 'fallen women.' It was conducted by the Reverend G. P. Merrick, MA, MB, chaplain of HM Prison, Millbank, and presented in a paper read before the ruri-decanal chapter of St. Margaret's and St. John's, Westminster — in the Jerusalem chamber — on Thursday, 17 July 1890. He clearly had to choose his words carefully when reporting such a subject to such an audience. The archdeacon points out in his introduction to the published version of the paper that the chaplain has managed to express himself 'with extreme delicacy and singular moderation.' And so he has, except that he contrives to mention within the first five pages that one of the 'victims of the Whitechapel murderer (better known as Jack-the ripper)' had been released from Millbank and 'received a gift of clothes from me within twenty-four hours of her murder.'" Merrick wrote of the women prisoners in his charge at Millbank, "I say I have not met a hundred women — perhaps out of a hundred thousand — who have said that they like their wicked and wretched mode of life. They loathe it, and their repugnance to it can only be stifled when they are more or less under the influence of intoxicating drinks. We must not forget that modesty is particularly a woman's natural possession, and it is only when she is impelled to do so by drink, or necessity or by her utilized affections that she allows it to leave her." The Rev. George Purnell Merrick, *Work Among the Fallen as Seen in the Prison Cell* (London: Ward Lock, 1890).

6. For a notable and entertaining study see Sian Rees, *The Floating Brothel: The Extraordinary Story of Female Convicts Bound for Botany Bay* (Sydney: Hachette, 2009). In July 1789, 237 women convicts mainly taken from London's overcrowded Newgate Gaol left England aboard *The Lady Juliana.* They were destined to provide sex and breeding for male convicts in the Australian colony.

7. *Singleton v. Ellison,* 1895.

8. May Churchill Sharpe, *Chicago May, Her Story* (London: Sampson Low, 1929). Crime historian and author Richard Whittington-Egan noted the Bella Freeman Ripper story.

9. *Charles Booth and the Survey into Life and Labour in London (1886–1903),* B347, p. 65. Archives Division of the Library of the London School of Economics and Political Science.

10. MEPO 3/141, ff. 158–63.

11. *Illustrated Police News,* October 20, 1888.

12. John Sweeney and Francis Richards, eds. *At Scotland Yard* (London: Grant Richards, 1904).

13. Howard Vincent, *A Police Code and Manual of the Criminal Law* (London: Cassell, Petter and Galpin, 1881).

14. Charles Van Onselen, *The Fox and the Flies: The Secret Life of a Grotesque Master Criminal* (New York: Walker, 2007).

15. For a complete and balanced assessment of Anderson's Jack the Ripper theories, see S.P. Evans and D. Rumbelow, *Jack the Ripper: Scotland Yard Investigates* (Stroud, UK: Sutton Publishing, 2006).

16. *Pall Mall Gazette,* July 1888.

17. *The Link,* June 23, 1888.

18. HO 144/221/A49301C, ff. 217–23; S.P. Evans and K. Skinner, *The Ultimate Jack the Ripper Sourcebook: An Illustrated Encyclopedia* (London: Constable & Robinson, 2001).

19. Ibid.

20. *The British Medical Journal,* December 8, 1888.

21. There is a discrepancy here between the number of victims and the mention of a previous case of mutilation. It seems that Hammond's source for the Whitechapel murders

were press reports on "the murder of an unknown woman in Christmas week 1887." She is regarded as Margaret Hames, victim of a nonfatal but serious attack in December 1887 and a friend of Emma Smith, the first Whitechapel victim, killed on April 3, 1888.

22. William A. Hammond, "Murder and Madness," *The North American Review* Vol. CXLVII, No. CCCLXXXV (December 1888).

23. For an impartial discussion on the comments and statements of these senior police officers see S.P. Evans and D. Rumbelow, *Jack the Ripper: Scotland Yard Investigates* (Stroud, UK: Sutton Publishing, 2006).

24. For the best coverage of the main documentary sources on the Whitechapel murders see S.P. Evans and K. Skinner, *The Ultimate Jack the Ripper Sourcebook: An Illustrated Encyclopedia* (London: Constable & Robinson, 2001); Paul Begg, *Jack the Ripper: The Facts* (London: Robson Books, 2006); Philip Sugden, *The Complete History of Jack the Ripper* (London: Robinson, 2002).

25. Sir Robert Anderson, *The Lighter Side of My Official Life* (London: Hodder & Stoughton, 1910), p. 146.

26. HO 144/221/A49301H, ff 7–14.

27. Though Macnaghten also noted a Polish Jew named Kosminski as a suspect, he is known to have favored Montague Druitt.

28. Colin Holmes, "East End Crime and the Jewish Community, 1887–1911," in Aubrey Newman, ed., *The Jewish East End 1840–1939* (London: Jewish Historical Society of England, 1981). Proceedings of the conference held on October 22, 1980, jointly by the Jewish Historical Society of England and the Jewish East End Project of the Association for Jewish Youth.

29. *Jewish Chronicle,* March 4, 1910.

30. *Jewish Chronicle,* March 11, 1910.

## *Chapter 3*

1. Sir Robert Anderson, *The Bible and Modern Criticism.* 5th ed. (London: Hodder and Stoughton, 1905), Chapter XII.

2. M Howells and K. Skinner, *The Ripper Legacy: The Life and Death of Jack the Ripper* (London: Sidgwick and Jackson, 1987).

3. Sir Robert Anderson used the term "supernatural" in his 1905 book *The Bible and Modern Criticism* to describe prophetic elements of the Old Testament. In his view, prophesy supported the belief in resurrection and miraculous events of the New Testament. It is a good example of the late Victorian literal use of the term as a belief in spiritual reality. Though the term has come to connote superstition, it originally connoted acceptance of the prospect of a life after death.

4. *The Times,* October 6, 1888.

5. *The Belfast News-Letter,* January 8, 1889.

6. Thomas De Quincey, "The Avenger," *Blackwood's Edinburgh Magazine,* 1838.

7. *The New York Times,* October 8, 1888.

8. *The New York Times,* November 11, 1888.

9. Clerics prosecuted and incarcerated during the early Victorian period on charges of ritualism and popery.

10. *Birmingham Daily Post,* January 17, 1889.

11. Arthur Griffiths, *Mysteries of Police and Crime.* 2 Vols. (London: Cassell, 1898). Before publishing his well-known reference on Macnaghten's suspects without names, Griffiths wrote two magazine articles mentioning the Whitechapel murders which he also sourced for *Mysteries of Police and Crime.* In the early 1895 issue of *Windsor Magazine,* writing under the pseudonym Alfred Aylmer, he addressed the Whitechapel murders in relation to the theory of Robert Anderson. "Although he has achieved greater success than any detective of his time, there will always be undiscovered crimes, and just now the table is pretty full. Much dissatisfaction was vented upon Mr. Anderson at the utterly abortive efforts to discover the perpetrator of the Whitechapel mur-

ders. He has himself a perfectly plausible theory that Jack the Ripper was a homicidal maniac, temporarily at large, whose hideous career was cut short by committal to an asylum." In the following year in an article titled "Unsolved Mysteries of Crime" located by researcher Nick Connell in an 1896 issue of *Cassell's Family Magazine,* Griffiths wrote, "No real solution has been offered as yet of the notorious Whitechapel murders; no reasonable surmise made of the identity of that most mysterious monster 'Jack the Ripper.' Given certain favorable conditions, say the police, thus contradicting their other contention — conditions such as were present in that long series of gruesome atrocities — and a murderer will always escape retribution, if only he has the good luck to escape observation at the moment. If he is able to remove himself quickly from the scene of action, and can cover up his tracks promptly and cleverly, detection is, and must be, at fault. Various theories, based upon these alleged conditions, were put forward by the police in the Whitechapel affair. One was that the murderer only visited London at certain intervals, and that at all other times he was safe beyond all pursuit. Either he was at sea — a sailor, a stoker, of foreign extraction, a Malay or Lascar — or he was a man with a double personality; one so absolutely distinct from, and far superior to the other, that no possible suspicion could attach to him when he resumed the more respectable garb. It was, in fact, a real case of Dr. Jekyll and Mr. Hyde. Granted, also, that this individual was afflicted with periodic fits of homicidal mania, accompanied by all the astuteness of this form of lunacy, it was easy to conceive of his committing the murders under such incontrollable impulse, and of his prompt disappearance by returning to his other altogether irreproachable identity. No doubt this was a plausible theory, but theory it was, and nothing more. It was never, even inferentially, supported by fact."

12. *Illustrated Police News,* January 28, 1899. This report is also suggestive of the private information that Macnaghten claimed to have received on suspect M.J. Druitt.

13. *Chicago Tribune,* October 27, 1887.

14. Stead developed his Jesuit Jack the Ripper theory until it appeared in a 1907 letter from Ernest Crawford to journalist and author George R. Sims. See Chapter 6.

15. *Pall Mall Gazette,* September 19, 1888.

16. *The City Press,* December 19, 1888.

17. There is no clear indication or proof that the chalk writing on the wall and portion of Catherine Eddowes's apron are linked or that the killer wrote it. However, it is the basis of dubious theories. It was erased, according to statements of Metropolitan Police Commissioner, Sir Charles Warren, to avoid riots.

18. *East London Observer,* September 15, 1888.

19. *The Times,* October 2, 1888.

20. *Jewish Chronicle,* October 5, 1888.

21. Robin Odell first published his Shochet Jewish butcher theory in *Jack the Ripper in Fact and Fiction* (London: Harrap, 1965). Odell gives an enlightening overview of the debate of crime historians and an updated position on his theory in *Ripperology: A Study of the World's First Serial Killer and a Literary Phenomenon* (Kent, OH: Kent State University Press, 2006), pp. 103–06.

22. *Jewish Chronicle,* October 12, 1888.

23. *Illustrated Police News,* October 20, 1888.

24. *The Times,* October 25, 1888.

25. Derek Reid, "General Jewish Superstitions in the East End," in *The Jewish East End 1840–1939,* Aubrey Newman, ed. (London: Jewish Historical Society of England, 1981).

26. *The Philadelphia Times,* December 3, 1888. Cited in Chapter 25 of Stewart P. Evans and K. Skinner, *The Ultimate Jack the Ripper Sourcebook* (London: Robinson, 2001). George Lewis was also employed as a solicitor for Parnell at the Special Commission. Lewis was accused of libel in 1889 by Charles Le Grand, a private detective (and a small-time crook) employed by the Whitechapel Vigilance Committee who inquired into the murder of Elizabeth Stride. Widely

syndicated press reports claimed in 1892 that Le Grand was Jack the Ripper, though Sergeant Stephen White had investigated him and presumably cleared him at the time of Stride's murder. Le Grand was noted in Gerry Nixon, "Le Grand of the Strand," *Ripperologist*, No. 42, August 2002.

27. *The Chicago Tribune*, October 7, 1888.

28. For further reading on ritual murder from an investigator's stance, see Kenneth V. Lanning, "Appendix II: 1992 FBI Study of Satanic Ritual Abuse," in *Satanism Today*, James R. Lewis, ed. (Santa Barbara, CA: ABC-CLIO, 2001).

29. Sir Walter Scott, *Letters on Demonology and Witchcraft*. 2nd ed. (London: Routledge, 1885). Though early prosecution and punishment of witchcraft was violent in Scotland, Ireland and continental Europe, Anglican England was less prone to belief in religious miracles as evidence in a criminal court. Rather, English courts were confined to charges of sedition and rebellion inspired by Catholics' belief in miracles and witches. Since the Witchcraft Act of 1735, English witchcraft and occult traditions have been regarded as superstitions unworthy of legal stature, except where necessary to protect subjects of the Crown from exploitation. With Matthew Hopkins, the self-appointed "Witch Finder General" active during the English Civil War, Puritanism was the major early persecutor of English witches, most of whom women. The practice was finally refuted with the works of an Anglican clergyman, Francis Hutchinson, who had studied witch trials and questioned their procedures. In *An Historical Essay Concerning Witchcraft* (1718), Hutchinson stated that charges of witchcraft were based on "the very dregs of pagan and popish superstitions." For further reading see Andrew Sneddon, *Witchcraft and Whigs: The Life of Bishop Francis Hutchinson, 1660–1739* (Manchester, UK: Manchester University Press, 2008).

30. For a background study see Spiro Dimiolanis, "Jack the Necromancer and the Victorian Occult Revival," *Ripperologist* No. 58, March 2005.

31. R. Hayward, "Demonology, Neurology, and Medicine in Edwardian Britain," *Bulletin of the History of Medicine*. Vol. 78, No. 1, Spring 2004, pp. 37–58.

32. William Morris, "Police Spies Exposed," *The Commonweal*, Vol. 4, No. 104, January 7, 1888. Theodor Reuss, a baritone singer who used the stage name "Charles Theodore," joined the English Socialist League in 1885 as an anarchist and was involved as a librarian and labor secretary. On May 7, 1886, he was expelled as a police spy in the pay of the Prussian Secret Police. On October 5, 1887, the *London Evening News* published an article by Reuss on the designs of London anarchist circles, confirming suspicions he was a Prussian spy sent to England to watch socialists. Reuss was acquainted with British occultist Aleister Crowley during the late 1890s and early 20th century.

33. Black magic or satanic worship in London during the late Victorian period is an obscure phenomenon from which a Jack the Ripper suspect would be expected to emerge. Black magic Ripper theories are rather based on popular speculative fictions and the reactions of pseudo-religious subcultures to the evil crimes of a serial killer. Period literary sources on the phenomenon were mostly commentaries on medieval Latin grimoires in the works of Éliphas Lévi with English translations by occultist and author Arthur E. Waite. In the 1896 English translation of Lévi's 1856 *Transcendental Magic: Its Doctrine and Ritual*, Waite notes a passage in Lévi's 1868 French manuscript, *Le Grand Arcane, ou l'Occultisme Devoile*, published posthumously in 1898: "Black magic is the occult continuation of proscribed rites belonging to the ancient world. Immolation [ritual killing] is the basis of the mysteries of necromancy, and bewitchments are magical sacrifices where the magnetism of evil is substituted for stake and knife. In religion it is faith which saves; in black magic it is faith which kills ... black magic is the religion of death." Ripper suspect Roslyn D'Onston alluded in a late 1888 article to a Lévi commentary on *Le Grand Grimoire* (The Grand Grimoire), also called *Le Dragon Rouge, ou l'art de commander les esprits celestes, aeriens, terrestres, inferaux* (The Red Dragon, or the Art of Controlling Celestial, Aerial, Terrestrial, and Infernal Spirits), which was published in Paris by Antonio Venitiana in 1845 and "printed from a manuscript of 1522." In an English translation of *Le Grand Grimoire* titled *The Book of Black Magic and of Pacts* (London: Redway, 1898), Waite declared the work "one of the most atrocious of its class; it has a process in Necromancy which is possible, say some occult writers — in the geniality of a lucid interval — only to a dangerous maniac or an irreclaimable criminal. It must be admitted that the Rite is highly unreasonable, but in dealing with such literature it seems unsafe to advance the objection, for it applies much too widely."

34. The Icelandic *Dracula* preface was noted and translated in *Dracula and the Lair of the White Worm*, Richard Dalby, ed. (London: W. Foulsham, 1986). In the first edition of *Dracula* (London: Archibald Constable, 1897), developed from as early as 1890, Bram Stoker writes, "Seeing that Dr. Seward keeps his newspapers, I borrowed the files of the Westminster Gazette and the Pall Mall Gazette, and took them to my room. I remember how much the Dailygraph and the Whitby Gazette, of which I had made cuttings, helped us to understand the terrible events at Whitby when Count Dracula landed, so I shall look through the evening papers since then, and perhaps I shall get some new light. I am not sleepy, and the work will help to keep me awake." For a background study on the influence of the Whitechapel murders and press portrayal of Jack the Ripper on development of *Dracula*, see Robert Eighteen-Bisang, "Dracula, Jack the Ripper and a Thirst for Blood," published in *Ripperologist* No. 60, July 2005, and available at http://www.casebook.org/dissertations/rip-thirst.html. The *Pall Mall Gazette* article of Roslyn D'Onston and other widely circulated occult Ripper theories had an influence on journalist Stoker as manager of the Lyceum Theatre. It staged productions of *Dr. Jekyll and Mr. Hyde* that were assumed to have later inspired the murderer. Dracula is also portrayed as a supernatural sexual killer reveling in blood, an image of the novel that established later gothic legends of Jack the Ripper. In a letter Stoker wrote to Gladstone on 24 May 1897 with a copy of *Dracula*, he states "...and these may in some way interest you who have made as bold a guess at 'immortaliability.'" See also: Eighteen-Bisang, R., and E. Miller. *Bram Stoker's Notes for Dracula: A Facsimile Edition*. McFarland, 2008.

35. *East London Advertiser*, October 6, 1888. The *Journal de Psychologie Normale et Pathologique*, May-June 1907, argued that medieval werewolves were criminal sadists who were predecessors of Jack the Ripper.

36. A published interview with F.C. Hughes-Hallett described Martha Tabram's murder as a "sacrifice." Hughes-Hallett, a member of Parliament in the House of Commons, claimed to have investigated her murder and suspected a West End clubman tentatively linked to Ripper suspect Francis Tumbelty. See Joe Chetcuti, "Tumblety in London: Trailing an Infiltrator, Part 1," *Ripperologist*, No. 59, May 2005.

37. *The Times*, September 27, 1888.

38. For the outcome of the police investigation on the coroner's theory, see S.P. Evans and D. Rumbelow, *Jack the Ripper: Scotland Yard Investigates* (Stroud, UK: Sutton, 2006). Further details on the identity and legitimate business of the American doctor were given in the *Chicago Tribune*, October 7, 1888.

39. *The Curse Upon Mitre Square: 1530–1888* was first published by Simpkin, Marshal and Co. in 1888. In 1889, the Lovell Company of New York reprinted it. It was reprinted again in 1999. It is now in the public domain, and an online version with an introduction (2002) by Cindy Collins Smith, can be found at http://www.hollywoodripper.com/pdf/CurseUponMitreSquare.pdf.

40. *Penny Illustrated Paper*, November 3, 1888. There are some discrepancies in the actual location of the historic altar steps and the exact site of Catherine Eddowes's murder.

41. *The Star,* November 9, 1888. A "shilling shocker" was a cheap populist pamphlet of the Victorian period, which usually featured stories that blended the macabre, murder and other crimes. Although they are of historic interest as primary sources, these sensationalist pamphlets cannot be relied on for facts.

42. Loren Coleman, *The Copycat Effect: How the Media and Popular Culture Trigger the Mayhem in Tomorrow's Headlines* (New York: Pocket Books, 2004).

43. *Lucifer,* Vol. III, No. 16, December 1888, pp. 341–342.

44. *Lucifer,* Vol. VI, No. 35, July 1890, pp. 353–364.

45. *The Theosophical Forum,* November 1892. Reprinted in *Theosophy,* Vol. 33, No. 11, September 1945.

46. *Lucifer,* Vol. IV, No. 20, April 1889, pp. 89–99.

47. *Lucifer,* Vol. VII, No. 38, October 1890, pp. 89–98.

48. Minutes of a meeting of the Ghost Club, June 7, 1895. Reproduced courtesy of the Ghost Club historic archives.

49. Daniel H. Caldwell, ed., *Madam Blavatsky's Esoteric Papers: A Comprehensive Compilation* (Whitefish, MT: Kessinger Publishing, 2005).

50. An earlier mention of the term "elixir of life" in relation to the Whitechapel murders similar to that of Arthur Diosy was brought to the attention of police and reported in the *Chicago Tribune,* October 7, 1888. Without corroboration of the vague account it is not known to be of any substance. Stewart Evans and D. Rumbelow, *Jack the Ripper: Scotland Yard Investigates* (London: Sutton, 2006), p. 93.

51. *Pall Mall Gazette,* December 3, 1888.

52. Churchill Archives Centre. CHAR 28/78/25.

53. *The Times-Democrat,* August 10, 1884.

54. *The Japan Times,* September 25, 1998.

55. Robin Odell, *Ripperology: A Study of the World's First Serial Killer and a Literary Phenomenon* (Kent, OH: Kent State University Press, 2006).

56. Peter Costello, *The Real World of Sherlock Holmes: True Crimes Investigated by Arthur Conan Doyle* (London: Robinson, 1991). The passage about lights bestowing invisibility is derived from press reports of German "thieves candles" made of human fat.

57. Bookseller Bernard Quaritch and printer Charles Wyman founded the Sette of Odd Volumes in 1878. It was an eccentric dining club for lettered men and its members were referred to as the "odd volumes." The literary club sponsored lectures and exchanged papers on a range of subjects, some of which were privately printed and are now very rare.

58. Peter Costello, *The Real World of Sherlock Holmes: True Crimes Investigated by Arthur Conan Doyle* (London: Robinson, 1991), p. 69. Costello cites the letter of James B. Atlay preceded with a mention that "several members were closely connected with the case: G. R. Sims, Sir Melville McNaughton [sic], Lord Aberconway, Major Arthur Griffiths, Arthur Diosy, and even a relative of one of the putative suspects, the Duke of Kent." This gives the impression that Atlay is referring to the duke, a relative of Prince Albert Victor. This cannot be the case as the Atlay letter was written before H.R.H. Prince George, the duke of Kent, was elected a member of Our Society. For a further background study on the topic see Evans, Stewart. "On the Origins of the Royal Conspiracy Theory." http://www.casebook.org/dissertations/dst-evansorigins.html

59. *The London Magazine,* 1923.

60. S. Ingleby Oddie, *Inquest* (London: Hutchinson, 1941).

61. Stephen P. Ryder, "Emily and the Bibliophile: A Possible Source for Macnaghten's Private Information," *Ripperologist,* No. 37, October 2001.

62. William Le Queux, a journalist and novelist who later developed his own Jack the Ripper theory, wrote on the release of Major Arthur Griffiths' *Mysteries of Police and Crime* (1898): "During the period of the 'Jack the Ripper' murders, in pursuing my profession as journalist, I immediately visited the scenes of each of the crimes, spent many exciting days and nights in Whitechapel, and accompanied several of the detectives — who were my personal friends — on their active

investigations. I, therefore, saw more of these revolting crimes, their details, and the methods of the police than any of the outside public, and I can only add to the Major's statement that the police were utterly mystified, overwhelmed by a jumble of false and absurd clues, and from first to last were entirely without any real suspicion of the identity of the murderer. It was only long after the final crime that the theory above given [drowned in the Thames] was started in order to satisfy the public, and to account for the failure to make an arrest. The truth is, that the mystery of 'Jack the Ripper' is as inscrutable today as it ever was." *Manchester Times,* February 10, 1899.

63. Daniel Dunglas Home was a famous Scottish physical medium who, it was claimed, could levitate. The reference in the Mahatma letter is to a private session held in 1868 at the home of Lord Adare that was witnessed by Captain Wynne and Lord Lindsay, who recorded his impressions. Sir Arthur Conan Doyle also took an interest in Home's abilities and later wrote about the claims that were brought to the attention of the Society for Psychical Research. The legend of Home's levitations was expanded and published in England, America and France after his death on June 21, 1886.

64. Letter No. VIII, received through Madame Blavatsky about February 20, 1881. In *The Mahatma Letters to A. P. Sinnett from the Mahatmas M. and K.H.*, 2d ed., A.T. Barker, ed. (London: Rider, 1926).

65. Mabel Collins was also a founding member of the London Lodge of the Theosophical Society.

66. Letter No. LXXXVII. In *The Mahatma Letters to A. P. Sinnett from the Mahatmas M. and K.H.* 2d ed. A.T. Barker, ed. (London: Rider, 1926). Though the letter is undated, it was probably written in 1887.

67. The Roslyn D'Onston Jack the Ripper theory has had extensive coverage since the 1970s. Apart from expanded fictional treatments, it has also been noted in books about crime, such as Brian Lane's *The Encyclopedia of Occult and Supernatural Murder* (London: Brockhampton Press, 1997), pp. 144–145. Influential compilations on the Whitechapel murders that repeat the D'Onston and Cremers theories without appraisal in context of the Victorian period include P. Begg, M. Fido, and K. Skinner, *The Complete Jack the Ripper A to Z* (London: Blake Publishing, 2010).

68. *The Ceylon Observer,* May 31, 1880.

69. *The Theosophist,* August 1, 1880.

70. Dr. Elliott Coues was president of the Washington branch of the Theosophical Society, a former member of the Society for Psychical Research and a rival of Helena Blavatsky. He had published in the U.S. press caustic letters between Mabel Collins and Blavatsky after she was expelled from the Theosophical Society in early 1889. Cremers claimed that Collins lived with Ripper suspect Roslyn D'Onston.

71. Letter No. CVI. (Undated, probably 1887.) In *The Mahatma Letters to A. P. Sinnett from the Mahatmas M. and K.H.*, 2d ed., A.T. Barker, ed. (London: Rider, 1926).

72. Letter No. CVI. In *The Mahatma Letters to A. P. Sinnett from the Mahatmas M. and K.H.*, 2d ed., A.T. Barker, ed. (London: Rider, 1926). These English Jesuit conspiracy theories seem part of the root of later French fabrications on the Priory of Sion and its spiritual war with the Vatican. W.T. Stead also developed a Jesuit Ripper theory.

73. Blavatsky's "Mahatma letters" were claimed to be of mystical origin. They were much talked about, and in 1885 the Society for Psychical Research mounted an investigation. A study indicates they were written through living persons during what is known as "the Great Game," a strategic rivalry between the British Empire and Russia for control in Central Asia. For further reading see K. Paul Johnson, *The Masters Revealed: Madam Blavatsky and the Myth of the Great White Lodge* (Albany: State University of New York Press, 1994).

74. Om Prakash Ralhan, *Encyclopaedia of Political Parties: Post-independence India* (New Delhi: Anmol, 2002).

75. For further details of the fascinating life of Duleep

Singh, see Christy Campbell, *The Maharajah's Box* (New York: HarperCollins, 2001).

76. Colin Wilson, *The Occult* (New York: Random House, 1971), p. 329.

77. Victorian legends and theories of an occult Jack the Ripper have given rise to a numerous modern developments. Melvin Harris wrote three books considering Scotland Yard suspect Roslyn D'Onston and the accounts of Vittoria Cremers. There is also a fringe Ripperology of fiction works. Most notable of this genre were the 1909 French novels about "Sar Dubnotal," a psychic investigator and occult detective. One of Dubnotal's enemies was a Jack the Ripper figure named "Tserpchikopf the Hypnotist." These works were credited to author Norbert Sevestre and were based on the early criminology methods of Cesare Lombroso. Later examples of criminology mixed with fiction and unsound historic treatments of the Victorian occult revival include Christopher Smith, "Jack the Ripper and the Alembic Connection," *The Criminologist*, Vol. 17, No. 1, 2, and 3, 1992–93; Simon Whitechapel, "Guts 'n' Roses: The Coming Apocalypse of the Ripper Millennium," in *The Mammoth Book of Jack the Ripper*, M. Jakubowski and N. Braund, eds. (London: Robinson, 1999); and Ivor Edwards, *Jack the Ripper's Black Magic Rituals* (London: John Blake Publishing, 2002).

## Chapter 4

1. Robert Donston Stephenson was born in Sculcoates, Hull, East Riding, on April 20, 1841. His parents, Richard and Isabella Stephenson, were bone and seed crushing manufacturers and proprietors of Dawber & Stephenson, Dawber being his mother's maiden name. His siblings were Elizabeth, William, Isabella and Richard; Robert was the youngest. He married Anne Deary, his mother's domestic servant, in Islington in 1876. They soon separated, and are not known to have had any children. His father died in 1889 and his mother followed in 1891. Regarded as a black sheep in the family, he inherited none of the Stephenson estate, which added to his constant financial difficulties. He died on October 9, 1916, at Islington Infirmary.

2. According to census returns, Inspector Thomas Roots was born in 1849 in West Malling, Kent, and married Eliza Stephens of Hertford at North Aylesford, Kent, in 1868. In 1871 he was living at 141 Beresford Street, Newington, London, and had attained the rank of police sergeant. In 1881 he lived at 25 Carter Street, Newington, with his wife and five children and is noted as "Inspector Met. Police." His household included two boarders, and both were also inspectors with the Metropolitan Police. Thomas Roots died at the age of 41 in late 1890 at Fulham. His wife is noted as a widow the following year, and does not appear to have remarried by 1901.

3. Michael Ostrog has been conclusively eliminated as a credible Jack the Ripper suspect because he was incarcerated in France during the murders. See Philip Sugden, *The Complete History of Jack the Ripper* (London: Robinson, 2002).

4. Stewart P. Evans and K. Skinner, *The Ultimate Jack the Ripper Sourcebook* (London: Robinson, 2002), Chapters 38 and 39.

5. Corporation of London Record Office, Police Box 3.23, No. 390. London Metropolitan Archives, reference code CLA/048/CS/02/390. The text of the letter appears in S.P. Evans and K. Skinner, *Jack the Ripper: Letters from Hell* (Stroud, UK: Sutton, 2004), pp. 204–205.

6. It is not known why D'Onston would accuse Davies of being Jack the Ripper. He was a distinguished Welshman who held posts at the London Hospital (although not during D'Onston's stay). Davies is noted in the London Hospital Medical College register of students ref: MC/S/1/5, from 1873 to 1879, and was awarded his M.D. degree at the University of Aberdeen. Davies was not listed as a house surgeon or physician at the London Hospital in 1888 or 1889. It seems that, at that time, he was visiting his friend Dr. Evans in Davis ward, where he likely met D'Onston. Davies also did

voluntary work at the London Hospital and in the East End, particularly among poor Welsh residents. At one time he lived at 10 Goring Street, Houndsditch, Bishopsgate, London, though he moved to Castle Street, Houndsditch, as noted in D'Onston's statement. D'Onston is noted in the December 26, 1888, police report as "a doctor of medicine upon diplomas of Paris & New York." These credentials were easily obtained; women, whom England barred from entering the medical profession, would apply for these diplomas. D'Onston may have felt outshined by Davies's medical standing, and this might have prompted him to elaborate on police suspicions and press theories that Jack the Ripper was an upper-class doctor.

7. D'Onston described the Davis ward in the police statement as a "private ward," meaning a smaller ward. Private-paying patients and wards were not introduced at the London Hospital until the 1930s. Inpatients were admitted and treated free of charge during the 1880s.

8. D'Onston's Scotland Yard statement is reproduced in Robin Odell, *Ripperology: A Study of the World's First Serial Killer and a Literary Phenomenon* (Kent, OH: Kent State University Press, 2006), p. 13.

9. There is a discrepancy between the accounts of George Marsh and D'Onston. Marsh noted that he saw a letter about Stead refusing the offer to track the Whitechapel murder, but D'Onston told Roots that the proprietor of the *Pall Mall Gazette*, Henry Yates Thompson, had refused based on a letter Roots had seen dated November 30, 1888. As Roots's police report would appear to be correct, this shows that Stead encouraged *Pall Mall Gazette* reporters to hunt Jack the Ripper.

10. Roots is referring Swanson to documentation filed with the Metropolitan Police Orphanage on the suspect for use in further Scotland Yard inquiries. A check with the orphanage archives did not yield details on D'Onston's 1886 file and application. The historical records had been destroyed for all but a short list of 372 candidates, and D'Onston's name is not among them. For further details see Melvin Harris, *The True Face of Jack the Ripper* (London: Michael O'Mara, 1994).

11. The Newgate Calendars were pamphlets widely read by the Victorian populace. They listed recent crimes and described executions.

12. Stead is referencing his own earlier article on the Whitechapel murders titled "Murder as an Advertisement," alleging that Jack the Ripper was a Jesuit. *Pall Mall Gazette*, September 19, 1888.

13. *Pall Mall Gazette*, September 24, 1888.

14. William Waddell, a spurned lover of Jane Beadmore, was convicted and executed for this case. He imitated the mutilations of Jack the Ripper. However, a century later, crime writer Patricia Cornwell introduced a theory and regarded the case as unsolved. She believed artist Walter Sickert was complicit in the Whitechapel murders. For further details on the Gateshead murder see Alan Sharp, "A Ripper Victim That Wasn't: The Capture of Jane Beadmore's Killer," *Ripper Notes*, January 2006, http://www.casebook.org/dissertations/rn-beadmore.html.

15. *The Times*, September 27, 1888.

16. *The Times*, September 26, 1888.

17. *Evening News*, September 27, 1888.

18. The initial details given to Baxter during the Chapman inquest were passed on to Scotland Yard and dismissed. The London correspondent of *The Chicago Tribune*, reported on October 7, 1888, "I learned today from a Scotland Yard man working on the case that the mysterious American who was here a few months ago offering money for specimens of the parts taken from the bodies of the victims has been discovered. He is a reputable physician in Philadelphia with a large practice, who was over here preparing a medical work on specific diseases. He went to King's College and Middlesex Hospitals and asked for specimens, and merely said he was willing to pay well if he could not get them otherwise.

The statement that he offered £20 each or named any other large sum seems to be a delusion of the Coroner. These facts were given the police by an eminent London physician, who saw a great deal of the Philadelphian when he was here, but would only divulge the information on a written guarantee from Sir Charles Warren that neither his name nor the name of the physician in question should be given to the public. He said the doctor had gone back to America, and his mission here was purely legitimate."

19. *The Times,* September 19, 1888. Cited in S.P. Evans and K. Stewart, *The Ultimate Jack the Ripper Sourcebook* (London: Robinson, 2001), p. 107.

20. Stead wrote in his journal on September 25, 1888, "Our stand regarding Trafalgar Square hit us in advertisements and also in circulation. The Star starting soon after also hit us. The result is that we are now down to the figure we were before, with fewer advertisements. This is failure, I admit. From my proprietor's point of view I have failed to make his paper a property. He has a right to send me away. He gave me notice from October 1 and yesterday I got the letter saying that he wanted some serious conversation with me about it today." Reprinted in R.W. Robertson Scott, *The Life and Death of a Newspaper* (London: Methuen, 1952).

21. *East London Advertiser,* September 29, 1888.

22. Even if D'Onston was not Jack the Ripper, he may have written the "From Hell" letter sent with a kidney portion to George Lusk. This is surmised despite the fact that his handwriting, which was known from his October 16, 1888, letter to the City Police, did not match that of the "From Hell" letter. In his December 1 *Pall Mall Gazette* report on the Whitechapel murders, D'Onston alludes to works of the French occultist Éliphas Lévi, so a possible source for the Lusk letter may be an 1884 English translation of Levi's short work, *Letters from Hell,* translated by J. M. Wheeler and published by Ramsay and Foote, London. The Ripper letters are discussed with further details in S.P. Evans and K. Skinner, *Jack the Ripper: Letters from Hell* (Stroud, UK: Sutton, 2004).

23. *Evening News,* October 18, 1888. This is a reprint of a letter to the editor of the *Daily Chronicle.* The Athenaeum club may have been responsible for medical pranks during the period of the Whitechapel murders. For further details see ref. GB 0387 MC/U, Royal London Hospital Archives and Museum.

24. *Pall Mall Gazette,* December 31, 1888. This report led to the theory that D'Onston wrote "Ripper letters," but his handwriting does not appear to match any known Ripper letters, so the theory is dubious.

25. The details contained in the original historic registers are reproduced courtesy of the Royal London Hospital Archives and Museum. They resulted from e-mail correspondence, August 27, 2006, between the author and Jonathan Evans, the chief archivist, and have been verified by independent researchers.

26. Royal London Hospital Archives register of inpatients of 1888, document reference LH/M/1/16.

27. This indicates that the patient did not have a letter of referral or ticket from a governor of the London Hospital. The patient was admitted via the hospital's Receiving Room on the authority of the medical officer who had examined him.

28. It seems to have been the practice at the London Hospital during the Victorian period to record the civil state as "U" (unmarried) for older or perhaps divorced patients and "S" (single) for younger patients. However, Donston's 1889 register records him as "S" for single.

29. The Victorian practice at the London Hospital on ward transfers was to strike out the ward name and replace it with that of the new ward. D'Onston was transferred from Currie to Davis ward. His October 16, 1888, letter to the City Police with the return address of Currie Wards confirms that he was transferred from a large ward to a smaller one sometime after that date. The transfer is consistent with a diagnosis of neurasthenia, which would have been treated with rest, quiet and privacy that he may not have had in the large Currie Ward.

30. The term "neurasthenia" was coined by New York neurologist George Beard in 1869. It was considered a disorder related to the stress of modern life and was sometimes called "the American disease." See Christopher G. Goetz, "Poor Beard!!: Charcot's Internalization of Neurasthenia, the 'American Disease,'" *Neurology,* 57 (3) (August 14, 2001): pp. 510–514. Some further examples are found in James Burnett, "Some Aspects of Neurasthenia," *The Medical Times and Hospital Gazette,* February 3, 1906, pp. 58–59. John A. Price's *A Dictionary of Terms Used in Medicine and the Collated Sciences,* 13th edition (London: Whittaker, 1899), defines neurasthenia as "Nervous exhaustion, characterized by over-sensitiveness, irritability, mutability, etc." Pierre Janet, an early pioneer of psychiatry, wrote an article titled "La Force et la faiblesse psychologiques," in which he asserted: "If a patient is poor he is committed to a public hospital as psychotic; if he can afford the luxury of a private sanatorium, he is put there with the diagnosis of neurasthenia; if he is wealthy enough to be isolated in his own home under constant watch of nurses and physicians he is simply an indisposed eccentric." If nothing else, we can be sure he had some kind of debilitating condition complicated by apparent alcoholism and drug addiction that was serious enough to require hospitalization. Inspector Thomas Roots confirmed that D'Onston "drinks very heavily, and always carries drugs to sober him and stave off delirium tremens."

31. Dr. Henry Gawen Sutton, 1836–1891, was elected assistant physician of the London Hospital in 1867 and physician in 1876. Though the hospital had no specialist consultant posts in the period, Sutton lectured in pathology at the London Hospital Medical College and was said to have gained experience in morbid anatomy. He specialized in renal disease and worked with a Ripper suspect, Sir William Gull, at Guy's Hospital prior to his appointment at the London Hospital. He had also worked at a temporary hospital at Commercial Street, Whitechapel. Sutton was born in Yorkshire, as D'Onston was, and died on June 9, 1891, of influenza and bronchitis.

32. The condition on discharge of "Relieved" indicates that the patient was not cured of the diagnosed condition when discharged. It is roughly equivalent to a discharge against medical advice. He was still ill when he approached Scotland Yard. Inspector Roots's report of December 26, 1888, confirms that D'Onston continued to use medication. The following year, the register lists his treatment as concluded and his discharge status as "Cured" but for the diagnosis of "Chloralism."

33. Royal London Hospital Archives register of inpatients 1889 document reference LH/M/1/17.

34. D'Onston altered his occupation from the 1888 "Journalist" to this 1889 register entry of "Author." This likely reflects his move from newspaper writing to more literary pursuits in his later years, as a writer of articles for W.T. Stead's specialist periodicals and his own book, *The Patristic Gospels.*

35. "Chloralism" was defined in the 13th edition of Price's *A Dictionary of Terms Used in Medicine and the Collated Sciences* (London: Whittaker, 1899) as "a general term for the paralysed condition induced by the prolonged use of hydrate of chloral." The book also defines chloral as "a colorless oily liquid prepared by the mutual action of chlorine and alcohol."

36. Claire Daunton, ed., *The London Hospital Illustrated: 250 Years* (London: Batsford, 1990).

37. Royal London Hospital Archives and Museum, ref. LH/A/15.

38. *Report from the Select Committee of the House of Lords on Metropolitan Hospitals, Provident and other Public Dispensaries, and Charitable Institutions for Sick Poor.: together with the proceedings of the Committee, minutes of evidence and appendix.* Chair: William Mansfield, 1st Vct. Sandhurst. House of Commons Papers. Reports of Committees 392. Vol. XVI.1, 1890.

39. Royal London Hospital Archives and Museum, ref: LH/N/4/1.

40. *The Star*, October 4, 1888.

41. *The Star*, December 19, 1888.

42. Royal London Hospital Archives and Museum, ref. LH/A/1/17.

43. Frederick Whyte, *The Life of W. T. Stead. Vol. 2* (London: Jonathan Cape, 1925), pp. 341–342.

44. An example was the *Evening News* bought out by the Conservative Newspaper Company Ltd in 1882. National Archives ref. BT 31/3010/16991.

45. *Pall Mall Gazette*, December 3, 1888.

46. This is a reference to D'Onston's theory, which he described in a letter to the City Police on October 16, 1888, two days after the claims of Arthur Diosy on supposed use of the victims' extracted uteri for black magic. It seems likely that D'Onston blended other Victorian and medieval sources to create his theory. He may also have embellished Diosy's uterus theory based on the reference of W.T. Stead on December 3, 1888. It shows that D'Onston at least read widely on the occult, probably as a part of his early Christian biblical studies on Alexandrian Gnostic traditions and the Essenes. These historic elements were also explored by the Theosophical Society, the Society for Psychical Research and in the background literature of the team that issued the English Revised Version of the Bible in 1881.

47. D'Onston noted an opposing claim in a statement to Scotland Yard on December 26, 1888, that he regarded Mary Kelly a part of the Jack the Ripper series.

48. *Pall Mall Gazette,* December 1, 1888.

49. *Pall Mall Gazette*, October 3, 1888.

50. Ignatius L. Donnelly, born of an Irish immigrant to America, became a lawyer, U.S. congressman, editor and publisher of newspapers. He also wrote about more esoteric subjects, including the work referred to here: *The Great Cryptogram: Francis Bacon's Cipher in Shakespeare's Plays.* Donnelly maintained that ciphers in the works of Shakespeare indicated that their true author was Francis Bacon.

51. *Pall Mall Gazette,* December 6, 1888.

52. Esther Delaforce has referred by mistake to another letter sent to the *Pall Mall Gazette* on December 6, 1888, in response to the article "The Whitechapel Demon," which was published on December 1, 1888, in that newspaper.

53. *Pall Mall Gazette,* December 12, 1888.

54. In *The History of Spiritualism* (London: Cassell, 1926), Sir Arthur Conan Doyle said of Stainton Moses, "There is no writer who has left his mark upon the religious side of Spiritualism so strongly as the Reverend W. Stainton Moses. His inspired writings confirmed what had already been accepted, and defined much which was nebulous. His writings, under the signature of 'M.A. Oxon,' are among the classics of Spiritualism. They include 'Spirit Teachings,' 'Higher Aspects of Spiritualism,' and other works. Finally, he became editor of Light, and sustained its high traditions for many years. His mediumship steadily progressed until it included almost every physical phenomenon with which we are acquainted. Stainton Moses aided in the formation of the Society for Psychical Research in 1882, but resigned from that body in 1886 in disgust at its treatment of the medium William Eglinton. He was the first president of the London Spiritualist Alliance in 1884, a position he retained until his death."

55. Later police accounts report that Catherine Eddowes was murdered in "Mitre Court" rather than in "Mitre Square." "The earliest appearance of the name 'Mitre Square' appears to be in 1830," according to the C & J Greenwood Map of London, 1827 (updated 1830). See "Mitre Square Revisited," *Ripperologist* 104, July 2009.

56. *Light*, December 8, 1888, p. 506.

57. Éliphas Lévi, *Transcendental Magic: Its Doctrine and Ritual* (London: Rider, 1896). Translated, annotated and introduced by Arthur Edward Waite.

58. Éliphas Lévi, *The Mysteries of Magic: A Digest of the Writings of Éliphas Lévi,* translated and edited by Arthur Edward Waite (London: George Redway, 1886). In another early English translation of an 1896 work by Éliphas Lévi, *The Magical Ritual of the Sanctum Regnum* (London: George Redway, 1896; edited by W. Wynn Westcott) it is stated in the preface that, "The Mysteries of Magic, a Digest of the Writings of Eliphaz Levi, by Mr. A. E. Waite, published by Mr. Redway in 1886, has had so large a circulation among English readers, that the editor anticipates a cordial reception for this little volume." The chapter titles in *The Mysteries of Magic* were: "Initiatory Exercises & Preparations," "Religious & Philosophical Problems & Hypotheses," "Scientific & Magical Theorems," "The Doctrine of Spiritual Essences, or Kabalistic Pneumatics," "With the Mysteries of Evocation, Necromancy, and Black Magic," "The Great Practical Secrets, or Realizations of Magical Science."

59. The relevant passage for comparison of the 1886 English translation of Éliphas Lévi's *The Mysteries of Magic* with D'Onston's article is: "A leaden cup blazoned with the signs of the Moon, Venus, and Saturn, two candles of human fat set in crescent-shaped candlesticks of black wood, a magic sword with black handle, a magic fork, a copper vase holding the blood of the victim, a censer containing incense, camphor, aloes, ambergris, and storax, mixed and moistened with the blood of a goat, a mole, and a bat; four nails torn from the coffin of an executed criminal, the head of a black cat which has been fed on human flesh for five days, a bat drowned in blood, the horns of a goat cum quo puella concubuerit, and the skull of a parricide, are all indispensable." Lévi, a lapsed Catholic priest, also used as a source *Le Grand Grimiore,* containing *Le Dragon rouge, au l'art de commander les esprits celestes, aeriens, terrestres, infernaux.* It is dated 1521 and was published in 1822 in Avignon, France. The medieval manuscripts on which this recipe is based were contrived during the Inquisition as covers for beliefs deemed capital crimes by the Roman Church. They also held elements of earlier Christian, Pagan and Hebrew traditions. Some medieval European practitioners took the heretical suggestions literally, giving rise to a minority satanic tradition. Further distortions and translations from the original Latin informed the Victorian occult revival and were consulted by early novelists of supernatural horror.

60. In his first major story, "The Great God Pan," Arthur Machen included a mention of the Whitechapel murders. "The police had been forced to confess themselves powerless to arrest or to explain the sordid murders of Whitechapel; but before the horrible suicides of Piccadilly and Mayfair they were dumbfounded, for not even the mere ferocity which did duty as an explanation of the crimes of the East End, could be of service in the West." Arthur Machen, "The Great God Pan," first published with his *The Inmost Light* in Volume V, John Lane Keynotes Series, 1894. See also: Sage Leslie-McCarthy, "Chance Encounters: The Detective as 'Expert' in Arthur Machen's 'The Great God Pan,'" *Australasian Journal of Victorian Studies* 13(1) (2008). Machen would later describe his visits to the East End with his friend Arthur Waite during the Whitechapel murders in *The London Adventure: Or, The Art of Wandering* (London: Martin Secker, 1924).

61. Edward Bulwer-Lytton wrote a number of popular Victorian occult romances and novels, which probably influenced D'Onston as there is no evidence that he met him as claimed. In e-mail correspondence dated June 14, 2006, between myself and the curator of Rosslyn Chapel, Robert Cooper, he suggested, "The use of the name Roslyn is interesting and as both [Lytton and D'Onston] seem to have been interested in the Romantic Movement, the Roslyn may have come from the works of Sir Walter Scott who wrote about the chapel and was one of the main figures of the Romantic Movement." Cooper is also curator of the Grand Lodge Museum and Library and was not able to locate D'Onston in the records of that organization. For further details on the traditions of Rosslyn Chapel, see Robert L.D. Cooper, *The*

*Rosslyn Hoax?: Viewing Rosslyn Chapel from a New Perspective* (Addlestone, UK: Lewis, 2007).

62. Roslyn D'Onston, *The Patristic Gospels: An English Version of the Holy Gospels as They Existed in the Second Century* (London: Grant Richards, 1904). The title page says: "Collated from 120 of the Greek and Latin Fathers, from the Second to the Tenth Century; the 26 Old Latin (Italic) Versions of the Second Century; the Vulgate; 24 Greek uncials and some cursives: the Syriac, Egyptian, and other ancient versions and corrected by comparing all the critical Greek texts from Stephanus (A.D. 1550) to Westcott and Hort, 1881; all the English versions from Wiclif (Fourteenth Century) to the American Baptist Version of 1883; as well as every commentator English and Foreign, who has ever suggested a practicable rendering."

63. In his *Patristic Gospels,* D'Onston refers to a work of: Westcott and Hort's *The New Testament in the Original Greek* (New York: Harper & Brothers, 1881). He also mentions consulting Westcott, an Anglican bishop, on his English translation of the New Testament. D'Onston's book had some interest in 1904 but has been superseded in biblical studies with responses to innovations of the Authorized King James Version. In comparison, Sir Robert Anderson opposed the trend of the "Higher Criticism" of biblical developments in his religious writings.

64. *Pall Mall Gazette,* January 3, 1889.

65. *Pall Mall Gazette,* February 15, 1889.

66. Stead later reprinted D'Onston's early 1889 *Pall Mall Gazette* articles on "She" and the Obeeyah, and they were further discussed in *The English Mechanic and World of Science,* Vol. 49, September 1, 1899.

67. Sir Henry Rider Haggard, *The Days of My Life: An Autobiography* (New York: Longmans, 1926).

68. Tau-triadelta (pseud. Robert Donston Stephenson), "African Magic," *Lucifer* 7, November 1890, p. 231.

69. The *Review of Reviews* was a monthly journal founded by W.T. Stead in London in 1890. He eventually established editions in America and Australia and dreamed of a global publishing empire. However, the publisher, Sir George Newnes, M.P., objected to Stead's scathing attacks on *The Times,* and withdrew his support, saying that the venture was "turning his hair grey." Stead bought out Newnes's share and stamped the *Review of Reviews* with his brand of toboid journalism in articles such as "Ought Mrs. Maybrick to Be Tortured to Death?" and "Baby-killing as an Investment."

70. Franz Hartmann, M.D., 1838–1912, was a German physician, Theosophist and author of esoteric works and biographies on Jakob Bohme and Paracelsus. He translated the Bhagavad Gita into German and edited the *Lotusbluten* journal. He spent time with Helena Blavatsky in Adyar, India, and founded the German Theosophical Society in 1896. His article, which Stead and D'Onston responded to in *Borderland,* "Seelenbraute und Vampirismus ['Soul brides' and Vampirism]," was published in: *Lotusbluthen* Vol. 6, Issue 38 (1895), p. 785. Mabel Collins later joined the German branch of the Theosophical Society. It was thought that Hartmann was a cofounder, with Theodor Reuss, of the German O.T.O., but this was misleading information disseminated by Ruess, who was in the pay of the Prussian secret police.

71. This article was signed "Tau-triadelta: A Pupil of Lord Lytton," *Borderland,* April 1896.

72. *Borderland,* April 1896.

73. *Pall Mall Gazette,* February 8, 1889.

74. *Lucifer,* Vol. 1 (January 1888), pp. 395–397; J. Fitzgerald Molloy, *A Modern Magician: A Romance,* 3 Volumes (London: Ward and Downey, 1887). Molloy (1858–1908), a prolific author of historical and dramatic works, wrote also under the pseudonym Ewan Wilding. His *A Modern Magician* was an occult romantic novel of interest in the Theosophical Society.

75. The article was published in French as "Un Magicien Moderne: Autobiographie" in *Le Voile d'Isis,* 1923–24. A

translator's note says that the identity of the author was not known.

76. The monthly periodical *Le Voile d'Isis: Revue de Philosophie Esoterique* published its first issue on November 12, 1890. Described as the official organ of the Independent d'etudes Esoterique de Paris, it was founded and edited by occult author Dr. Gerard Anaclet Encausse. Encausse wrote widely under the name "Papus," which is derived from the "Nuctemeron of Appolonius of Tyana," a supplement published in Éliphas Lévi's "Dogme et Rituel de la Haute Magie." The works of Lévi and the French occult revival also influenced Encausse. He joined the Theosophical Society and was a founding member of its French branch in 1887, but left soon after. Encausse wanted to establish an association to disseminate teachings of occultism "according to the ways of the Western Christian tradition," a departure from Blavatsky's eastern leanings. D'Onston alludes to this French background in his writings and adoption of the pseudonym Tau-triadelta. For further reading on the Victorian roots of alternative intellectual and religious movements, see Mark Sedgwick, *Against the Modern World: Traditionalism and the Secret Intellectual History of the Twentieth Century* (Oxford: Oxford University Press, 2004).

77. Sir Robert Anderson's 1902 book, *The Bible and Modern Criticism,* is based on a series of earlier letters to the press. He gives the background in a footnote: "The Times correspondence quoted in this chapter originated with a 'declaration on the truth of Holy Scripture,' signed by Dean Goulbourn and a number of other clergymen, which appeared in The Times of December 18, 1891. My object in intervening was to point out that these clergymen in taking their stand upon the ground that the Church was 'the witness and keeper of Holy Writ,' betrayed the cause they sought to defend, and were false to the Church of England, which in Article XX, claims only to be 'a witness,' &c. My second letter (The Times, January 23, 1892) was in reply to the letter of 'A Beneficed English Clergyman of Twenty-five Years' Standing,' who took infidel ground. Mr. Huxley's reply appeared in The Times of January 26th. Letters from the Duke of Argyll, Canon Girdlestone, and myself appeared on February 1st, and were answered by Mr. Huxley on February 3rd and 4th. My last letter (quoted above) appeared on February 8th, and Mr. Huxley's rejoinder on the 11th. The title 'The Bible and Modern Criticism' was assigned to the correspondence by the editor of The Times."

78. In regarding biblical sources as a basis for the Revised Version of 1881, Anderson gave an example which reflects his comments on a Jewish Ripper suspect: "But while the lawyer understands the value of indirect evidence, the layman is always inclined to disparage it in favor of the direct. Witnesses of credit and repute testify that they saw the accused commit the crime with which he is charged. What more can any one want? The average juryman is ready at once to convict; and he cannot imagine why the judge should allow further time to be spent upon the case. But the judge knows well that evidence of this kind is apt to err, and needs to be tested with the utmost care." Here Anderson adds a footnote: "Of course, if the accused is seized at the time, evidence of eye-witnesses is conclusive. The conflict between direct and indirect evidence arises where the accused is arrested after an interval, and his identity becomes the salient question in the case." Sir Robert Anderson, *The Bible and Modern Criticism,* Fifth Edition (London: Hodder and Stoughton, 1905), p. 106.

79. For an in-depth study of this period in the East End, see Donald Rumbelow, *The Houndsditch Murders and the Siege of Sidney Street* (Harmondsworth, UK: Penguin Books, 1990).

80. Sir Robert Anderson, *The Bible and Modern Criticism,* Fifth Edition (London: Hodder and Stoughton, 1905), p. 45.

81. In a series of newspaper articles published in 1895 in *Reynolds News,* Patrick McIntyre, a former detective sergeant

of the Political Department at Scotland Yard, described Anderson as an obsessive religious moralist in his capacity as Metropolitan Police assistant commissioner and head of CID.

## Chapter 5

1. Melvin Harris, *The True Face of Jack the Ripper* (London: Michael O'Mara, 1994).

2. Author Robin Odell noted that Bernard O'Donnell had told him he was beaten to the draw by Donald McCormick and decided to allow an interval to pass before he launched his own theory, "in which the identity of the Ripper will be definitely established." Robin Odell, *Ripperology: A Study of the World's First Serial Killer and a Literary Phenomenon* (Kent, OH: Kent State University Press, 2006). McCormick published his book *The Identity of Jack the Ripper* (London: Jarrods) in 1959.

3. R. Whittington-Egan, *A Casebook on Jack the Ripper* (London: Wildy & Sons, 1975); S. Knight, *Jack the Ripper: The Final Solution* (London: Harrap, 1976).

4. Melvin Harris, *The True Face of Jack the Ripper* (London: Michael O'Mara, 1994).

5. J. Overton Fuller, *The Magical Dilemma of Victor Neuburg* (London: W.H. Allen, 1965).

6. Daniel H. Caldwell, compiler, *Madam Blavatsky's Esoteric Papers: A Comprehensive Compilation* (Whitefish, MT: Kessinger Publishing, 2005).

7. The extract is: "There has been a great row in the Theosophical Society, Madam Blavatsky expelled Mrs. Cook (Miss Mabel Collins) and the President of the Lodge for flirtation (Mrs. Cook has a husband living), and Mrs. Alicia [sic] Cremers, an American, for gossiping about it. As a result, Madam Blavatsky is in high spirits. The society is like the "happy family" that used to be exhibited round Charing Cross Station—a cat in a cage full of canaries. The Russian cat is beginning to purr now and smoothen [sic] its fur again—the canary birds are less by three—the faithful will be more obedient than ever." Vittoria Cremers is also mentioned in the letters of author Katherine Mansfield, indicating Cremers's wide literary, mystical, and artistic associations during the period. "Letter to Miss Tynan, 21 April 1889," in *The Letters of W.B. Yeats*, ed. Allan Wade (London: R. Hart-Davies, 1954), p. 41.

8. Lord Lindsay, earl of Crawford and Balcarres, was implicated in the "Mahatma Letters" incident of the Indian Branch of the Theosophical Society. Crawford held an administrative position with the Theosophy Society. See Chapter 3.

9. Mabel Collins's letter is reprinted courtesy of the Alice Marshall Women's History Collection, Penn State Harrisburg Library, Middletown, PA. The year of the letter is assumed from a postmark found on the envelope.

10. For further reading on Dr. Anna Kingsford see Alan Pert, *Red Cactus: The Life of Anna Kingsford*, 2nd edition (Watsons Bay, NSW: Books & Writers, 2007). Her 1886 published work, *Pasteur: His Method and Its Results: A Lecture*, is available at: http://ocp.hul.harvard.edu/dl/contagion/006181268.

## Chapter 6

1. There are no definitive works on the role of conspiracy theories in shaping the history of Jack the Ripper and the Whitechapel murders apart from this book. For an insightful and informative look at conspiracy theories and the 20th century see David Aaronovitch, *Voodoo Histories: The Role of the Conspiracy Theory in Shaping Modern History* (London: Jonathan Cape, 2009).

2. The Edwardian period covered the brief reign of King Edward VII from 1901 to 1910 though it is sometimes extended through the end of the First World War in 1918. The period was characterized by rapid developments in fashion, the arts, travel and leisure for the upper classes, and by the founding of the Labor Party as representatives for the lower classes. The Edwardian period also saw the forging of many Jack the Ripper press theories.

3. The first organization for the accreditation of journalists, the Chartered Institute of Journalists, was formed in England in 1883.

4. *The Star,* September 10, 1888.

5. The "Swanson Marginalia" is a set of annotations ostensibly made by retired Chief Inspector Donald Swanson, supervisor of the Whitechapel murders inquiries, in his copy of Sir Robert Anderson's memoirs. The book is now deposited in the New Scotland Yard Crime Museum.

6. *The Star,* September 24, 1888. Letter to the editor from George Bernard Shaw.

7. The editor is drawing parallels between Irish Coercion policies of the Tory Party and Chief Secretary of Ireland Arthur Balfour and the quelling of socialist riots in Trafalgar Square in November 1887 by Metropolitan Police Commissioner Sir Charles Warren and Home Secretary Henry Matthews. Such comparisons with the official handling of the Whitechapel murders were widely reported. They have come to inform and influence the development of published theories on Jack the Ripper.

8. *The Star,* September 24, 1888. It is a curious fact that this editorial was written one day before the famous "Dear Boss" letter is dated. This is at odds with the assertion that journalists of *The Star* had fabricated the letter (with the knowledge of editor T.P. O'Connor) to keep up the paper's circulation figures. As accredited Victorian newspapermen they were obliged to uphold certain standards in reporting as the editorial demonstrates.

9. Scottish intellectual Thomas Davidson, founded the Fellowship of the New Life movement in 1883. Members included poet Edward Carpenter, animal rights activist Henry Stephens Salt, sexologist Havelock Ellis, later Fabian Society secretary Edward R. Pease and future prime minister Ramsay MacDonald. The Fellowship of the New Life was disbanded in the early 1890s after the Fabian Society was formed in 1884 for political campaigns.

10. The Fabian Society, founded in London on January 4, 1884, was named after the Roman general Quintus Fabius Maximus Cunctator on the suggestion of Frank Podmore, a cofounder of the Society for Psychical Research. Fabius, nicknamed "the delayer," advocated tactics of attrition rather than head-on confrontation with the armies of Hannibal. The Fabian Society adopted these measures in parliamentary agitation for social reforms and contributed to the formation of the Labor Party. With the Russian Revolution of 1917, English socialism fell largely out of favor, and it was viewed with suspicion during the growth of communism. Portrayals of Jack the Ripper as a serial murderer who killed to expose the poverty and conditions of the East End, and the supposed incompetence and apathy of responsible authorities, had by the turn of the 20th century become politically partisan. This, of course, had little to do with actual events investigated by Scotland Yard in 1888. See Carl Levy, ed., *Socialism and the Intelligentsia, 1880–1914* (New York: Routledge & Kegan Paul, 1988).

11. Sir Melville Macnaghten, *Days of My Years* (London: Edward Arnold, 1914). One of the earliest novels based on the Whitechapel murders was *Lord Jacquelin Burkney: The Whitechapel Terror* (New York: Anton, 1889), by "Rodissi," the pseudonym of Jacob Ringgold. In the novel, the eminent surgeon Lord Burkney, the murderer, refers to himself as "The Avenger." Marie Belloc Lowndes would also name her Jack the Ripper "The Avenger" in her 1913 novel *The Lodger.* Thomas De Quincey, the early Victorian author and eccentric, wrote a short fiction titled "The Avenger," seemingly based on an 1816 German serial murder case. Its preface read, "Why callest thou me murderer, and not rather the wrath of God burning after the steps of the oppressor, and cleansing the earth when it is wet with blood?"—possibly presaging

Jack the Ripper and the religious mania later found in Lowndes's work. Thomas De Quincey, "The Avenger," *Blackwood's Edinburgh Magazine*, 1838. East End–born Sir Alfred Hitchcock adapted Lowndes's novel as his first major successful silent movie, *The Lodger: A Story of the London Fog* (1927). The novel was further adapted in three sound movies, *The Phantom Fiend* (1932), *The Lodger* (1944) and *Man in the Attic* (1953).

12. *The New York Times*, May 1, 1910, responded to Anderson's disclosures: "When Sir Robert Anderson, formerly the head of Scotland Yard, confessed in Blackwood's Magazine for April that he was the author of The London Times articles on 'Parnellism and Crime,' he cleared up one of the most interesting political mysteries since the Letters of Junius. He also established what was always morally certain, the complicity of the English Government officials in the conspiracy to run the Irish leaders for the purpose of securing coercive anti–Irish legislation. Why Sir Robert Anderson has chosen to make this confession is a mystery to the dismayed and angry Conservatives. Apparently he had no object except to gratify a garrulous vanity. He is now writing his reminiscences for Blackwood's, and in the April issue he quite casually remarks, apropos an anecdote which he places in 1893: 'To the present hour I do not know whether the Home Secretary was then aware of my authorship of The Times articles of 1887 on "Parnellism and Crime," for in relation to that matter I acted with strict propriety in dealing with Mr. Monro and not with the Secretary of State.'"

13. *Hawera & Normanby Star*, June 14, 1910.

14. Ref. H0144/221/A49310C, f225. Stewart P. Evans and Keith Skinner, *The Ultimate Jack the Ripper Sourcebook: An Illustrated Encyclopedia* (London: Robinson, 2001), Chapter 23.

15. *Pall Mall Gazette*, May 7, 1895.

16. *Penny Illustrated Paper*, August 6, 1910.

17. *Penny Illustrated Paper*, October 15, 1910.

18. *Penny Illustrated Paper*, July 2, 1910.

19. *Pall Mall Gazette*, March 24, 1903.

20. For further reading on the invention and growth of the telegraph see Tom Standage, *The Victorian Internet* (New York: Walker, 1998).

21. George R. Sims, "Who Was Jack the Ripper?" *Lloyd's Weekly News*, September 22, 1907. Stewart P. Evans and Keith Skinner discovered this article thanks to a reference in the letter from Ernest Crawford to G.R. Sims sent two days later.

22. Ernest Crawford's 1907 letter to George R. Sims was first published in Melvin Harris, *The True Face of Jack the Ripper* (London: Michael O'Mara, 1994), pp. 153–154. Crawford was born in Bath in 1867 and was around 41 years of age when he wrote to Sims about Jack the Ripper. The 1891 and 1901 census returns note his address as 2 Rose Hill Terrace, Walcot, Bath, and his occupation as portrait and landscape photographer, in which capacity he probably had contact with W.T. Stead.

23. Stewart P. Evans and K. Skinner, *The Ultimate Jack the Ripper Sourcebook* (London: Robinson, 2001), Chapter 39.

24. W.T. Stead, *The Pope and the New Era: Being Letters from the Vatican in 1889* (London and New York: Cassell, 1890). On March 23, 1890, *The New York Times* printed an in-depth review and rebuttal of Stead's pamphlet on the papacy. Stead, D'Onston and Helena Blavatsky were noted as also supportive of Garibaldi and the 1860s Italian campaigns against the Vatican. Stead took advantage of the contemporary focus on the Irish question to promote his theory of a Jesuit Jack the Ripper. He used the Whitechapel murders as opportunities for social commentary rather simply reporting the facts. Because news reports are a vital primary source on the Whitechapel murders, a clear distinction needs to be made between such commentary and the historic recording of actual events.

25. For a complete background on the early development of crime and detective fiction see Albert Borowitz, "The History & Traditions of Fact Based Crime Literature," *Legal Studies Forum*, Volume 29, Number 2 (2005). This essay was first published as the introduction to Borowitz's *Blood and Ink: An International Guide to Fact Based Crime Literature* (Kent, OH: Kent State University Press, 2002).

26. Peter Bagnall, "Joseph Conrad and Jack the Ripper, or The Unfortunate Alias of Martin Ricardo," unpublished Ph.D. thesis, University of Oxford, 1999.

27. Joseph Conrad, *The Secret Agent* (London: Methuen, 1907). Conrad wrote his author's note to a new edition in 1920. For further reading see Norman Sherry, *Conrad's Western World* (Cambridge, UK: Cambridge University Press, 1980).

28. This referred to a Norwegian seaman named Fogelma who believed he was Jack the Ripper, but no evidence existed to support his claim.

29. *Empire News*, October 23, 1923.

30. Betty May Sedgewick (also known simply as Betty May and nicknamed "Tiger Woman" for her feline features) was born in about 1892 in the East End. Her father ran a brothel in Limehouse that serviced sailors from the London docks. As a teenager, she became an artist's model. She went to France, where she joined a gang that robbed rich men. On her return to London, she resumed professional modeling and posed for the sculptor Jacob Epstein. In 1914 she met Crowley at the Café Royal. Stories of her disputes with Crowley were widely circulated in the press. In 1929 she published her autobiography, *Tiger Woman: My Story*, which included the story of Vittoria Cremers. Betty May had also met Nina Hamnett and probably Walter Sickert and others of that artistic circle who knew Cremers and had heard her Jack the Ripper story, as Crowley noted.

31. Aleister Crowley was born Edward Alexander Crowley on October 12, 1875, to wealthy parents in Warwickshire, England. His parents were Plymouth Brethren, a strict puritanical Christian sect. Crowley's mother reportedly dubbed him the "Beast," derived from the biblical book of Revelation. He turned 13 during the Whitechapel murders and held a lifelong interest in the crimes of Jack the Ripper as a metaphor for Victorian hypocrisy and occult theories.

32. Jean Overton Fuller, who had met Vittoria Cremers in the early 1930s, noted that she likely met Crowley at the public performances of *The Rites of Eleusis* at Caxton Hall in London during October and November 1910. She wrote: "It was during these performances that Cremers, having recently arrived from the United States, made her first appearance in the Crowley circle." Jean Overton Fuller, *The Magical Dilemma of Victor Neuburg* (London: W.H. Allen, 1965).

33. Aleister Crowley, "Jack the Ripper." Completed 1943 but first published posthumously in 1974, in the limited circulation Thelemic magazine *Sothis* 1(4). Crowley drew from a variety of noted sources originating with Vittoria Cremers to complete his article. He also had brief wartime contact with the daughter of Sir Melville Macnaghten, Lady Christabel Aberconway, who retained a draft copy of the Macnaghten Memorandum. Crowley does not appear to have queried Aberconway on Jack the Ripper, even though he knew of her father's police career and involvement in the investigation. Crowley recorded their early 1944 meeting in his unpublished diary. See also Christabel Aberconway, *A Wiser Woman: A Book of Memories* (London: Hutchinson, 1966).

34. Crowley's previous articles on Jack the Ripper were published in the *Empire News*, the paper for which Bernard O'Donnell worked as a crime reporter. They appeared on February 11, 1934, and May 19, 1934. Titled "Cross of Seven Points," they were included in a series of articles published during the period 1933–34 in the *Sunday Dispatch and Empire News*.

35. After Grant Richards rejected the novel, it was published in 1922 by William Collins & Sons, London.

36. Betty May, *Tiger Woman: My Story* (London: Duckworth, 1929). May notes that a "Bernard" approached her

on her return to London in late 1923 offering £500 to publish her stories in a Sunday periodical. She also recalled making tea for staff working at his Fleet Street office. It appears that Bernard O'Donnell knew of Cremers's Ripper story earlier than he notes in his unpublished manuscript and that it was based not on Cremers's reputed memoirs but on reports of Crowley's unpublished autobiography, which Betty May claimed to have seen.

37. The first publication of Betty May's Jack the Ripper story, in a series of articles in the *World's Pictorial* in 1925, apparently was ghost-written by Bernard O'Donnell. Melvin Harris, *The True Face of Jack the Ripper* (London: Michael O'Mara, 1994).

38. The original wanted poster, circa 1913, of Vittoria Cremers issued by Aleister Crowley is now in a private collection. It displays a crude caricature of her and includes text stating that Cremers was wanted for theft, embezzlement, and other crimes, and offered £5 for information leading to her apprehension and conviction. It included accusations of sexual harassment of young girls and involvement in "white slave" blackmail gangs.

39. Walter Sickert's Jack the Ripper lodger story was noted in the autobiography of Sir Osbert Sitwell, *Noble Essences: A Book of Characters* (London: Macmillan, 1950). Sickert frequented the Café Royal with the bohemians of the Bloomsbury Group and other artists, writers and musicians. Crowley was also often in attendance. For an interesting portrayal of the period and characters with mentions of Nina Hamnett and Betty May, see Virginia Nicholson, *Among the Bohemians: Experiments in Living 1900–1939* (New York: HarperPerennial, 2005).

40. Ref: NS12 (b). Crowley's letters, Yorke Collection. The Warburg Institute. University of London.

41. Aleister Crowley, *Moonchild: A Prologue* (London: Mandrake Press, 1929).

42. John Symonds and Kenneth Grant, eds. *The Confessions of Aleister Crowley* (London: Jonathan Cape, 1969), Chapter 78. It was originally planned as six volumes, but ran into difficulties and was published as a limited edition of two volumes as *The Spirit of Solitude: An Autohagiography. Laterly Re-Antichristened The Confessions of Aleister Crowley* (London: Mandrake Press, 1929).

43. Aleister Crowley, *Moonchild: A Prologue* (London: Mandrake Press, 1929), Chapter 14.

44. Aleister Crowley, *Moonchild: A Prologue* (London: Mandrake Press, 1929), Chapter 21.

45. The most notable were published as interviews with Betty May in the *Sunday Express*. Crowley was portrayed in the British press as "The Wickedest Man in the World" and as "A Man We'd Like to Hang."

46. A newspaper that interviewed Betty May in 1923 stated, "The Sunday Express promises Crowley that it intends to pursue its investigations with the utmost ruthlessness, and that next Sunday it will endeavour to supply him with considerable further material on which to base any action which he may care to bring," and that May "was given money by the British Consul to return to England.... The Sunday Express is putting the facts of this tragic case in the hands of Scotland Yard."

47. Allegations and lewd libels reached court in April 1911 in what became known as "The Looking Glass Affair." By 1917, New Scotland Yard had raided Crowley's Regent Street premises while he was in America.

48. This account of the Ripper's ability to become invisible was drawn from earlier (1919) press reports released on the death of Sergeant Stephen White. It first appeared in the 1929 autobiography of Betty May and recurred in O'Donnell's and Crowley's writings. It was blended with reports of German occult "thieves candles," made of human fat, that could render criminals invisible.

49. Crowley is referring to Olivia Haddon, whose brother became the executor of Vittoria Cremers's will, and to Victor Neuburg, with whom she lived in Wales. They had all fallen

out with Crowley by 1913, and he regarded this as a betrayal for the remainder of his life.

50. John Symonds and Kenneth Grant, eds., *The Confessions of Aleister Crowley* (London: Jonathan Cape, 1969), Chapter 71. Jean Overton Fuller also noted Crowley's Jack the Ripper story when researching the life of Victor Neuburg. See *The Magical Dilemma of Victor Neuburg* (London: W.H. Allen, 1965).

51. "'Jack the Ripper: Another Version of the Mystery' by Pierre Girouard (Late Paris Police)," *East Anglian Daily Times,* November 30, 1929. The complete article was published in Melvin Harris, *The True Face of Jack the Ripper* (London: Michael O'Mara, 1994).

52. Nina Hamnett, *The Laughing Torso* (London: Constable, 1932).

53. The incident was recorded in Mark Goulden, *Mark My Words!* (London: W.H. Allen, 1978).

54. Percy Reginald Stephenson, *The Legend of Aleister Crowley: Being a Study of the Documentary Evidence Relating to a Campaign of Personal Vilification Unparalleled in Literary History* (London: Mandrake Press, 1930).

55. *The Freethinker,* August 24, 1930.

56. Jean Overton Fuller, *The Magical Dilemma of Victor Neuburg* (London: W.H. Allen, 1965).

57. In a recent study by British historian Andrew Cook, *Jack the Ripper: Case Closed* (Stroud, UK: Amberley Publishing, 2009), the author argues on the basis of the letters to the press that Jack the Ripper was a fictional character created by journalists to sensationally link unrelated murders in hopes of boosting newspapers sales — particularly *The Star.* This is highly unlikely as the portrayal of Jack the Ripper had been developing for over a century and because at the time of the murders in 1888, the police had independently linked the murders in Whitechapel to at least six victims of the same killer. Though contemporary journalists did sensationalize the murders, as journalists certainly do today, they also recorded details that would otherwise be lost to history. When period press reports are compared to official files, a more comprehensive view emerges that a serial killer did in fact exist independent of press sensations.

58. *Harvard Law Review,* Vol. 66, No. 3 (January 1953), p. 560.

59–65. *The Old Bailey and Its Trials* (New York: Macmillan, 1950); *Cavalcade of Justice* (London: Clerke & Cockeran, 1951); *The World's Worst Women* (London: W.H. Allen, 1953); *The Trials of Mr. Justice Avory* (London: Rich & Cowan, 1953); *Crimes That Made News* (London: Burke Publishing, 1954); *Should Women Hang?* (London: W.H. Allen, 1956); *The World's Strangest Murders* (London: Frederick Muller, 1957).

66. Frederick P. Wensley, *Detective Days* (London: Cassell, 1931). Published as *Forty Years of Scotland Yard* in the United States.

67. "Scotland Yardsman," *Time,* July 8, 1929.

68. The first police officer to rise through the ranks to become chief constable of Scotland Yard was actually Adolphus Frederick Williamson in 1886. He held that position during the Ripper murders. He died on December 9, 1889. The erroneous story that Wensley was the first was widely circulated in the press on his retirement in 1929. This indicates the heavy reliance of O'Donnell and other authors of the time on newspaper accounts as sources of information.

69. Bernard O'Donnell, "Black Magic and Jack the Ripper (or alternatively) This Man was Jack the Ripper," Unpublished manuscript, 1958. Extract reprinted courtesy of Peter O'Donnell.

70. Robert Bloch, "Yours Truly, Jack the Ripper," *Weird Tales,* July 1943. Bloch's mentor was H.P. Lovecraft, who drew extensively from Victorian occult treatises for development of his Cthulhu Mythos novels. Bloch was also the author of the short story "Psycho" that was inspired by the case of Ed Gein and made into the famous movie by Alfred Hitchcock. For further reading on Bloch and Jack the Rip-

per, see Eduardo Zinna, "Yours Truly, Robert Bloch," http://www.casebook.org/dissertations/dst-bloch.html.

71. Stephen Knight had early access to all the official Whitechapel murders files then extant, and published Roslyn D'Onston's Scotland Yard statements in 1976. He dismissed D'Onston as a suspect on the premise that he and D'Onston's own suspect, Dr. Morgan Davies, were not pursued. According to Knight, this supported the theory that Scotland Yard knew the murders had ended with Mary Kelly and that Jack the Ripper was caught.

72. Bernard O'Donnell told crime author Robin Odell that Donald McCormick's Jack the Ripper book was released when O'Donnell completed his manuscript in 1958, so he decided to hold off on publication. Robin Odell, *Ripperology: A Study of the World's First Serial Killer and a Literary Phenomenon* (Kent, OH: Kent State University Press, 2006).

73. Notes on suspect Roslyn D'Onston and Bernard O'Donnell's unpublished manuscript are courtesy of Richard Whittington-Egan.

74. A good summary of the restoration of official police documentation on the Whitechapel murders investigation can be found in S.P. Evans and Donald Rumbelow, *Jack the Ripper: Scotland Yard Investigates* (London: Sutton, 2006), p. 261. For transcriptions of all extant official material on the Whitechapel murders see S.P. Evans and Keith Skinner, *The Ultimate Jack the Ripper Sourcebook* (London: Robinson, 2001).

75. Notable works on Jack the Ripper, misdirection and other clandestine intrigues during the cold war are the books and novels of journalist Donald McCormick (1911–1998). He occasionally fabricated his own sources and also wrote popular histories on espionage and occult subjects under the pseudonyms Richard Deacon and Lichade Digen. In addition, Chapman Pincher, an investigative journalist with the *Daily Express* who specialized in espionage, wrote *The Private World of St. John Terrapin: A Novel of the Café Royal* (London: Sidgwick & Jackson, 1982), which included as characters Jack the Ripper, Inspector Abberline, Walter Sickert and Aleister Crowley. During the cold war Pincher also fabricated press reports on the first British H-bomb testing in the Pacific in 1957.

76. *Reynolds's Newspaper,* December 1, 1889.

77. Richard Whittington-Egan, *A Casebook on Jack the Ripper* (London: Wildy & Sons, 1975).

78. Kelly Alexander, comp., *Jack the Ripper: A Bibliography and Review of the Literature* (London: Association of Assistant Librarians, 1973, reprint 1984).

79. Other notable bibliographical compilations are the books of Ross Strachan, *Jack the Ripper: A Collector's Guide to the Many Books Published* (privately published, 1997) and *The Jack the Ripper Handbook: A Reader's Companion* (privately published, 1999).

80. Author, crime historian and former police officer Donald Rumbelow gives a fascinating outline of the efforts to retrieve and store historic police documentation and materials in the epilogue to Evans and Rumbelow's *Jack the Ripper: Scotland Yard Investigates*. Rumbelow found the Mary Kelly and Catherine Eddowes police photos dumped in a disheveled attic at Snow Hill police station. Stewart P. Evans, also an author, crime historian and former police officer has, in collating and cataloging primary and secondary sources on Victorian crime and the history of Scotland Yard, preserved and published fragile and important historic records. It is through the efforts of crime historians and the National Archives that available official source material on the Whitechapel murders has survived.

81. For a background to the missing suspects files and a compilation of available photocopies and notes see S.P. Evans and Keith Skinner, *The Ultimate Jack the Ripper Sourcebook: An Illustrated Encyclopedia* (London: Robinson, 2001).

82. Colin Wilson and Robin Odell, *Jack the Ripper: Summing Up and Verdict* (London: Bantam Press, 1987).

83. Robin Odell, *Ripperology: A Study of the World's First Serial Killer and a Literary Phenomenon* (Kent, OH: Kent State University Press, 2006).

84. Martin Howells and Keith Skinner, *The Ripper Legacy: The Life and Death of Jack the Ripper* (London: Sidgwick & Jackson, 1987).

85. Robin Odell, *Ripperology: A Study of the World's First Serial Killer and a Literary Phenomenon* (Kent, OH: Kent State University Press, 2006).

86. Sir Shane Leslie, *Sir Evelyn Ruggle-Brise* (London: John Murray, 1938).

87. Melvin Harris, *Jack the Ripper: The Bloody Truth* (London: Columbus Books, 1987).

88. Melvin Harris (1930–2004) was a noted British author, broadcaster and television investigative researcher who worked on the popular Yorkshire Television series *Arthur C. Clarke's Mysterious World* and *Arthur C. Clarke's World of Strange Powers*. Among his research interests were medieval forgeries, the Amityville Horror hoax, Nostradamus, Jeane Dixon, alleged ghost manifestations, psychic charlatans, spiritualists and reincarnation.

89. Melvin Harris, *Sorry, You've Been Duped!* (London: Weidenfeld and Nicolson, 1986).

90. Paul Begg, *Jack the Ripper: The Facts* (London: Robson Books, 2006).

91. Melvin Harris, *The True Face of Jack the Ripper* (London: Michael O'Mara, 1994), p. 2.

92. Melvin Harris, letter to Colin Wilson, circa 1989, sent from Ireland.

93. Melvin Harris, *The True Face of Jack the Ripper* (London: Michael O'Mara, 1994), Chapter 23.

94. In 1988 the FBI prepared for the television special *The Secret Identity of Jack the Ripper* a psychological criminal personality profile which can be read here: http://foia.fbi.gov/foiaindex/jacktheripper.htm A later notable criminal profile was Robert D. Keppel, et al., "The Jack the Ripper Murders: A Modus Operandi and Signature Analysis of the 1888–1891 Whitechapel Murders," *Journal of Investigative Psychology and Offender Profiling* 2 (2005), pp. 1–21.

95. Paul Begg, *Jack the Ripper: The Uncensored Facts* (London: Robson, 1988); Martin Fido, *The Crimes, Detection & Death of Jack the Ripper* (London: Weidenfeld & Nicolson, 1987).

96. Patricia Cornwell, *Portrait of a Killer: Jack the Ripper—Case Closed* (London: Time Warner, 2003).

97. *Daily Express,* December 31, 1993.

98. Melvin Harris, *The True Face of Jack the Ripper* (London: Michael O'Mara, 1994), p. 79.

99. Kate Jackson, *George Newnes and the New Journalism in Britain, 1880–1910: Culture and Profit* (Aldershot, UK: Ashgate, 2001).

100. On December 6, 1993, questions were asked in the House of Commons: "Mr. Parry—To ask the Secretary of State for the Home Department (1) what inquiries have been conducted by the Metropolitan Police into the alleged diaries of Jack the Ripper; and if he will make a statement; (2) if the report of the Metropolitan Police on the Jack the Ripper diaries has been sent to the Director of Public Prosecutions; and if he will make a statement. Mr. Charles Wardle replied; I understand from the Commissioner that the Metropolitan Police have conducted inquiries into the origin and authenticity of the manuscript diary purporting to have been written by Jack the Ripper, and into the circumstances surrounding the publication of the manuscript. A report has been prepared and will be submitted shortly to the Crown Prosecution Service." HC Deb 06 December 1993 vol. 234 c5W.

101. *The Sunday Times,* September 19, 1993.

102. *The Sunday Times,* May 4, 2008.

103. Melvin Harris, "The Maybrick Will: The Crucial Key to a Shabby Hoax," *Ripperologist,* December 1996.

104. Keith Skinner, "A Nest of Forgers," January 19, 1997, http://www.casebook.org/dissertations/maybrick_diary/kskinner.html.

105. Ibid.

106. Melvin Harris, "The Maybrick Hoax: Donald Mc-Cormick's Legacy," 1999, http://www.casebook.org/dissertations/maybrick_diary/mb-mc.html.

107. Nigel Morland, *This Friendless Lady* (London: Frederick Muller, 1957).

108. *MacKill's Mystery Magazine*, Vol. 4, no. 3, May 1954.

109. "Whitechapel at Whitehall," *St. Stephen's Review*, August 17, 1889.

110. David Fisher, *The War Magician* (New York: Berkley, 1983). Reprinted as *The War Magician: The Man Who Conjured Victory in the Desert* (London: Weidenfeld & Nicolson, 2004).

111. Major Jasper Maskelyne, R.E., "Deceptive Camouflage Ideas 1941–1945." Maskelyne's unpublished scrapbook included his published reports on the supernatural. Maskelyne was also noted as a member of the religious Movement for Moral Rearmament, which used theater for boosting community confidence after the war.

112. Jasper Maskelyne, *Magic: Top Secret* (London: Stanley Paul, 1949). Maskelyne's exploits and the British use of stage magicians during World War II are somewhat dramatized in his memoirs. For more factual studies of these fascinating events see Nicholson Rankin, *Churchill's Wizards: The British Genius for Deception, 1914–1945* (London: Faber and Faber, 2009); Thaddeus Holt, *The Deceivers: Allied Military Deception in the Second World War* (London: Weidenfeld & Nicolson, 2004).

113. Richard Stokes, a military historian and magician, refuted David Fisher's claims in a series of articles in *Genii Magic Journal* in the 1990s. Stokes posted on his web site, www.Maskelynemagic.com, details of a reported discussion with Doreen Montgomery, the literary agent of Rupert Crew who was responsible for the Maybrick Diary. The information on the web site indicates that Frank S. Stuart had ghostwritten the 1949 memoirs of Jasper Maskelyne for that agency. Attempts to contact Stokes to verify the claims were not met with a response, so ostensible links with "The Diary of Jack the Ripper" are, though curious, speculative and without confirmation.

114. An interesting case for official consideration of wartime counterintelligence uses of popular delusions was drawn from programs of World War II. See Jean M. Hungerford, *The Exploitation of Superstitions for Purposes of Psychological Warfare (U)*, U.S. Air Force, Project Rand, Research Memorandum RM-365, ASTIA Document Number ATI 210637, April 14, 1950. This research paper referenced *Magic: Top Secret* by Jasper Maskelyne (ghost-written by Frank S. Stuart).

115. Richard Stokes, "Confessions of a Ghost Hunter," 2005. www.Maskelynemagic.com. Unfortunately, Stokes rarely provides references for his sources. As such, the material cited has as far as possible been checked but cannot be relied on as accurate. Efforts to contact Stokes were not successful.

116. Detective Inspector Herbert T. Fitch completed an earlier work, *Traitors Within: The Story of the Special Branch, New Scotland Yard* (New York: Doubleday, Doran, 1933). Another version was released, titled *Traitors Within: The Adventures of Detective Inspector Herbert T. Fitch* (London: Hurst & Blackett, 1933).

117. Herbert T. Fitch, *Memoirs of a Royal Detective* (London: Hurst & Blackett, 1935).

118. *Notes and Queries*, February 2, 1935, p. 78.

119. *Notes and Queries*, February 16, 1935, p. 123.

120. *Cassell's Saturday Journal*, June 11, 1892.

121. *Atchison* (Kansas) *Daily Globe,* October 27, 1888.

## Chapter 7

1. For a complete background to the resignation of Sir Charles Warren during the Whitechapel murders see Stewart P. Evans and Donald Rumbelow, *Jack the Ripper: Scotland Yard Investigates* (Stroud, UK: Sutton, 2006).

2. HO 144/221/A49301D, ff. 23–6.

3. For a complete and objective study of Anderson's position on Jack the Ripper see "Did Anderson Know?," Chapter 16 in Stewart P. Evans and Donald Rumbelow, *Jack the Ripper: Scotland Yard Investigates* (Stroud, UK: Sutton, 2006).

4. Sir Edward George Jenkinson was a private secretary to Earl Spencer, Lord Lieutenant of Ireland. He was appointed assistant undersecretary for police and crime at Dublin Castle after the 1882 Phoenix Park murders. He was then employed at the Home Office to organize the secret political crime department and to build a system of spies and informers, which conflicted with Scotland Yard and Metropolitan Police Commissioner James Monro. Jenkinson was sacked in December 1886 for what were regarded as extralegal activities. Though he remained unofficially involved in later developments, he was not trusted by the conservative Salisbury government because he had Liberal and Irish Home Rule sympathies. He was seen as a rival of Sir Robert Anderson.

5. *Birmingham Daily Post*, September 4, 1888.

6. *The Times*, March 10, 1883.

7. There is a mention of Home Office files in Stewart P. Evans and Donald Rumbelow, *Jack the Ripper: Scotland Yard Investigates* (Stroud, UK: Sutton, 2006): "The Home Office did, however, once have items that have been missing almost since the time of the murders. A note on file A49301 shows that out of forty-eight items, twenty-two were destroyed or missing when filed in 1893" (p. 264). It is a curious fact that the date of filing reflected a change of government after August 15, 1892.

8. Miss Elizabeth Cass was arrested by PC Endacott of Tottenham Court Road Police Station on June 28, 1887, and charged with solicitation and prostitution. Cass denied the charges and Endacott maintained his testimony. The matter came before the home secretary after complaints were made to Metropolitan Police Commissioner Sir Charles Warren. Endacott was suspended after the government was defeated in the House of Commons opposing a call for a public inquiry into the affair. The surviving papers on the case are located at the National Archives: HO 144/472/X15239 (Police Inquiry) and HO 144/472/X15239B (Prosecution of PC Endacott).

9. *The New York Times*, October 7, 1888.

10. *The New York Times*, November 11, 1888.

11. *The New York Times*, June 24, 1888.

12. *Reynold's Newspaper*, "Scotland Yard: Its Mysteries and Methods by Patrick McIntyre (Late First Detective-Sergeant, Political Department, Scotland Yard)." A series of weekly articles from February 3, 1895, to May 26, 1895.

13. Detective Sergeant Patrick McIntyre joined the Metropolitan Police in 1878. He was recruited in 1883 to the Political Department of Scotland Yard under the direction of Chief Inspector John George Littlechild and Chief Superintendent Adolphus Frederick Williamson. During McIntyre's 17-year police career, he was involved with investigations of Fenians, anarchists, and radical extremists as well as the protection of royalty, important dignitaries and informers. He was also employed on the Lambeth Poisoner murder case. In his series of articles, which included information on the Berner Street murder of Elizabeth Stride, McIntyre stated, "I shall endeavour to put forth, as clearly as possible, events that have come under my direct personal observation. In dealing with these I wish to be perfectly impartial, and not in any way to bring in that which would be injurious to the service that I have belonged to for seventeen years."

14. *Reynold's Newspaper,* April 7, 1895.

15. Hansard, HC Deb 19 April 1910 vol. 16 cc1867–70.

16. Anonymous, *The Times: Past Present Future* (London: Printed and Published at the Office of The Times, Printing House Square, 1932).

17. *The Times Parnell Commission: Speech Delivered by*

*Michael Davitt in Defence of the Land League* (London: Kegan Paul, Trench, Trubner, 1890).

18. *Murray's Magazine* was a conservative publication. The following excerpt can be taken as illustrative. The magazine was referred to in Hansard, HC Deb 25 June 1888 vol. 327 ccl148–249: "This Plan [Plan of Campaign — Irish Land League initiative] had inflicted nameless horrors and disabilities on people who declared when persons went to visit them that they had been forced to join it and wished they saw the end of it, If hon. Members wished proof of that fact, and proof which could not be challenged, let them go to Murray's Magazine and read in the article by Mrs. Bishop, a lady who visited Ireland the other day, and who was not of the same way of thinking as he was, what she had to say about a dozen well-to-do families whom she found living under these circumstances, who had been forced out of their comfortable homes, who bitterly lamented it, and prayed God that the Plan might soon come to an end."

19. Hansard, HC Deb 21 April 1910 vol. 16 cc2335–435.

20. Ibid.

21. Authors Paul Begg and Martin Fido have been most vocal in supporting the veracity of Sir Robert Anderson's "insane Jewish Ripper" theory. It is conceded that Anderson at least wrote the 1887 articles on the American part of the case. In the contract drawn up by *The Times*'s solicitor Joseph Soames for payment to Le Caron as witness before the Special Commission, a note was included from *The Times*'s manager John Cameron MacDonald to Anderson. Dated January 10, 1889, it read: "Disclosures are now pressing on us in such a way that if your man [Le Caron] is not available as quickly as steam can carry him the case will have been virtually concluded and that section of it embraced in your articles ["Parnellism and Crime"] no longer needful to be gone into." Cited in Christy Campbell, *Fenian Fire: The British Government Plot to Assassinate Queen Victoria* (New York: Harper-Collins, 2003), p. 323.

22. Sir Robert Anderson, *The Lighter Side of My Official Life* (London: Hodder & Stoughton, 1910).

23. For a complete background to what is known as the "Jubilee Plot," see Christy Campbell, *Fenian Fire: The British Government Plot to Assassinate Queen Victoria* (New York: HarperCollins, 2003). The plot failed, and according to Anderson and James Monro of Scotland Yard it was due to their vigilance. The resulting international press that implicated the Irish Party was the "public exposure of the conspiracy" to which Anderson refers in this letter to *The Times*. Until Anderson admitted he wrote the "Parnellism and Crime" articles in 1910, it was believed that either *The Times* journalist John Woulfe Flanagan or Richard Pigott were solely responsible.

24. Sir Robert Anderson, *Sidelights of the Home Rule Movement* (London: J. Murray, 1906; New York: Dutton, 1906).

25. Anderson became aware of "a rule of the Civil Service" after Sir Charles Warren was reprimanded in accord with the same rule in November 1888. The rule was previously issued to the Prisons Department of which he was secretary in 1887. However, Anderson persisted without censure to write publicly for *The Times* on official matters. Winston Churchill quoted the rule in considering the abolition of Anderson's pension for unauthorized publication of his *Blackwood's Magazine* articles on Jack the Ripper in 1910.

26. To Anderson, the Salisbury Tory administration and Scotland Yard under the direction of the Home Office, the defensive ends that justified the means show to an extent the real danger some Irish Republicans posed. By 1888, Special Branch had infiltrated all major terrorist and anarchist secret societies and had begun a campaign to disseminate press and official propaganda reversing the effectiveness of mainland terrorist plots. In his memoirs, Anderson stated, "The moral of my story will be understood by any one who will read Mr. Swift MacNeill's 'Irish Parliament,' or even the extracts from it given in my book 'A Great Conspiracy.' The grant of Gladstonian Home Rule to Ireland would soon lead to an agitation more vehement and dangerous than any which the present generation has experienced." *The Lighter Side of My Official Life* (London: Hodder & Stoughton, 1910), Chapter 12. This strict control of the Victorian situation may have been a contributing factor and motive for Scotland Yard to consider that the Whitechapel murders as political terrorist acts.

27. It is supposed that Anderson was mistaken in attributing to Sir William Harcourt acceptance of his position on the matter, as Henry Matthews was the home secretary at the time. However, Anderson is correct, as Harcourt had brought up the question of Le Caron's papers in early 1889 in the House of Commons in response to Le Caron's Special Commission testimony. According to the *Hansard* transcripts, Harcourt did not accept Anderson's explanation, as he claimed. Home Secretary Matthews rather gave advance notice that he would appear before the commission to testify. Anderson did not appear, and in a scathing letter to *The Times*, he threatened to expose the previous administration, of which Harcourt was the home secretary, with official documents that he had privately retained.

28. HO 144/926 James Monro wrote a letter dated April 13, 1910, to Sir Edward Troup denying his official support for Anderson's publication of the "Parnellism and Crime" articles. When the articles were printed, Anderson was officially secretary to the Prison Commissioners and Monro was the Metropolitan Police assistant commissioner. Anderson thus did not require Monro's sanction, as he claimed, unless publication had involved unofficial secret service discussions at the Home Office. Pigott's Special Commission testimony confirmed unofficial government sanction for their publication.

29. Anderson regarded Balfour as more philosophical than religious. Balfour was a president of the Society for Psychical Research and wrote extensively on spiritual subjects, adopting an intellectual and critical view. Anderson abhorred any innovative approach to the conservative and prophetic Christianity that he practiced and on which he had written widely. Balfour's and Anderson's differences influenced their official capacities, views of Catholicism, and handling of the Irish question. At the time of Anderson's 1910 "definitely ascertained fact" on the identity of a Jewish Jack the Ripper, Balfour was framing the "Balfour Treaty," which later established a Jewish homeland in Israel.

30. *The Times*, April 30, 1910.

31. Hansard, HC Deb 20 March 1889 vol. 334 cc256–323.

32. In May 1888 the Official Secrets Bill was introduced in Parliament. After protracted resistance to debate from the opposition benches due to sparse details from the Tory government, it was finally enacted in September 1889. However, it did not reach its current form with amendments until 1911, when it was rushed through Parliament. Though the bill was primarily defended as a measure to protect military secrets, the legislation included amended provisions for the nondisclosure of official secrets by civil servants, journalists, spies and police. It did not refer to pending serious criminal investigations such as the Whitechapel murders even though they were under investigation by Special Branch. Nevertheless, it was the Treasury rule in its 1884 form that directly affected the public statements of senior police officials on Jack the Ripper.

33. *The Leeds Mercury* of February 24, 1888, reported on a meeting of Fenians in New York City. It was headlined "news of the dynamite party."

34. In an interview Sir Robert Anderson gave his views: "Asked generally as to the difficulties he had known to hinder crime investigation, Sir Robert at once mentioned the difference between the legal status and powers of our own as compared, for instance, with the French police. 'In Paris,' he remarked, 'if a murder were to take place, the house would be at once surrounded by a cordon of officers, the doors would all be sealed, the Chief of Police would be at once

informed, and no one would be allowed to touch anything until he had completed his investigation. Everything would be left just as it was found; the most skilled police officers would see everything as the criminal left it; they would note the methods of his work by the evidence remaining, and would have placed before them all that would help them to unravel the story. See the difference here. "An Englishman's home is his castle," as we know, and when the crime investigator desires to enter a house he has to take off his cap ceremoniously, and say, "If you please." Something of the same kind happened in the Ripper crimes. In two cases of that terrible series there were distinct clues destroyed — wiped out absolutely — clues that might very easily have secured for us proof of the identity of the assassin. But, as I said, there is first of all a legal question involved. No law hinders a police officer from going into a private house or private grounds to arrest a criminal. But the law gives him no right to enter for the investigation of the crime and the securing of evidence that may lead to the detection of the criminal. That brings me, of course, to the question of an alteration of the law and the reconstitution (if that be necessary) of the Criminal Investigation Department; and that is too big a question to be settled, or even discussed, profitably here.'" "Crime Detection: How the Police Are Hindered in Their Investigations," *Daily Chronicle*, September 1, 1901.

35. An early example of Robert Anderson's writing on criminal reform was "Morality by Act of Parliament," *Period Review*, January 1891.

36. *The Times*, March 21, 1889.

37. *Birmingham Daily Post*, February 7, 1889.

38. Hansard, HC Deb 19 April 1910 vol. 16 cc1867–70.

39. Andy Spallek, "The West of England MP Identified," *Ripperologist* 88, February 2008. George Broderick was subpoenaed to appear in the 1893 libel case *Gatty v. Farquharson*. Farquharson's 1891 Ripper story is a likely source for Sir Melville Macnaghten's private information on suspect M.J. Druitt.

40. Broderick is mistaken on this point, as Parnell had chosen not to institute a libel action. However, Parnell did begin libel action in Scotland later, and was eventually vindicated and compensated by *The Times* on closing of the Special Commission.

41. This appears to be a reference to the Russell Club of Oxford University.

42. George C. Brodrick, *Memories and Impressions* (London: James Nisbet, 1900). An entry in Special Branch ledgers refers to O'Brien and the Whitechapel murders and may relate to Irish MP and proprietor of *United Ireland*, William O'Brien, whose Special Commission contempt of court application made by the Attorney General on December 14, 1888, was countered by Mr. Reid QC against George Brodrick for comments on the Whitechapel murderer. A further entry alleges that Lord Randolph Churchill was Jack the Ripper, indicating how Victorian political gossip entered official records.

43. Scotland Yard crime index information on the Whitechapel murders is courtesy of Stewart P. Evans. In Sir Robert Anderson, *Pseudo-Criticism: or, The Higher Criticism and Its Counterfeit* (London: Fleming H. Revell, 1904), Anderson asserts that medical experts, in his experience, can "blunder." He adds, "Among the 'undiscovered murders' the enumeration of which in that category may be thus explained, would be one of the cases reckoned among the exploits of the now historic 'Jack the Ripper.' The popular history of the' Whitechapel Murders,' I may add, is based largely on the theories of experts. And, while the author of these crimes was horribly real, 'Jack the Ripper' is a myth." Anderson had commissioned medical reviews of the Whitechapel murders independent of the inquest inquiries and verdicts. With the "suggested complicity of the Irish Party" investigated by Scotland Yard CID, the implication is that Anderson was concerned with the mutilation of the victims done, presumably or actually, with surgical knives — the weapons used in the

Phoenix Park murders of 1882, a case whose leading perpetrators had escaped. As these crime index references on a Whitechapel murder can be dated to the murder of Mary Kelly on November 9, 1888, the Irish Party suspicions at the Parnell Special Commission linked allegedly with the Whitechapel murders can be contended with some historical confidence.

44. S.P. Evans and Keith Skinner, *The Ultimate Jack the Ripper Sourcebook* (London: Robinson, 2001), p. 476.

45. Ref. HO 144/221/A49301C, ff. 217–23.

46. A classic example of Anderson's contradictory statements on the status of the killer, is found in his article in the February 1908 issue of *Nineteenth Century* magazine, titled "Criminals and Crime: A Rejoinder." Anderson mentions "my book entitled 'Criminals and Crime,' the special subject of which is organized and systematic crime, and in this country crime of that character does not include offences against the person." He adds a footnote saying that, "the 'Whitechapel murders' were the only exception to this in recent times, and, as I have recorded in my book, the author of those murders was a lunatic, and if evidence had been available to bring him to justice he would have been sent to Broadmoor." (Broadmoor was a criminal asylum.) Yet in Anderson's book *Criminals and Crime*, he wrote that, "no amount of silly hysterics could alter the fact that these crimes were a cause of danger only to a particular section of a small and definite class of women, in a limited district of the East End; and that the inhabitants of the metropolis generally were just as secure during the weeks the fiend was on the prowl, as they were before the mania seized him, or after he had been safely caged in an asylum." Anderson elsewhere adds, "In my first chapter I alluded to the fact of that fiend's detention in an asylum. Now the inquiry which leads to the discovery of a criminal of that type is different from the inquiry, for example, by which a burglar may often be detected." Of course, after his retirement Anderson could write whatever he pleased in open and public statements.

47. Sir Robert Anderson, "The Problem of the Alien Criminal," *Nineteenth Century* Vol. XIX, February 1911, pp. 217–225.

48. The 1887 Coercion Act enabled the forcible eviction of Irish peasant tenants in the wake of Parnell's Land League "Plan of Campaign." The Land League resisted inequitable treatment by English Protestant landlords. It was partly a motive espoused by extremist Irish Republican secret societies for active retaliation on British imperial and commercial interests. The violent movement grew in opposition to the parliamentary efforts of the Irish Party and the will of the Irish people generally. On March 8, 1887, *The New York Times* added, "The Parnellites propose to call the attention of the House to articles in the London Times charging Mr. Parnell, Mr. Sexton, Arthur O'Connor, and others with guilty knowledge of and complicity in a series of murders in Ireland. The Times began the series of articles entitled 'Parnellism and Crime' with an outspoken denunciation of the League leaders as having intimate, notorious, and continuous relations with avowed murderers. One passage is as follows: 'The National League movement is based upon a scheme of assassination, carefully calculated and coolly applied; murderers provide their funds; murderers share their inmost counsels; murderers have gone forth from League offices and set their bloody work afloat.' This violence of language pervades the whole attack, which is designed to assist the passage of a crimes bill."

49. The marquess of Salisury's "Alien Bill," reintroduced in the House of Lords in 1894, generated heated debate and revealed his approach to immigration, which was not apparent during his tenure as prime minister during the Whitechapel murders. The first lord of the Treasury and lord president of the council, the earl of Rosebery, remarked on the debate: "These, I think, were important elements of the noble Marquess's statement. Now, as regards the influx of pauper aliens into London, they are, so far as I can ascertain,

almost restricted to two quarters—part of St. George's-in-the-East and part of Whitechapel. Now, I do not deny that there is a strong feeling in a part of the East End of London, and notably in these parishes, against the influx of these pauper aliens, but you must remember that, whether the number be great or small, they do not become chargeable to the rates. These Polish Jews do, no doubt, some of them, come in a state of some poverty to this country, but they do not become chargeable to the rates, because the race to which they belong undertakes their support when they are placed in circumstances of poverty, and therefore any argument which may be based on this ground, and which is practically alluded to in the provisions of this Bill for excluding pauper aliens, does not bear at all upon the influx of Jewish pauper aliens or Jewish poor people into the East End of London. But this is, perhaps, only a side issue, though I think the noble Marquess laid some stress upon it in his speech the other day. What I want to point out is, that the whole case is exceedingly small, far too small for legislation now, and not likely to become great enough for legislation in the future." HL Deb 17 July 1894 vol. 27 cc117–56.

50. *The New York Times* reported on August 21, 1887, that "London itself is far more engrossed in the case of Israel Lipski than with the fate of the Salisbury Government. Up to the present there is no indication that Mr. Matthews intends extending the doomed man's reprieve of one week, which was reluctantly given the prisoner's solicitor to find new testimony. The solicitor has spent the most of the week in overcoming the obstacles put in his way by the police, but has really brought to light a number of facts pointing strongly to Lipski's innocence. More time is needed to examine these, which Mr. Matthews yesterday declared he was resolved not to grant. The worst feature of the refusal is that it is almost confessedly based upon anger at the way the Pall Mall Gazette took the case up. Mr. Matthews does not of course say this, but his manner shows that he is deeply wroth at the paper, and his apologists in the press and among lawyers declare that the man must be hanged, if only to show proper contempt for the insolence of newspaper interference. Belief in the young Jew's innocence seems almost universal now. If he is hanged the effect on the public mind will be of a most painful character. The only hope now is the interest taken in the case by powerful Hebrews, some of whom, like Baron Henry de Worms, are Tory members of Parliament. If they are unable to change Mr. Matthews's mind or get at the Queen, Lipski will be hanged early on Monday morning."

51. Donald Rumbelow, *The Houndsditch Murders and the Siege of Sidney Street* (Harmondsworth, UK: Penguin Books, 1990).

52. Sir Robert Anderson, *The Lighter Side of My Official Life* (London: Hodder & Stoughton, 1910).

53. The works of historian Bernard Porter are among the most exhaustive studies of Victorian Britain's secret service available as of this writing.

54. S.P. Evans and D. Rumbelow, *Jack the Ripper: Scotland Yard Investigates* (Stroud, UK: Sutton, 2006), pp. 241–242.

55. Sir Robert Anderson was noted advocating an adoption of the French system of blending secret service with domestic policing. (In England these functions were separate.) Increased powers of arrest and detention would be effective in building a case against suspects, he said, and used as an example the Whitechapel murders investigation.

56. The permanent Special Branch was formally created on February 3, 1887. Its permanent crime ledgers date from early 1888. For further reading see Bernard Porter, *The Origins of the Vigilant State: The London Metropolitan Police Special Branch before the First World War* (London: Weidenfeld & Nicolson, 1987). On its origins Porter noted, "At the beginning of February 1887 James Monro was given a staff of 'special' high-ranking police officers: one chief inspector and three second-class inspectors. For the purposes of administration these men had to be members of the CID 'and not

be ostensibly distinguished from other Constables of that Force'; but they were financed (secretly) out of Imperial and not Metropolitan Police funds. This group was consequently now formally part of the Metropolitan Police, but it was still kept separate—at least for some purposes—from the Irish Branch. On most of the returns that were made of 'special duty' CID strength thereafter, right through to 1911, it appears as a distinct category, known as 'Section D,' as against the Irish Branch, which was known as 'Section B.' (Section C was the port police). It was also referred to as the 'Special Confidential Section,' the 'Special (Secret) Branch,' and, on some printed notepaper in November 1887, as 'Home Office. Crime Department. Special Branch.' The first Special Branch that bore this name was this little cadre of four police inspectors under Monro, who took over Jenkinson's duties in February 1887, and not the Special Irish Branch of the CID which—on paper and for accounting purposes—was quite different. Section D's brief was to take care of the observation of anarchists and Fenians. To head up this group Chief Inspector John Littlechild was taken from Scotland Yard's 'Irish Branch' and not replaced there."

57. Hansard, HC Deb 12 July 1888 vol. 328 cc1202–9; HC Deb 12 November 1888 vol. 330 cc913–41.

58. The Metropolitan Police Special Branch historic ledgers, marked "Special Account," are held at the internal archive of the Specialist Operations Department. They consist of: Volume 1, 1888–1894; Volume 2, 1894–1901; Volume 3, 1901–1912.

59. Hansard, HC Deb 12 November 1888 vol. 330 cc913–41.

60. Hansard, HC Deb 04 June 1889 vol. 336 cc1808–57.

61. Sir Robert Anderson, *The Lighter Side of My Official Life* (London: Hodder & Stoughton, 1910).

62. James Monro, 1903. Unpublished memoirs held at the Metropolitan Police Historical Collection.

63. For a full examination of claims of the assistant commissioner of the Metropolitan Police on the Whitechapel murders see S.P. Evans and D. Rumbelow, *Jack the Ripper: Scotland Yard Investigates* (Stroud, UK: Sutton, 2006), p. 243.

64. An entry in the *Metropolitan Police Estimates Book, 1885–92*, records: "A46472D/3. Mr. Macnaghten allowed L100 in addition to salary as Ass C.C. while acting as Confidential Assistant to Asst Commr. of C.I.D. total not to exceed L600 p.a. Ref. HO 395/1." Cited in S.P. Evans and K. Skinner, *The Ultimate Jack the Ripper Sourcebook* (London: Robinson, 2001), p. 644.

65. The main Metropolitan Police Special Branch historic crime ledger was the Chief Constable's CID Register for the period 1888–1892. It is held at the internal archive of the Specialist Operations Department.

66. Sir Melville Macnaghten, *Days of My Years* (London: Edward Arnold, 1914).

67. *The Times*, July 13, 1893.

68. *Star*, November 17, 1888.

69. *Sun*, February 19, 1894.

70. Kosminski, Druitt and Ostrog, the three suspects that Macnaghten felt were "more likely than Cutbush" to have been Jack the Ripper (in the official Scotland Yard report dated February 23, 1894), have been whittled away over time and history as *less* likely than anyone else who came to the attention of the police, particularly Ostrog, who was in France at the time of the murders. Philip Sugden, *The Complete History of Jack the Ripper* (London: Robinson, 2002).

71. *Pall Mall Gazette*, March 31, 1903.

72. MEPO 3/140, ff. 177–83.

73. Author Stewart P. Evans discovered the Littlechild letter, dated September 23, 1913, in February 1993. It introduces Francis Tumblety, a previously unknown suspect in the Whitechapel murders whom John George Littlechild, a former chief inspector of Scotland Yard and head of Special Branch, regarded as "among the suspects, and to my mind a very likely one.... He was ... at one time a frequent visitor to

London and on these occasions constantly brought under the notice of police, there being a large dossier concerning him at Scotland Yard." For further reading see S.P. Evans and Paul Gainey, *Jack the Ripper: First American Serial Killer* (London: Arrow, 1996).

74. *Chicago Daily Tribune,* November 25, 1888.

75. *Rocky Mountain News,* October 10, 1888.

76. *Evening Star* (Washington, D.C.), November 19, 1888.

77. The "Modern Babylon exposures" were a Victorian euphemism for male homosexuality, which at that time in England was a criminal offense under the provisions of the Criminal Law Amendment Act. The expression was derived from a series of investigative reports in the *Pall Mall Gazette* in 1885, titled "The Maiden Tribute of Modern Babylon." The articles exposed organized child prostitution that led to the passing of legislation raising the age of consent for girls from 13 to 16. The act also gave police firmer powers in arresting streetwalkers and brothel-keepers, though it made "indecent" acts between males illegal until 1967. Francis Tumblety was arrested and charged for offenses of gross indecency on November 7, 1888, two days before the murder of Mary Kelly. He was bailed under supervision. A court warrant was issued on November 14, and after bail was posted on November 16, he absconded to the U.S. The first press release on these arrests was cabled from London on November 17, 1888. It included details about Tumblety being suspected of complicity in the Whitechapel murders.

78. *San Francisco Chronicle,* November 18, 1888.

79. *The New York World,* November 19, 1888.

80. *The New York Times,* November 19, 1888.

81. *The New York Times,* November 23, 1888. There is a discrepancy in the date that Crowley sent the dispatch. A comparison of the reports indicates that November 19 was likely the date Crowley contacted Scotland Yard after reading reports of Tumblety's arrests. However, press reports of police inquiries are not always an accurate reflection of the facts, particularly on the investigation of a suspect.

82. *The Brooklyn Daily Eagle,* April 27, 1890.

83. David Edgar Herold was the name of the conspirator involved in the Lincoln assassination plot. His name was misspelled as "Harold" on the wanted poster. The "low, licentious sheet published in New York" mentioned by Tumblety was *The New York Times* which reprinted his *Washington Star* letter, slightly rewritten, backdating it and spelling the conspirator's name "Herrold." The reasons for the vilification appear to be the political climate after the American Civil War. (Most of the recruits for early Fenian groups and the Irish Republican Brotherhood came from America.) As Tumblety was Irish and had sympathies with the Irish Nationalist movement, he easily became the target of press editorial opinion. His status as a quack doctor fed into the prevailing prejudices between established medical practice and herbal homeopathic remedies for which Tumblety was a public advocate. His eccentric dress, ways and homosexuality were the stuff of rumors and legends. For further reading see Timothy B. Riordan, *Prince of Quacks: The Notorious Life of Dr. Francis Tumblety, Charlatan and Jack the Ripper Suspect* (Jefferson, NC: McFarland, 2009).

84. *The Chicago Tribune,* July 11, 1865.

85. *New York Herald,* November 19, 1888.

86. American researcher Roger J. Palmer discovered the interview with Francis Tumblety in *The New York World,* January 29, 1889. "Tumblety Talks," *Ripperologist* No. 79, May 2007.

87. *Ripperologist,* No. 82, August 2007.

88. This is a reference to the 1888 Special Commission and the "Parnellism and Crime" articles with which Sir Robert Anderson admitted involvement in 1910.

89. Francis Tumbelty, *Dr. Tumblety: A Sketch of the Life of the Gifted, Eccentric and World-Famed Physician* (New York: Brooklyn Eagle Book and Job Printing Department, 1889).

90. *Pall Mall Gazette,* December 31, 1888.

91. Guy B.H. Logan, *Masters of Crime Studies of Multiple Murders* (London: Stanley Paul, 1928), p. 33.

92. Walter Dew, *I Caught Crippen* (London: Blackie & Sons, 1938).

93. ref. PRO HO/134/10. Official letter dated November 23, 1888, from the Home Office to Scotland Yard discovered by author Keith Skinner in 1996, relating to extradition of Roland Gideon Israel Barnett.

94. *San Francisco Chronicle,* November 23, 1888.

95. The earliest full examination of a Fenian connection to the Whitechapel murders was Nick Warren, "The Great Conspiracy." in *The Mammoth Book of Jack the Ripper,* Maxim Jakubowski and Nathan Braund, eds. (London: Robinson, 1999). Though the article was speculative, it brought together several high-level conspiracy threads. It has since been followed with further documentary support for a Scotland Yard inquiry into Irish extremist involvement with the Whitechapel murders. Warren's conspiracy is centered on the use of surgical knives in the 1882 Phoenix Park murders and the medical suspicions that Jack the Ripper used similar knives.

96. Major Arthur Griffiths was the first to publish on the Polish Jew Ripper theory, in *Mysteries of Police and Crime,* 2 Volumes (London: Cassell, 1898).

97. For a biography see Donal McCracken, *Inspector Mallon: Buying Irish Patriotism for a Five-Pound Note* (Dublin: Irish Academic Press, 2009).

98. Frederick Moir Bussy, *Irish Conspiracies: Recollections of John Mallon (The Great Irish Detective) and Other Reminiscences* (London: Everett, 1910).

99. *The New York Times,* November 4, 1888.

100. *The Irish Times,* November 13, 1888. The report was reprinted in the *Daily News,* November 13, 1888.

101. Hansard, HC Deb 23 November 1888 vol. 331 cc15–6.

102. *Thomson's Weekly News,* December 1, 1906. Cited in S.P. Evans and Donald Rumbelow, *Jack the Ripper: Scotland Yard Investigates* (Stroud, UK: Sutton, 2006).

103. The Coroners Act of 1887 states: "By a circular from the Home Office in September 1884, coroners were requested, in all cases in which a verdict of manslaughter or murder should be returned, to send a copy of the depositions to the director of public prosecutions with or without remarks which the coroner might think fit to offer." *The Coroners' Act, 1887, with Forms and Precedents, Being the Fifth Edition of the Treatise by Sir J. Jervis on the Office and Duties of Coroners,* R.E. Melsheimer, ed. (London: H. Sweet & Sons, 1888), p. 52. See also: R. Henslowe Wellington, *The King's Coroner: Being the Practice and Procedure in His Judicial and Ministerial Capacitites. Volume II* (London: Bailliere, Tindall and Cox, 1906).

104. *Return of Working of Regulations for Carrying Out of Offences Acts.* For the years 1888, 1889, 1890 and 1891. House of Commons Parliamentary Papers.

105. Noted as Catherine Mylett in the DPP returns.

106. There is a further entry made on the application by an "E.K. L—, Custom House, E.C." for a "Whitechapel murder" simply designated "Re—W." The result of the application noted, "Letter sent to Commissioner of Police." Larkins was known to be active in promoting his theories to the authorities.

107. Appears to be noted in DPP returns as *Alice M----* on August 27, 1889.

108. The application was made on June 26, 1890. In the "Result of Application" column, it is stated: "Applicant had previously told same story to Metropolitan Police, the City Police, and to a solicitor in Bedford—row. The Director took his statement in presence and at request of the solicitor; the Director was of opinion, though the solicitor thought otherwise, that the applicant was under hallucinations, but forwarded statement to Metropolitan Police."

109. Anderson wrote: "A Police Commissioner has no powers save those which are expressly conferred on him by

the Police Acts, or which pertain to him as a magistrate. For under the Metropolitan Police Acts each of the Commissioners is a magistrate for all the Home Counties; and he has all the legal powers of a magistrate, though forbidden by statute to act in Sessions. I may add here that when I was appointed I was surprised to find that my colleagues had never taken the oath, for as a lawyer I held this to be essential. Being snubbed for declaring my view of the matter, I naturally pressed it, and the Law Officers, to whom it was referred, supported me. Accordingly we all took the oath as magistrates before the Lord Chancellor." *The Lighter Side of My Official Life* (London: Hodder & Stoughton, 1910), Chapter IX.

110. *The Prosecution of Offences Act, 1879.* R. Henslowe Wellington, *The King's Coroner: Being a Complete Collection of the Statutes Relating to the Office Together with a Short History of the Same* (London: William Clowes & Sons, 1905). The Coroners Act of 1887 states: "And if the director of public prosecutions gives notice to the coroner that he has undertaken criminal proceedings, he must transmit the inquisition to him."

111. Douglas G. Browne was given access (with original coauthor Ralph Straus, who had died during preparation of the book), to closed official Scotland Yard files as noted in the introduction of the book *The Rise of Scotland Yard: A History of the Metropolitan Police* (London: Harrap, 1956).

112. A notable exception to this historical omission is inclusion of Browne's information in S.P. Evans and D. Rumbelow, *Jack the Ripper: Scotland Yard Investigates* (Stroud, UK: Sutton, 2006).

113. Sir Basil Thompson, *The Story of Scotland Yard* (London: Grayson & Grayson, 1935).

114. G. Douglas Browne, *The Rise of Scotland Yard: A History of the Metropolitan Police* (London: Harrap, 1956).

115. *The Irish Times* on April 12, 1883, printed transcripts of the Irish attorney general's speech to the jury on the Phoenix Park murders trial of Joseph Brady in Dublin. The speech included details of the autopsy reports. "The medical examination of the bodies disclosed the circumstance that both men had been despatched by the same means. Both of them had been stabbed to death by pointed weapons of great sharpness, keenness, and strength, but not very large, not very wide, and not necessarily more than ten or twelve inches in length. The wound that had been fatal in the case of Mr. Burke, and which, let us trust, was the first he received, was one behind his back, which passed there very near the shoulder, traversed right through his body, piercing the pericardium and the heart, and came out in front. But there were many other wounds upon him. I shall not unnecessarily attempt to harrow your feelings by a detail of them. There were many wounds inflicted by a weapon of a similar kind; but there was one wound—and I shall ask your attention to this, because you will see the bearing of it upon the evidence—there was one wound inflicted not by a thrust or stab, but inflicted by a cut which was upon the throat. His throat was cut. In the case of Lord Frederick Cavendish, the wounds upon his body were also numerous. The wound from which he died was one under the axilla or armpit—I know not on which arm—which severed the large artery which supplies the limb, and which must have produced death in a very short time by rapid bleeding. There was also an important wound upon his person which I must describe, or to which I must at least ask your attention, because it too has a vital bearing upon the case the Crown here presents to you. Upon the left arm there was a wound which was not a stab, but which was, as it is described by the eminent surgeon who examined his body after his death, it was a slash. It was a wound which not alone severed flesh and sinew and cut and sliced the bone, but it punctured the bone of the arm with terrific force. It was a wound, not a stab, but a slash, and it must have been inflicted, as you will hear proved by the doctors, by a man of almost Herculean strength, assuming it was inflicted by a weapon not of itself of any great

weight or size. That is all I intend to say as to the wounds on the bodies of these gentlemen, and I shall say nothing more."

116. Anderson was a millenarist and an advocate of the new century as it figured in his Book of Daniel prophetic calculations. Believing that religion influenced the criminal justice system, Anderson wrote, "We need to shake free once for all stupid and cruel punishment-of-crime system—an evil legacy from the pagan codes on which our law is based—and to recognize that punishment is merely a means to an end, and that the great end to be kept in view is the protection of the community. Fitting the penalty to the offence was a distinctive feature of the Divine law of the Theocracy. A process of negative induction will point us to the influence of the Bible [King James Version] in moulding our national life and character. For in a wholly peculiar sense and degree we have been for centuries 'the people of the book.' And this conclusion receives striking confirmation from the fact that present-day tendencies to class hatred and class war have developed side by side with a movement to disparage the Bible, and to dethrone it from the place it has held for so many generations in the estimation of the British people." *The Lighter Side of My Official Life* (London: Hodder & Stoughton, 1910).

117. Bernard Alderson, *Arthur James Balfour: The Man and His Life* (London: Grant Richards, 1903).

118. Detective Sergeant Patrick McIntyre, in his series of articles for *Reynold's Newspaper*, on May 12, 1895, gives an account of events during the Special Commission and the Pigott forgeries with Sir Robert Anderson's discreet approval that does not appear in any other study of the period. The account outlines convoluted Victorian intrigues and politics that had an impact on sources and the police investigation of the Whitechapel murders. McIntyre wrote, "Our mission to Paris was after the failure of the Pigott letters. It was arranged apart from Mr. Soames, the solicitor who had conducted all the Times's legal business during the Commission. The person responsible for our Paris enterprise was a near relative of Mr. John Walter, the late proprietor of the Times. She still continued to believe implicitly in the genuineness of the forged letter, even after Pigott had blown his brains out, and she instigated this quiet commission of her own. Mr. Houston asked the consent of Mr. Anderson to my going with himself and Le Caron. This was done secretly, as the Scotland Yard authorities did not wish to be in any way mixed up with the expedition. Mr. Anderson consented, and so we three fishers went sailing to the gay French capitol. We opened up communication with Patrick Casey, a man who knew all that was going on in connection with the letters. Casey communicated with John Hayes in America, and when Hayes knew that his expenses would be guaranteed, he came over to this side of the Atlantic. Mr. Graham, one of the barristers who represented the Times, was also then in Paris. It is difficult for me to make clear to the readers the exact position of all the parties in this game. The complications are extraordinary. Hayes, for instance, was really an agent of the British Government, and he had been followed from New York by two detectives of Pinkerton's agency, who were employed for the purpose by the Mulcahy section of the Clan-na-Gael. They were watching Hayes, who was believed by some of them to have come over in connection with some traces that existed in England of the murder of Dr. Cronin in Chicago. Casey appeared to act with us who were working in the interests of the Times, but he was all along informing his brother Joseph of what was going on. Joseph was repeating this information to Mr. Michael Davitt, who, in his turn, was communicating it to some of his friends in the Irish Parliamentary party. It only remains to be said that one of these Parliamentary colleagues was kindly supplying Mr. Soames with the whole story. Who this traitorous M.P. was it is not for me to say. And thus the information went round and round in a way that could never be adequately explained in an article like this. What I have

described should, however, be sufficient to convince my readers of the difficulties that attended the unravelling of the great Irish problems of a few years ago."

119. *The New York Times*, June 16, 1887.

120. *Brooklyn Eagle*, March 30, 1887.

121. *The New York Times*, April 15, 1887.

122. Clan-na-Gael member Dr. Patrick Cronin went missing on May 4, 1889, and was found murdered on May 22, 1889, after he had accused Alexander Sullivan, the president of Clan-na-Gael, of embezzlement. The main period sources for the case and trial are Henry M. Hunt, *The Crime of the Century: Or, the Assassination of Dr. Patrick Henry Cronin* (Chicago: H.L. & D.H. Kochersperger, 1889); John T. McEnnis, *The Clan-Na-Gael and the Murder of Dr. Cronin, Being a Complete and Authentic Narrative of the Rise and Development of the Irish Revolutionary Movement, and an Impartial Account of the Crime in the Carlson Cottage* (Chicago: F.J. Schulte & J.W. Iliff, 1889).

123. *The Irish Times*, October 29, 1887.

124. *Chicago Tribune*, November 5, 1887.

125. *Chicago Tribune*, January 19, 1888.

126. "Number One" of the Invincibles was rumored to be Patrick Joseph Percy Tynan. If so, he is then a candidate for the Macnaghten Balfour reference on Jack the Ripper. However, there are doubts about his claims that Parnell and the Land League were cooperating on the Phoenix Park murders despite firm denials from Invincible, Thomas Doyle and testimony of the 1888–89 Special Commission. Tynan was suspected of being a Tory informer and his claims were strongly refuted, notably in *The New York Times* of June 4, 1894. He escaped trial for the Phoenix Park murders due to ineffective motions of extradition from the U.S. In the winter of 1887–88, Tynan wrote an Irish history titled *The Irish National Invincibles and Their Times*. There was an English "curtailed edition" (London: Messrs. Chatham, 1894) and an American full edition (New York: Irish National Invincible Publishing, 1894). An addendum to the English edition commented on an update then being made to the American edition: "In the city of Troy, New York, during the American political campaign of 1888, an Irishman and a graduate of Trinity College, Dublin, addressing a political meeting, openly avowed his sympathy with the Irish Invincible movement. He there publicly declared that not only had he been a member of that organisation, but that he was the purchaser of the irregular weapons [surgical knives] of warfare used by the Invincibles in the Phoenix Park, Dublin." The Phoenix Park murders of the new Liberal-leaning chief secretary of Ireland, Lord Frederick Cavendish, and his permanent under-secretary, Thomas Henry Burke, had effectively disrupted the Home Rule campaigns of Gladstone, Parnell and the lord lieutenant, Earl Spencer, for the ensuing decades.

127. *Pall Mall Gazette*, April 21, 1887.

128. *The Belfast News-Letter*, January 8, 1889.

129. *The Irish Times*, March 17, 1888.

130. Christie Campbell, *Fenian Fire: The British Government Plot to Assassinate Queen Victoria* (London: HarperCollins, 2003).

131. *Western Mail* (Wales), May 21, 1888.

132. *The Chicago Daily Tribune*, June 6, 1888.

133. *The Chicago Daily Tribune*, June 14, 1888.

134. Cited in: S.P. Evans and D. Rumbelow, *Jack the Ripper: Scotland Yard Investigates* (Stroud, UK: Sutton, 2006).

135. *Birmingham Daily Post*, August 11, 1888.

136. "The Work of the Irish Leagues: The Speech of the Right Hon. Henry James, Q.C., M.P., Replying in The Parnell Commission Inquiry." (London: Cassell. Published for the Liberal Unionist Association, 1890).

137. *The New York Times,* September 18, 1888.

138. *The Washington Post*, January 8, 1889.

139. *Butte Weekly Miner*, September 17, 1896.

140. Metropolitan Police document. *Chief Constable's CID Register — Special Branch.* 1888–c. 1892. Specialist Operations Internal Archive, New Scotland Yard. Cited in Lind-

say Clutterbuck, "An Accident of History?: The Evolution of Counter Terrorism Methodology in the Metropolitan Police from 1829 to 1901, With Particular Reference to the Influence of Extreme Irish Nationalist Activity" (unpublished Ph.D. thesis, University of Portsmouth, June 2002). According to researcher Chris Phillips, 57 Bedford Gardens was in Kensington and was an artist's studio. William Macgrath was an Irish artist traveling in England and Ireland at the time of the Whitechapel murders. On March 26, 1889, artist Moffat Peter Lindner wrote a letter addressed to 57 Bedford Gardens, Kensington arranging a meeting of artists: "Dear Symons, We cannot get the Café Royal for May 1st, & McNab thinks we ought to have a meeting of Dinner Committee to decide on some other place — Next Friday at 6.30 will suit McLean, so please come if you can. I have written to the other men — McNab only had a definite reply from the Café Royal y'day. Underdown has consented to take the chair. Sincerely yours M.P. Linder." (MS Whistler L151, Glasgow University Library.) It is not surprising that nationalistic artists, poets, musicians, authors and journalists were kept under Special Branch surveillance during the period nor that they would be suspected of the Whitechapel murders. The artist James Abbott McNeill Whistler associated with Irish artists in London during the period of the Whitechapel murders and was brought to the attention of Scotland Yard on several occasions, according to his correspondence. Some of his early letters were retained in the Fenian Briefs of the Dublin Castle State Papers Office. In 2001, Metropolitan Police Deputy Assistant Commissioner John Grieve publicly advised crime author Patricia Cornwell to research Walter Sickert, known to frequent the Café Royal and an associate of Whistler, as a suspect for the Whitechapel murders.

141. *Reynold's Newspaper*, March 10, 1895.

142. *Reynold's Newspaper*, March 5, 1895.

143. *Brooklyn Eagle*, October 9, 1887.

144. *The Washington Post*, May 28, 1889.

145. Of H. Llewellyn Winter, Detective Sergeant Patrick McIntyre wrote: "When I have been at branches of the Irish National League, I have heard members of this gang making the most violent, anti-English orations. I remember one Sunday night attending a League meeting where the President got up and denounced me as a spy. The same individual, as I afterwards leaned, was one of the gentlemen employed by Winter.... There were in every branch of the League one or more of Winter's men. They were well fed and had plenty of money at their command. What a wonder then that crime was not manufactured in big quantities ... when they were being egged on by men who only joined the League for the purpose of associating it with dynamite conspiracies and other crimes." (*Reynold's Newspaper*, May 5, 1995). The situation at the change of government in 1886 was that Sir Edward Jenkinson, head of the Home Office secret criminal department and a system of street informers, rivaled the detective department of Scotland Yard. Consequently, Assistant Commissioner James Monro took steps to dismantle it. On the appointment of Henry Matthews as home secretary, Jenkinson sent him a memo stating, "An expose of my past relations with the detective department of Scotland Yard would create a public scandal and my examination in open court might bring under public notice many things connected with my system of secret work." Jenkinson memo to Matthews, July 22, 1886, ref. HO 144/721.

146. *The Chicago Daily Tribune*, September 2, 1889.

147. *Chicago Daily Tribune*, January 25, 1890.

148. *Chicago Daily Tribune*, February 17, 1890.

149. *The New York Times*, September 26, 1890.

150. *Birmingham Daily Post*, September 26, 1890.

151. *The New York Times*, September 14, 1894.

152. *The Bristol Mercury and Daily Post*, February 2, 1893.

153. *Liverpool Mercury*, July 25, 1888.

154. *Reynold's Newspaper*, May 26, 1895. Former detective sergeant Patrick McIntyre's articles ended with an editorial notice: "One of Mr. McIntyre's articles has appeared each

week since February 3, and they have, therefore, taken the form of a narrative of seventeen chapters. The story is now brought to a close, and will shortly be published in book form, with considerable additions." McIntyre's book apparently never appeared. He had previously been demoted on a technically by Robert Anderson and had quarreled with Anderson's informer Le Caron. McIntyre's knowledge as an experienced Special Branch detective during the Whitechapel murders was to go the way of Chief Inspector John Littlechild and two commissioners of the Metropolitan Police, Sir Charles Warren and James Monro: historic silence.

# Bibliography

Aaronovitch, David. *Voodoo Histories: The Role of the Conspiracy Theory in Shaping Modern History.* London: Jonathan Cape, 2009.

Aberconway, Christabel. *A Wiser Woman: A Book of Memories.* London: Hutchinson, 1966.

Alderson, Bernard. *Arthur James Balfour: The Man and His Life.* London: Grant Richards, 1903.

Alexander, Kelly, comp. *Jack the Ripper: A Bibliography and Review of the Literature.* London: Association of Assistant Librarians, 1973, reprint 1984.

Anderson, Sir Robert. *The Bible and Modern Criticism.* Fifth Edition. London: Hodder and Stoughton, 1905.

_____. *The Coming Prince.* London: Hodder & Stoughton, 1895.

_____. *The Lighter Side of My Official Life.* London: Hodder & Stoughton, 1910.

_____. *Pseudo-Criticism: or, The Higher Criticism and its Counterfeit.* New York: Fleming H. Revell, 1904.

_____. *Redemption Truths.* Grand Rapids, MI: Kregel Publications, 1980.

_____. *Sidelights of the Home Rule Movement.* London: J. Murray, 1906; New York: Dutton, 1906.

Barker, A.T. ed. *The Mahatma Letters to A.P. Sinnett from the Mahatmas M. and K.H.* Second Edition. London: Rider, 1926.

Begg, P.. *Jack the Ripper: The Facts.* London: Robson Books, 2006.

_____, M. Fido, and K. Skinner, *The Complete Jack the Ripper A to Z.* London: Blake, 2010.

Bermant, Chaim. *Point of Arrival: A Study of London's East End.* London: Macmillan, 1975.

Booth, Charles. *Charles Booth and the Survey into Life and Labor in London (1886–1903).* Archives Division of the Library of the London School of Economics and Political Science.

Booth, Martin. *A Magick Life: A Biography of Aleister Crowley.* London: Hodder & Stoughton, 2001.

Borowitz, Albert. *Blood and Ink: An International Guide to Fact Based Crime Literature.* Kent, OH: Kent State University Press, 2002.

Brady, Maziere W. *Rome and Fenianism: The Pope's Anti-Parnellite Circular.* London: Robert Washbourne, 1883.

Brewer, J.F. *The Curse Upon Mitre Square: 1530–1888.* London: Simpkin, Marshal, 1888; New York: Lovell, 1889.

Brodrick, George C. *Memories and Impressions.* London: James Nisbet, 1900.

Browne, G. Douglas. *The Rise of Scotland Yard: A History of the Metropolitan Police.* London: Harrap, 1956.

Bussy, Frederick Moir. *Irish Conspiracies: Recollections of John Mallon (The Great Irish Detective) and Other Reminiscences.* London: Everett, 1910.

Caldwell, Daniel H., comp. *Madam Blavatsky's Esoteric Papers: A Comprehensive Compilation.* Whitefish, MT: Kessinger, 2005.

Campbell, Christy. *Fenian Fire: The British Government Plot to Assassinate Queen Victoria.* London: HarperCollins, 2003.

_____. *The Maharajah's Box.* London: HarperCollins, 2001.

Chapman Pincher. *The Private World of St. John Terrapin: A Novel of the Café Royal.* London: Sidgwick & Jackson, 1982.

Clutterbuck, Lindsay. *An Accident of History? The Evolution of Counter Terrorism Methodology in the Metropolitan Police from 1829 to 1901, with Particular Reference to the Influence of Extreme Irish Nationalist Activity.* Unpublished Ph.D. Thesis, University of Portsmouth, June 2002.

Conan Doyle, Sir Arthur. *The History of Spiritualism.* London: Cassell, 1926.

Conrad, Joseph. *The Secret Agent.* London: Methuen, 1907.

Cooper, Robert L.D. *The Rosslyn Hoax? Viewing Rosslyn Chapel from a New Perspective.* Addlestone, UK: Lewis, 2007.

Cornwell, Patricia. *Portrait of a Killer: Jack the Ripper—Case Closed.* London: Time Warner, 2003.

Costello, Peter. *The Real World of Sherlock Holmes: True Crimes Investigated by Arthur Conan Doyle.* London: Robinson, 1991.

Crowley, Aleister. *Moonchild: A Prologue*. London: Mandrake Press, 1929.

_____. *The Spirit of Solitude: An Autohagiography. Laterly Re-Antichristened The Confessions of Aleister Crowley*. London: Mandrake Press, 1929. Reissued as: *The Confessions of Aleister Crowley*. Symonds, John, and Kenneth Grant, eds. London: Jonathan Cape, 1969.

Curtis, L. Perry. *Jack the Ripper and the London Press*. New Haven: Yale University Press, 2001.

Dalby, Richard, ed. *Dracula and the Lair of the White Worm*. London: W. Foulsham, 1986.

Daunton, Claire, ed. *The London Hospital Illustrated: 250 Years*. London: Batsford, 1990.

Dew, Ex-Chief Inspector Walter. *I Caught Crippen*. London: Blackie, 1938.

D'Onston, Roslyn (pseud. Robert Donston Stephenson). *The Patristic Gospels: An English Version of the Holy Gospels as they existed in the Second Century*. London: Grant Richards, 1904.

Edwards, Ivor. *Jack the Ripper's Black Magic Rituals*. London: John Blake, 2002.

Emsley, Clive, and Haia Shpayer-Makov, ed. *Police Detectives in History, 1750–1950*. Aldershot, UK: Ashgate, 2006.

Evans, S.P., and Paul Gainey. *Jack the Ripper: First American Serial Killer*. London: Arrow, 1996.

Evans, Stewart P., and Donald Rumbelow. *Jack the Ripper: Scotland Yard Investigates*. Stroud, UK: Sutton, 2006.

Evans, Stewart P., and Keith Skinner. *The Ultimate Jack the Ripper Sourcebook: An Illustrated Encyclopedia*. London: Constable & Robinson, 2001.

_____, and _____. *Jack the Ripper: Letters from Hell*. Stroud, UK: Sutton, 2004.

Farnell, Kim. *Mystical Vampire: The Life and Works of Mabel Collins*. Oxford: Mandrake, 2005.

Fido, Martin. *The Crimes, Detection and Death of Jack the Ripper*. London: Weidenfeld & Nicolson, 1987; New York: Barnes & Noble, 1993.

Fisher, David. *The War Magician*. New York: Berkley Books, 1983. Reprinted as: *The War Magician: The Man Who Conjured Victory in the Desert*. London: Weidenfeld & Nicolson, 2004.

Fishman, William J. *East End 1888: A Year in a London Borough Among the Labouring Poor*. London: Duckworth, 1988.

_____. *East End Jewish Radicals, 1875–1914*. London: Duckworth, 1975.

Fitch, Herbert T., and Frank S. Stuart, with a foreword by Baroness Orczy. *Memoirs of a Royal Detective*. London: Hurst & Blackett, 1935.

Foster, R.F. *Lord Randolph Churchill: A Political Life*. Oxford: Oxford University Press, 1988.

Gardner, Gerald. *Witchcraft Today*. London: Rider, 1954.

Gould, F.J. *The Life-Story of a Humanist*. London: Watts, 1923.

Goulden, Mark. *Mark My Words!* London: W.H. Allen, 1978.

Griffiths, Arthur. *Mysteries of Police and Crime*. Two Volumes. London: Cassell, 1898.

Haggard, Sir Henry Rider. *The Days of My Life: An Autobiography*. New York: Longmans, 1926.

Hamnett, Nina. *The Laughing Torso*. London: Constable, 1932.

Harris, Melvin. *Jack the Ripper: The Bloody Truth*. London: Columbus Books, 1987.

_____. *The Ripper File*. London: W.H. Allen, 1989.

_____. *Sorry, You've Been Duped!* London: Weidenfield and Nicolson, 1986.

_____. *The True Face of Jack the Ripper*. London: Michael O'Mara Books, 1994.

Harrison, Shirley, and Michael Barrett. *The Diary of Jack the Ripper*. London: Smith Gryphon, 1993.

Hattersley, Roy. *Blood and Fire: William and Catherine Booth and Their Salvation Army*. New York: Doubleday, 1999.

Hibbert, Christopher. *Queen Victoria: A Personal History*. New York: HarperCollins, 2001.

Horowitz Murray, Janet. *Strong-Minded Women And Other Lost Voices from 19th-Century England*. Harmondsworth, UK: Penguin, 1984.

Howells, M. and K. Skinner. *The Ripper Legacy: The Life and Death of Jack the Ripper*. London: Sidgwick & Jackson, 1987.

Hunt, Henry M. *The Crime of the Century: Or, the Assassination of Dr. Patrick Henry Cronin*. Chicago: H.L. & D.H. Kochersperger, 1889.

Jackson, Kate. *George Newnes and the New Journalism in Britain, 1880–1910: Culture and Profit*. Aldershot, UK: Ashgate, 2001.

Jakubowski, M. and N. Braund, eds. *The Mammoth Book of Jack the Ripper*. London: Robinson, 1999.

Johnson, K. Paul. *The Masters Revealed: Madam Blavatsky and the Myth of the Great White Lodge*. Albany: State University of New York Press, 1994.

Kaczynski, Richard. *Perdurabo: The Life of Aleister Crowely*. Tempe, AZ: New Falcon Publications, 2002.

Knight, Stephen. *Jack the Ripper: The Final Solution*. London: Harrap, 1976.

Koven, Seth. *Slumming: Sexual and Social Politics in Victorian London*. Princeton, NJ: Princeton University Press, 2006.

Lane, Brian. *The Encyclopedia of Occult and Supernatural Murder*. London: Brockhampton Press, 1997.

Lanning, Kenneth V. *Lanning Report*. Behavioral Science Unit, National Center for the Analysis of Violent Crime, FBI Academy, Quantico, Virginia, 1992.

Le Caron, Major Henri. *Twenty-five Years in the Secret Service: The Recollections of a Spy*. London: William Heinemann, 1895.

Leslie, Sir Shane. *Sir Evelyn Ruggle-Brise: A Memoir of the Founder of Borstal*. London: John Murray, 1938.

Lévi, Éliphas. *The Magical Ritual of the Sanctum Regnum.* Edited by W. Wynn Westcott. London: George Redway, 1896.

_____, and Arthur Edward Waite. *The Mysteries of Magic: A Digest of the Writings of Eliphas Levi.* London: George Redway, 1886.

_____, and _____. *Transcendental Magic: Its Doctrine and Ritual.* London: Rider, 1896.

Levy, Carl, ed. *Socialism and the Intelligentsia, 1880–1914.* New York: Routledge & Kegan Paul, 1988.

Linder, Seth, Keith Skinner, and Caroline Morris. *The Ripper Diary: The Inside Story.* Stroud, UK: Sutton, 2003.

Macnaghten, Sir Melville. *Days of My Years.* London: Edward Arnold, 1914.

Magellan, Karyo. *By Ear and Eyes: The Whitechapel Murders, Jack the Ripper and the Murder of Mary Jane Kelly.* Derby Longshot, 2005.

Maskelyne, Jasper. *Magic: Top Secret.* London: Stanley Paul, 1949.

May, Betty. *Tiger Woman: My Story.* London: Duckworth, 1929.

Mayall, David. *English Gypsies and State Policies.* Hatfield: Gypsy Research Centre, University of Hertfordshire Press, 1995.

_____. *Gypsy-Travellers in Nineteenth-Century Society.* Cambridge, UK: Cambridge University Press, 1988.

McCracken, Donal. *Inspector Mallon: Buying Irish Patriotism for a Five-Pound Note.* Dublin: Irish Academic Press, 2009.

McEnnis, John T. *The Clan-Na-Gael and the murder of Dr. Cronin, being a complete and authentic narrative of the rise and development of the Irish revolutionary movement, and an impartial account of the crime in the Carlson cottage.* Chicago: F.J. Schulte & J.W. Iliff, 1889.

Merrick, George Purnell. *Work Among the Fallen as Seen in the Prison Cell.* London: Ward Lock, 1890.

Monro, James. Unpublished memoirs. Metropolitan Police Historical Collection, 1903.

Newman, Aubrey, ed. *The Jewish East End, 1840–1939.* London: Jewish Historical Society of England, 1981.

Oddie, Ingleby. *Inquest.* London: Hutchinson, 1941.

Odell, Robin. *Jack the Ripper, in Fact and Fiction.* London: Harrap, 1965.

_____. *Ripperology: A Study of the World's First Serial Killer and a Literary Phenomenon.* Kent, OH: Kent State University Press, 2006.

O'Donnell, Bernard. *Black Magic and Jack the Ripper (or alternatively) This Man Was Jack the Ripper.* Unpublished manuscript, 1958.

_____. *Cavalcade of Justice.* London: Clerke & Cockeran, 1951.

_____. *Crimes That Made News.* London: Burke, 1954.

_____. *The Old Bailey and Its Trials.* New York: Macmillan, 1950.

_____. *Should Women Hang?* London: W.H. Allen, 1956.

_____. *The Trials of Mr. Justice Avory.* London: Rich & Cowan, 1953.

_____. *The World's Strangest Murders.* London: Frederick Muller, 1957.

_____. *The World's Worst Women.* London: W.H. Allen, 1953.

Overton Fuller, J. *The Magical Dilemma of Victor Neuburg.* London: W.H. Allen, 1965.

Owen, Alex. *The Darkened Room: Women, Power, and Spiritualism in Late Victorian England.* London: Virago Press, 1989. Rpt. Chicago: University of Chicago Press, 2004.

Pearsall, Ronald. *The Table-Rappers: The Victorians and the Occult.* London: Michael Joseph, 1972. Rpt. Stroud, UK: Sutton, 2005.

_____. *The Worm in the Bud: The World of Victorian Sexuality.* Harmondsworth, UK: Penguin, 1983.

Pert, Alan. *Red Cactus: The Life of Anna Kingsford.* 2nd edition. Watsons Bay, NSW: Books & Writers, 2007.

Porter, Bernard. *The Origins of the Vigilant State: The London Metropolitan Police Special Branch Before the First World War.* London: Weidenfeld & Nicolson, 1987.

_____. *Plots and Paranoia: A History of Political Espionage in Britain, 1790–1988.* Boston: Unwin Hyman, 1989.

Priestley, Philip. *Victorian Prison Lives: English Prison Biography 1830–1914.* London: Methuen, 1985.

Rees, Sian. *The Floating Brothel: The Extraordinary Story of Female Convicts Bound for Botany Bay.* Sydney: Hachette, 2009.

Riordan, Timothy B. *Prince of Quacks: The Notorious Life of Dr. Francis Tumblety, Charlatan and Jack the Ripper Suspect.* Jefferson, NC: McFarland, 2009.

Sharpe, May Churchill. *Chicago May, Her Story.* London: Sampson Low, 1929.

Robertson Scott, R.W. *The Life and Death of a Newspaper.* London: Methuen, 1952.

Rumbelow, Donald. *The Complete Jack the Ripper.* London: Penguin, 2004.

_____. *The Houndsditch Murders and the Siege of Sidney Street.* Harmondsworth, UK: Penguin, 1990.

Scott, Sir Walter. *Letters on Demonology and Witchcraft.* Second Edition. London: Routledge, 1885.

Sedgwick, Mark. *Against the Modern World: Traditionalism and the Secret Intellectual History of the Twentieth Century.* Oxford: Oxford University Press, 2004.

Shelden, Neal. *Jack the Ripper and His Victims.* Hornchurch, Essex, UK: Neal Shelden, 1999.

Short, K.R.M. *The Dynamite War: Irish-American Bombers in Victorian Britain.* Dublin: Gill & Macmillan, 1979.

Sitwell, Sir Osbert. *Noble Essences: A Book of Characters.* London: Macmillan, 1950.

Sneddon, Andrew. *Witchcraft and Whigs: The Life of Bishop Francis Hutchinson, 1660–1739.* Manchester, UK: Manchester University Press, 2008.

Standage, Tom. *The Victorian Internet.* New York: Walker, 1998.

Stead, W.T. *The Pope and the New Era: Being Letters from the Vatican in 1889.* London and New York: Cassell, 1890.

Stephenson, Percy Reginald. *The Legend of Aleister Crowley: Being a Study of the Documentary Evidence Relating to a Campaign of Personal Vilification Unparalleled in Literary History.* London: Mandrake Press, 1930.

Strachan, Ross. *Jack the Ripper: A Collector's Guide to the Many Books Published.* Privately published, 1997.

_____. *The Jack the Ripper Handbook: A Reader's Companion.* Privately published, 1999.

Sugden, Philip. *The Complete History of Jack the Ripper.* London: Robinson, 2002.

Sweeney, John, and Francis Richards, ed. *At Scotland Yard: Being the Experiences During Twenty-Seven Years Service of John Sweeney Late Detective Inspector, Criminal Investigation Department, New Scotland Yard.* London: Grant Richards, 1904.

Thompson, Sir Basil. *The Story of Scotland Yard.* London: Grayson & Grayson, 1935.

*The Times: Past Present Future.* London: The Times, Printing House Square, 1932.

Treves, Sir Frederick. *The Elephant Man and Other Reminiscences.* London: W.H. Allen, 1980.

Tully, James. *The Real Jack the Ripper: The Secret of Prisoner 1167.* London: Magpie Books, 2005.

Tynan, Patrick J.P. *The Irish National Invincibles and Their Times.* New York: Irish National Invincible Publishing; London: Messrs. Chatham, 1894.

Van Onselen, Charles. *The Fox and the Flies: The Secret Life of a Grotesque Master Criminal.* New York: Walker, 2007.

Vincent, Howard. *A Police Code and Manual of the Criminal Law.* London: Cassell, Petter and Galpin, 1881.

Walkowitz, Judith R. *City of Dreadful Delight: Narratives of Sexual Danger in Late-Victorian London.* London: Virago Press, 1992.

Wensley, Frederick P. *Detective Days.* London: Cassell, 1931.

Whittington-Egan, R. *A Casebook on Jack the Ripper.* London: Wildy, 1975.

Whyte, Frederick. *The Life of W.T. Stead.* London: Jonathan Cape, 1925.

Wilson, Colin, and Robin Odell. *Jack the Ripper: Summing Up and Verdict.* London: Bantam Press, 1987.

Woodhall, Edwin T. *Crime and the Supernatural.* London: J. Long, 1935.

Yeats, W.B. *The Letters of W.B. Yeats.* Edited by Allan Wade. London: R. Hart-Davies, 1954.

Yost, Dave. *Elizabeth Stride and Jack the Ripper: The Life and Death of the Reputed Third Victim.* Jefferson, NC: McFarland, 2008.

# Index

Numbers in *bold italics* indicate pages with photographs.

PROPERTY OF
SENECA COLLEGE
LIBRARIES
@ YORK CAMPUS